Introduction to
Psychology and Counseling

Introduction to Psychology and Counseling

Christian Perspectives and Applications

Second Edition

Paul D. Meier, M.D.
Frank B. Minirth, M.D.
Frank B. Wichern, Ph.D.
Donald E. Ratcliff, Ed.S.

MONARCH
Tunbridge Wells

Unless indicated otherwise, Scripture quotations are from
the Holy Bible, New International Version. Copyright 1983
by the International Bible Society.

Printed in the United States by Baker Book House for
Monarch Publications. Owl Lodge. Langton Road,
Speldhusrt, Kent TN3 0NP.

British Library Cataloguing in Publication Data
A catalogue record for this book is available from the
British Library.

ISBN 1 85424 178 8

To our teachers
(spiritual and professional)
who have taught us
and who have guided our lives
over the past thirty years.

Contents

Figures

Tables

Preface to the First Edition

A few years ago I wrote in the introduction to *Christian Psychiatry* that I suspected the field of Christian counseling would gain in popularity in the years to come. Indeed, counseling has become an area of intense interest among conservative evangelicals. Recognizing the scarcity of textbooks in this field, my colleagues and I have written this textbook on Christian psychology and counseling.

As was true of *Christian Psychiatry*, our work continues to be based on the Bible. We regard the Bible as the inerrant Word of God and as our foundation and guide for life.

We have continued to focus on keeping a balance in our approach to counseling—a balance between feelings and behavior, between the past and present, and between theory and practice. Our various educational backgrounds help to insure that balance.

Our prayer is that God will bless this book to the glory of his Son, Jesus Christ. We pray that God will use it to influence Christian young people so they can be healthy and competent counselors.

FRANK MINIRTH, M.D.

Preface to the Second Edition

In recent years "psychology bashing" has become the favorite pastime of certain Christians. Dave Hunt and a host of others have decried the use or even study of psychology by Christians. Could psychology be part of a New Age conspiracy?

Students sometimes come to Christian colleges and seminaries asking, "Why should I study psychology? I plan to be a pastor (or missionary, or Christian educator, or . . .), so why study anything but the Bible?" Is psychology relevant for Christians? Should Christians even consider studying psychology?

On the other hand, many Christians like James Dobson, a clinical psychologist, have not compromised their faith as they have studied and used psychology. In fact, some have made use of this discipline to become more effective Christian leaders. Perhaps the danger is not psychology but faulty priorities. Making psychology one's god is just as misguided as dismissing it as the devil's work. Certainly not every idea psychologists have suggested should be immediately accepted, but just as surely the discipline cannot be rejected outright.

For many, the first edition of *Introduction to Psychology and Counseling* helped to sort out these issues, identifying the valuable aspects of psychology and showing their practical value. The first edition met with an enthusiastic reception. Many colleges and seminaries adopted it as a textbook and it sold well to the general public. In six years it went through seven printings. For this we can be thankful.

In this new edition, the first section of the book has been expanded to include other relevant information that Christians should consider, as well as many additional applications that church leaders can use. The latter section of the book has been condensed and reorganized to comport with the standard manner in which general psychology is taught. In the process we have attempted to keep those portions that have helped make this a popular book with the general public as well.

15

New to this edition are special "spot-light" sections which feature relevant persons, ideas, and applications. Many of these emphasize the use of psychology in the church. They should not be considered final answers in any sense, since most situations are more complex than these simplified descriptions suggest. Yet it is hoped that by considering one psychological concept in one specific situation, the student can begin to apply the basic ideas. In actual situations several psychological concepts will have to be considered, along with principles from the Bible, in order to obtain a more complete understanding and application.

The distinctives of this text are readily apparent and can be summarized as three Cs. The most important distinctive is that this text is *Christian*. We have attempted to write a book that is wholly Christian—from foundational perspectives to specific applications. The authors believe the Bible is the most important source of Truth and is completely trustworthy. There is an emphasis upon applications within Christian contexts, including the church.

The *classic* studies of psychology are emphasized throughout this work. The most recent research is not always the best research, and perhaps the concentration upon the latest findings in many introductory texts results in their quickly becoming dated. While the present book does not neglect the most significant recent research, the authors believe that introductory students need to be grounded in the classical psychological studies that have helped shape the discipline and will continue to be foundational to newer research.

The third distinctive is the book's *clinical* orientation, as emphasized in the latter part of the title. While not neglecting other perspectives and topics, the authors place a priority on Christian counseling in the text, and two of the longest chapters are completely devoted to this topic. This orientation stems in part from the background of the primary authors (psychiatry) and in part from a conviction held by all of the authors that counseling is one of the most important areas where psychology can help humanity.

We wish to thank the following people for their help on the first edition: Judy Slease for her editorial help in the early drafts; Betty DeVries, who served as the senior editor and production coordinator; Walter R. Hearn, the editor; and Daniel J. Malda, the designer.

We also wish to thank Allan Fisher, director of publications, for his help on the second edition, and Maria E. denBoer for copyediting. We also appreciate those psychologists who reviewed the first draft of the second edition and provided many helpful comments.

We trust that this second edition will be even more beneficial than the first. Christians need psychology as a tool to help them understand themselves and others. It is our prayer that this edition will, like the first, help us reach that goal.

DONALD RATCLIFF, ED.S.

1

Introduction
to Psychology

Psychology can be defined as the scientific study of the behavior and thinking of organisms. Psychology might be thought of as the study of how living creatures interact with their environment and each other, and how they cope (successfully or unsuccessfully) with that environment. Psychology thus overlaps with philosophy and religion as well as with other sciences such as physiology, anthropology, and sociology. Psychologists are interested in the differences among various animal species and in the ways that human beings differ from both animals and machines.

The Growth of Psychology

Psychology has had an almost exponential growth during the last few decades. A plethora of books on psychology, both technical and popular, has poured from publishers. Psychology courses are among the most popular in colleges and universities. Enrollment of graduate students in psychology programs has been increasing at a tremendous rate. Essentially every school of higher education on the North American continent devotes at least some aspects of its curriculum to the study of human behavior or the behavior of organisms.

The progress of scientific psychology is remarkable, considering that Wilhelm Wundt first established psychology as an independent and self-sufficient academic discipline in 1879. He founded a psychological laboratory at the University of Leipzig in Germany, where many early students of psychology took their training. Around the turn of the century the effect of the science of psychology began to be felt across much of Europe and America.

Early psychologists tried to do exactly what the term "psychology" implies—study ("logy") the mind ("psyche"). While his predecessors emphasized either the philosophy of the mind or the physiology of the brain, Wundt used both emphases to develop an experimental approach to understanding human behavior. Wundt made use of introspection or self-observation in which the individual experiences an event and then attempts to describe it. By repeating or replicating the same experiences with different people, Wundt attempted to specify the components of consciousness and see how those components combined in complex thought. He also did research on decision making and reaction time. Once Wundt's work became known, similar laboratories developed throughout Europe and the United States.

Eleven years after the founding of the first psychological laboratory, William James, an American psychologist and philosopher, wrote the first general psychology textbook, entitled *The Principles of Psychology* (1890). This work, which is recognized as a landmark in psychology, emphasized the *function* of consciousness, not the *components* of consciousness as Wundt's work had done. This perspective came to be known as functionalism; it emphasized the practical application of research to everyday situations.

During the second decade of this century a third perspective, behaviorism, was developed by American psychologist John B. Watson. While accepting the methods of experimentation, Watson rejected the study of consciousness because he believed that it could only be examined indirectly. Since behavior could be directly studied and precisely measured, he maintained that it was the only scientific object psychologists could justifiably consider. Watson argued that human behavior was due to certain laws, all derived from the fundamental principle that stimuli (events before a behavior occurs) produce a response (the behavior itself). His approach, as a result, is often designated S-R theory. Watson's theory became very popular in the 1920s, remained dominant in American psychology for several decades (especially after B. F. Skinner broadened the

perspective considerably), and continues to have ardent supporters even today.

While the United States became enamored of behaviorism, Freud's radically different views began to emerge in Europe. Freud saw unconsciousness as the basic cause of behavior, and held that people generally have no idea of the real causes of their actions because these causes are hidden from consciousness. His theory, called psychoanalytic psychology, was derived from case histories of people he counseled rather than experimentation, which is probably why it did not become popular in the more experimentally oriented United States. While Freud's views have never dominated American psychology, his emphasis on early childhood experiences has powerfully influenced many psychologists (although few completely accept his ideas about how those experiences affect people).

With the dominance of behaviorism in America well into the 1960s, some were prone to quip that psychology had "lost its mind," since mental phenomena were minimized by behaviorists. In the 1970s the mind again became an object of serious study by psychologists (Zimbardo 1982), although the way the mind was understood was significantly different from the view of early psychologists. Today the cognitive approach has become increasingly popular. This theory focuses on memory, thought processes, problem solving, feelings, and other aspects of consciousness. Humanistic psychology, a perspective that emphasizes human freedom and a positive view of human nature, became popular during the 1960s. Throughout the history of psychology a biological approach has also been considered important in determining at least some kinds of human behavior; the nervous, endocrine, and musculoskeletal systems obviously must be taken into account when studying human activity. Today it is more likely that a psychologist will hold to some combination of theories rather than only one.

Ways of Knowing

Before psychology was recognized as a distinct discipline, it was considered to be a branch of philosophy. A basic issue that philosophers have considered over the centuries is epistemology, or the question of how people know. The scientific method, upon which psychology is based, is but one way of forming conclusions.

Ray and Rivizza (1985, 3–7) identify six ways of knowing: (1) tenacity, (2) authority, (3) a priori beliefs, (4) reason, (5) common sense, and (6) the scientific method.

First, we can know by tenacity, by accepting something as true because it has always been that way. Regardless of evidence to the contrary, the individual adamantly refuses to consider the facts. The basic attitude is "I said it; I believe it; that settles it for me!" Tenacity is even found among a few psychologists who refuse to consider anything other than their own conclusions, as well as among a few Christian antipsychology crusaders of recent years.

A second way of knowing is by authority. This involves taking someone's (or something's) word on the matter. Christians appeal to the authority of the Bible as a way of knowing about God and humanity. Many of our conclusions are based upon authority because it takes too much time to check everything out first-hand. A car repair manual, a favorite Bible scholar, and even a general psychology textbook could all be considered potential authorities in this sense. Some Christians elevate a pastor or a denomination to this level.

We can also know by a priori beliefs. These are the presuppositions we all begin with, such as assuming that the senses are generally reliable and that the world we live in actually exists. A priori beliefs are held by everyone, including scientists, because they are reasonable and because we must have some kind of foundation before appealing to any other way of knowing. The famous philosopher Descartes began with the assumption "I think, therefore I am." Christians such as the late Francis Schaeffer have often emphasized the need to examine our basic beliefs and assumptions to see if they are trustworthy.

Scientists also make assumptions and build their structure of knowledge on those assumptions. Christians should be aware of the assumptions made by scientists and compare them with their own. Publicly and plainly stated assumptions enable others to detect any bias experimenters may have introduced into their research design. If Christian psychologists construct a test of spiritual maturity, they should be willing to state publicly exactly what assumptions they have made about spiritual maturity.

Reason and logic can also be used to know things. These can be of great benefit as long as the original assumptions are correct. Common sense is also valuable, and is certainly superior to sheer tenacity in that our own experience is used as a basis for drawing conclusions. Unfortunately, one person's experience is necessarily too limited to make this the only way of knowing. Furthermore, what we perceive in a given situation is often as much the result of our assumptions and expectations as it is the actual experience.

The last way of knowing is the scientific method. Psychological research has been greatly influenced by this approach to knowing, and while a theory cannot be "proven" in the absolute sense, experimental and other kinds of research can provide evidence for or against certain conclusions. Perhaps the greatest value of the scientific method is being able to test ideas and then discard those which are not trustworthy.

The Christian can find value in each of the above ways of knowing. Even tenacity may be acceptable when it comes to affirming the existence of God, although we need to find other reasons to believe as well. The scientific method is predominant in modern psychology, yet we must realize that science rests upon certain a priori beliefs (such as the concept of an orderly universe) and authority (such as trusting accounts of what other researchers have found). The scientific method also involves reason and may even make use of common sense to form propositions to be tested.

The Scientific Method

Essentially science involves the proposal of an idea, called a hypothesis, which is then tested in some way; finally, the results of that test are evaluated to determine if the original idea is confirmed. As a result of using this method the prevailing concepts that guide research, called theories, are either substantiated, modified, or rejected.

The scientific method can make use of several different research approaches (Martin 1985, 3–16). One such approach would be to carefully observe human behavior to see if one action occurs regularly with another. For example, we might ask if annual income is in any way related to church attendance. The relationship between the two factors (or variables) is expressed as a correlation. A perfect correlation could be designated as a +1.00 (all those with a high income go to church; all those with a low income do not attend church) or a –1.00 (all those with a low income go to church; all those with a high income do not attend church). If there is no relationship between the two variables,

the correlation is .00 (income level is completely unrelated to church attendance). Correlations between .00 and .30 (or between .00 and –.30) generally indicate little or no relationship, while correlations above .70 (or below –.70) generally indicate a strong relationship (Hinkle, Wiersma, and Jurs 1988, 85).

Of course, a correlation does not imply anything about cause and effect. For example, even if spanking was found to be related to delinquency, we could not thereby conclude that spanking caused delinquency. It may be the case that delinquents misbehaved more as children and thus received more spankings.

We can also determine a correlation by having people fill out surveys or by interviewing them. Surveys and interviews can also be used to discover how many people favor a particular option (as is done in opinion polls) or simply to generate new ideas ("How can we raise funds for the youth group?").

Another method of conducting research is the case study, which involves an in-depth account of a given individual (Martin 1985, 14–16). This approach rejects the use of statistics in favor of verbal descriptions obtained by interviewing, self-report, or possibly examination of certain records. The case study was central to Freud's work and is still commonly used in abnormal psychology and counseling research.

The predominant research method in contemporary psychology is the experiment. Experimental design involves manipulating the level of the independent variable (the suspected cause) and holding as many other factors as possible constant. An experiment is a set of controlled observations, and may consist of a few observations or many. In practice scientists make some kind of measurement in two or more groups of subjects (usually a "control" group and an "experimental" group).

Spotlight 1.1.
An Experiment: *Learning Worship Service Roles*

Ratcliff (1985) undertook a study to determine if preschool children could learn worship service roles, such as preaching, song leading, ushering, and leading in prayer. Two experimental groups were used in order to compare two ways of teaching children.

The independent variable was how the children learned church roles: (1) by being told where they made mistakes and then practicing the role; (2) by an adult performing the role followed by the children practicing it; or (3) by allowing the children to practice the roles without any feedback. The third group was the control group because it was the standard or norm against which the first two groups (the experimental groups) would be compared. The dependent variable was how well each group performed the roles. This required measurement; thus the aspects of each role had to be defined. For example, the role of leading in prayer included: (1) saying "God," "Jesus," or "Lord"; (2) praying with closed eyes; (3) bowing of the head; and (4) saying "amen" at the end of the prayer. One point was given for each aspect.

By comparing the total points for each group after instruction, the differences between methods of teaching could be compared. (Note that such totals are only comparable if the children in each of the groups are equivalent in such areas as age, gender, and previous knowledge of the roles. Furthermore, each group must be treated identically [other than the independent variable, of course]. The other sources of bias mentioned in the text must also be considered.)

In this experiment, the children who were shown how to perform the role scored higher than those who were told what their mistakes were. The control group did not do as well as either experimental group, but this may have been due to the particular children studied.

The control group serves as the norm or standard against which observations of the experimental group are compared. The experimental group is the group that is directly tested by the experimenter. The independent variable is whatever the experimenter changes in the experimental group, or the factor which makes it different from the control group. The dependent variable is the variable that is expected to change as a result of variations in the independent variable.

The experimenter will try to find out whether the independent variable produces a variation in the dependent variable by comparing experimental and control groups. Presumably all other variables have been controlled. Put another way, the subjects have all been treated exactly the same except for the independent variable.

Sources of Bias

Certain factors in psychological research must be carefully controlled. The first is subject selection. Bias or distortion can be introduced into research by the way the scientist chooses the subjects or groups. For example, because human subjects are reluctant to volunteer, researchers might take whomever they can get, perhaps even their own relatives. As a result, they may reach conclusions that do not represent the opinions or behavior of people in general. Common biases in subject selection relate to racial, ethnic, educational, vocational, and religious backgrounds. Any one of these biases may

---

Spotlight 1.2. Research in the Church

There is a genuine need for research in the church today. It is quite possible to have good worship services and for Christian leaders to be very active, and yet the real job is never accomplished because the needs and opinions of church members are never considered.

The material in this chapter is not sufficient to prepare an individual for doing research in the church. Top-quality research takes more detailed training than reading a chapter in a textbook or attending a class period or two in introductory psychology. A good place to begin preparation for doing research is Engel's *How Can I Get Them to Listen?* There are also specialized courses in research methods.

How can research be used to help the church? Consider a key research method in psychology, the experiment, in which some factor is changed in order to determine what the result will be. (It is important to remember that results of any experiment must be measurable or at least describable in terms of tangible behavior in order to be useful.) In a church service there are many variables with which a church leader may want to experiment, such as the way the offering is taken (passing plates, placing plates at the door, or providing an offering box on the rear wall). A church may experiment with different kinds of services such as a fellowship or testimony meeting rather than the standard Sunday evening sermon. A series of sermons on a topic might be compared with having guest speakers or missionary services. Recorded music might be played over the PA system before a service to see if the congregation feels more worshipful as a result. Different methods of presenting sermons or Sunday school lessons could be tried, such as using an overhead projector to display the main points of the message. Or films and videotapes could be compared with live presentations to see which is most effective and helpful.

Experimentation could be extended beyond the church service to determine what kinds of fellowship are best for the church. Do Bible studies, church dinners, parties, or other special functions promote fellowship? The pastor might experiment to see if his visitation is more effective than lay visitation. Does any kind of visitation increase attendance or does it have some other kind of benefit? Do

completely nullify the effect of the independent variable.

A second source of bias is the placebo effect. No matter what the independent variable or what the experimenter does to the experimental group, there may be a change in the dependent variable. The placebo problem strongly affects research on the effectiveness of psychotherapy. For example, some clients get better just knowing that they will get psychotherapy, without ever seeing a doctor.

A third source of bias is the experimenters themselves and their assumptions. Experimenters must control what they can, be as open as possible about

---

bus ministries, junior church, or new methods of evangelism improve the impact of the church either numerically or in terms of spiritual growth? How does a new curriculum compare with the old?

While many other ideas could be suggested, the important thing is that you measure your impact *before* you start the experiment so that afterwards you will have something with which to compare the results. Your findings should be in some way measurable or at least be described in terms of tangible behavior to be most useful.

It might also be helpful to conduct a general survey of the church to learn people's preferences and opinions before the experiment (Engel's book is most helpful for this). The survey could be repeated after changes have been implemented in order to obtain people's reactions. They may be able to put things down on paper which they would be reluctant to say. Keep in mind that an increase (or decrease) in attendance is not the only criterion. More important than sheer numbers is whether people are growing spiritually.

It is important to give experiments sufficient time to work. One or two attempts may not be adequate. People may need some time to warm up to an idea, or it may be a bad week. Usually several weeks are required before results can be ascertained. There are exceptions, of course: if the minister preaches in a clown suit and no one attends, the idea probably should be rejected!

There are other ways of conducting research besides the experiment. One method is a qualitative approach known as ethnography. This method is standard procedure for most anthropologists when they study a new tribe or culture. Careful observation or interviews can determine what is actually being accomplished in church or Sunday school. Church activities may have results which are quite different from what was originally intended. While Van-Leeuwen (1982, 114–35) lays the groundwork for this approach, the specifics demand detailed guidelines (Lofland and Lofland 1984).

While research may not be exciting, the results can be highly informative and valuable. Certainly missionaries and those in other church ministries can make use of the experimental approach as well. What works in one place may not work in another. How better to find out what really does work than research?

bias, and accept the limitations under which all scientists work.

Is the Scientific Method Appropriate?

VanLeeuwen (1982, 94–98) notes that above psychological theory stands the paradigm. A paradigm is the overall assumptions and general approach that psychologists share. While theories may change, the broader paradigm rarely does. The current paradigm for psychology is the scientific method, a paradigm borrowed from the natural sciences.

VanLeeuwen doubts whether the approach used by physicists and biologists is appropriate for the study of human behavior and thinking. If the paradigm is faulty, the methods of research and theories that are produced by that paradigm are then also suspect.

VanLeeuwen suggests that psychology is presently in the midst of a paradigm change. Researchers are beginning to realize that people are not merely machines or animals. Thus the natural science approach is insufficient; Christians consequently have a valuable opportunity to influence the paradigm change.

VanLeeuwen questions the strict cause-and-effect assumptions of natural scientists, and instead favors recognition of the freedom of choice people exercise. She notes the presence of reflexivity—the tendency of participants in experiments to think about the experiment and thus change their behavior from what it would be otherwise (1982, 115–16).

To counter reflexivity, some researchers have misled participants into thinking the psychologist is studying something other than what is actually being studied. This is done so that the behavior the participants change will be unrelated to the variables being researched. While this seems to work for a while, VanLeeuwen points out

the obvious ethical issue of deception. In addition, as psychological research and accounts of deception in that research are disseminated, reflexivity becomes an even greater problem. People who participate in psychological research may come to distrust what researchers tell them at the beginning of a study and wonder what is really being investigated.

Ethics in Research

In recent years ethics has become an intense concern in psychological research. Most universities, for example, require the approval of an ethics committee prior to conducting research. An ethics committee considers such issues as informed consent, potential dangers to those being studied, debriefing of participants after research, and whether the potential findings are worth the difficulties involved. Not only is human research carefully monitored by such groups, but increasingly research involving animals is screened to insure that unnecessary cruelty is avoided.[1]

Yet a critical issue remains: Are Christians to trust any research conducted under a paradigm originally intended for sciences like physics and biology? Is human behavior in any way similar to the functioning of machines and animals?

Christianity and the Scientific Method

Schaeffer, in *The God Who Is There*, maintains that people are in some ways like God and in other ways more like animals and machines (Schaeffer 1968; Koteskey 1983, 26–28). God is both personal and infinite; while people have the first attribute, they do not have the latter. Thus people are quite different from animals and machines in certain ways and yet resemble them in others (see fig. 1.1).

1. For a Christian perspective on research involving animals, see Boyce 1985.

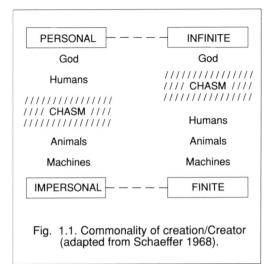

Fig. 1.1. Commonality of creation/Creator (adapted from Schaeffer 1968).

Francis of Assisi expressed this well when he spoke of being brother to the animals and heavenly bodies. This means that we can make use of psychological research (even animal research) based on the natural science paradigm if we bear in mind that human behavior is distinctive. We share a commonality of creation with animals and machines, but we also share the image of God with our Creator.

Indeed, VanLeeuwen (1985, 245–48) makes it clear that she is not advocating wholesale rejection of the existing approach, but instead the broadening of psychology's paradigm to embrace the entire range of human functioning, including those aspects that elude the mainstream scientific method. Creative theorizing and contact with other subject areas are needed, as well as adoption of such Christian assumptions as the existence of human freedom, the necessity of ethical and truthful research approaches, and the complementary use of other research methods.[2]

Is psychology likely to be influenced by Christianity in a paradigm change, as Van-Leeuwen has suggested? There are a number of indications that this might be possi-

2. Evans 1989 presents much the same argument.

ble. Several years ago, Zimbardo (1982, 59) stated that "now that cognitive psychology has taken the head once lopped off by radical behaviorism and returned it to the body of psychology, we might in the next 10 years consider implanting a heart or a little soul in the same body." Certainly Zimbardo is not speaking directly of a need for Christianity, but his statement does reflect a desire to address issues currently missing in the discipline. Certainly the heart and soul are considered at length in the Scriptures.

Menninger (1973) has written a now classic book entitled *Whatever Became of Sin?* (although he concentrates upon what he regards as social sin rather than personal sin). More recently Peck (1978, 1983), beginning from an essentially secular position but finding himself confronted with the reality of the spiritual world, has written best-sellers that relate spiritual issues to psychology. Books written by Christian psychologist James Dobson have sold widely—even in secular bookstores. Perhaps an infusion of Christianity into psychology has begun, or will soon begin.

Psychology and Christianity

The discipline of psychology not only embraces a diversity of subjects and interests, but also provides practical knowledge for everyday living. The fact that both psychology and the Bible provide information for daily living as well as information about how human beings can be expected to think and behave in various environments has sometimes produced tension.

In a sense, psychology is wide open. Psychologists themselves debate about how to study their science, how to utilize it in everyday life, and where it should go as a discipline. It is appropriate for Christians trained in the discipline to present a Christian viewpoint of the field of psychology. Of course, many writers have attempted to popularize the information produced by psychological research and Christians have often reacted "for" or "against" certain discoveries on the basis of inadequate information. Conflict between theology and science has existed for centuries, as evidenced by the problems of Copernicus and Galileo. Many Christians have tended to take a viewpoint opposite of whatever scientific position has been presented. The viewpoint of Christians on certain issues has been largely misinformed and has sometimes sprung from irrelevant theology.

As a result of these tensions, the Christian community has often been suspicious of or even hostile toward psychology and the social sciences. Such hostility has at times been justified because of the outrageous claims and interpretations of social scientists. Sometimes the church has felt itself a bastion of human rights amid a sea of depersonalization fostered by the reductionism of the scientific method.

Ways of Relating Psychology and Theology

Carter and Narramore (1979), adapting the analysis of history developed by Niebuhr (1951), suggest that there are four possible ways of relating psychology and theology.

The first position is the Christianity against psychology position. In recent years a number of prominent Christians have written polemics against psychology, accusing it of being at best a competitor of Christianity and at worst a new age conspiracy of Satan. Jay Adams, a well-known Christian counselor, made similar attacks on mainstream psychology in the early 1970s. He commented on Dobson's *Dare to Discipline* (1970) by saying that "his near total capitulation to behaviorism is couched in Christian terms but really introduces an equally godless system in Christian terms. . . . Dobson's approach is cold and godless. It centers upon manipulation" (1973, 82).

Spotlight 1.3.
Christians Take on Psychology

A few years ago a small-town newspaper printed a letter written by a local pastor advocating that Christians avoid psychologists. After reading some materials written by Jay Adams, he came to the conclusion that sin was the source of every problem and repentance was the only solution. Reading the Bible, not talking to a counselor, was what was needed, he wrote. He also said that psychology teaches people to be humanistic, thus following the "hollow and deceptive philosophy, which depends on human tradition and the basic principles of this world" (Col. 2:8). The pastor felt that people should turn from psychology to God.

As Christians we may need to inform a brother or sister who has not seen the opposite side of an issue. Following the example of Priscilla and Aquila, such correction should preferably be done in private (Acts 18:26) so that the erring person has the opportunity to emend his position. Yet, if the individual fails to undertake needed action and the error is serious, public correction may be needed (1 Tim. 5:20).

Spotlight 1.4.
Psychologists Take on Religion

Some psychologists assume a psychology against Christianity position. They tell people to stop using religion as a crutch, and to begin to develop inner strength. They may recommend that clients stop reading the Bible and begin reading self-help literature. They may even suggest that people stop attending church (but, of course, continue attending counseling sessions!).

Perhaps it is because of such unfortunate experiences that people are attracted to the Christianity against psychology perspective. Yet going to the other extreme may not help much—troubled individuals will probably continue to have problems.

It might be helpful to recognize that most psychologists are tolerant, if not supportive, of a client's religious beliefs. Either a Christian counselor or a sympathetic non-Christian psychologist might be considered.

It is unfortunate that some counselors are strongly opposed to Christianity. It should be a top priority for anyone involved in Christian ministry to check out the attitudes about Christianity held by local psychologists. It is also good to be acquainted with their specialties. Local hospital chaplains are often helpful sources of such information. Insight might be gleaned from members of the local ministerial association. Of course, there is no substitute for getting acquainted firsthand if there is a local mental health association.

If local counselors are not appropriate, there may be a Christian psychologist within driving distance. Regardless, it is a good idea to know of someone, preferably several people, who are trustworthy yet competent in counseling. As a last resort, ask the secretarial staff at the local mental health center. Though they are not allowed to discuss individual cases, they may be able to provide the general orientation of the counselors they work for.

Those who take the Christianity against psychology position see no value in psychology and thus reduce all problems to the spiritual arena (sometimes adding the possibility of physical problems). Benner (1988, 44) asserts that this spiritual reductionism makes all psychotherapy contrary to God's purposes. Like the approach of Job's "comforters," this position invariably traces the problem to personal sin.

A second position is the psychology against Christianity position. Here psychology is thought to have the answers while Christianity is viewed as either unimportant or detrimental to healthy living. This position is exemplified by Freud, who asserted that Christianity is pathological. Watson, and to a lesser extent Fromm, also belong in this category (Benner 1988, 47–48). Like the Christianity against psychology position, this one is reductionistic. Both positions oversimplify by reducing everything to one viewpoint.

As a contemporary example of the psychology against Christianity position, consider this prepublication blurb describing *Neuropsychological Bases of God Beliefs* (Parsinger 1987):

Spotlight 1.5. Science and the Bible

A case for the scientific method can be made from the Bible. We will examine only a sample of the many passages that relate conceptually to the principle of careful investigation that is behind the scientific method.

For example, consider Ecclesiastes 11:6:

Sow your seed in the morning,
    and at evening do not let your hands be idle,
for you do not know which will succeed,
    whether this or that,
    or whether both will do equally well.

We as Christians must be careful to base our conclusions on research, not guesswork.

Judging by casual appearance is not sufficient (John 7:24). Proverbs 25:2 says "to search out a matter is the glory of kings." If this is true for kings, why not the rest of us? Why not make use of the scientific variety of "searching" called research?

Isaiah 28:26 implies that God is at work in a person's careful analysis of cause and effect. God "instructs him and teaches him the right way," God counsels us by helping us discover what works.

We might look to the mining and refining allegory in Job 28:1–3 as a model for the Christian study of psychology. We need to mine the accumulated insights of psychology and refine them with both further research and biblical understanding.

An intriguing section of Scripture parallels the Christian's use of psychology. In 2 Samuel 8:7–14 we have an account of David's conquering his enemies and taking shields of gold from them. After he took the shields, he dedicated them to God. In Crabb's terms, he "spoiled the Egyptians." The passage concludes by stating that God protected David wherever he went, apparently with the help of the shields. We may likewise make use of the findings of psychology for both personal insight and helping others. We must not worship the shields, but we can be assured that God will use that knowledge if it is first dedicated to him.

The author skillfully blends modern neurophysiology with critical behavioral psychology to offer an objective explanation of why people believe in God. . . . The author begins with the biological component of the explanation for God beliefs. From the start, he asserts that God Experiences are products of the human brain. He explains that when certain portions of the brain are stimulated, God Experiences, tempered by the person's learning history, are evoked. He shows that the God Experience correlates with transient electrical instabilities within the temporal lobe of the brain.

A third perspective may be described as the Christianity and psychology viewpoint, which affirms the two disciplines as separate but equal ways of finding truth. Benner (1988, 41) emphasizes the dualistic nature of this separation which is contrary to biblical holism. The Bible teaches that people are not segmented but rather function as wholes. Benner adduces Minirth and Tournier as examples of people holding this view.

The final approach is the psychology integrates Christianity view. Here the person is seen fundamentally as a unity. While we may speak of levels of analysis—meaning that people can be explained from several perspectives at one time (MacKay 1979, 30)—humans are fundamentally a unity (Benner 1988, 41). Some Christians have adopted the monist theological correlate of this position, which denies the possibility of the self existing apart from the body after death (Myers and Jeeves 1987, 24–30), although this conclusion is not necessitated by Christian holism.

Carter and Narramore favor the fourth approach; other noteworthy evangelical writers have developed the perspective further (Farnsworth 1985; Collins 1981; Kirwan 1984). Yet there is a danger in adopting this model uncritically. Integration can easily become syncretism, a mixing of paganism and Christianity to produce a sub-Christian, compromising faith.

Rather than accepting any of the four models entirely, it may be better to adopt an eclectic approach, taking the best features of each of the four models. Crabb (1977, 47–52) speaks of "spoiling the Egyptians," referring to the Old Testament account of the Israelites taking gold and other precious materials from Egypt and leaving the leeks and onions behind. Perhaps we as Christians should make use of those psychological concepts that are useful and compatible with Scripture and leave behind those that conflict with our faith.

While each model has weaknesses, each also has some value. The first underscores the importance of the Bible and God. The second model emphasizes the importance of being open to psychological investigation to avoid rationalizing less than Christian behavior (for example, do people attend church because of their beliefs, desire for relief from guilt, or the need for socioeconomic validation?). A psychological reflection upon biblical content may reveal insights not discovered otherwise (such as the behavioral emphasis in the Book of Proverbs).

The separation model also has value. The differences in the questions asked and approaches to answering them would lend themselves to a creative interface when the integrity of both Christianity and psychology is maintained. Finally, there is obvious value in the integration model's holistic approach. A person is a unity, not a dichotomy (at least while in this life). This approach is likely to encourage a cross-fertilization of ideas from both psychology and Christianity, enhancing creativity and intellectual productivity.

Sources of Data

As we examine the relationship between psychology and Christianity, it may help to consider a diagram of Christian eclecticism (see fig. 1.2). Here the ultimate source of knowledge is God as he has revealed truth. Two sources of revelation are generally identified by theologians: special revelation (the Bible) and general revelation (God's creation—nature/humanity). Other forms of revelation might be possible ("God told me") but are usually considered secondary and subordinate to the two primary revelations. These two sources of information constitute data bases of potential information to be considered: the data of the Bible and the data of nature/humanity. While the Bible has the advantage of being inspired and inerrant, nature/humanity has the disadvantage of being fallen and imperfect (Ackerman 1988).

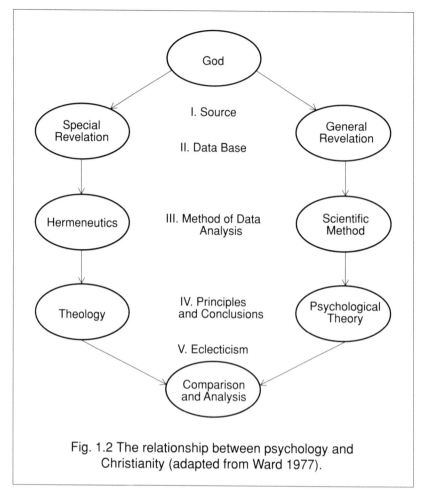

Fig. 1.2 The relationship between psychology and Christianity (adapted from Ward 1977).

Each of these sources has a distinct method of data analysis. Hermeneutics is used to study the Bible, while the scientific method is used to study nature/humanity. Thus we should study the Bible by considering issues such as cultural context, historical context, language, literary forms, and so on.[3] The methodology of the scientific method is quite different.[4]

Since the data sources and the methods of analysis are different, we would expect to find differences in the conclusions reached by each discipline. This is, in fact, sometimes the case. These conclusions, in the form of psychological theories and theological constructs, are at once interpretive, tentative, and summarize the best data in each area.

The final level of analysis is the comparison of the conclusions from the two areas to find where they are similar, complementary, interactive, and at odds. There is theological and biblical reflection upon psychology and psychological reflection upon theology and the Bible. The guiding principle is that both are products of God's revelation and both portray humanity (although neither is exhaustive in its description). Conflicts between theology and psychology are due either to error in biblical interpretation, error in using the scientific

3. Several fine books on hermeneutics written from an evangelical/psychological perspective are available. See Virkler 1981; Johnson 1983.

4. Yet it should be noted that psychology would benefit from an analysis of its hermeneutical methods. See Evans 1989, 45–66, 138–42.

method, or both. Since both are derived from God's revelation, accurate findings in each will not conflict. All truth is God's truth. We do best, therefore, to adopt an eclectic approach, tentatively accepting those psychological principles that have good research evidence and do not conflict with biblical data. These principles must also be congruent with general biblical principles. Theological conclusions must be tested using both biblical and valid psychological insights. There is also room for deferring judgment on a particular idea until more information is available. Some of the areas of potential comparison and compatibility are outlined in table 1.1.

Sources of Tension Between Psychology and Christianity

Some of the antipathy felt by Christians toward psychology results from the difficulty of defining precisely where psychology as a discipline begins and where it ends. Many psychologists are not comfortable delineating a difference between psychology and physiology, neurology, sociology, or philosophy. Because psychology tends to cover a wide range of subject matter, it is difficult to focus on specific contact points between psychological knowledge and Christian belief and practice. As Christians have attempted to integrate the divergent models of contemporary psychology and to identify their common underlying assumptions, they have sometimes picked up implications and assumptions about the nature of humanity that are inconsistent with the Scriptures.

Another source of strain is that both psychology and theology sometimes use concepts which, by their nature, are not directly observable, but which nevertheless help them to make sense of observable events. Consider the theoretical concept of depression, which may accurately describe feelings of sadness, waking up early in the morning hours, a general feeling of vague discomfort, loss of appetite, and several other behavioral events. Some people think of depression as an objective entity, but it is best regarded as a symptom of a number of possible problems. For example, when individuals are experiencing a great deal of stress, they may manifest depression (that is, sadness, inability to sleep, loss of appetite, and so on). Although such individuals are depressed, they probably do not have the condition of depression. Depression in that sense is a theoretical construct.

Theoretical constructs permit operational definitions and model building by scientists. Models frequently represent the mental framework of the individual con-

Table 1.1 Areas of Potential Comparison and Compatibility		
Theology	**Psychology**	**Example**
Sin	Abnormal psychology	Peck 1983
Salvation and spiritual growth	Developmental psychology	Darling 1969; Benner 1988
The church	Social psychology	Bolt and Myers 1984; Griffin 1982
Angels	Parapsychology	Koteskey 1980
Christ and the Holy Spirit	Counseling	McKenna 1977; Gilbert and Brock 1985
Nature of man	Personality	Burke 1987
Future things	Behavioral psychology	Bufford 1981

Source: Adapted from Carter and Mohline 1976; Collins 1981.

structing the model. Theology provides us with other theoretical constructs to aid us in building models about creation which can guide our further examination of creation. The problem, of course, is that theological and psychological constructs can and do conflict. The important thing to remember, however, is that it is the constructs we develop in each of these disciplines that cause the problems, not the truth behind those constructs.

A final source of tension is that many social scientists do not believe in God. Probably more scientists in the natural sciences such as geology, chemistry, and physics believe in God than do scientists in the social sciences. The extent to which scientists exclude from their thinking the concept of God will directly influence the kind of models they build to cope with the data they observe. For example, reliance upon strict cause-and-effect assumptions precludes divine intervention and miracles.

The Evaluation of Psychology

An individual who accepts the presupposition that God exists can understand truth to some extent from God's perspective and thus be more receptive to the truth found in his creation. In addition, the Christian should excel in scientific endeavors since that excellence is part of commitment to God. God is the ultimate source of truth. Because truth exists in God, his creation can represent only an abstraction of it. Our apprehension or knowledge of that creation (that is, the way we observe the creation) is a second level of abstraction. We Christians benefit in our understanding of truth by accepting both presuppositions: that God is the source of truth, and that God is the Creator. When we observe creation, we also observe God's truth.

Christians also benefit from the assumption of a special revelation from God in the Scriptures. In that special revelation, God has revealed himself, presented his message of Jesus Christ, and offered salvation and forgiveness to all humankind. Christians who believe in the inerrancy of the Scriptures have not only their own observation of God's truth through creation but also God's Word to guide their study of creation.

The Christian psychologist thus has several advantages over the secular psychologist. Not only do Christians approach the world from the perspective that truth is revealed in God's creation, but they also have a "grid," the Word of God, through which to evaluate what they observe within creation. With that grid they can sift truth from error.

All persons, whoever they are, who diligently study creation, will come to a knowledge of some truth. Paul states: "since what may be known about God is plain to them, because God has made it plain to them. For since the creation of the world God's invisible qualities—his eternal power and divine nature—have been clearly seen, being understood from what has been made, so that men are without excuse" (Rom. 1:19–20).

Thus both Christians and non-Christians who study creation will be observing God's truth. Christians place their ultimate faith in God, who is revealed in the Bible. This gives them an accurate understanding of the truth of God in creation. Secular scientists who can also observe truth in creation, do make important discoveries, such as penicillin or X-radiation, even without such clear guidance. Such discoveries of God's truth, although not contained in the Bible, are still representative of the grace of God toward humankind. That they are made by non-Christian scientists does not change the fact that they are examples of God's grace, mercy, and truth.

Often, of course, the theoretical conceptual systems of humans will be imperfect because of their abstraction and also because of the implicit presuppositions underlying them. A scientist may make a valid discovery, but be led by personal presuppositions to interpret and apply that discovery in an incorrect manner.

Of course, try as it might, the science of psychology will never explain the purpose and meaning of human existence. Such questions go beyond the level of the science of psychology to engage the field of theology. To expect that the science of psychology might reveal the answers or even that the scientists who study psychology could comment accurately about such questions is a misunderstanding, not necessarily of science, but of the levels of explanation we can have for certain questions in life. Ultimately, the questions of human existence are theological questions for the Christian, grounded in faith and the Word of God. Ideally, the explanations of science and the Christian's understanding of the Bible should complement one another.

Christians should never raise a scientific truth to the same level as that of Scripture. We hold the Scripture to be God's inerrant Word; apparent scientific truth has often later been proved inaccurate. In the study of any science, of course, Christians should be firmly grounded in the Word of God. We must build from special revelation a grid of knowledge that will allow us to test whether the scientific models and theoretical constructs presented by scientists are indeed in agreement with God's creation.

Human Beings in Holistic Perspective

A holistic model assumes that human behavior might be described in different ways by different disciplines, each accounting essentially for the same behavior. For example, within the domain of theology we might categorize a specific human behavior as sexual immorality. Since Scripture is very clear about what constitutes sin, sexual immorality can be described as sin from a theological viewpoint. Within the science of psychology, sexual immorality or promiscuous sexual behavior might be described as a result of early childhood experiences. It might be accounted for on the basis of an identity crisis or by the fact that adolescents are striking out and rebelling against their parents. It might also be attributed to frustration; overcrowding of an urban ghetto, for example, which causes extreme boredom and a lack of productive effort, might also be expected to lead to sexual immorality. All such descriptions from within the domain of the science of psychology could accurately apply to the behavior of sexual immorality. Another discipline such as physiology, however, might conceivably discover that the chromosomal makeup of certain individuals is associated with increased sexual drive, leading them to engage in sexual immorality. To say that the theological, psychological, or genetic description of sexual immorality is most accurate would be naive. To a Christian, all valid descriptions bring credit to God as the Creator.

Several different disciplines may in fact be able to give a valid account of the same event or phenomenon. Such equally valid but incomplete accounts are said to be complementary. The fact that an adolescent is in rebellion against a parent does not change the fact that sexual immorality is sin. In other words, the psychological description is not in conflict with the theological description, but the two descrip-

---

Spotlight 1.6. Pastoral Counseling

Beyond the research and teaching efforts of Christian professionals in the field of psychology, another strong tradition of Christian psychology exists within the domain of theology. Usually called pastoral psychology or pastoral counseling, this discipline is represented by individuals who have attempted to develop a Christian psychology from a theological perspective. Frequently pastors or theologians have attempted to formulate a Christian psychology out of a need to help their parishioners. On the whole such efforts have been outstanding and can be considered a worthwhile contribution to applied psychology.

Within the tradition of pastoral counseling would fall the significant work of Anton T. Boisen, a minister who as a result of several mental breakdowns concluded that the church was neglecting the field of mental health. He became a social worker at the Boston Psychopathic Hospital and made many observations on the relationship between religious experience and mental health. Other leaders in the field have been Clyde M. Narramore and Henry R. Brandt. Their writings have convinced many evangelical Christians that psychology can be both biblical and functional. Presently most conservative seminaries have departments of pastoral psychology and counseling.

Broad categories of pastoral counselors can be differentiated to some extent on the basis of their use of biblical absolutes in counseling and their use of psychology in counseling.

---

tions actually complement or complete one another.

In the past, Christian philosophy has often been characterized by Platonic dualism, by a strong differentiation between body and soul. Among biblical scholars, however, a consensus is growing that the Scriptures present human nature not as two distinct substances, but as one whole entity. A close examination of Old Testament and New Testament terminology reveals a distinctly holistic picture.

In Christian psychology, problems are often categorized as spiritual, psychological, or physical. Such categories correspond to the biblical concepts of spirit, soul, and body, respectively. Although those divisions are useful in helping us think about human experiences, we need to remember that in reality a person is a whole and must be dealt with as such. Theologians have long argued about whether human beings are dichotomous (with material and nonmaterial components) or trichotomous (with spirit, soul, and body components). The basic difference seems to be between those who are impressed with such divisions and those who are not! Any division of human experience or of human personality encountered in this text should be regarded as arbitrary and operational only. The predominant emphasis in the Bible is upon the *whole* person.

Christian Contributions to Psychology

We might get the impression that Christians today are discovering psychology for

One category would include CPE (clinical pastoral education). This organization has well-developed and extensive training programs available in many hospitals and seminaries. Some of the instructors hold to a liberal theological orientation.

A second category includes the evangelical popularizers of counseling, often popular speakers, whose presentations contain practical advice on daily living. Bill Gothard's "Institute of Basic Youth Conflicts" seminars are a well known example. Keith Miller, Bruce Larson, Tim LaHaye, Norman Wright, and Charles W. Shedd are known in evangelical circles as both popular speakers and prolific writers. In general they have a conservative theological orientation and strongly advocate the use of biblical absolutes as guides to daily living. Their impact on the Christian is on the whole beneficial, helping to solve many of the basic problems people face.

A third group includes those pastoral counselors who seek a middle course, advocating a balance of theology and psychology. Although Adams strongly emphasizes directive counseling based on Scripture, his methods have much in common with psychology (although he would never admit as much). Professional psychologists such as Gary R. Collins, Maurice Wagner, Paul D. Morris, Donald F. Tweedie, and H. Newton Malony have done much to advance the integration of theology and psychology. Their influence has been instrumental in expanding the psychological insights of Christians.

the first time. Actually Christians are reclaiming territory that rightfully belongs to them (Sovine 1988). It was the rise of science that first began to polarize psychology and theology; when science lost its original theistic base the divorce became complete.

Christians have been actively involved in both psychology and theology for centuries. VandeKemp (1984) annotates hundreds of sources dating from 1672 to 1965 dealing with these two areas. Christians have historically been involved in the care of the mentally ill. The clergy were the primary caretakers of the mentally disturbed during the Middle Ages. Christians in Belgium formed the community of Gheel in the twelfth century, where the insane were treated with prayer, the laying on of hands, and kindness. Teresa of Avila, a sixteenth-century Spanish nun, introduced the idea of "mental illness." William Tuke, a Quaker, developed a humanitarian institute for the insane in England. His ideas were borrowed by Americans in the form of "moral treatment."

Benjamin Rush was a leader in the use of moral treatment. This proclaimed "father of psychiatry" was significantly influenced by Christian thinking (Theilman and Larson 1984). Likewise Johann Heinroth, who also lived in the nineteenth century, made significant contributions to modern psychology.

Earlier in this century we witnessed the birth of the pastoral counseling movement, and while it has sometimes identified too closely with modernist theology, it is another example of how Christianity relates to psychology.

Today we continue to see an increased interest in psychology on the part of Christians. Dobson has produced numerous books, films, and radio programs. An entire encyclopedia of psychology has been written from a Christian perspective (Benner 1985), and dozens of other books by Christian psychologists have sold widely. Two journals are actively involved in interfacing Christianity and psychology: the *Journal of Psychology and Theology* and the *Journal of Psychology and Christianity*.

The *Journal of Psychology and Theology* is associated with the Rosemead Graduate School of Psychology, accredited by the American Psychological Association (APA). The *Journal of Psychology and Christianity* is associated with the Christian Association of Psychological Studies (CAPS), which has members in a number of countries. There are several other scholarly journals which publish articles that relate psychological and religious issues.

Fuller Theological Seminary offers doctoral degrees in psychology and is APA-accredited. Michigan State University has a Christian psychiatric program, and

---

Spotlight 1.7.
The Father of Psychiatry?

An outstanding Christian pioneer in the field of psychiatry was Johann Christian August Heinroth, who published books and scholarly papers in Germany in the early 1800s. Heinroth was the first psychiatrist to coin the word "psychosomatic" to describe the relationship between spiritual/psychological conflicts and physical illnesses. Heinroth's description of man's tripartite nature, based on Romans 7, divided human personality into: (1) the *Überuns* (conscience), (2) the ego (mind, emotions, and will), and (3) the *Fleisch* (basic drives, including sinful nature). Freud's division of personality into superego, ego, and id merely duplicated Heinroth's model.

Johann Christian August Heinroth (1773–1843)

Heinroth and Freud both described the struggle between the human conscience and selfish drives and impulses. Their solutions were different, however. Freud taught that since the ego (will) was an unconscious slave to the id (basic drives), the solution was to accept that fact and live a pragmatic life, deadening the conscience; otherwise guilt would cause mental illness. Heinroth felt that the ego was a slave to the *Fleisch* (Rom. 7), but that victory could be obtained through the power of the Holy Spirit in a born-again believer (Rom. 8).

Since his discoveries preceded Freud's by a hundred years, Heinroth could be considered the father of psychiatry as well as the father of *Christian* psychiatry. But because most modern psychiatrists consider Heinroth's solutions (faith in Christ and yielding to the Spirit) ridiculous, Freud is considered the father of psychiatry.

many Christian colleges and seminaries have graduate and undergraduate programs in psychology. Many of these schools (particularly those at the graduate level) have waiting lists for entry into their psychology programs, while most other college majors are begging for students. The American Psychological Association has a division which is designated for those psychologists interested in religious issues. Recently there has been a rebirth of interest in the psychology of religion.

Clearly Christianity and psychology are renewing their acquaintance. The long-divorced disciplines are again taking an interest in one another. Is a remarriage possible?

References

Ackerman, P. 1988. The integrated model for relating psychology and Christianity. *Creation Social Science and Humanities Quarterly* (Summer): 7–13.

Adams, J. 1973. *The Christian counselor's manual*. Grand Rapids: Baker.

Benner, D., ed. 1985. *Baker encyclopedia of psychology*. Grand Rapids: Baker.

———. 1988. *Psychotherapy and the spiritual quest*. Grand Rapids: Baker.

Bolt, M., and D. Myers. 1984. *The human connection*. Downers Grove: Inter-Varsity.

Boyce, J. (with C. Lutes). 1985. Animal rights. *Christianity Today* (Sept. 6): 35–39.

Bufford, R. 1981. *The human reflex*. New York: Harper and Row.

Burke, T. 1987. *Man and mind*. Hillsdale, Mich.: Hillsdale College Press.

Carter, J., and R. Mohline. 1976. The nature and scope of integration. *Journal of Psychology and Theology* 5 (Winter): 3–14.

Carter, J., and B. Narramore. 1979. *The integration of psychology and theology*. Grand Rapids: Zondervan.

Collins, G. 1981. *Psychology and theology*. Nashville: Abingdon.

Crabb, L. 1977. *Effective biblical counseling*. Grand Rapids: Zondervan.

Darling, H. 1969. *Man in triumph*. Grand Rapids: Zondervan.

Dobson, J. 1970. *Dare to discipline*. Wheaton, Ill.: Tyndale.

Engel, J. Forthcoming. *How can I get them to listen?* 2d ed. Grand Rapids: Zondervan.

Evans, C. 1989. *Wisdom and humanness in psychology*. Grand Rapids: Baker.

Farnsworth, K. 1985. *Whole-hearted integration*. Grand Rapids: Baker.

Gilbert, M., and R. Brock. 1985. *The Holy Spirit and counseling*. Peabody, Mass.: Hendrickson.

Griffin, E. 1982. *Getting together*. Downers Grove: Inter-Varsity.

Hinkle, D., W. Wiersma, and S. Jurs. 1988. *Applied statistics for the behavioral sciences*. 2d ed. Boston: Houghton Mifflin.

James, W. 1890. *The principles of psychology*. New York: Holt.

Johnson, C. 1983. *The psychology of biblical interpretation*. Grand Rapids: Zondervan.

Kirwan, W. 1984. *Biblical concepts for Christian counseling*. Grand Rapids: Baker.

Koteskey, R. 1980. *Psychology from a Christian perspective*. Nashville: Abingdon.

———. 1983. *General psychology for Christian counselors*. Nashville: Abingdon.

Lofland, J., and L. Lofland. 1984. *Analyzing social settings*. 2d ed. Belmont, Calif.: Wadsworth.

MacKay, D. 1979. *Human science and human dignity*. Downers Grove: Inter-Varsity.

McKenna, D. 1977. *The Jesus model*. Waco: Word.

Martin, D. 1985. *Doing psychology experiments*. 2d ed. Monterey, Calif.: Brooks/Cole.

Menninger, K. 1973. *Whatever became of sin?* New York: Hawthorne.

Myers, D., and M. Jeeves. 1987. *Psychology through the eyes of faith*. San Francisco: Harper and Row.

Niebuhr, H. 1951. *Christ and culture*. New York: Harper and Row.

Parsinger, M. 1987. *Neuropsychological bases of God beliefs*. New York: Praeger.

Peck, M. 1978. *The road less traveled*. New York: Simon and Schuster.

———. 1983. *The people of the lie*. New York: Simon and Schuster.

Ratcliff, D. 1985. The use of play in Christian education. *Christian Education Journal* 6: 26–33.

Ray, W., and R. Rivizza. 1985. *Methods toward a science of behavioral experience*. 2d ed. Belmont, Calif.: Wadsworth.

Schaeffer, F. 1968. *The God who is there*. Downers Grove: Inter-Varsity.

Sovine, C. 1988. *Integration of psychology and theology*. Staley lecture series, Toccoa Falls College, Mar. 22.

Theilman, S., and D. Larson. 1984. Christianity and early American care for the insane. *Journal of Psychology and Christianity* 3 (Fall): 27–34.

VandeKemp, H. 1984. *Psychology and theology in Western thought, 1672–1965*. White Plains, N.Y.: Kraus International.

VanLeeuwen, M. 1982. *The sorcerer's apprentice*. Downers Grove: Inter-Varsity.

———. 1985. *The person in psychology*. Grand Rapids: Eerdmans.

Virkler, H. 1981. *Hermeneutics*. Grand Rapids: Baker.

Ward, W. 1977. *The Bible in counseling*. Chicago: Moody.

Zimbardo, P. 1982. Psychology today: The state of the science. *Psychology Today* 16 (May): 58–59.

The Biological Basis
of Behavior

The relationship between biology and human behavior has been extensively explored in recent years. One aspect of this topic, how the brain functions, has been popularized by a number of books, as well as by a spectacular PBS television series entitled "The Brain" (Restak 1984). This most complicated organ of the human body has mystified and fascinated people for thousands of years. Yet in spite of considerable advances in knowledge, certain aspects of its functioning continue to elude biologists and psychologists.

Before considering specific mental processes, we should first examine the nervous system. The human nervous system is highly complex, made up of billions of nerve cells containing a small sea of chemicals that relay messages throughout the body. Anatomically the nervous system has two major functional components. The peripheral nervous system consists of specific nerves from the brain stem which control primarily the head and the various senses (the cranial nerves), the nerves from the spinal cord which relay impulses to and from various parts of the body, and the autonomic (involuntary) nervous system. The central nervous system consists of the brain and spinal cord. The brain itself is composed of two cerebral hemispheres, the brain stem, the cerebellum, and the limbic system.

The Neuron

The microscopic unit of the nervous system is the nerve cell or neuron (see fig. 2.1). The neuron is composed of a cell body which contains the nucleus; an axon, a long unbranched fiber extending from the cell body which carries impulses to other neurons, glands, and muscles; and dendrites, shorter branching fibers projecting from the cell body which receive impulses from other neurons. Nerve cell bodies are usually arranged in clusters. Aggregates of nerve cell bodies outside the brain and spinal cord are called ganglia.

Some nerve fibers lack a covering, but most are encased in a

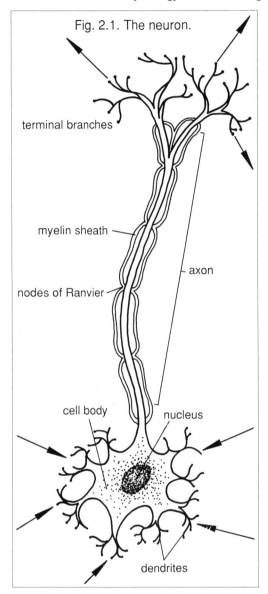

Fig. 2.1. The neuron.

terminal branches

myelin sheath

axon

nodes of Ranvier

cell body

nucleus

dendrites

tion of a dendrite, the inside of the axon becomes chemically positive. This change in polarity occurs in a chain-reactionlike sequence all along the axon (see fig. 2.2). After the impulse has been delivered along the axon via that chemical reaction, the original chemical state of the axon is restored and it is ready for the next impulse transmission. This process is called axonal transmission because it takes place within the axon.

In the process of axon depolarization, chemical changes take place in the terminal branches of the axon (see fig. 2.2). Each terminal branch contains neurotransmitter substances which are released

sheath. Many peripheral fibers have a sheath made of a fatty substance known as myelin. The space between the dendrites of one neuron and the axon of another neuron is called the synapse.

Impulses are carried along the surface of the axon at rates of speed approximating two hundred miles per hour, with speeds varying according to the diameter of the axon and whether it is myelinated. Chemically the inside of the resting neuron is negatively charged. Upon stimula-

---

Spotlight 2.1. Christian Sources on the Brain

Several Christians have considered the relationship between the brain and faith. For example, Donald MacKay, who chaired an interdisciplinary team studying the brain at Keele University in England, pioneered research in this area. MacKay participated in an early debate with B. F. Skinner on William F. Buckley's television program (1971) and wrote an excellent book on the brain from a Christian perspective (MacKay 1980).

MacKay asserts that neuropsychology, as well as psychology and science in general, examine the world at a different level than philosophers and theologians (see chap. 1). Thus the description of physical brain activity is only conclusive at that level of analysis; it certainly does not rule out the religious realm since that is yet another level of analysis.

Several other Christians have written important works on neuropsychology. More philosophical in nature, Custance (1980) and Myers and Jeeves (1987, 19–30) consider the issues of

into the synapse and migrate to a receptor site on the receiving dendrite of the next axon. A chemical reaction takes place, allowing the impulse to continue on to the next neuron and from there to a different part of the nervous system. This process is called synaptic transmission since it occurs within the synapse.

Nerve fibers of the brain and spinal cord having a common origin and destination constitute a tract. Within the tracts, nerve fibers that conduct impulses toward the cell body are called afferent (sensory) fibers, while those that conduct impulses away from the cell body are called efferent (motor) fibers.

The Central Nervous System

The Upper Brain

The average brain of a young adult male weighs 1,380 grams. Its approximately 110 billion cells include 14 billion neurons. The two cerebral hemispheres are incompletely separated into left and right portions. Each of these hemispheres has distinct functions (see fig. 2.3), although they are not as discrete as was once thought (Levy 1983). The hemispheres are connected by the corpus callosum, a broad band of crossing fibers. The surface of each hemisphere is wrinkled and has crevices called fissures. A layer of

---

monism and dualism. The latter along with MacKay make a case for monism from psychological research; they believe that people are fundamentally a unity and that it is illegitimate to separate the soul or spirit from the body.* In contrast, Custance believes that the evidence from brain research points to some kind of separation, which he holds to be the biblical position.

It should be noted that the holistic perspective, which the writers of this book advocate, does not require that we dismiss the possibility of life after death. Exactly what existence we have immediately after death is unknown, although the Bible clearly tells us that Christians will be present with the Lord. We also have the certainty of a future bodily resurrection. Even if we assume that the self is the result of brain activity, this same self could be the result of another source apart from the brain at the moment of death. If the conscious self is the result of the present body, another kind of body could manifest

*See Demski's (1990) critique of the "semi-materialism" implicit in MacKay's (as well as Myers' and Jeeves') conclusions.

that same self. Regardless, the Bible is clear that someday we will be reunited with our earthly bodies, although they will be transformed as Christ's was after his resurrection. This conclusion is generally acceptable to all of the above writers.

D. Gareth Jones, formerly an anatomist at the University of Western Australia, wrote *Our Fragile Brains* (1981). Jones carefully describes brain functions and influences, continually emphasizing Christian and biblical perspectives in the process. For example, he discusses the need for respect for the brain, citing the theological doctrine of people being made in the image of God. He applies this concept to the issues of brain damage, brain control, and personhood.

Collins (1985) has written an excellent book on the mind as it relates to the brain and Christianity. Collins goes beyond mere neurological concerns and surveys almost all of psychology. His approach underscores the primacy of the mind in the study of human thought and behavior, which is, of course, the definition of psychology.

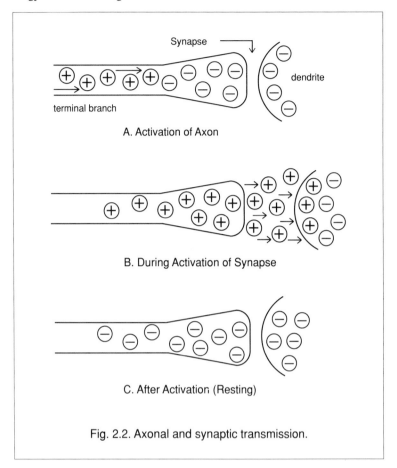

A. Activation of Axon

B. During Activation of Synapse

C. After Activation (Resting)

Fig. 2.2. Axonal and synaptic transmission.

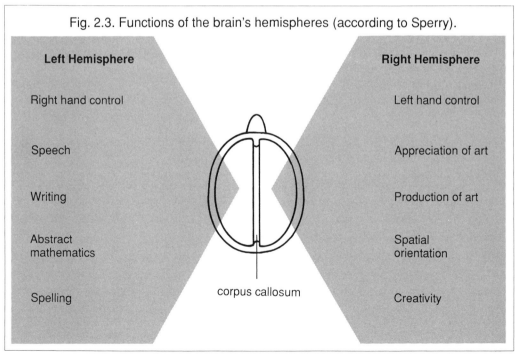

Fig. 2.3. Functions of the brain's hemispheres (according to Sperry).

Left Hemisphere	Right Hemisphere
Right hand control	Left hand control
Speech	Appreciation of art
Writing	Production of art
Abstract mathematics	Spatial orientation
Spelling	Creativity

corpus callosum

Spotlight 2.2.
Localizing Religion in the Brain

Since the two hemispheres of the brain apparently have quite different functions, can we locate faith and religion in some particular part of the brain?

Lee (1985), Owens (1983), and Meyer (1975) associate the right hemisphere with immediate experience and the symbolization of religion. Collins (1985, 28) suggests the possibility that the right hemisphere may also be involved in understanding the complexities of evil and morality. The left hemisphere, in contrast, is more verbal and thus more theological. The above writers claim that certain churches emphasize one hemisphere to the neglect of the other. Because of this proclivity, individuals may lose their sensitivity to other ways of worshiping and serving God; their religion is less than complete.

Certainly we have all been to churches where everything was strictly cerebral; we listen and perhaps even learn but we are not moved. Other churches have moving services, but there is little theology or content to the experience. Clearly we need churches that are intellectually stimulating, experiential, and mystical.

On the other hand, a clear connection between religion and brain function has not been found (Dodrill 1976; Wong 1984). This may be due in part to the fact that the activities of the two hemispheres are not as neatly divided as many would believe.

Regardless, we can conclude that true faith necessarily involves the whole person and thus the whole brain. Christ is in the work of transforming the entire person and thus the whole of the individual should be involved in the worship of and service to God.

cerebral cortex 1.3 to 4.5 millimeters thick covers the entire surface of the cerebrum.

The two major grooves on the lateral surface of the brain are the fissure of Sylvius and the fissure of Rolando. By using them as landmarks, each hemisphere can be divided into four lobes (see fig. 2.4). The frontal lobe is anterior to the fissure of Rolando and above the lateral fissure of Sylvius, while the occipital lobe is at the most posterior part of the hemisphere. The parietal lobe lies between the frontal lobe and the occipital lobe, while the temporal lobe is below the fissure of Sylvius.

The four lobes of the brain all play a part in the receiving, processing, and sending out of the messages which constitute human thinking. Golden (1981, 26–45), following the famous neurologist Luria, delineates the functions of these four lobes in a fairly comprehensive manner.

Tactile sense data (pain, pressure, touch) is conveyed to the primary region of the parietal lobe. A touch on the left side of the body arrives at the parietal lobe on the right side of the brain. If the head is touched, the sensation arrives at the lower part of the parietal area near the fissure of Sylvius; if a leg is touched, the sensation

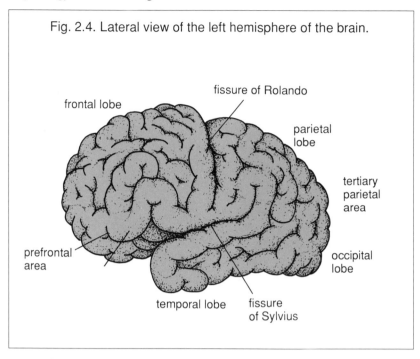

Fig. 2.4. Lateral view of the left hemisphere of the brain.

frontal lobe

fissure of Rolando

parietal lobe

tertiary parietal area

prefrontal area

occipital lobe

temporal lobe

fissure of Sylvius

arrives near the top of the fissure of Rolando. If the primary parietal area is damaged, a person may not be able to perceive being touched or may not recognize objects by touch. This area is closely related to the frontal lobe, which controls motor output. Sensory input is thus closely linked to muscle control in the production of coordinated movement.

The secondary parietal area is located farther back in the parietal lobe. Damage in this area may result in faulty processing of tactile information.

At the rear of the brain is the occipital lobe. The primary occipital area is farthest back; it receives visual information from the eyes. In a sense, then, we all have "eyes in the back of our heads"—that is where information from the eyes enters the brain. If the primary occipital area is damaged, partial or complete loss of vision results even though the eyes themselves are perfectly normal.

The secondary occipital area is located in front of the primary area. This area codes and integrates visual data. If it is

damaged the person is able to see but often misinterprets visual data.

Below the parietal lobe and in front of the occipital lobe is the temporal lobe. The primary area of this lobe is located in the middle-rear section of this part of the brain. The primary temporal area receives information from the ears. Curiously, even though the ears and the temporal lobes are physically close together, most of the information from each ear goes to the opposite temporal lobe. An injury to the primary parietal lobe is often associated with deafness in the opposite ear, even though the ear itself functions normally.

The secondary temporal lobe is located in front of the primary area, and it processes auditory information. When this part of the brain is probed, the person may hear voices or sounds that are not actually present. Because this area is close to the limbic system in the lower part of the brain, damage can produce certain kinds of emotional problems (such as depression or uncontrollable violence). Decoding of speech may also be affected; the individual may hear but not understand speech, or may have difficulties with pitch and rhythm (Golden 1981). Damage to this area may also affect speech because of inaccurate auditory feedback.

While the three lobes considered thus far are concerned with the reception and processing of sensory inputs, the frontal lobe controls sensory output to muscles in the body. The primary frontal area is located anterior to the fissure of Rolando, just opposite the primary parietal area. Like the latter, muscle output corresponds with the part of the body affected; the lower sections connect to muscles in the head while upper areas connect to the legs and feet. Again, the left frontal lobe controls the right side of the body and vice versa. If a stroke victim loses control of the left side of the body, for example, the damage occurred in the right hemisphere. While each frontal lobe controls the opposite half of the body, it is sometimes possible for the same side to take over some functions. Damage to the primary region may cause speaking and singing deficits.

The secondary frontal area, located in front of the primary section, is responsible for organizing behavior. As Golden (1981, 42) describes it, this area sends out "executive orders" to the muscles, constantly adjusting those orders on the basis of feedback from the other lobes. Damage to this area can produce jerky movements or perseveration (repeated movements or speech).

Penfield (1975), in the process of doing brain surgery, found that as he touched certain areas of the brain with an electrode, some individuals would remember specific events. Sometimes an individual would remember the feeling that occurred with a given event. And sometimes an individual would recall only the feeling, such as elation or depression, without any specific recollection of the precipitating event.

Penfield concluded that specific memories and emotions are recorded and stored in precise areas of the brain, although many today question his assumption that memory is like a tape recording (see chap. 7).

The Split Brain

Sperry (1970) conducted research with seizure-disordered individuals in which he severed the corpus callosum of the brain. The epileptic seizures became less frequent as a result. In effect, because of the surgery the left and right hemispheres functioned quite independently of one another. Sperry used this information to delineate the specific functions of each half of the upper brain (see fig. 2.3). The following characteristics were found for those who process language in the left hemisphere (about 90 to 95 percent of right-handed people); characteristics can be different for others.

Sperry discovered that the left half of the brain controls the right half of the body and vice versa. He also found that when split-brain individuals handled objects with their left hand (without seeing the object), they could show through motions what the object was used for but could not name it. He thereby concluded that the right hemisphere could recognize things but was unable to control speech. When objects were placed in their right hand, these individuals could immediately name them; thus the left hemisphere was related to speech.

Sperry maintained that the left hemisphere was involved in the understanding of abstract concepts and complicated calculations, while the right hemisphere was concerned with simple words and was very limited in its ability to carry out calculations. However, the right hemisphere was far superior to the left in assembling designs, identifying emotions on faces, and drawing. While several of his findings

Spotlight 2.3. Epilepsy and Christians

Epilepsy is a significant brain disorder that affects a large number of people. Although there are several kinds of epilepsy, the best-known form produces grand mal seizures in which the individual falls to the floor and begins convulsing for several minutes. Afterward the person is usually dazed or sleeps, then resumes normal activity. Until recent decades little could be done for epileptics, but today a number of medications are prescribed to control seizure activity.

Epilepsy has several possible causes. In some forms seizures are due to electrical storms of neural activity. If an individual has a particularly severe form of epilepsy, the corpus callosum may be surgically cut, which results in a decline in seizure activity.

Is epilepsy the same thing as demon possession? Those who do not accept the Scriptures literally often conclude that epilepsy is described as demon possession because that was the commonly accepted perspective in the New Testament era. But to posit this conclusion is to admit to the possibility of error in the Bible, which we cannot accept.

Since epilepsy can be linked with biological malfunction, it is difficult if not impossible to associate it with the presence of demons as well. Yet there are New Testament accounts of demon possession that include seizure activity. How is this to be explained?

The existence of supernatural evil forces is to be granted. Furthermore, these forces can manifest themselves in ways similar to epilepsy. We know, for example, that fevers can produce epileptic-like seizures. If we accept the biblical record at face value, then, demon possession can also imitate epileptic seizures.

Regardless, the prejudice from which many epileptic individuals suffer is unwarranted. Some states continue to restrict their driving privileges, in spite of the fact that with proper medication most epileptics can be excellent drivers (far safer than someone under the influence of alcohol, for example). Christians must not be prejudiced against others because of physical abnormalities such as epilepsy.

have been verified by recent research (Diehl and McKeever 1987), it is important to note that the differences are not as distinct as once thought (Gazzaniga 1972). In addition, left-handed people often have an altogether different arrangement of hemispheric abilities.

The Lower Brain

The brain stem, below the cerebral hemispheres and the cerebellum, has many connected structures. The medulla oblongata sits at the base of the brain stem and attaches to the spinal cord. The medulla controls heart and respiratory rate, and contains reflex centers for vomiting, sneezing, coughing, and swallowing. The pons lies just above the medulla and contains ascending and descending nerve tracts plus the crossing fibers between the brain stem and the cerebellum. The midbrain, just above the pons, is a reflex center for pain, vision, and hearing. The thalamus and hypothalamus are also part of the lower brain. The thalamus produces conscious recognition of cruder, less critical sensations of pain, temperature, and touch. Relaying sensory impulses to the cerebral cortex, it plays a part in the mechanism responsible for emotions by associating sensory impulses with feelings of pleasantness or unpleasantness. It also plays a part in the arousal mechanism. The hypothalamus, just in front of and beneath the thalamus, is very important in regulating appetite, thirst, sex drive, sleep patterns, body temperature, and emotions. Running throughout the entire brain stem is another specialized system called the reticular activating system, which monitors incoming information in order of importance and directs critical stimuli to higher brain centers (see chap. 5).

The cerebellum, the second largest part of the brain, is located just behind the brain stem. It has many small convolutions. Its primary function is the automatic control of body position and coordination. Thus, walking, reaching, hitting a ball, and maintaining balance all depend to a large degree on cerebellar function.

The spinal cord, connected to the brain stem, runs through the center of the spinal column made up of the spinal vertebra. It provides basic connections between motor and sensory neurons and serves as the pathway for nerve impulses traveling from the extremities of the body to the brain via nerve fibers.

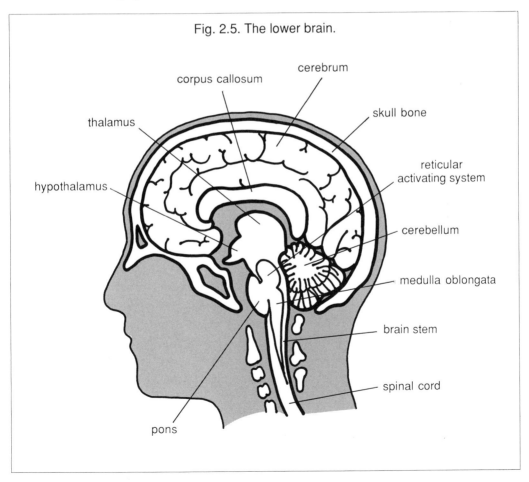

Fig. 2.5. The lower brain.

cerebrum

corpus callosum

skull bone

thalamus

reticular activating system

hypothalamus

cerebellum

medulla oblongata

brain stem

spinal cord

pons

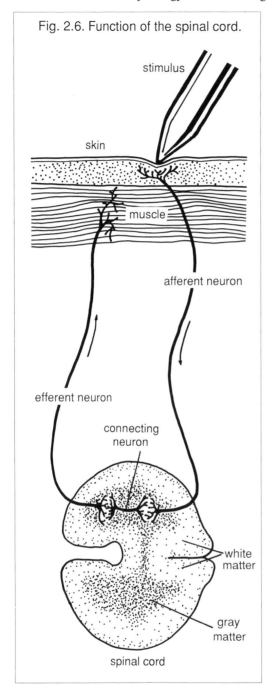

Fig. 2.6. Function of the spinal cord.

stimulus

skin

muscle

afferent neuron

efferent neuron

connecting neuron

white matter

gray matter

spinal cord

If the spinal cord is viewed in cross-section, two distinct areas are noted. A dark area forms an H-shaped core known as the gray matter, composed of cell bodies and nerve fibers without myelin sheaths. The white matter, composed of nerve fibers having myelin sheaths, encases the gray matter and carries impulses to and from the brain. The spinal cord is a mediator for reflex activity such as the quick withdrawal of the hand from a hot object. Any action more complicated than such a simple reflex would be referred to a higher brain center. The peripheral nervous system functions partly through the spinal cord.

One section of the lower brain is the limbic system, which includes the hippocampus, the amygdala, and the hypothalamus. The limbic system connects the rest of the lower brain to the temporal lobes of the upper brain. Hunger, sexual response, rage, and fear are all intricately linked to the limbic system; the recall of memory is the basic function of the hippocampus (note that it *recalls* memory, but does not *store* memory). In many respects the limbic system is quite distinct in function and anatomy from the remainder of the lower brain, and thus may be considered a "third brain" of sorts (Maclean 1970).

Brain Development

Golden (1981, 173–81), best known for his Luria Nebraska neuropsychological test, has suggested a stage theory of development. Each stage is the product of biological brain maturation and environmental experience. There are five stages of development, each corresponding to the maturation of certain brain areas.

The first stage involves the maturation of the lower brain structures, particularly the reticular system. By twelve months after conception, arousal and attention have developed. Should this area of the brain be damaged, physical hyperactivity will result (in contrast to learned hyperactivity, which develops in later childhood).

The second stage of development begins at the same time as the first stage and likewise is generally completed by twelve months after conception. This involves the maturation of the four primary areas of the cerebral cortex. The early life of the infant is essentially dominated by several basic reflexes (such as crying, grasping, and so on). As secondary areas mature in the third stage, these reflexes are replaced by purposeful, learned actions.

The third stage is concurrent with the first two, but continues through early childhood to about age five. Children begin to discriminate between different objects as soon as they are sufficiently able to concentrate (stage 1). Fear of strangers, preference for certain people, coordination, crawling, and walking are examples of behavior resulting from secondary development.

During the first years of life, most learning is the result of the maturation of the secondary areas of the brain. Tertiary (third) areas in each lobe are relatively immature at this time; thus what is learned is not truly integrative. The child learns by memorizing or acting out very concrete material, not through higher-level thought processes.

The fourth stage of brain development relates to the tertiary parietal area at the rear of the parietal lobe (see fig. 2.4). This portion of the brain typically matures at about five to eight years of age, although maturation may occur as early as age two or three or as late as age ten or twelve. This area of the brain correlates the information that has been processed by the secondary areas in the parietal, temporal, and occipital lobes. Thus when the tertiary parietal area matures, genuine reading, writing, logic, and grammar result. Golden maintains that most IQ tests measure abilities primarily in this area of the brain.

This fourth stage produces a readiness for formal education. Yet if this part of the brain matures later than average, the child will probably have difficulty performing academic skills at the standard age. Such children are not retarded or learning-disabled; they might be thus misclassified, however, since the brain is not yet mature. It is probably best to wait to send such children to school rather than force them into formal education. Golden emphasizes that a large number of children are somewhat delayed; thus the designation of age six for learning skills related to the tertiary parietal lobe is less than ideal. This arbitrary definition as the entry age for school means that we classify 10 to 40 percent of children as abnormal. Hyperactivity may result from such unrealistic expectations, whereas setting a more realistic age for such skills (Golden recommends age eight) would result in fewer problems.[1]

Another source of difficulty in the fourth stage is previous injury to the tertiary parietal area. Major injuries produce mental retardation, while minor injuries result in learning disabilities such as dyslexia. Such injuries can occur any time after conception but only become apparent when the tertiary parietal area matures. Forcing developmentally immature children to learn formal education skills, however, can at times produce similar problems.

The fifth stage of brain development occurs in adolescence, when the prefrontal (or tertiary frontal) areas develop. The prefrontal region continues to mature throughout adolescence and is not completely mature until the individual is approximately twenty-four years old. This area regulates the planning and evaluation of behavior.

The prefrontal region can be damaged early in life but significant effects may not be evident until adolescence. Distractibility, mental inflexibility, apathy, hyperactivity, and lack of inhibition may result.

1. Moore 1985 and Elkind 1987 provide additional evidence for later entry into formal education.

Spotlight 2.4.
Neuropsychology and the Church

A teen-ager in a church is moody, impulsive, and uses obscene language indiscriminately. His parents say he became that way as he entered adolescence. They also recall an automobile accident in which he received a serious head injury and was hospitalized. They feel he needs "more religion" to overcome his problems; but he sincerely desires to serve God. What counsel should the parents and teen-ager receive?

It is possible that the boy received brain damage to the prefrontal area. He may need to be examined by a neurologist for a diagnostic workup and perhaps by a neuropsychologist for testing.

If his problem is brain damage, it could affect impulse control and therefore the teen-ager may not be able to control his language. This sometimes happens to elderly people; they cannot inhibit impulses and may begin to use words they abhor. The problem is not spiritual in origin, but physical. However, as is often the case, the adolescent may have developed spiritual problems due to the physical difficulty. We must not forget that humans are holistic; problems in one area often produce problems in others.

Consider another situation. A children's worker in the church observes that two children are having problems reading. She wonders if the children might be retarded or at least slow learners.

The tertiary parietal area of the brain may be delayed in development in these children, but there could be more severe problems. On the other hand, they may be unfamiliar with religious terms. Because of variations in the extent of religious knowledge, a good case can be made for ability rather than age grouping in religious education.

Different content requires different mental abilities and thus the use of different sections of the brain. If a part of the brain needed is immature, the child will fail to understand the material being taught. We need to be selective about what we teach children from the Bible, reserving content that requires adult thinking for adults.

Some who have a damaged prefrontal area will use confabulation; they retell a personal account by filling in forgotten segments with impossible or absurd details. Certain kinds of schizophrenia and manic depression have also been linked with prefrontal damage. Such problems may develop later in life because of degeneration of the prefrontal area, although of course this does not always happen.

The Peripheral Nervous System

The peripheral nervous system consists of the somatic system and the autonomic (involuntary) system. The somatic system controls voluntary muscles which in turn control most body movements. The autonomic system, on the other hand, controls involuntary muscles (for example, heart, stomach, skin) and the body's various secretory glands. It has two divisions: the sympathetic and the parasympathetic. Most involuntary muscles and glands are innervated by both sympathetic and parasympathetic fibers. Each participates directly in controlling and integrating the actions of the organs and glands (see fig. 2.7).

The sympathetic division is most active when responding to stress. Sympathetic fibers carry impulses preparing the body for "fight or flight": heart rate increases, respiration increases, pupils dilate, digestion stops, salivation decreases, urination is inhibited, the adrenal glands are stimulated, and peripheral blood vessels constrict. Parasympathetic fibers carry impulses that effect the opposite changes in the body. In addition to diminishing the emergency reaction, the parasympathetic division causes the organs and glands to

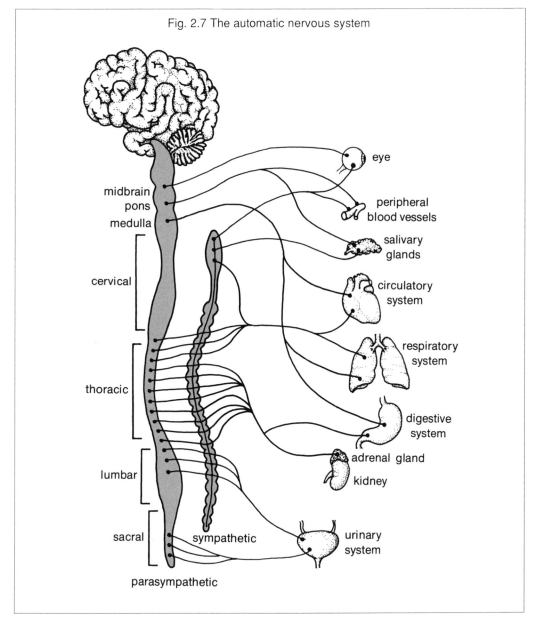

Fig. 2.7 The automatic nervous system

midbrain
pons
medulla

cervical

thoracic

lumbar

sacral

sympathetic

parasympathetic

eye

peripheral blood vessels

salivary glands

circulatory system

respiratory system

digestive system

adrenal gland

kidney

urinary system

return to normal function following a crisis.

The Endocrine System

Five sets of glands regulate the chemistry of the body in ways that affect psychological function. These glands produce hormones that are taken through the blood to various parts of the body. While these glands function in a holistic manner, it is helpful to discuss them individually.

The gonads (male testes, female ovaries) produce sperm or ova, but they also influence voice pitch, body hair, and the development of breasts. The pituitary gland functions as a master gland, and is controlled by the hypothalamus. If it malfunctions, growth may be accentuated or inhibited (Muller 1987).

The thyroid gland influences the rate of metabolism. An overactive thyroid results in a high energy level, increased stress reactions, and excessive hunger. When too few hormones are released, the individual becomes sluggish and food is transformed into fat rather than energy.

The pancreas, located at the rear of the stomach, controls the amount of sugar in the bloodstream. Fatigue results when the blood sugar level is too low, while too much sugar in the blood produces diabetes. The parathyroid glands also influence energy level.

The glands that make up the endocrine system are psychologically relevant. For example, an unusually low energy level may appear to be depression and may even be experienced as such, but may actually be a physical response to a malfunctioning gland rather than psychological difficulties.

Variations in Consciousness

The variation of the psychological and physiological dynamics of the brain may be termed consciousness. Consciousness has been said to be synonymous with being aware. Thus it is a faculty of perception that draws on information from the outside world directly through the sense organs and indirectly through stored memory traces. Consciousness may be viewed as a continuum from maximum alertness to unconsciousness or coma. We will briefly describe some of the important variations of consciousness.

Attention is a state of consciousness that is dependent on the amount of effort exerted in focusing on a specific experience. It varies from passive (automatic-reflexive) to active (voluntary).

Suggestibility is also a state of alerted consciousness. It occurs frequently in emotionally immature persons, making them seem particularly gullible. Willingness to be suggestible is used in hypnosis.

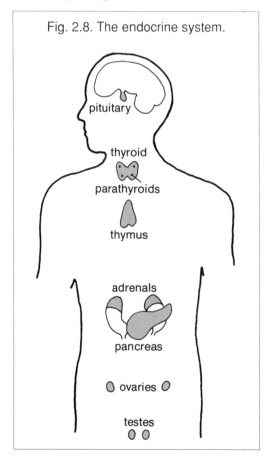

Fig. 2.8. The endocrine system.

pituitary

thyroid

parathyroids

thymus

adrenals

pancreas

ovaries

testes

As a patient becomes hyperattentive to the hypnotist, the hypnotist uses relaxation techniques and the patient's imagination to make the patient enter a trancelike state of heightened suggestibility. No one clearly understands the hypnotic state, yet its many clinical uses have ranged from recollection of repressed information to relief of pain (Kihlstrom 1985).

Dissociative states are also alerted states of consciousness but they occur spontaneously. Dissociation may vary from a brief trancelike episode in which a person temporarily escapes reality to a more prolonged state, such as multiple personality (see chap. 14).

Sleep is one of the most interesting variations in consciousness. We spend about one-third of our lives in sleep. The amount of sleep needed for proper mental functioning and alertness varies from individual to individual. On the average about eight hours of sleep per twenty-four-hour period are needed.

Many investigators have searched for a sleep-control mechanism in the brain. It is now known that the reticular activating system in the brain stem is intimately associated with the regulation of sleep and wakefulness (Moruzzi and Magoun 1949).

The electroencephalogram (EEG) was developed to measure the different waves emitted by the brain, which vary according to the levels, or stages, of sleep. In stage 1, a very brief period of falling asleep, brain waves become irregular, heart rate slows, and muscles relax. In stage 2, sleep is deeper, revealing characteristic sleep spindles on the EEG. In stage 3, sleep is even deeper and the EEG shows correspondingly different wave patterns. In stage 4, sleep is in its deepest level, producing delta waves on the EEG. This level of sleep occurs in fifteen- to twenty-minute intervals during the first four hours of sleep. The four stages, recurring in a regular pattern throughout the night, occupy about 75 percent of total sleep time. The remaining 25 percent is spent in REM (rapid eye movement) sleep. REM periods occur on the average of every hour and a half during sleep, lasting from five to twenty-five minutes. Stages 1 through 4 are referred to as non-REM or NREM sleep.

Although relaxation takes place in REM sleep, some muscles spontaneously twitch, and pulse and respiration rates increase as the blood pressure rises. Males often experience penile erection during REM sleep, without associated dream content. Dreaming tends to occur for an average of twenty minutes for each ninety minutes of sleep, but this varies considerably. The longer a person sleeps, the more likely that a dream will be recalled since the later periods of sleep are lighter.

Dreaming, like sleep, seems to be essential to mental health. Deprivation of either can lead to irritability and perceptual disturbances (Webb 1982). Sleep and dream patterns are usually altered in anxiety and depressive disorders.

Why do people dream? Psychologists have long debated this question. Freud (1900) believed that dreams may reveal the most hidden part of the personality, the unconscious mind, although the revelation is often symbolic (see chap. 15). If this is the case, by dreaming people reduce emotional tensions and partially satisfy unconscious conflicts—at least temporarily.

The Bible also attaches significance to dreams. God spoke through dreams on a number of occasions. Yet dreams are rarely mentioned in the Scriptures. Certainly people must have dreamed regularly, but apparently they did not grant special significance to their dreams except on rare occasions. Why certain dreams were considered particularly important is not clear from the biblical record.

Research indicates that dreaming helps aid in the retention of new or unusual information (Empson and Clarke 1970). In fact, it may be preferable to get a good night's sleep with plenty of dreams instead of cramming the night prior to an exam! One final theory suggests that dreams may simply be the brain's attempts to make sense out of random neuron firing (Lavie and Hobson 1986). If this is the case, most dreams may have little or no real significance.

Before concluding our discussion of dreams and sleep, we should mention insomnia, the inability to sleep. This problem may originate from several sources, but often anxiety or tension is to blame. It may also be possible that planning (a function of the prefrontal lobe) arouses the reticular activating system and prevents sleep. The insomniac needs to learn to relax and not do a great deal of planning after going to bed.[2] Occasional use of sleeping pills and nonstimulating thought may also be helpful.

In addition to laying the groundwork for our consideration of normal and abnormal mental processes, this chapter has shown the extraordinary complexity of the human nervous system. The Christian will stand in awe at God's wisdom and love shown in creation. The psalmist has appropriately said, "I praise you because I am fearfully and wonderfully made; your works are wonderful, I know that full well" (Ps. 139:14).

2. See the appendix for relaxation exercises.

References

Brand, P., and P. Yancey. 1984. *In his image*. Grand Rapids: Zondervan.

Buckley, W. 1971. Case against freedom. Transcript of Firing Line television program, Oct. 17. Columbia, S.C.: Southern Educational Communication Association.

Collins, G. 1985. *The magnificent mind*. Waco: Word.

Custance, A. 1980. *The mysterious matter of mind*. Grand Rapids: Zondervan.

Dembski, W. 1990. Converting matter into mind. *Perspectives on Science and Christian Faith* 42 (Dec.): 202–26.

Diehl, J., and W. McKeever. 1987. Absence of exposure time influence on lateralized face recognition. *Brain and Cognition* 6: 347–59.

Dodrill, C. 1976. Brain functions of Christians and non-Christians. *Journal of Psychology and Theology* 4 (Fall): 280–85.

Elkind, D. 1987. *Miseducation*. New York: Knopf.

Empson, J., and P. Clarke. 1970. Rapid eye movements and remembering. *Nature* 227: 287–88.

Freud, S. 1900 (repr. 1983). *The interpretation of dreams*. Laguana Beach, Calif.: Buccaneer.

Gazzaniga, M. 1971. One brain—two minds? *American Scientist* 60: 311–17.

Golden, C. 1981. *Diagnosis and rehabilitation in clinical neuropsychology*. Springfield, Ill.: Thomas.

Jones, D. 1981. *Our fragile brains*. Downers Grove: Inter-Varsity.

Kihlstrom, J. 1985. Hypnosis. *Annual Review of Psychology* 36: 385–418.

Lavie, P., and J. Hobson. 1986. Origin of dreams. *Psychological Bulletin* 100: 229–40.

Lee, J. 1985. *The content of religious instruction*. Birmingham, Ala.: Religious Education.

Levy, J. 1983. Language, cognition, and the right hemisphere. *American Psychologist* 38: 538–41.

MacKay, D. 1980. *Brains, machines and persons*. Grand Rapids: Eerdmans.

Maclean, P. 1970. The triune brain, emotion, and scientific bias. In *The neurosciences*, ed. F. Schmitt. New York: Rockefeller University Press.

Meyer, S. 1975. Neuropsychological worship. *Journal of Psychology and Theology* 3 (Fall): 281–89.

Moore, R. 1985. American schools: Some proven solutions. Paper for U.S. Secretary of

Education for meeting with educational leaders, June 24, Family Research Council, Washington, D.C.

Moruzzi, G., and H. Magoun. 1949. Brain stem reticular formation and reactivation of the EEG. *Electroencephalography and Clinical Neurophysiology* 1: 455–73.

Muller, E. 1987. Neural control of somatotropic function. *Physiological Review* 10: 962–1053.

Myers, D., and M. Jeeves. 1987. *Psychology through eyes of faith*. San Francisco: Harper and Row.

Owens, V. 1983. Seeing Christianity in red and green. *Christianity Today* (Fall): 281–89.

Penfield, W., et al. 1975. *The mystery of the mind*. Princeton: Princeton University Press.

Restak, R. 1984. *The brain*. New York: Bantam.

Schaeffer, F. 1969. *The God who is there*. Downers Grove: Inter-Varsity.

Sperry, R. 1970. Perception in the absence of neocortical commissures. In *Perception and its disorders*. New York: Association for Research in Nervous and Mental Disease.

Webb, W. 1982. Sleep and biological rhythms. In *Biological rhythms, sleep, and performance*, ed. W. Webb. Chichester, England: Wiley.

Wong, T. 1984. One brain's response. *Journal of Psychology and Theology* 12 (Fall): 208–10.

3

Sensation
and Perception

Sensation and perception were predominant issues in the early study of scientific psychology. English anthropologist Sir Francis Galton (1907) made some of the earliest investigations of color blindness and mental imagery. He found that certain persons, including at least one famous mathematician, had very poor visual imagery.

In sensation some physical stimulus (such as touch, sight, or taste) is detected and the energy of that stimulus is transformed into neural impulses to be transmitted by the nervous system. Perception is the interpreting and organizing of those neural impulses into an internal representation of reality. We sense the world around us and the way we perceive those sensations affects the way we behave.

Sensation

All types of stimuli impinge on us from our environment. In some metropolitan areas of the United States, for example, there may be as many as nine thousand radio signals in the air at a given time. Human sense receptors do not respond to such signals, so without a radio an individual remains unaware of them. Our receptors do respond to other stimuli, however. Lying in the sun, people may begin to get quite warm and then may feel a burning sensation. Yet the ultraviolet radiation, which has in part caused the burning sensation, is beyond the range of visual perception.

A stimulus from the environment must have a certain strength before sensory receptors can detect it. The magnitude of stimulus strength when a stimulus is strong enough to be detected 50 percent of the time is called the absolute threshold. Stimulus strengths close to but below that threshold are said to be subliminal.

Fechner (1860) concluded that a regular relationship must exist between changes in stimulus strength and changes in sensation; this conclusion was later confirmed by Stephens (1972).

Certain body organs have highly specialized receptor cells, usually

Spotlight 3.1. Subliminal Influence

Descriptions of subliminal influence date back to the 1950s, when reports circulated that messages such as "drink Coke" and "eat popcorn" were implanted in the pictures shown at movie theaters. Supposedly these messages appeared too quickly on the screen to be consciously seen yet they affected viewers' behavior. More popcorn was eaten and more Cokes were drunk (Meade 1976).

It should be noted, however, that these "experiments" lacked scientific rigor and the results were probably exaggerated. However, some evidence for the idea of subliminal influence is provided by recent research. Bornstein, Leon, and Galley (1987), for example, presented a picture of a given individual subliminally to a group of students and found that these students expressed greater attraction to that person later.

Other experiments indicate that individuals sweat more in response to subliminal syllables previously associated with pain (McCleary and Lazarus 1949). Philipchalk (1988, 52–53) summarizes the findings to date by emphasizing that subliminal influence is only possible when the situation is at least somewhat ambiguous, the individual is likely to use hunches in making a decision, and there is little or no cost for guessing.

Antirock crusaders today generally appeal to earlier subliminal research to emphasize the dangers of "backward masking" (words, sometimes satanic messages, recorded backward that are in certain songs). Yet research (Vokey and Read 1985) indicates that

sensitive to only one type of physical or chemical stimulus from the environment. The eye has receptors for pressure or touch as well as for visible light, however. Hence, although the eye is most sensitive to light waves it can also respond to the pressure of a finger.

Our bodies can sense changes in pressure, pain, and temperature. In addition to such cutaneous (skin) senses, we have kinesthetic senses (such as the sense of balance) and chemical senses (our taste buds, for example). The two senses about which most is known, however, are vision and hearing.

Vision

The eye contains two visual systems. Each system has its own distinctively shaped receptor cells located at the back of the retina. These light-sensitive cells are called rods and cones. The cones, which function only in relatively bright light, are responsible for color vision and high visual acuity. In dim light the cones cannot be stimulated so the rods make sight possible. Although the rods are very sensitive to dim light, they do not discriminate among colors. When only the rods are operating, everything appears to be achromatic—that is, black, white, or shades of gray.

Light enters the eye at the cornea and passes via the pupil, an opening controlled by the iris, through the lens and into the liquid that fills the eyeball. The light beam is focused by the lens onto the retina at the back of the eyeball. At the center of the

even when backward masking exists, the messages do not influence behavior.

One scientific study (Thorne and Himelstein 1984) contests the idea that the songs cited by evangelists even have backward masking. In this experiment, several songs commonly condemned by antirock crusaders were played backward so that the supposedly backward-masked words would become obvious.

Three groups heard the songs. One group was told to listen for satanic words; another group was told to just listen for words; and the third group was only told to listen carefully. What each group perceived depended upon what they were told to look for. As we will see later in this chapter, we often interpret experience in light of our expectations. Had there been actual backward masking, all three groups would have found satanic messages, not just the first group.

Is there danger from subliminal influence in rock music? While backward masking is apparently not a danger, there may be danger in the lyrics themselves. For example, young people considering immoral behavior might be influenced in this direction by hearing erotic songs. Taking Philipchalk's guidelines, such influence is most likely if they are not sure whether they should or not, if they are easily swayed by suggestion, and if they see no cost in following the immoral advice. Those are a lot of "ifs" and one wonders if adolescent peer pressure, lack of adequate moral values, and biological drives—not music—account for immoral behavior.

retina is the fovea, the most sensitive part of the eye in normal daylight vision. Of the more than 7 million cones in the retina, most are packed very closely together in the fovea, the rest decreasing in number toward the periphery of the retina. Rods

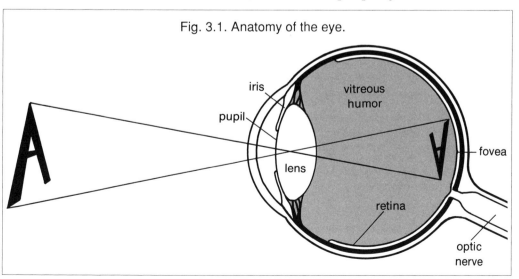

Fig. 3.1. Anatomy of the eye.

are found in all parts of the retina except the fovea.

It has been estimated that the retina contains approximately 130 million receptors, producing a tremendous convergence of information from the many receptors into the optic nerve. Since the rods and cones are located in an inner layer of the retina, light must actually travel through several layers of nerve fibers and blood cells before reaching the receptor cells. The receptors contain photopigments which absorb visible light. The cones seem to contain three pigments corresponding to the wave lengths of blue, green, and red light, respectively. Absorption of light breaks the photopigment down into its component parts and produces a nerve impulse. Thus millions of receptors responding to a visual stimulus provide the nervous system with information about such aspects of the visual image as brightness, color, form, and movement.

Visual perception requires selection of relevant stimuli from among all the irrelevant stimuli in the environment. Our visual perception mechanisms must spot the desired figure and discard all other distractions. As in other perceptual processes, the central principle seems to be that of economy. From the huge amount of possible information, only the essential information is transmitted; the nonessential information is discarded. Research on all of these mechanisms continues and much is yet to be learned about visual processes. Obviously a small disturbance in any receptor site can markedly impair the ability to perceive external stimuli.

Hearing

Hearing is made possible by the ear, a highly complex organ which senses the vibration of air molecules. Sound is the result of air molecules increasing in pressure and moving back and forth much like

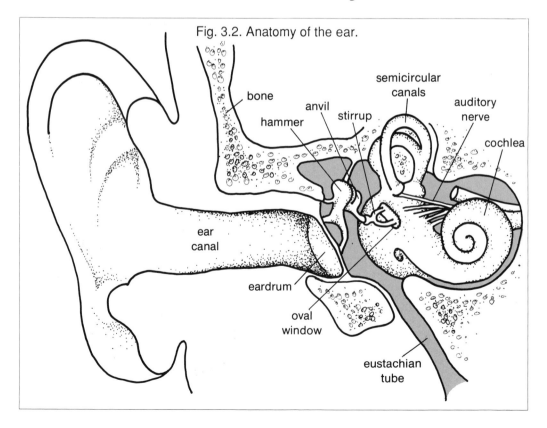

Fig. 3.2. Anatomy of the ear.

bone

anvil

hammer

stirrup

semicircular canals

auditory nerve

cochlea

ear canal

eardrum

oval window

eustachian tube

Spotlight 3.2.
Sensation and Christianity

In *Fearfully and Wonderfully Made* (Brand and Yancey 1980), a physician and a professional writer pool their efforts to describe the human body and to draw spiritual parallels from it.

In chapters 2 and 3, the senses of sight and hearing, particularly the cells which cooperate to produce these senses, are discussed. The amoeba, a one-celled organism, is more adaptive than a cell from the eye or ear. Yet the sense cell is much more specialized and, by combining its efforts with similar cells, can produce far greater feats. As Brand and Yancey put it, "in exchange for its self-sacrifice, the individual cell can share in . . . the ecstasy of community" (p. 24).

In the body of Christ, Christians have a unity. Even though we have different abilities (just as the various cells of the body are specialized), yet we can function as one within the single body of Christ. God seems to enjoy the variety of cultures, just as he planned the variety of cells.

Six chapters of Brand and Yancey's book are devoted to touch, one of the most important senses. Many wonderful details of this sensation are considered. Brand notes how much he has come to appreciate this ability so often lost by the leprous. Imagine being unable to pet a dog, feel feathers or wool, or sense the distinction between wet and dry or cold and hot.

The book cites the research of Harlow (to be considered in chap. 10) and Montagu (1986) to underscore the importance of touch to human development. We as the body of Christ need to physically touch those around us. Sensitive contact with others is a part of our function as Christians. Jesus, our example, often touched those he healed. Love is often expressed best through person-to-person touch.

---

waves crashing in on a beach. A large number of vibrations per second is correlated with a tone of high pitch, a smaller number per second with a lower pitch.

The ear's external shape is designed to concentrate slight air pressure variations in the ear canal, where they eventually contact the eardrum. Rapid variations in air pressure cause the eardrum to move in and out at the same frequency. These vibrations are picked up in the middle ear by three small bones—the hammer, anvil, and stirrup— which transmit them to another membrane. Beyond that membrane, called the oval window, lies the inner ear or cochlea. The stirrup acts like a piston, moving the oval window back and forth and setting up vibrations in the cochlear fluid. Movement of that fluid produces vibrations in a thin membrane within the cochlea, which contains the auditory receptors. The receptors are very minute hair cells. Moving those small hair cells excites them and produces nerve impulses in the fibers of the auditory nerve The impulses are then carried to the brain.

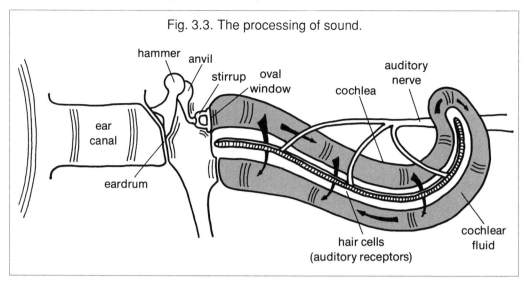

Fig. 3.3. The processing of sound.

Currently it is believed that different hair cells act like the individual strings of a piano. Thus only a certain set of receptors would be excited by a specific variation of air pressure or tone. It has also been suggested that some of the hair cells may operate in groups. As such receptors discharge their impulses at different times, the impulses are grouped by the auditory nerve to provide more information, again discriminating between relevant and irrelevant stimuli.

Other Senses

There are at least four cutaneous or skin senses. Warmth and cold seem to be detected as two separate sensations, with more spots on the skin sensitive to warmth than to cold. When a stimulus reaches a certain temperature, the warm fiber stops responding and the cold fiber begins responding. Pressure receptors operate when the skin is depressed or deformed.

Motion receptors, located in the semicircular canals of the inner ear, detect changes in motion of the body. Positioning of these canals at right angles to each other inside the ear enables an individual to detect body motion in any of the three dimensions of space.

Taste and smell are considered chemical senses since the receptors of both the nose and tongue are stimulated primarily by interaction with chemical molecules.

Taste receptors are located in taste buds distributed along the surface and sides of the tongue. There are basically four taste qualities—sweet, sour, bitter, and salty (McBurney and Gent 1979). Response to food is generally triggered by a combination of taste and aroma. Many factors influence our ability to taste, including learning. People seem to vary considerably in their taste sensitivity. Certain food additives apparently enhance the taste of some types of food.

Olfactory receptors are located in membranes in the upper part of the nasal cavity. The stimuli that excite the olfactory receptors are chemical molecules in gaseous form suspended in the air we breathe.

All the sense organs operate to present a constant stimulus picture to the brain. The brain has two ways of adjusting to the inputs from the various receptor sites. The first is called receptor adaptation. If you sit down in a tub of hot water, for example, initially you notice the warmth of the water. After a short time, however, the water does not feel so warm. That is because the nerve endings in the skin are firing less often as your skin warms up, approaching the temperature of the water. In short, because your skin and its nerve endings have adapted to the heat, the water will seem much less hot. Adaptation refers to reduction in the firing rate of receptor cells in response to a constant stimulus. The nervous system also adjusts to stimuli through the process of habituation. If you are sitting in a room with an air conditioner running, for example, the noise at first may be quite obvious. Yet because the noise is constant, it is more likely to be ignored.

Sensory Deprivation

Many investigators have studied what happens when sensations are diminished or cut off. Initial results from such sensory deprivation experiments were often inconsistent. In the best-known type of deprivation experiment, individuals are deprived of sleep while all other physical needs are met.

In a sensory deprivation study (Heron 1957) at McGill University, students were asked to lie on a bed in a small room with their eyes covered and their arms in cardboard tubes. Their bodily needs were provided for and they were told that they could leave the experiment at any time. They were encouraged to relax and be comfortable. Although the expectation was

Fig. 3.4. Sensory receptors.

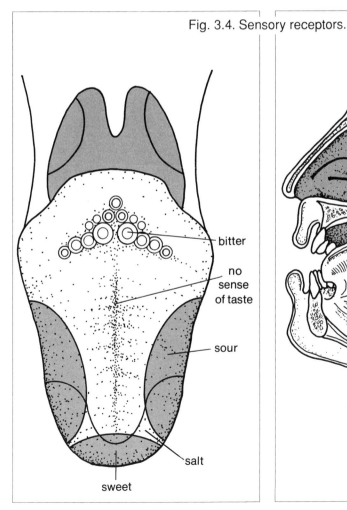

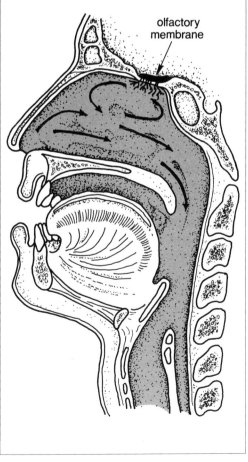

Spotlight 3.3. Parapsychology

Philipchalk (1988, 54–58) has identified certain phenomena that he calls "perception without sensation"—an area more commonly known as parapsychology. (He also describes "sensation without perception"—subliminal influence [see spotlight 3.1].) Parapsychology includes extrasensory perception (ESP) or, more specifically, telepathy (reading a person's mind), clairvoyance (sensing what occurs at another location), and precognition (knowing events prior to their happening).

Does perception without sensation actually occur? Most psychologists are skeptical. Some people are easily duped by charlatans while others may simply be naive. In contrast, Koteskey (1980, 74–75) believes these may be natural abilities that have spiritual counterparts. Philipchalk describes some possible counterparts, such as the "word of knowledge" being clairvoyance and the "word of prophecy" being precognition. He also links silent prayer with telepathy.

Yet Philipchalk recommends caution in making such associations. Parapsychology also includes psychokinesis (moving objects without physical contact), psychic healing, poltergeists (ghosts), and reincarnation. As we move through the areas considered by parapsychology the categories become more clearly occultic. The Bible emphatically warns us to avoid spiritism. Thus three options present themselves: parapsychology is trickery; parapsychology is supernatural (either demonic or from God); or parapsychology is a natural ability (as Koteskey claims). While we can certainly affirm God's supernatural abilities (for example, divine healing), parapsychology in general is dangerous territory because of its strong occultic associations. Since the occult is clearly forbidden in Scripture, it is probably best to avoid any participation in parapsychological activity.

that most students would be able to stand such isolation for several days, almost half the subjects quit during the first forty-eight hours. Those who stayed showed considerable intellectual impairment both during the sensory deprivation experience and afterward. They lost problem-solving abilities and had difficulty counting and concentrating. About 80 percent of the subjects began to hallucinate, seeing or hearing things that were not physically there. Their hallucinations were similar to those of individuals whose mental perceptions have been altered by drug experiences or psychotic episodes. One subject reported the impression that his body had turned into twins and that two bodies were lying on the bed.[1]

Perception

Specific sensations are building blocks to be organized and elaborated into a meaningful whole in the process of perception. Sensation apart from perception occurs all the time, as the reticular activating system filters out a large percentage of information from the brain's awareness (see chap. 2). Subliminal influence is also sensation without perception (see spotlight 3.1).

1. Results of recent experiments similar to those of Heron are not as extreme. See Suedfeld and Kristeller 1982.

Spotlight 3.4. Sensory Deprivation and Cult Activities

Many of us have heard of certain cults which deprive their members of sleep and food, as well as contacts with their families and other outsiders. They may be required to spend long periods in isolation, in some ways resembling the sensory deprivation experiments. There may also be certain parallels with prisons or concentration camps that make extensive use of solitary confinement.

Consider the famous case of Jim Jones, leader of a cultic church called People's Temple. In 1979 most of his group moved to Guyana, cutting off all contact with the outside world. Mass suicide was the result of Jones' inordinate control over group members.

Are there similarities between cult activities and sensory deprivation research? The changes in short-term behavior and thinking that result may be similar in some ways. Yet there are important differences. The similarities and differences may perhaps be best considered by examining the manipulative techniques of cult groups as outlined by Enroth (1977, 149–83).

First, Enroth describes the encouragement of personality regression among converts in many cults. At best the individual develops a childlike ego, much like the early adolescent, and at worst a trancelike state (though the latter does not always occur). Here we see some similarity to the hallucinatory and other unusual effects of sensory deprivation.

The cult member is required to make a number of personal sacrifices as a measure of faith. This may involve nonstop activity, for which such groups are noted, or celibacy may be strongly encouraged. Poor living conditions may be combined with hard work and a change in dress as a measure of loyalty. Certainly sacrifice is involved in sensory deprivation studies, but many enter into the research thinking they will be getting a nice rest.

Those in cultic groups may also be asked to invest their resources by giving the group their possessions. Their money and personal belongings cannot be returned to them in most cases. Resource investment was not present in the deprivation studies, other than the investment of time.

Another characteristic mentioned by Enroth is the breaking of previous relationships. This encourages increasing engagement with the group, while the outside world is perceived as corrupt. The terminology used by the group functions as a wall, clearly separating outsiders from insiders. The individual may be shielded from outside news; and diadic (two-person) relationships *within* the group may be discouraged due to the potential threat to the group. Family ties may be renounced. The sensory deprivation research did include the temporary severing of relationships, although only for a couple of days in contrast to the often permanent severing of ties in cults.

The sense of "we-ness" is accentuated within the group by encouraging members to work together for the sake of transforming the world. Often such groups encourage members to affirm positive aspects of the group and not mention negative factors. Rituals foster the feelings of we-ness, as do doctrines that state that the group is the only means of salvation. Real or imagined persecution and an initiatory process unify members. These factors are clearly absent in deprivation studies.

Mortification is also mentioned by Enroth, in which the previous identity of the person is taken away. Rituals of degradation or extreme physical activities weaken any resistance the person may have, while pressure to conform is intense, particularly for members who deviate. There is commonly an invasion of privacy. These characteristics are generally missing in sensory deprivation, particularly extreme physical activity.

Finally, Enroth notes an appeal to transcendence in the effort to build commitment to the group. Commitment to something greater than the self provides meaning and purpose for the participant. A central leader or group of leaders may command devotion and thus provide a means to such transcendence. This was completely missing in the deprivation research.

Certain aspects of cults are similar to sensory deprivation studies, including the fact that effects are usually temporary once the individual leaves the cult or deprivation context; but they are clearly different in other respects, such as the short-term involvement of deprivation and the sometimes long-term involvement in cults.

To illustrate how perception develops from sensations, consider what happens in visual perception. After light has entered the eye and excited the visual receptors, the resulting nerve impulses are conducted to the brain, which organizes them and generates some form of visual perception. A basic principle of visual perception seems to be that individuals tend to see what they expect to see.

Size Constancy and Depth Perception

A child learns early in life that objects remain constant in size whether they are near or far away. As an example of this principle of size constancy, consider your perception of a truck coming toward you. As the truck approaches, it continually appears larger, yet you do not regard the truck as actually growing in front of you. Having learned from experience that distance and size are correlated, as the truck gets larger in your visual field, you conclude that it must be getting closer to you. As objects move toward us the size of their image on the retina increases and as they move away the size of the image on the retina decreases. The brain does not interpret this as a change in size but integrates the image with past experience, allowing us to interpret the change as a change in distance.

Depth perception enables us to live in a three-dimensional world. The brain takes the two-dimensional images falling on the retina and constructs the third dimension. An important cue used by the brain in this process is the relative size of familiar objects. The apparent coming together of parallel lines as they approach the horizon is called linear perspective, another cue used by the brain to judge distance. Another kind of perspective is sometimes called aerial perspective, referring to the fact that fuzzy-appearing objects are typically seen as farther away than distinct objects. We also tend to see objects that are physically close and similar to each other as units.

Recognition of Stimuli

How does an individual recognize objects and people from stimuli? The theory of feature analysis states that specific components of a stimulus are separated and individually analyzed by the brain. Thus parts of the brain respond to vertical lines, for example, while other parts respond to horizontal lines. These are then put together at a more abstract level of processing to form identifications such as the letter T (one vertical and one horizontal line).

The template matching theory asserts that people have a complete mental pattern (a template) for different objects and ideas. Each new experience is superimposed upon the template, and if the fit is reasonably good, the stimulus is identified with the concept associated with the template. There is a template for the letter T; when a person sees a stimulus that is the same shape, it is considered to be the letter T. The template theory has been criticized both for its mechanistic aspects and because some examples do not resemble the supposed template. For example, this theory fails to account for an object being recognized even though the specific sensation is from a unique and distorted angle. Our mental patterns are more flexible than a template.

Perception as Active

Perception is active, not passive. We often hear people say they are "soaking up knowledge," but in reality they are actively involved in perceiving ideas. We sometimes hear of witnesses to an accident, all credible, who tell very different stories about what happened. In a sense, we "construct" what we learn. What we know is hardly a carbon copy of the world; if it were there would be fewer differences of opinion.

What is involved in the construction of information? A number of factors can be identified. Perception involves the grouping of data according to proximity, similarity, or other familiar categories. For example, some people associate obesity with being continually happy. This may make them more likely to perceive happiness in those who are obese and less likely to see indications to the contrary. Extending this idea beyond perception, such stereotypes might also influence the obese person to fulfill those expectations. Many people stereotype by saying such things as "he's just like . . . " or "I know her kind." Perhaps the verse "Do not judge, or you too will be judged" (Matt. 7:1) fits here.

It is possible to rearrange sensory input to the brain in order to produce a different organization of the data. Experiments have been performed with special glasses that turned everything upside down (Dolezal 1982). Those who used the glasses eventually adjusted to the new form of data. When they took the glasses off, there was again a time of readjustment to normal sensory input.

Perhaps there is a message here for churches that want new converts to immediately change their values: readjustment to a new lifestyle often takes time. Spiritual growth is more often a gradual process than a sudden, drastic change. How can the process of adjustment be speeded up? In one experiment (Held and Hein 1963) two kittens were given the same experiences, but only one of them actually acted on the environment. The restrained kitten did not perceive the new environment as well, while the one who moved freely in the environment learned more quickly. Perhaps we need to encourage new converts to be active in church, and not make them self-conscious about the mistakes they make. Involvement in the church demands more than passive listening.

The extent of the organization of information is often overlooked. Gestalt psychology speaks of the fact that we impose upon sense data the "figure" and "ground." This means that we determine which things are important (the figure) and what will fade into the background (the ground). This happens all the time in our perceiving. For example, proud parents may see their child's ability to play a trumpet as important (the figure) and the ability to do so skillfully as insignificant (the ground), whereas a music teacher would see just the opposite. Gestalt psychologists have developed drawings that portray this ability to shift figure and ground. For example, there are cards which initially look like geometric designs if the dominant color is perceived as ground, yet the card spells out the word "Jesus" if the dominant color is the figure.

Gestalt psychologists have developed a number of rules used by individuals to organize their perceptions (see fig. 3.5). When given a cluster of many objects, we tend to mentally group those objects which are similar (the rule of similarity).

A second rule is that of proximity: objects that are close to one another tend to be mentally associated. Other gestalt rules include continuation (grouping objects that form straight or curved lines) and closure (the tendency to mentally fill in the gaps between objects).

Not only do we organize sensory information, but the brain actively adds to incoming sense data. People do not merely see what actually exists, but they also interpret it by adding other information; they supplement although they may not realize it. For example, people listening to a political candidate interpret what he says by what they have heard about that

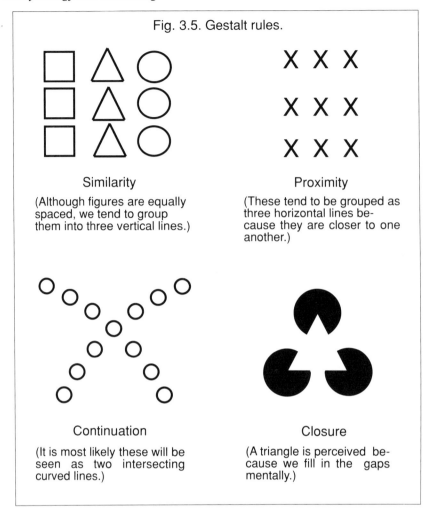

Fig. 3.5. Gestalt rules.

Similarity
(Although figures are equally spaced, we tend to group them into three vertical lines.)

Proximity
(These tend to be grouped as three horizontal lines because they are closer to one another.)

Continuation
(It is most likely these will be seen as two intersecting curved lines.)

Closure
(A triangle is perceived because we fill in the gaps mentally.)

candidate previously. In church a non-Calvinist might very well look for the Calvinist bias in a guest speaker rather than actually hearing what is said.

What Influences Our Perceptions?

What key factors influence the creative nature of perception? Certainly past experience influences us a great deal. This is illustrated by a classic experiment performed by Boring (1930). Two groups of people were shown drawings. One group saw a portrait of an older woman, while the other group saw a picture of a young woman. Both groups were then asked to identify an ambiguous combination of the two drawings. Those who had seen the first drawing identified it as an older woman, while those in the second group believed the ambiguous drawing to be that of a young woman.

A second influence is situation. For example, you may be walking at night in the inner city and suddenly see the shadowy outline of a thug in an alley (Geiwitz 1976, 89). Should you stop to investigate, the shadowy outline might well be a cat perched on a garbage can! Likewise when you are hungry, food is more quickly recognized than other objects (Lazarus, Yousem, and Arenberg 1953).

A third influence is that of the values held by the individual. An experiment by Bruner and Goodman (1947) indicated that

Spotlight 3.5. Perceptual Psychology and Christianity

There is a strong possibility that people can misunderstand the message of the gospel. What concepts of perceptual psychology can help us minimize this problem?

The most important thing is to keep the presentation as unambiguous as possible. Ambiguity invites additions to the original stimuli. Try to use familiar terms. Emphasizing common past experiences and values is more likely to result in acceptance of the message.

Even Christians are not immune to misperceptions of sensory data. One way in which this could happen is to read into the Bible what we want to see. Christians have their favorite topics and can creatively "add to" a text and thus find what they want to find.

A far better approach is to let the Bible interpret itself, as well as try to understand the context in which it was written rather than imposing upon it our own cultural and personal milieu. Our natural inclination is to find support for our own cultural, denominational, and doctrinal viewpoints, particularly when we read verses that could be taken several different ways. Being aware of that inclination can make us more aware of it and help us to avoid it as much as possible.

At many colleges and seminaries eternal security comes up for regular debate among students. Is it possible that *both* sides have perhaps mishandled Scripture? Is it possible that God wants us to trust in what he has done and not in our own efforts? Does he want us to be sensitive to our shortcomings and not become complacent? Perhaps the stance one takes on this issue is more the result of selective perception than the "obvious" message of Scripture.

Consider another matter in which perceptual influences play an important part. Suppose an evangelist comes to a church and causes division because of his style of preaching. Some in the congregation call his lively sermons "wild fire" while others say he is filled with the joy of God. Is it possible that both reactions are due to the past experiences (a crucial factor in perception) that both groups have had? Those who have associated lively preaching with negative experiences are most likely to perceive the evangelist as unpleasant, while the others have probably had altogether different past experiences.

There are Christians who believe their prayers are never specifically answered. They may pray and have a right heart, but they are not sure that God has responded. Yet others are just as sure that they receive answers to their prayers.

There can be psychological reasons for not perceiving answers from God. While past experiences with others who see their prayers as being answered can influence us to look for similar results, we also need to look at values. Does someone's value system allow for answers, or does that person assume that God is silent? Expectation also plays an important part. Expecting answers enables a person to look for answers to prayer. Conversely, we must be careful not to perceive answers when the situation is ambiguous; God may be asking us to wait for an answer and not immediately assume what we want to hear. Perhaps the same rationale could be used to account for the perception (or nonperception) of miracles (see spotlight 6.6).

The influence of different perspectives on achieving more accurate perceptions, emphasized at the close of this chapter, may be implied in Old Testament passages that require two or more witnesses against a transgressor of the law. Perceptual differences are also underscored in John 12:29: those who listened for God heard God, whereas those who were not perceptually oriented toward hearing God only heard thunder or thought an angel had spoken.

poor children exaggerated the size of coins more than middle-class children when they were asked to draw them. They exaggerated size because they valued the coins. If it was merely the lack of familiarity with coins that influenced their drawings, some children would have overestimated and others would have underestimated the size of the coins.

Finally, expectation also influences perception. If we expect certain things to happen, we will tend to interpret sensations accordingly—particularly if those sensations are ambiguous. This phenomenon can be seen in several of the previous examples as well.[2]

The Autokinetic Effect

Sherif's (1937) research on the autokinetic effect is a good example of the role of expectation in perception. People in his experiments were told that a spot of light projected on the wall would move and were instructed to estimate the amount of movement. Although the spot of light never actually moved, the people inevitably reported movement. When told that the spot of light would even trace out letters and words, participants began reporting words and sentences. Clearly their expectations resulted in the addition of a considerable amount of information to their sensations!

In an interesting variation on the above experiments, Sherif had groups of people watch the light and asked them to reach a consensus on how far it had moved. One year later when group members were again tested individually with the nonmoving spot of light, they invariably estimated the light moved the same distance the group had estimated a year before. The group's influence persisted, indicating the powerfully social nature of human beings. The groups we belong to greatly affect our perceptions of reality. No wonder the Bible is very clear that we are to "come out from them and be separate" as well as "not give up meeting together."

2. For an interesting account of how such influences are involved in the perception of magic tricks, see Korem and Meier 1980.

Perceptual Processes in Reading

Perception is essential in the process of reading. A reader takes in data bit by bit as the eyes stop, move on, stop, move on, and so forth. While the eyes are moving they do not take in data (Shebilski 1977); the individual fills in the gaps of information (the letters skipped between eye movements). This process is analogous to the gestalt rule of continuation.

The number of letters a reader sees with every eye movement influences reading speed. Shebilski (1975) found that average college students move their eyes every four or five letters when reading, while faster readers move their eyes every nine or ten letters. Many speed-reading classes attempt to teach students to observe more letters with each eye movement.

We tend to take the perceptual complexity of reading for granted, unless we are working with children who are first learning to read. There the complexity of the task is obvious. The child might learn by the whole word method, where words are considered stimuli to be recognized; or the child might learn by the phonics method, where parts are combined to produce entire words. Many people use both approaches, teaching children to recognize common words without sounding them out while using phonics with less common words. Considering the many perceptual processes taking place with either method, it is amazing anyone learns to read!

Perception as Veridical

There are dangers in wholeheartedly accepting standard perceptual theory. Hodges (1986) notes that if this perspective is accepted completely, then our trust in science (and psychology) will be undermined. After all, scientists also use perception to make their observations of reality. True, we cannot always trust our perceptions. How, then, can we become more accurate in our understandings?

Hodges cites Gibson's theory of perception as a possible answer. Gibson (1979) emphasizes that things are known in relation to absolutes. In other words, our perceptions are constrained by what actually exists. The goal, then, is to make our perceptions veridical or more consistent with the real world.

What must be done to achieve this goal? First, we need to gain multiple perspectives on events. Certainly the Scriptures give us a perspective we can fully trust (see chap. 1). In addition, we need to realize that perception is by its very nature progressive.

Hodges notes that the history of the world is a progressive revelation of God's purposes. Likewise our interpretations of events may become more accurate as we gain more experience. This demands humility on our part; to learn we must acknowledge that what we presently know is partial and possibly in error. Third, social interaction can enhance knowing. Through community we can interact and thus share more perspectives; with more perspectives we are more likely to achieve knowledge. Clearly the community of believers is important in developing Christian perceptions of the world, God, and Christian living.

References

Boring, E. 1930. A new ambiguous figure. *American Journal of Psychology* 42: 444–45.

Bornstein, R., D. Leon, and D. Galley. 1987. The generalizability of subliminal mere exposure effects. *Journal of Personality and Social Psychology* 53: 1070–79.

Brand, P., and P. Yancey. 1980. *Fearfully and wonderfully made*. Grand Rapids: Zondervan.

Bruner, J., and C. Goodman. 1947. Value and need as organizing factors in perception. *Journal of Abnormal and Social Psychology* 42: 33–44.

Dolezal, H. 1982. *Living in a world transformed*. New York: Academic.

Enroth, R. 1977. *Youth, brainwashing and the extremist cults*. Grand Rapids: Zondervan.

Fechner, G. 1860. *Elements of psychophysics*. Cited in R. Fancher. 1990. *Pioneers of psychology*, 2d ed. New York: Norton.

Galton, F. 1907. *Inquiries in human faculty and its development*. London: J. M. Dent and Sons.

Geiwitz, J. 1976. *Looking at ourselves*. Boston: Little, Brown.

Gibson, J. 1979. *The ecological approach to visual perception*. Boston: Houghton Mifflin.

Held, R., and A. Hein. 1963. Movement-produced stimulation. *Journal of Comparative and Physiological Psychology* 56: 872–76.

Heron, W. 1957. The pathology of boredom. *Scientific American* (Jan.): 52—56.

Hodges, B. 1986. Perception, relativity, and knowing and doing the truth. In *Psychology and the Christian faith*, ed. S. Jones. Grand Rapids: Baker.

Korem, D., and P. Meier. 1980. *The fakers*. Grand Rapids: Baker.

Koteskey, R. 1980. *Psychology from a Christian perspective*. Nashville: Abingdon.

Lazarus, R., H. Yousem, and D. Arenberg. 1953. Hunger and perception. *Journal of Personality* 21: 312–28.

McBurney, D., and J. Gent. 1979. On the nature of taste qualities. *Psychological Bulletin* 86: 151–67.

McCleary, R., and R. Lazarus. 1949. Autonomic discrimination without awareness. *Journal of Personality* 18: 171–79.

Meade, E. 1976. How to keep from being manipulated. *Christian Life* (May): 16–17, 47–48.

Montagu, A. 1986. *Touching*. 3d ed. New York: Harper and Row.

Myers, D., and M. Jeeves. 1987. *Psychology through the eyes of faith*. San Francisco: Harper and Row.

Philipchalk, R. 1988. *Psychology and Christianity*. Lanham, Md.: University Press of America.

Shebilski, W. 1975. Reading eye movements. In *Understanding language,* ed. D. Massaro. New York: Academic.

—————. 1977. Visuomotor coordination in visual direction and position constancies. In *Stability and constancy in visual perception,* ed. W. Epstein. New York: Wiley.

Sherif, M. 1937. An experimental approach to the study of attitudes. *Sociometry* 1: 90–98.

Stephens, S. 1972. *Psychophysics and social scaling.* Morristown, N.J.: General Learning.

Suedfeld, P., and J. Kristeller. 1982. Stimulus reduction as a technique in health psychology. *Health Psychology* 1: 337–57.

Thorne, S., and P. Himelstein. 1984. The role of suggestion in the perception of satanic messages in rock and roll recordings. *Journal of Psychology* 116: 245–48.

Vokey, J., and J. Read. 1985. Subliminal messages: Between the devil and the media. *American Psychologist* 40: 1231–39.

4

Emotions

We are all familiar with emotions, but they are difficult to define. Emotion involves the affective or feeling part of experience; we *feel* emotional. Yet feelings are closely related to thinking since thinking certain thoughts can produce positive or negative emotions. Biologically there is arousal when emotions are felt, so this is yet another aspect of emotion. Emotion is also closely related to motivation. Emotions make us more likely to act in certain ways. While some might feel emotions are the same thing as moods, they can be distinguished by the fact that emotions do not last as long as moods and tend to be more intense (Morris 1987).

Perhaps the best way of describing what we mean by emotion is to give examples of the most common emotions. Positive emotions include wonder, elation, tenderness, joy, and surprise, while negative emotions are fear, disgust, anger, sadness, anxiety, and depression.

Americans are feeling-oriented, perhaps more so than people in other cultures. We applaud individuals who go against the evidence and follow their feelings to find the truth of the matter (Sovine 1988). People often get married because of feelings. When a couple no longer has those feelings, they may move on to new partners. Some rely on feelings in assessing spirituality; they are disappointed if they do not "feel God's presence" in their lives.

The results of overreliance on feelings are obvious: broken homes, serial relationships, and shallow faith. It would be easy to conclude that feelings should have little or no part in the mature Christian's life. The evangelistic booklet "The Four Spiritual Laws" portrays the emotions as an optional caboose to the train (representing Christian living), while fact is the engine. Are Christians to be fact-oriented, with little or no emotion?

The Bible emphasizes knowledge over feeling (Sovine 1988). The Greek word for "feeling" occurs only twice in the New Testament, while "knowledge" is found 491 times. Yet many specific emotions

---

Spotlight 4.1. The Bible and Emotions

While the specific word for emotion is rare in the New Testament, there are a number of references to specific emotions, often linking them with parts of the body. This underscores the importance of emotions to the holistic nature of human existence.

Consider Genesis 43:30. Joseph was "deeply moved at the sight of his brother." The phrase "deeply moved" in the original Hebrew is a word that refers to a number of body organs. This particular word is repeated a number of times in the Old Testament in the context of emotional response. Clearly the visceral organs are powerfully affected by our emotions.

We can see the same idea in the New Testament (Phil. 1:8; Philem. 7, 20; 1 John 3:17–19). Christ can remove the negative emotions of anxiety and stress when we trust in him. Casting our burdens upon him results in rest.

Psychosomatic illness may be prevented by our resting in Christ, relaxing in the assurance of his forgiveness and acceptance. The Book of Proverbs speaks of health being more likely for those who believe in God (Prov. 3:8). Clearly the Bible has much to say about human emotions, and many of its comments relate physiological response (literally or metaphorically) to felt emotion.

---

are emphasized throughout Scripture. The Book of Lamentations is a depressive lament; Ecclesiastes has similar emotional overtones. Christ himself experienced the full range of emotions, as the Gospels clearly indicate. Perhaps there is a middle ground where emotions can be important yet not dominate a person's life.

Theories of Emotion

Although the concept of emotion is difficult to define objectively, it is widely accepted. Emotion generally refers to intrapsychic feelings which range from love or hate to fear or sadness. Which comes first: the biological arousal or the perception of feelings? William James believed that emotional feelings are mostly a matter of the individual consciously noting the messages sent from various parts of the body. Hence he proposed that our feelings follow biological-neural arousal. This has become known as the James–Lange theory of emotion. A contrasting approach is the Cannon–Bard theory (Bard 1938), which suggests that the experience of emotions and physiological arousal occur simultaneously. For example, if you observe a car accident, your perception is apt to occur at the same time you experience your emotions.

A third theory of emotion suggests that cognition (thinking) is involved in what emotion is felt. Schachter and Singer (1962), while basically agreeing with the James–Lange theory, believe that the physical arousal associated with emotion is not specific (at least initially); upon cognitive analysis, the exact emotion is specified. Thus the mental interpretation of an event is the key to labeling the emotion felt.

An experiment conducted by Schachter and Singer serves as an illustration of this process. Individuals were injected with a general stimulant (they were told it was a vitamin) and then were asked to wait in an area with someone who either acted angry or performed amusing antics. Those who received the stimulant interpreted their arousal as either anger or happiness depending upon the other person's response. We tend to interpret our feelings according to context.

Schachter and Singer's cognitive theory is not without its weaknesses, however. Attempts to repeat their classic experiment have been unsuccessful (see Hogan and Schroeder 1981). Furthermore, cognition does not always determine emotion; if it did we could change emotions by simply thinking good thoughts. Although thought substitution sometimes helps (see chap. 7), it is not automatic. "Whistling a happy tune" will not help chronic depressives!

The cognitive theory underscores an important aspect of emotions known as cognitive appraisal. Evaluation automatically follows the event being appraised and determines both the emotional reaction and the subsequent response. Thus cognition takes a stronger role than suggested by Schachter and Singer, as it involves not only labeling but also the reaction and degree of arousal.

A final theory emphasizes the physiological basis of emotion. The autonomic nervous system (see chaps. 2 and 5) is activated by emotions, thus producing a faster pulse, sweating, and many other biological responses. The facial muscles also receive messages unrelated to the autonomic nervous system (resulting in different facial grimaces and expressions), and the blood supply to the face can be affected (producing blushing or paleness) (Zajonc 1985). The facial reactions are then transmitted to the brain where they are interpreted and labeled. Thus the physiological theory has much in common with the James–Lange theory.

Which theory best describes emotions? This issue is still hotly debated among psychologists. Perhaps the best conclusion is to say that emotions depend upon circumstances. The competing theories actually complement one another; sometimes arousal occurs prior to emotion; sometimes thinking produces emotion; and sometimes the processes are simultaneous.

Nonverbal Communication

We may communicate our feelings by describing them to others. However, we also communicate feelings in other ways. Facial expressions, body movements, gestures, and vocal characteristics are all effective modes of communication. The words, "I love you," for example, can be interpreted in many different ways, depending on whether they are said in a whisper, in a teasing tone of voice, in a cry, or with a hug.

Nonverbal communication is any expression that does not rely on words or word symbols, generally referring to an entire range of physical behaviors that can be used in conjunction with verbal utterances. One part of nonverbal expression deals with "paralanguage," those aspects of communication that are vocal but nonverbal (voice qualities, pitch, intensity, and rate of speech, for example). Another aspect of nonverbal expression is eye contact, which helps define the nature of the relationship between people (for example, positive or negative, intimate or distant). People tend to exchange glances with someone they like, but will try to avoid looking at someone they dislike. Body cues can be rather subtle indicators of psychological status. Sitting up straight rather than reclining may indicate anxiety, for example. Individuals who are open and outgoing tend to have a relaxed, open posture or sitting style. Individuals who cross their arms and legs frequently communicate that they are closed or distrustful.

Many other nonverbal behaviors beside body position and gestures can convey emotional status. People often concentrate so much on verbal content that they forget about what their bodies may be saying. Sometimes what a person says contradicts what the hearers perceive with their eyes. We usually take for granted that the different channels of communication (verbal, vocal, facial, and motor) are all saying the same thing. That is, when people say they are depressed, we expect their eyes to be teary, their voice to be cracking or low, and their hands to be slightly trembling or clutched together. It has been estimated that only 7 percent of a person's communication involves verbal impact; 38 percent involves vocal impact; and 55 percent involves facial impact (Mehrabian 1971). People tend to trust our nonverbal and facial communication the most and our words the least. Sarcasm is an example of inconsistent communication. A positive thing is said verbally but a negative tone of voice or facial expression discounts any positive implication.

The Positive Emotions

Koteskey (1980) identifies positive emotions with our Godlikeness. The emotion of love is found in the account of the prodigal son, as the father runs and kisses his wayward son. Christ wept at the tomb of Lazarus because of his great love for his friend.

A second positive emotion is that of joy. Scripture tells us that heaven rejoices when a sinner repents. The joy a believer has is deeper than what the world gives because it does not depend upon outward circumstances. It is a joy that cannot be taken from us.

Peace and awe are also identified as positive emotions by Koteskey although these are rarely mentioned by modern psychologists. Awe and reverence are denoted hundreds of times in the Bible by the phrase "the fear of God."

While Koteskey associates these emotions with the image of God, they are not always an expression of that image. For example, there is perverted love, joy from adultery, peace from the use of illegal drugs, and awe for worldly power. While positive emotions may generally be more desirable, they do not insure Godlikeness.

Indeed, Sovine (1988) maintains that several emotions listed by Koteskey are not emotions at all. The emotion of love tends to be associated with circumstances, but love in the Bible is associated with actions and attitudes rather than feelings (see Matt. 5:44; 1 Cor. 13:4). Joy is based upon position in Christ rather than emotional state (Luke 10:17–20). Peace is not just getting along with other people, but the realization that God is in control.

The Negative Emotions

Koteskey lists a number of less desirable emotions. These too can be linked with God, as he is described as hating, being angry, and being jealous. Yet generally humanity has misdirected these more negative emotions. Kirwan (1986) notes that four negative emotions are directly linked with the fall: fear, guilt, depression, and anger (Gen. 3:10; 4:6).

Among the negative emotions described by Koteskey is hatred. God certainly has a hatred of sin, and we are called upon to hate evil (though not to hate those who do evil). Sorrow is also seen as godly; Christ was known as a "man of sorrows." Yet the grief felt by Christians is not hopeless as is that of the non-Christian.

Envy and jealousy are important aspects of human behavior, although psychologists have often ignored these emotions. Selfishness is a basic characteristic of mankind, but we can become more altruistic with God's help. Coveting is a tendency that all of us must beware of, Christian or not.

God is described as angry in a number of passages, Koteskey notes, and this anger is justified because of sin and suffering. Yet God is "slow to anger" and we need to be like him in this respect. How we deal with anger is closely related to our parents' reactions, since imitation of parental behavior plays a primary role in personality development. Children easily pick up the tendency to repress anger from a parent, particularly a parent of the same sex. Many parents discourage their children from sharing angry feelings, even appropriately. Having learned to fear anger, such children grow up feeling that being aware of their anger or expressing it will result in rejection or punishment. Repressing anger often leads to displacing it on something or someone else. Unconscious grudges can lead to physical symptoms such as insomnia, fatigue, or loss of appetite.

Paul warns us that we must not sin in anger (Eph. 4:26). While anger is allowed, we must "not let the sun go down" while we are still angry. Those who can maturely rid themselves of anger seldom become clinically depressed. Usually grudges are unconscious because of our fear of admitting them. Pent-up anger may be directed either toward others (holding grudges) or toward self (true or false guilt).

Children who identify with chronically depressed parents will learn similar attitudes. Their anger eventually affects their

---

Spotlight 4.2. Grief Reactions

The stress of adjusting to serious loss is exemplified by the entire Book of Job. Job lost his children, estate, health, and essentially everything he had. With the Lord's help Job was able to overcome his loss and become effective again.

The grief reactions normally experienced by persons suffering a significant loss are not clinical depressions. A grief reaction can turn into depression, however, if short-circuited. The five stages experienced by most people who grieve, described by Kübler-Ross (1969), should be regarded as healthy safeguards against chronic depression. In the first stage (denial), individuals refuse to believe what is happening to them. The second stage is an angry reaction toward someone other than self, an anger turned outward. This stage almost always includes some anger toward God for allowing the loss to occur. After acceptance of the reality of the loss and angry reaction toward God or whoever else is held responsible, grieving persons begin to feel guilty. This third stage of bargaining generally includes a combination of false and true guilt, and is usually worked through fairly quickly. The fourth stage, depression or genuine grief, is vitally necessary. Individuals who suffer a significant loss should definitely have a good cry. Not grieving can lead to a low-grade depression that can last for many years. The fifth stage, resolution, is relatively brief and almost automatic once the stages of denial, anger turned outward, anger turned inward, and genuine grief have been worked through. During resolution, zest for life is regained. Continued depression after a significant loss comes from handling anger irresponsibly by not dealing with it or trying to repress it.

nervous systems, which adjust to the depressed lifestyle and may produce harmful and far-reaching effects.

Why should we have to experience fear, anger, grief, anxiety, and other negative emotions? Are these needless experiences? Actually, negative emotions can serve as a warning that something is needed (Sovine 1988). Fear tends to prepare us to run or to enter into combat (the "fight or flight" response); guilt can indicate sin that needs correction; and grief is the natural result of loss that indicates that readjustment is required.

Negative emotions may produce physical problems if not attended to, problems sometimes labeled "psychosomatic reactions." For example, some (but not all) cases of high blood pressure, heart problems, colitis, arthritis, ulcers, asthma, skin rashes, headaches, and even cancer can be related to the prolonged stress associated with other negative emotions. The problems are genuine, not imagined, but they are produced by psychological struggles.

Express or Repress?

How should we deal with the negative emotions? Some psychologists have advocated complete expression, often in encounter groups where total honesty is required. The "let it all hang out" and "say how you feel" approach makes it less likely that emotions will be bottled up, but it also brings with it several dangers. Direct attack does not facilitate healthy relationships, which require a measure of discretion. Indeed, some who "tell it all" may tell more than they actually feel. As noted before, feelings can be difficult to identify precisely and the individual who does not reflect upon feelings may overreact.

The other extreme of holding in all emotion is also unhealthy. Psychosomatic difficulties may result, or the underlying feelings may be expressed indirectly through defense mechanisms (see chap. 12). Defense mechanisms do not facilitate good relationships.

Perhaps a third position—"controlled verbal expression"—is possible. Here the emphasis is upon *your* feelings, not upon what the other person said or did. There is a recognition of the actual emotions felt, along with confession and restitution.

Common Depression

One emotion that everyone has felt from time to time is depression. This is not the clinical extreme (discussed in chap. 14), but the more common variety. Normal depression may show up after the birth of a baby, following the death of a loved one, after falling short of goals, or after some major project is completed. Feeling "blue" on Mondays or rainy days is the norm for some people.

THE BIBLICAL PERSPECTIVE

The Bible has a great deal to say about depression. Psalm 38:1–18 contains a vivid description of the symptoms of fairly severe depression:

> O Lord, do not rebuke me in your anger or discipline me in your wrath. For your arrows have pierced me, and your hand has come down upon me. Because of your wrath there is no health in my body; my bones have no soundness because of my sin. My guilt has overwhelmed me like a burden too heavy to bear. My wounds fester and are loathsome because of my sinful folly. I am bowed down and brought very low; all day long I go about mourning. My back is filled with searing pain; there is no health in my body. I am feeble and utterly crushed; I groan in anguish of heart. All my longings lie open before you, O Lord; my sighing is not hidden from you. My heart pounds, my strength fails me; even the light has gone from my eyes. My

friends and companions avoid me because of my wounds; my neighbors stay far away. Those who seek my life set their traps, those who would harm me talk of my ruin; all day long they plot deception. I am like a deaf man, who cannot hear, like a mute, who cannot open his mouth; I have become like a man who does not hear, whose mouth can offer no reply. I wait for you, O LORD; you will answer, O LORD, my God. For I said, "Do not let them gloat or exalt themselves over me when my foot slips." For I am about to fall, and my pain is ever with me. I confess my iniquity; I am troubled by my sin.

Spotlight 4.3. Suicide

Depression is the leading cause of suicide, which, in turn, is the tenth leading cause of death in the United States. Since over 10 percent of persons who make a suicide gesture eventually commit suicide, anyone who threatens suicide should be taken seriously. Eighty percent of those who do commit suicide have warned someone of their intentions. The incidence of suicide is higher among the divorced, widowed, and upper socioeconomic groups. It is most common among single, white adult males over forty-five years of age. Although women attempt suicide five times more frequently than men, twice as many suicidal men die. Men tend to use a violent means of suicide such as a gun or a car crash while women tend to use a moderate form such as drug overdose. Women are more apt to use suicide as a manipulative gesture.

Several warning signs can alert a counselor to suicidal individuals. Most suffer from intense emotional pain, as seen in depression, and have overwhelming feelings of hopelessness. They may have a severe health problem or have experienced a significant loss such as the death of a spouse or loss of a job. An excess number of disturbing life events in a short time period can precipitate suicide. Individuals with an intense need to achieve, or who exhibit chronic self-destructive behavior (for example, drug or alcohol abuse), may show suicidal tendencies. A prior history of suicide attempts or threats is an obvious clue. Suicidal individuals often follow a pattern, beginning with fleeting thoughts of suicide that are given greater and greater consideration until an actual attempt is made.

Individuals who exhibit suicidal tendencies should be encouraged to change their self-destructive thoughts and behavior. Christians regard suicide as a sin equivalent to murder. "Thou shalt not kill" applies to a person's own life as well as the lives of others. Of the suicides recorded in Scripture, none of the perpetrators was in the will of God at the time of death. Of those suicides—Abimelech (Judg. 9:54), Samson (Judg. 16:30), Saul (1 Sam. 31:4), Saul's armor-bearer (1 Sam. 31:5), Ahithophel (2 Sam. 17:23), Zimri (1 Kings 16:18), and Judas (Matt. 27:3–5)—several could be regarded more as battle casualties than as true suicides.

It is crucial that indications of suicide be recognized by Christian counselors and threats be taken seriously. It is generally best to refer suicidal individuals to someone with specialized training.

Spotlight 4.4. Emotions, Impressions, and Decision Making

Most Christians recognize the need to follow God's direction in making decisions. But how can we discern his will? Some Christians believe that God leads through impressions, which Dobson (1980) links with emotions. Others assert that God sends certain bodily sensations to indicate his will. One group, in fact, has identified several hundred specific bodily sensations, each of which corresponds with a message from God. They even built a church on the basis of architectural details derived from this process! Should we rely upon feelings and impressions in discerning God's will?

Two books have provided a number of insights in this area. Although they take very different approaches and even contradict one another at points, they are both valuable. Dobson's book (1980) has an important chapter that summarizes many of the more traditional conclusions in this area. Friesen (1980) provides a less traditional treatment.

Dobson cites three sources of impressions—God, Satan, and self—although he acknowledges that self is involved in the other two sources to some extent. Yet it is often difficult to determine from which source an impression derives. How can we be sure that what we sense is what God is saying?

To determine God's will, Scripture must be consulted early in the process to preclude any option not in accordance with God's revealed Word. It may help to ask God to make plain which option he desires. He may choose to do this, but he may allow us to do some of our own decision making and exercise our judgment.

It is perhaps more than likely that we will make our own decisions in minor areas. There are students, for example, who change their majors a dozen times while in college, because of their uncertainty about God's will. Of course, a dozen changes might possibly be his will; an individual might get a variety of classes that would be

---

Elsewhere in the Bible we find other descriptions of depression. Consider, for example, the description of Cain in Genesis 4:6–7.

Depressed individuals may cry often and their faces usually reflect their feelings. They also tend to be pessimistic and engage in other kinds of painful thinking (see Ps. 42:5). Those who are depressed often think repeatedly about their past mistakes, sometimes feeling guilty even when innocent. They are often preoccupied with themselves and avoid other people.

Common depression is also described in terms of its physical effects. Consider Psalm 102:3–7:

> For my days vanish like smoke; my bones burn like glowing embers. My heart is blighted and withered like grass; I forget to eat my food. Because of my loud groaning I am reduced to skin and bones. I am like a desert owl, like an owl among

unlikely any other way. (This is not recommended, it is just mentioned as a possibility!)

Yet God will probably give assurance in major decisions. True, this is coming dangerously close to relying upon feelings, but a sense of assurance is reported by many Christians on particularly important matters. In contrast, when a major change of life is anticipated and an individual is overwhelmed with worry, it may well be that caution is called for. Sometimes it is best to wait and consider the matter more carefully.

How does confirmation of a decision come to an individual? It may be through Scripture. Schaeffer, for example, came upon Isaiah 2:2 as a confirmation that he was to open L'Abri, the famous Swiss retreat for youth that began his worldwide ministry. On the other hand, confirmation may come from godly Christians who are sensitive to the Holy Spirit and have good insight. A spouse may be a source of confirmation. Confirmation may come from circumstances. An example is Gideon's fleece. (It should be noted that Gideon did not *receive* God's will by the fleece, but rather the fleece *confirmed* God's will.) Yet we must be careful that we do not make a god of circumstances.

It is easy to think that our own ideas are God's when trying to determine his will. Strong personal preferences may override prayer or reading Scripture. We must stay open to God's leading, regardless of what that may entail, by remaining teachable.

We must also be willing to let God say, "Wait awhile." God may very well open all the right doors suddenly and there will be no question about what he wants. More characteristically, however, he asks us to wait rather than make quick decisions. Finally, it should be noted that there may not be one single will for an individual's life (as the "Four Spiritual Laws" booklet implies). Perhaps God has several possible plans.

---

the ruins. I lie awake; I have become like a bird alone on a roof.

Sleep, appetite, and digestion may be affected adversely by depression.

CAUSES

Depression may be a powerful way of manipulating others, or perhaps even a vent to relieve anger. It can also be a way of getting attention. On the other hand, common depression can be the result of biological changes. Genetic influences may cause mood swings. Certain endocrine disorders are known to result in depression, as is depletion of certain chemicals in the neurons. Viral infections and fatigue can also bring on depressive symptoms.

In the majority of cases, however, common depression is the result of life stresses. The biblical Job is a good example of how life stresses can take an emotional toll on an individual. External influences, such as a divorce or other major life

Spotlight 4.5.
Christian Books on Emotions

A number of books have been published in recent years dealing with emotions and the Christian.

The best-known discussion of emotion from a Christian perspective is Dobson's best-seller, *Emotions: Can You Trust Them?* (1980). This book was originally a series of booklets for teen-agers and adults which was eventually published in book form. Guilt, romantic love, and anger are covered in separate chapters. The ideas and suggestions are vivid, interesting, and practical. A final chapter deals with impressions and how to determine God's will (see spotlight 4.4).

A more scholarly, but still very readable, approach is taken by VanderGoot in *Helping Children Grow Healthy Emotions* (1987). While the title indicates an emphasis on children, the first two and final three chapters treat emotions in a more general fashion.

A philosophical approach to the topic is detailed by Murphree in *Made to Be Mastered* (1984). Murphree deals with loneliness, emotional dependence, suffering, failure, and success. While maintaining more of a philosophical/theological emphasis, Murphree also discusses some of the psychological factors involved.

Seamand's best-seller, *Healing for Damaged Emotions* (1981), is an excellent resource for laypersons. He includes the topics of guilt and depression, and also considers the problems of perfectionism and poor self-esteem. This book can be profitably used for a series of Sunday school lessons. Seamand's other books are also very helpful.

Backus and Chapian (1980) explain how people can find their way out of anger, fear, and anxiety through "misbelief therapy." This approach to overcoming emotional problems has much in common with rational-emotive therapy (see chap. 16). The book has sold well, as evidenced by several followup volumes.

A number of Christian books have devoted one or more chapters to the topic of emotions. Roberts (1986) compares emotions to the fruit of the Spirit in a chapter by that same title. Collins (1985) devotes a chapter to emotions in his excellent book on the mind and brain. Five chapters of his comprehensive guide to Christian counseling (1980) consider anxiety, loneliness, depression, anger, guilt, and grief. A chapter of Koteskey's excellent book, *General Psychology for Christian Counselors* (1983), gives practical counseling applications from the study of emotions. Significant sections of both Kirwan (1984) and Philipchalk (1988) also consider the role of emotions in the Christian life. A chapter of Myers and Jeeves (1987) is concerned with emotions. For a Christian perspective on men's emotions, see Jones and Phillips-Jones (1988).

crises, often produce depressive reactions. Guilt may also produce depression, as can taking a wrong perspective on events (see Ps. 73:1–3). Depression can also be a satanic attack.

Minirth and Meier (1978, 135–95) suggest some guidelines for overcoming depression:

1. Accept Christ, who is the Source of strength.
2. Read the Bible, letting it reprogram your mind.
3. Pray; call upon the power of God.
4. Avoid sin.
5. Stop playing God; depression can be an attempt to punish self.
6. Recognize underlying anger and deal with it by verbalizing the anger and forgiving others.
7. Focus on actions; actions may determine feelings.
8. Change mental self-statements.
9. Fellowship with other Christians and build close friendships.
10. Stop getting even.
11. Learn to be properly assertive and deal with dependency needs.
12. Recognize an unhealthy fear of rejection.
13. Respond rationally; do not react aggressively.
14. Change your environment to reduce stress.
15. Develop new interests and activities.
16. Do not be overly introspective.
17. Accept responsibility for depression.
18. Realize that no one is perfect.
19. Learn to laugh; laughter relaxes.
20. Get help; counseling can instill hope.

References

Backus, W., and M. Chapian. 1980. *Telling yourself the truth.* Minneapolis: Bethany.

Bard, P. 1938. Studies in the cortical representation of somatic sensibility. *Harvey Lectures* 33: 143–69.

Collins, G. 1980. *Christian counseling: A comprehensive guide.* Waco: Word.

———. 1985. *The magnificent mind.* Waco: Word.

Dobson, J. 1980. *Emotions: Can you trust them?* Ventura, Calif.: Regal.

Friesen, G. 1980. *Decision making and the will of God.* Portland: Multnomah.

Hogan, R., and D. Schroeder. 1981. Seven biases in psychology. *Psychology Today* 15: 8–14.

James, W. 1884. What is emotion? *Mind* 19: 188–205.

Jones, G., and L. Phillips-Jones. 1988. *Men have feelings too!* Wheaton, Ill.: Victor.

Kirwan, W. 1984. *Biblical concepts for Christian counseling.* Grand Rapids: Baker.

———. 1986. "Counseling today" (cassette tape), spring.

Koteskey, R. 1980. Toward the development of a Christian psychology: Emotion. *Journal of Psychology and Theology* 8 (Winter): 303–13.

———. 1983. *General psychology for Christian counselors.* Nashville: Abingdon.

Kübler-Ross, E. 1969. *On death and dying.* New York: Macmillan.

Mehrabian, A. 1971. *Silent messages.* Belmont, Calif.: Wadsworth.

Minirth, F., and P. Meier. 1978. *Happiness is a choice.* Grand Rapids: Baker.

Morris, W. 1987. *Mood.* New York: Springer-Verlag.

Murphree, J. 1984. *Made to be mastered.* Grand Rapids: Baker.

Myers, D., and M. Jeeves. 1987. *Psychology through the eyes of faith.* San Francisco: Harper and Row.

Philipchalk, R. 1988. *Psychology and Christianity.* Lanham, Md.: University Press of America.

Roberts, R. 1986. Emotion and the fruit of the Spirit. In *Psychology and the Christian faith,* ed. S. Jones. Grand Rapids: Baker.

Schachter, S., and J. Singer. 1962. Cognitive, social and physiological determinants of emotional state. *Psychological Review* 69: 379–99.

Seamands, D. 1981. *Healing for damaged emotions.* Wheaton, Ill.: Victor.

Sovine, C. 1980. Integration of psychology and theology. Staley lecture series, Toccoa Falls College special class session, Mar. 23.

VanderGoot, M. 1987. *Helping children grow healthy emotions.* Grand Rapids: Baker.

Zajonc, R. 1985. Emotion and facial effects. *Science* 228: 15–21.

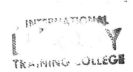

5

Motivation

What makes people do the things they do? The concept of motivation has been a difficult one for psychologists to define. The meaning of the word seems to change according to the individual psychologist's orientation to the study of the human being. Those who focus on human biological functioning tend to think of motivation primarily in relation to bodily needs. Other psychologists perceive humans as motivated primarily by inner feelings and rational decision making. Scientists who focus on humans as social beings tend to relate motivation to interpersonal functioning.

Motivation may have a variety of sources; hunger often stems from a biological drive whereas altruism may develop from interpersonal relationships, from a moral value system, or from belief in God. According to Scripture, the Holy Spirit motivates Christians to genuine love and altruistic acts.

Motivation is difficult to discuss because psychologists tend to make inferences about underlying psychological and physiological processes. Such inferences are then formalized in the concept of motivation. Much of what has been said about motivation hence may represent only an abstraction. Yet motivation is real and has two characteristics. The first is that it influences and directs behavior. For example, if a boy is walking barefoot on a hot sidewalk and his feet get too hot, he may begin to walk on the grass. As the sensation of heat, perceived through sensory organs in the feet, is transferred to his brain, the boy is motivated to walk on the cooler grass. Therefore his behavior has been altered. The second characteristic of motivation is that it describes purposeful behavior. That is, the boy not only realizes that his feet are hot but also moves to alleviate that condition in a purposeful way.

The two major theories of motivation are the drive theory and the arousal theory. Each relates to biological influences, although learned drives and cognitive arousal play a larger role in current theories of

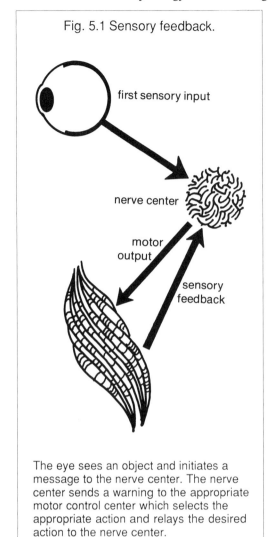

Fig. 5.1 Sensory feedback.

first sensory input

nerve center

motor output

sensory feedback

The eye sees an object and initiates a message to the nerve center. The nerve center sends a warning to the appropriate motor control center which selects the appropriate action and relays the desired action to the nerve center.

motivation. After considering these two basic theories, Maslow's hierarchy of needs will serve as a useful contrast.

Theories of Motivation

The Drive Theory

In its simplest form, drive theory focuses on certain biological needs that are basic to life. All other wants and needs are assumed to be learned through attempts to reduce the physiological arousals produced by those basic needs. Needs considered primary by drive theorists would include air, food, water, and proper body temperature. When such primary needs are not met, a primary drive builds up within the body, motivating the individual to satisfy that need. According to drive theory, as long as all of the body's primary needs are met, it is presumably in a state of balance. Whenever one of your primary needs is not satisfied, you are likely to experience a state of arousal or excitation. Generally speaking, the longer you are deprived of something, the greater the drive becomes and the more aroused you may feel. Eventually that arousal influences you to satisfy your needs. Once you do so, the drive level falls back toward zero and the drive state of excitation is greatly reduced.

Crucial to the drive concept is the idea of homeostatic activity. Homeostasis basically refers to maintenance of normal or unexcited levels, or the process of accomplishing a physiological balance or equilibrium (see fig. 5.2). Any action taken by an individual to reduce a drive is, therefore, homeostatic.

The Arousal Theory

In general, arousal theory differs from drive theory by suggesting that the homeostatic level may vary throughout life. Thus, need for stimulation changes according to past experiences and present condition. As an example, let us consider a woman who eats chocolate ice cream every night. During the first few nights she experiences a great deal of pleasure in eating the ice cream. By the sixth or seventh night, however, she may comment that she does not enjoy the chocolate ice cream as much. An arousal theorist would say her homeostatic level has shifted.

The reticular activating system in the brain (see fig. 2.4) sorts sensory information, either passing it on to the upper brain or blocking that information. The

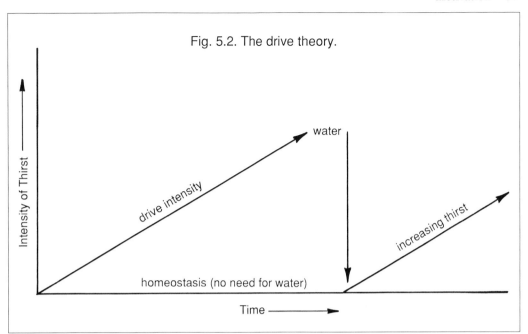

Fig. 5.2. The drive theory.

reticular activating system arouses the cortex or central area of the brain, making the individual vigilant and aware of what is happening in the environment.

Certain studies of arousal levels seem to have important implications for our functioning. For example, when arousal is very low, we usually do not have a good guide

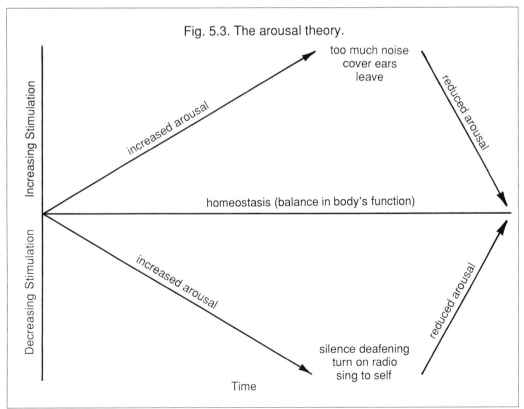

Fig. 5.3. The arousal theory.

for behavior. That is why when you get up early in the morning you may stub your toe trying to cross the room to turn on the light; the arousal level of your reticular activating system is low. At an intermediate level of arousal, usage of cues is optimal because the most useful information is taken from the sensory organs to guide behavior. The quarterback in a football game may be experiencing optimal arousal, making him aware of the charging defensive linemen and enabling him to throw his pass before they tackle him. At some point, however, increasing arousal becomes ineffective. When we become too aware of the environmental situation, our arousal can inhibit proper performance. If a fire breaks out in a crowded room, for example, panic may ensue and people may stampede for the doorways. The relationship between arousal and effective performance is described as an inverted-U function, meaning that it goes through a maximum and then diminishes (fig. 5.4).

Maslow's Theory

Other theories of motivation largely embrace what the drive and arousal theorists have said but add the more subjective variable of feelings. Although neural activity may begin when blood sugar is low, few of

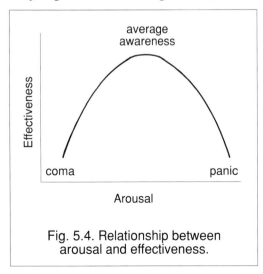

Fig. 5.4. Relationship between arousal and effectiveness.

us begin stuffing goodies in our mouths at that point. Often we begin to eat because we see a food commercial on television. Drive theorists and arousal theorists place little importance on feelings, emotions, or perceptions in defining drives and arousals. Hence many psychologists have gone beyond simple biologically based theories of motivation to more sophisticated theories which include emotions, perceptions, and relevant past experiences.

A number of psychological theories have combined such factors in order to explain motivation. For example, behavioral psychology describes the ways behavior is learned, and thus underscores some learned motivational factors (see chap. 6). The ideas of humanists, Freudians, and others could be included here, but for the sake of brevity we will consider only one theory because it is closely related to the two biological theories considered thus far.[1]

Maslow (1970) has suggested five levels of human need. These needs are placed in a hierarchy, beginning with the most basic ones. At any given step in the hierarchy there must be a degree of satisfaction before the individual is motivated to satisfy the next level.

At the bottom of the hierarchy are physical needs. These are such basic needs as air, food, and water. If these needs are not satisfied, the individual cannot survive. If an individual must spend a great deal of time trying to find food to subsist, it is unlikely that higher cravings will be realized.

The second level of need is that of safety. There must be some degree of protection from the environment. The person without shelter, for example, is unlikely to be interested in more advanced kinds of needs.

The third level is that of love needs. Love and acceptance are critical to a full

1. See chap. 12 for a survey of other applicable theories.

Spotlight 5.1.
The Drive and Arousal Theories in the Church

The biological theories of motivation have their place in the church. Those who nod off during a sermon exemplify lack of arousal. What might cause this lack of arousal? The obvious answer would be lack of sleep, but this is certainly not always the case. It is perhaps more likely that the message was not relevant and interesting. Good sermons are noted for their practical applications rather than for mere abstractions. Boredom may result in inattentiveness and a low degree of arousal. In contrast a good illustration, a lively joke, or an interesting story is more likely to get attention.

The arousal theory also has relevance for church leaders who have difficulty sleeping at night. Church leaders often experience an obsessive rethinking of daily experiences and planning for the future. These kinds of activities, which involve the frontal lobe of the brain, are likely to send a message to the reticular activating system that arousal is needed. Those who struggle with such obsessive rethinking should turn their thoughts to more mundane matters. Systematic relaxation exercises, described later in this chapter (as well as in the appendix), may help as this is likely to decrease the arousal of the reticular system.*

It is perhaps superfluous to point out that biological drives can also interfere with the reception of a message in church. One thinks of sleepy Sunday schools that would be greatly helped by breakfast rolls and coffee. It is all too easy for a teacher or pastor to conclude that people are uninterested due to lack of spirituality when the problem is actually biologically based.

*See Collins 1977 for further discussion on relaxation; and Coates and Thoreson 1977 for more information on insomnia.

life. Esteem needs are also important. Once we feel loved, we desire to be respected by others. Self-respect is also described as an aspect of this fourth level of the hierarchy.

The highest level is that of self-actual-

Spotlight 5.2.
Maslow's Hierarchy and Christianity

Is Maslow's hierarchy valid for Christians? Certainly we can acknowledge that people's needs are not identical and that it is difficult to satisfy people's higher needs (including spiritual needs) when they are hungry and homeless. Yet Christians sometimes neglect some of the lower levels of the hierarchy. The Bible speaks of fasting for spiritual purposes. It also describes Christ as not having anywhere he could call home and that ultimately our home is heaven. The Scriptures state that we must leave the love of friends and family for God's kingdom. Christ was not esteemed by those of this world and his followers have historically been regarded poorly by unbelievers.

Are peak experiences, characteristic of Maslow's highest level, to be central to the Christian life? Is not life in general more important than emotions and ecstatic experiences? This contradiction may be explained in part by the fact that Maslow does not mean that all of a person's needs at a given level must be fulfilled prior to moving to the next higher level. As Darling (1969) points out, 85 percent of physical needs could be satisfied, 70 percent of safety needs, 50 percent of love needs, 40 percent of self-esteem needs, and 10 percent of self-actualization needs.

Maslow's hierarchy does challenge certain aspects of Christianity. Yet in terms of evangelism and social concern, certain aspects of the hierarchy may help as we seek to meet people's needs. There is quite a difference between voluntary deprivation willingly accepted after salvation, and ignoring involuntary deprivation of the poor. Christians must minister to the whole person; Maslow's hierarchy could be used to determine where people's needs are most acute at a given moment in time.

ization, in which we move beyond love to expressions of individuality and harmony of the self (Darling 1969, 85). This level, which few acquire, is marked by "peak experiences," mystical states which mark the most fully developed individuals (see chap. 13).

In general, comprehending the motivation of any behavior requires an understanding not only of the physiological basis of that behavior, but also of psychological factors.

Biological Drives

Humans have a number of biological drives or needs similar to those of ani-

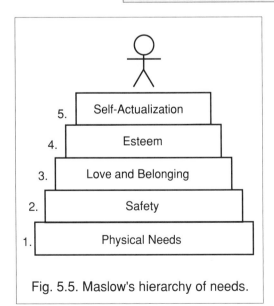

Fig. 5.5. Maslow's hierarchy of needs.

mals. Hunger, thirst, pain, and pleasure are common biological motivators. Here we will discuss hunger, stress (and anxiety), and sex.

Hunger

Hunger has received much attention as a motivator from both psychologists and physiologists, perhaps because the mechanism of the reduction of this drive is easily explained. Consumption of food is the response that reduces or temporarily eliminates the hunger drive. Certain internal body messages must cause us to begin to search our environment for food. What internal states do we "read" to know we are hungry?

Early research by Cannon (1934) indicated that hunger pangs were related to stomach contractions. As noted in chapter 2, the hypothalamus reacts to low blood sugar levels to induce eating behavior, and causes us to stop eating when the blood sugar level goes up.

Research by Zeigler (1975) indicates that the hypothalamic centers may be influenced by neural inputs from the trigeminal nerve, which runs through the cheek and face and controls chewing and swallowing responses. Damage to the trigeminal nerve causes loss of appetite.

The search for still other factors influencing eating behavior has led to studies

---

Spotlight 5.3.
Using Maslow's Theory in the Church

The biological needs of people in the church can be understood in terms of Maslow's theory. At noon it may be easier to think about Sunday dinner than it is to listen to the conclusion of the sermon. Maslow's first stage is more acute than his higher stages!

Or consider a missions committee that is attempting to establish priorities in the church's overseas work. Several committee members might feel that widespread hunger is a primary concern while others emphasize the need for love and belonging. To apply Maslow's theory would be to assess where the people to be reached are at present. If they are starving, the need for food would be primary. However, higher needs should also be considered since people do not have to be perfectly satisfied at lower stages before other needs are met. However, the physical needs of the hungry should be a priority.

Perhaps the youth group in a church has filled out a questionnaire asking what each person worries about the most. Many are concerned that their parents do not respect them; others describe the lack of justice in society; and still others worry about being desired by the opposite sex. These concerns reflect different stages of Maslow's hierarchy: the desire for respect is indicative of stage 4, a concern for justice is more common in stage 5, and wanting to be desired by others is a stage-3 concern. A youth leader would do well to see where young people are in the hierarchy and help meet needs at that level as well as encourage the progression upward.*

*For additional ideas on using Maslow's theory in the church, see McDonough 1979. Also see Crabb's (1977) chapter on motivation and his conclusion that only Christians can be truly self-actualized.

of external cues. Schachter (1971) has done considerable research on the eating behavior of obese and normal people. Schachter's findings indicate that obese people are much more aware of the external cues of their environment (such as clocks) and eat "because it is time to," consume large portions, and are affected by the taste of food. Average weight people usually eat when they feel hungry, take smaller amounts of food, and generally are more aware of internal cues (such as sensations of being full). It seems reasonable to conclude that the environment influences eating behavior.

Before moving on, a note about obesity and overeating may be appropriate. Clearly the Bible and the Judeo-Christian tradition strongly discourage gluttony. A Gallup poll revealed that 55 percent of American women and 38 percent of American men described themselves as overweight. Parents who believe a fat infant is a healthy one may establish a lifelong pattern of overeating. In adult life, wives may see themselves as successful if their husbands are "fat and happy." Sexual frustration can influence an adult to overeat, or obesity may be an unconscious way to avoid intimacy. Many individuals become obese soon after a broken engagement or divorce, thus guaranteeing that no member of the opposite sex will approach them for genuine love or for a sexual experience. Obesity may avert the temptation to have an extramarital affair.

Clearly, many psychological and physiological reasons may be given for why people overeat. But whatever the reasons, God still expects us to exercise self-control and promises to help us with temptation. In spite of many prohibitions against being overweight, the influences to overeat are often strong. The monitoring of eating habits, so important to physical health,

"Oh, my! What a healthy baby!"

hence may also be an indicator of self-control.

Is an attempt to lose weight likely to be successful? Recent evidence indicates that most people who lose a significant amount of weight gain it back shortly (Wing and Jeffery 1979). Furthermore, it is more difficult to lose weight the next time (Brownell et al. 1986). The body is designed to compensate for famine by adding extra fat cells in times of plenty. After a famine (going on a diet), the body stores fat so that weight will remain relatively stable during a subsequent famine. This process is of benefit to people who suffer in times of actual famine, but in planned famine, it works against efforts to lose weight.

Not much can be done about this problem. The dieter is fighting powerful genetic and psychological influences. While some individuals are genuinely able to lose weight and keep it off, many find themselves caught in a vicious and ever more difficult cycle of binging and dieting. The latter is probably more physically dangerous than being a little overweight.

Stress

Fear will be discussed in some detail when we consider the learning process.

Here it will be considered as one aspect of stress and anxiety. At the physiological level, defenses are controlled by the autonomic nervous system—the sympathetic and parasympathetic systems (see chap. 2). The sympathetic nervous system prepares a person for fighting, fleeing, feeding, and sexual behavior. The parasympathetic nervous system slows down those body functions that are aroused by the sympathetic system. The two systems influence much of what we do and feel. When a person becomes excited or emotionally aroused, the sympathetic system causes a release of adrenalin and noradrenalin, the arousal hormones secreted by the adrenal glands. The two hormones have generally similar excitatory effects on physiological reactions such as blood pressure and heart rate. Such arousal puts us under a variety of biological, psychological, and behavioral stresses, which if continued too long can exhaust us.

THEORIES OF STRESS

Holmes' Social Readjustment Rating Scale is used to determine the level of stress in relation to adjustment to change (Holmes and Rahe, 1967; see tab. 5.1). An accumulation of two hundred or more life change units in a single year is often fol-

---

Spotlight 5.4.
Christians and Weight Loss

In recent years there have been a number of popular books written by Christians on how to lose weight. While some of these are frivolous, equating weight with spirituality (adding guilt to the problem of being overweight is, by itself, unlikely to foster change), many such books are trying to meet a genuinely felt need. Unfortunately, many of these lack a good psychological foundation.

Of the Christian books on losing weight perhaps the best is that by Dobbert (1977), which includes an introduction by Dobson. This book needs to be supplemented, however, with other sources that include good psychological and medical orientations, such as Cordell and Giebler (1977) and Jeffrey and Katz (1977).

If you want to lose weight, we encourage you to do so, not just to follow a fad, but to be a healthier person. After a good physical examination by a physician, the following steps may be helpful:

1. Record what and when you eat or drink for a week. Also, keep a record of your exercise.
2. Note what rewards or pleasure you find in eating, including interaction with people around you.
3. Eat smaller amounts at different times.
4. Increase your physical exercise so that you begin to expend more energy in exercise than you take in by eating.
5. If you feel that interpersonal factors such as family or peers contribute to overeating, see a counselor or psychologist to discuss those issues.
6. Finally, do not expect to lose too much too fast. Probably a pound or two a week is appropriate. A good motto to tell yourself is that you "will not gain another pound."

Table 5.1
Holmes' Social Readjustment Rating Scale

Events	Scale of Impact
Death of a spouse	100
Divorce	73
Marital separation	65
Jail term	63
Death of close family member	63
Personal injury or illness	53
Marriage	50
Fired at work	47
Marital reconciliation	45
Retirement	45
Change in health of family member	44
Pregnancy	40
Sex difficulties	39
Gain of new family member	39
Business readjustment	39
Change in financial state	38
Death of close friend	37
Change to different line of work	36
Change in number of arguments with spouse	35
Mortgage over $10,000	31
Foreclosure of mortgage or loan	30
Change in responsibilities at work	29
Son or daughter leaving home	29
Trouble with in-laws	29
Outstanding personal achievement	28
Wife begins or stops work	26
Begin or end school	26
Change in living conditions	25
Revision of personal habits	24
Trouble with boss	23
Change in work hours or conditions	20
Change in residence	20
Change in schools	20
Change in recreation	19
Change in church activities	19
Change in social activities	18
Mortgage or loan less than $10,000	17
Change in sleeping habits	16
Change in number of family get-togethers	15
Change in eating habits	15
Vacation	13
Christmas	12
Minor violations of the law	11

lowed by development of psychiatric disorders. For example, a change of residence is actually a kind of loss that causes stress, so children subjected to repeated moves often become depressed.

The most stressful change is loss of a spouse, parent, or other close relative. The mortality rate actually increases markedly during the first year of a bereavement. Children suffer greatly from loss of a parent, often exhibiting overt depression, misconduct, or clinging behavior. The more insecure such children feel, the more they may cling to those who remain. They may also be more subject to depression later in life.[2]

Selye (1976) has suggested that the body goes through three distinct stages when stressed. The first is the alarm reaction, in which the body's defenses are mobilized by activity in the limbic and sympathetic systems and through the secretion of adrenalin and noradrenalin. The second stage is one of resistance, which occurs if the stress continues over a long period; during this stage the body may try to repair any damage the arousal causes while defending itself. Finally, a stage of exhaustion occurs if the emergency condition lasts too long. Psychological and environmental arousal states can be just as exhausting as physiological stresses. For example, a fear of being attacked or even of failure can drain our available resources as drastically as a case of mononucleosis.

Reactions to fear in stress situations may also depend on perceptions of control. The locus of control construct as developed by Rotter (1966) defines two kinds of individuals. Internals are people who believe they are autonomous. Since they believe they control what happens to them, they are aroused by threats and try to overcome those threats. Externals are

2. Holmes' methodology has been criticized by some psychologists, who question the validity of his scale.

those who see themselves primarily as being acted on by their environment. They tend to wait for an external agent to take care of them. Much internal or external behavior appears to be learned at an early age. Although some externals are prone to extreme helplessness, with retraining many can learn to cope with stressful situations sensibly and effectively. Meditation or relaxation training can help individuals reduce their alarm reactions by taking cognitive control over the arousal. Another way of controlling feelings of helplessness, which can be extremely stressful, has been to encourage individuals to experience mastery of the stressful situations. Finally, learning to predict when certain stressful situations will occur can significantly improve ability to deal with stress.

Clearly, fear or stress can be a significant motivator of human behavior. Psychological stresses such as major life changes can be quite harmful, depending on the individual's locus of control. Stress is a major problem for many in professional ministry, including missionaries (Foyle 1987). Christians, however, can have confidence that God does not allow them to experience any trials greater than they can bear (1 Cor. 10:13). Calling on fellow believers for help in times of need can aid in the management of stressful situations.

When excessive stress occurs repeatedly, the parasympathetic nervous system does not bring the body back to its normal resting state. As a result, there is some degree of general arousal from the continual release of hormones into the system. This continued state of arousal from the sympathetic system is known as anxiety.

All of us experience anxiety at times. Anxiety, which often accompanies depression, is an emotion characterized by uneasiness, apprehension, dread, concern, tension, restlessness, and worry. The anxious individual often anticipates misfortune, danger, or doom.

What can be done about anxiety? A number of principles from Scripture can be harnessed to overcome the effects of excessive stress and anxiety (see spotlight 5.5). Medications and relaxation exercises can also help. Many people do not know how to genuinely relax because they have been stressed for so long that their body has actually adjusted to the tension.

PROGRESSIVE RELAXATION TECHNIQUE

In progressive relaxation, the individual is instructed to tense a particular muscle group and then use that tension as a signal to relax. Muscles throughout the body (eyelids, jaw, neck, upper arms, hands, chest, stomach, back, upper legs, and feet) are systematically addressed. Over and over the phrase, "tension is a signal to relax," is repeated as the individual tenses the muscles and then relaxes them. Eventually the message ("tension is a signal to relax") becomes subconscious and automatic.

A relaxing and comfortable setting is important in progressive relaxation. Individuals are sometimes instructed to picture a very relaxing and calm environment (near an ocean or waterfall). A counselee might slowly count down from 10 to 0, breathing in and out with each number, relaxing a little more with each exhalation.

Sex

Although human beings have the same biological drive to reproduce that is found in animals, the social role of sex in human societies complicates any discussion of sex as a motivator. Masters and Johnson (1979) report that healthy sexual behavior requires a committed relationship. Such findings seem to complement what we know from God's revelation. The biblical record indicates that human sexual behav-

---

Spotlight 5.5.
Principles That Decrease Anxiety

A number of biblical principles, taken from Paul's writings, can help believers decrease anxiety (Markell 1982; Collins 1973; Minirth and Meier 1978).

1. Obey God. God commands us not to be anxious (Matt. 6:25–34; Phil. 4:6; 1 Tim. 6:6).
2. Pray (Phil. 4:6).
3. Realize that God can guard our hearts and minds as we obey him (Phil. 4:7).
4. Meditate on positive thoughts (Phil. 4:8). There is no better place to find positive thoughts than in the Bible.
5. Focus on godly behavior (Phil. 4:9). Anxious individuals need to avoid sin and join small fellowship groups.
6. Realize there is a twofold responsibility (ours and Christ's) in doing anything (Phil. 4:13). An individual can overcome anxiety through Christ.
7. Realize God will supply our needs but not always our wants (Phil. 4:19).

A number of common-sense suggestions can also help decrease anxiety.

1. Get adequate exercise—ideally three times per week.

---

ior has rarely met God's standards, however. Many believe that the Song of Solomon presents an appropriate model of human sexual behavior within marriage.

There is a diversity of definitions of sexual behavior. Although reproductive activities are necessary for the continuation of the species, obviously not all sexual behavior is reproductive. An understanding of sexual motivation must account for both reproductive and other aspects of sexual behavior.

Physiologically, sex hormones are produced in the gonads (testes in the male and ovaries in the female). Male sex hormones are collectively called androgens. The female sex hormones include both estrogens and progesterone. At puberty, secretion of sex hormones produces the physical and behavioral characteristics that we associate with maleness and femaleness. Throughout most of the rest of life, these hormones continue to be secreted.

Research by Olds (1969) suggests that "pleasure centers" exist in the brains of animals and humans. Sexual pleasure seems to be correlated with neural firing in certain regions of the brain. Thus, although hunger or stress as motivated behavior seems to be aimed at reducing tension or arousal, sexual behavior appears to be based on a complex interaction of hormonal influence, pleasurable sensory input, and learning.

Until recently, research concerning instinctual sexual responses in humans was almost nonexistent. Various studies by Harlow, as well as by Masters and Johnson, however, suggest that early experience

2. Get adequate sleep. Most people need eight hours of sleep per night.
3. Do what you can to deal with the fear or problem causing the anxiety. Examine different alternatives or possible solutions and try one.
4. Talk with a close friend at least once a week about your frustrations.
5. Get adequate recreation—ideally two to three times per week.
6. Live one day at a time (Matt. 6:34).
7. Imagine the worst thing that could possibly happen. Then more realistic possibilities will not look so bad.
8. Divert attention from self to others. As individuals get their minds off their own problems by helping others, their anxiety often decreases.
9. Do not put things off.
10. Set a time limit on your worries. Set aside a definite period of time each day in which to focus on a given problem. If the issue surfaces any other time, say, "I cannot consider that issue right now. I will consider it later during the designated time period, but I refuse to consider it at this moment." By doing so you set free much of the mental energy that would otherwise be wasted in worry.

is at least as significant as the effects of hormones in determining sexual behavior. Thus what a child learns early in life about appropriate sexual behavior is extremely important. Parents who fail to teach their children about appropriate sexual behavior probably contribute to later problematic sexual behavior.

The learned component of sexual behavior is of course important to sexual self-control, a topic often emphasized in conservative churches. In fact, many young people believe that in the eyes of the church, sin is synonymous with sex. Such a distorted concept does double damage. It enables people to ignore whole categories of sin that the Bible warns against (greed, jealousy, gossip), and it may make sexual enjoyment within marriage more difficult.

Christians recognize that in a fallen world, all human motivations are affected by rebellion against God, not merely sexual motivation. The believer's response to any situation of suspect motivation should be to turn to God, seeking his grace through Jesus Christ. We can be comforted by 1 John 1:9, which tells us that if we confess our sins he will forgive us and "purify us from all unrighteousness." When we find ourselves in sin we should act in obedience to God's will by confessing our twisted motivation and then ending immoral or destructive behavior.

Hyperactivity

The arousal theory provides a good basis for understanding the common problem of hyperactivity in children.

While the term "hyperactivity" is commonly used for this disorder, the most precise designation of the problem is "attention-deficit hyperactivity disorder" (DSM III-R, 50).

Although hyperactivity is sometimes the result of an overactive reticular activating system, it is more often due to an *under*active reticular system. Golden and Anderson (1979, 105) maintain that children with an underaroused RAS have what they call "stimulation hunger." The desire for more stimulation results in hyperactive behavior in an attempt to get more data to the brain. Thus when certain stimulants are given to a hyperactive child, the brain gets adequate data from normal behavior and the hyperactivity ceases. Ritalin, the drug most commonly prescribed for hyperactivity, is a stimulant which calms hy-

Spotlight 5.6.
Christians and Sexuality

While many Christians have long considered the issue of sexuality to be a delicate subject, the general tendency has changed dramatically in recent years. While significant earlier contributions by Christians should not be overlooked, such as that by Miles (1967), it was in 1973 that Maribel Morgan published her controversial *Total Woman,* which emphasized the dominant male and the sexually provocative female. In 1976 Tim and Beverly LaHaye's landmark *Act of Marriage,* written from a conservative evangelical perspective, made the topic of sex practically a household word.

This book was soon followed by a number of other significant volumes that emphasized a Christian perspective on sexuality, such as Smedes (1976) and Dillow (1977). Ed and Gaye Wheat (1981), a medical doctor and his wife, wrote what was described as "the definitive Christian sex manual," which included graphic descriptions and diagrams of love making.

Sexual problems have been considered by several Christian authors from a counseling perspective (Mayo 1987; Wilson 1984). The topic of homosexuality has been considered at length by numerous authors in Christian magazines and scholarly journals. Generally these writers have concluded that Christianity demands a forsaking of homosexual behavior upon conversion, but that the transformation of homosexual thinking is either impossible or takes considerable time, effort, and counseling. Rekers (1982a, 1982b), a well-known sex role researcher, has emphasized the importance of family influences in the development of homosexual or heterosexual behavior.

Joy has also published a book on children and sexuality (1988), a useful addition to his trilogy on marital bonding (1985, 1986, 1987). Joy believes that the stages of a relationship begin before marriage and culminate in a sexual relationship within marriage. Joy emphasizes the need to take each stage in the bonding process slowly and completely before moving on to the next stage of sexual intimacy.

Spotlight 5.7. Hyperactivity

Tolerance for children's activity levels varies from adult to adult. Furthermore, the ability to learn varies from child to child; some children learn in an active and noisy environment better than others. Diagnosis of genuine hyperactivity requires expert medical and psychological opinion. After diagnosis of the problem, interventions may be medical, psychological, or—more often—both.

How can we determine if hyperactivity is biological or learned? Golden and Anderson (1979, 174) suggest that the brain disorder that produces biologically based hyperactivity occurs within twelve months after conception (see chap. 2). They believe that if the child has an unusual activity level prior to age three (either underactive or hyperactive) and then is hyperactive after age three, this is probably biological hyperactivity. On the other hand, if the child has a normal activity level throughout infancy and then becomes hyperactive, the latter is probably due to inappropriate discipline techniques rather than a malfunctioning RAS.

While some adults overreact to normally active children, other adults may be insensitive (especially if they do not teach the child). An adult who knows of a hyperactive child may conclude that the child needs a good spanking instead of being placed on medication. Such a person needs to be informed that true hyperactivity (the unlearned variety) is a biological dysfunction, not simply a discipline problem. It is often necessary to slow down the hyperactive child with medication so that concentration is possible and proper discipline can have its intended effect. It might also be pointed out that medication is a temporary intervention, and is usually discontinued in early adolescence.

---

peractive behavior and increases attention span. Determining the optimum dosage of Ritalin, however, may require a number of adjustments by a physician.

We do not know the precise physiological cause of attention-deficit hyperactivity disorder. It may indeed be related to an overactive or possibly even an underactive RAS. However, the most current theory is that attention-deficit disorder is related to an imbalance in the neurotransmitter dopamine.

Hyperactivity is not always a biologically based problem. It may be the consequence of a combination of learned behavior and poor discipline techniques. Hyperactivity can be caused by medical,

psychological, or a combination of both factors. If biology is the problem, medication is needed; if learning is the problem, new child management skills are required; and if both learning and biology are involved, medication and management techniques must be combined.

We should not conclude from this chapter that all drives and needs are biological. For example, curiosity is a drive that we have from birth, and while it is adaptive it does not have a clear-cut biological basis. Furthermore, many needs are learned, such as the need for affiliation and the need for achievement.

Motivation lies behind most, if not all,

of human behavior. In this chapter we have concentrated on the biological aspects of motivation, keeping in mind that its psychological aspects are a necessary complement to understanding ourselves holistically. For the Christian, the spiritual components of motivation must also be considered; God is in the process of developing and purifying the motives of those who seek to grow spiritually.

References

Brownell, K., et al. The effect of repeated cycles of weight loss and regain in rats. *Physiology and Behavior* 38: 459–64.

Cannon, W. 1934. Hunger and thirst. In *A handbook of general experimental psychology*, ed. C. Marchison. Worcester, Mass.: Clark University Press.

Coates, T., and C. Thoresen. 1977. *How to sleep better*. Englewood Cliffs, N.J.: Prentice-Hall.

Collins, G. 1973. *Overcoming anxiety*. Santa Ana, Calif.: Vision.

———. 1977. *Relax and live longer*. Santa Ana, Calif.: Vision.

Cordell, F., and G. Giebler. 1977. *War on fat*. Niles, Ill.: Argus.

Crabb, L. 1977. *Effective biblical counseling*. Grand Rapids: Zondervan.

Darling, H. 1969. *Man in triumph*. Grand Rapids: Zondervan.

Diagnostic and statistical manual of mental disorders. 1987. 3d rev. ed. Washington, D.C.: American Psychiatric Association.

Dillow, J. 1977. *Solomon on sex*. Nashville: Nelson.

Dobbert, J. 1977. *The love diet*. Old Tappan, N.J.: Revell.

Foyle, M. 1987. *Overcoming missionary stress*. Wheaton, Ill.: Evangelical Missions Information Service.

Golden, C. 1981. *Diagnosis and rehabilitation in clinical neuropsychology*. Springfield, Ill.: Thomas.

Golden, C., and S. Anderson. 1979. *Learning disabilities and brain dysfunction*. Springfield, Ill.: Thomas.

Holmes, T., and R. Rahe. 1967. Social readjustment rating scale. *Journal of Psychosomatic Research* 2: 213–18.

Jeffrey, D., and R. Katz. 1977. *Take it off and keep it off*. Englewood Cliffs, N.J.: Prentice-Hall.

Joy, D. 1985. *Bonding*. Waco: Word.

———. 1986. *Rebonding*. Waco: Word.

———. 1987. *Lovers—Whatever happened to Eden?* Waco: Word.

———. 1988. *Parents, kids and sexual integrity*. Waco: Word.

LaHaye, T., and B. LaHaye. 1976. *The act of marriage*. Grand Rapids: Zondervan.

McDonough, R. 1979. *Keys to effective motivation*. Nashville: Broadman.

Markell, J. 1982. *Overcoming stress*. Wheaton, Ill.: Victor.

Maslow, A. 1970. *Motivation and personality*. 2d ed. New York: Harper and Row.

Masters, W., and V. Johnson, 1979. *Homosexuality in perspective*. Boston: Little, Brown.

Mayo, M. 1987. *A Christian guide to sexual counseling*. Grand Rapids: Zondervan.

Miles, H. 1967. *Sexual happiness in marriage*. Grand Rapids: Zondervan.

Minirth, F., and P. Meier. 1978. *Happiness is a choice*. Grand Rapids: Baker.

Morgan, M. 1973. *The total woman*. Old Tappan, N.J.: Revell.

Olds, J. 1969. The central nervous system and the reinforcement of behavior. *American Psychologist* 24: 114–32.

Rekers, G. 1982a. *Growing up straight*. Chicago: Moody.

———. 1982b. *Shaping your child's sexual identity*. Grand Rapids: Baker.

Rotter, J. 1966. Generalized expectancies for internal and external control of reinforcement. *Psychological Monographs* 80: 211.

Schachter, S. 1971. Some extraordinary facts about obese humans and rats. *American Psychologist* 26: 129–44.

Selye, H. 1976. *The stress of life*. New York: McGraw-Hill.

Smedes, L. 1976. *Sex for Christians*. Grand Rapids: Eerdmans.

Stafford, T. 1988. *The sexual Christian*. Wheaton, Ill.: Christianity Today.

Walen, S., N. Hauserman, and P. Lavin. 1977. *Clinical guide to behavior therapy.* Baltimore: Williams and Wilkins.

Wheat, E., and G. Wheat. 1981. *Intended for pleasure.* Rev. ed. Old Tappan, N.J.: Revell.

Wilson, E. 1984. *Sexual sanity.* Downers Grove: Inter-Varsity.

Wing, R., and R. Jeffery. 1979. Outpatient treatments of obesity. *International Journal of Obesity* 3: 261–79.

Zeigler, H. 1975. Trigeminal deafferentiation and hunger in the pigeon. *Journal of Comparative and Physiological Psychology* 89 (1975): 827–44.

Learning

Learning and thinking greatly influence human behavior, although debate continues about to what degree human behavior is instinctive. In this chapter we will consider learning to be a relatively permanent change in behavior as a result of experience.

From birth on we learn to make prescribed movements of our bodies. Literally hundreds of motor skills, from speech to athletic performance, are gained by learning. We learn to walk, run, write, read, and drive a car. We learn to cope with the complexities of language and to manipulate the abstract symbols of mathematics. If we could not learn, no changes in our behavior would occur except those brought on by normal developmental processes. Unable to profit from experience, we would be doomed to follow our previous patterns.

For Christians, learning has additional dimensions. Fellowship and sharing with other believers can provide a broad base of experience. Also, Christians have the Scriptures to guide their development and learning. Hence an understanding of learning mechanisms should be of special importance to Christian believers, helping them not only to grow personally but also to be more effective in their ministry to others.

The three basic models of learning are classical conditioning, operant conditioning, and observational learning.

Classical Conditioning

Credit for the development of classical conditioning theory is usually given to Russian physiologist Ivan P. Pavlov (1849–1936). In the early 1900s, however, E. B. Twitmyer at the University of Pennsylvania began to investigate the knee jerk reflex. Physicians use this reflex for diagnostic purposes. An abnormal response would suggest that the patient has suffered damage to the spinal cord. Twitmyer believed that this reflex might be influenced by the emotional or motivational state of an individual. In observing many subjects, Twitmyer discovered by accident that if a warning signal sounded without the hammer dropping on the knee, a response would occur anyway. Twitmyer did not realize at the time that he had discovered the conditioned reflex, a response pattern upon which a number of psychological theories would later be built. Lack of acceptance of Twitmyer's findings by American psychologists discouraged him from further research.

Pavlov's Investigations

Pavlov was awarded the Nobel Prize in 1904 for his investigation of how the nervous system coordinates digestive responses. Pavlov was studying the physiology of digestion in dogs when he noticed that dogs began to salivate at the sight and sound of the experimenter. He found that

Ivan Pavlov (1849–1936)

stimulations that regularly preceded the food always produced salivation. Pavlov then studied the secretion of saliva under carefully controlled conditions and discovered much of what we know about the type of learning called classical (or respondent) conditioning (Pavlov 1927).

Pavlov found that if food powder was placed in a dog's mouth, the animal would automatically salivate. Pavlov called the food an unconditioned stimulus (US) because its ability to elicit the unconditioned response (UR) was reflexive (instinctual) and not dependent on the condition of learning. A diagram of the situation might look like this:

$$\text{US (Food)} \xrightarrow{\hspace{2cm}} \text{UR (Salivation)}$$

Pavlov discovered that if he sounded a musical tone just before placing food in an animal's mouth, eventually the dog would salivate almost as much in response to the music alone as it would to the tone plus the food powder. Pavlov deduced that the animal had learned to associate the sound of the music with the stimulus of the food powder. The sound became a dinner bell that let the dog anticipate that it would be fed. Conditioning was more effective when the tone was sounded immediately before food was presented, a half-second being the optimal interval. Pavlov called the sound a conditioned stimulus (CS) because its power to evoke salivation was learned by its being paired with the food a number of times. After the two stimulus inputs had been paired frequently enough, the sound became a conditioned stimulus (CS) and the salivation a conditioned response (CR).

$$\text{CS (Sound)} \xrightarrow{} \text{US (Food)} \xrightarrow{} \text{UR (Salivation)}$$

$$\text{CS (Sound)} \xrightarrow{\hspace{2cm}} \text{CR (Salivation)}$$

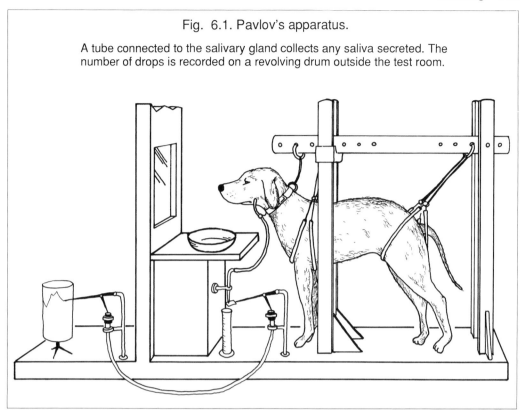

Fig. 6.1. Pavlov's apparatus.

A tube connected to the salivary gland collects any saliva secreted. The number of drops is recorded on a revolving drum outside the test room.

During the period in which learning takes place, called the acquisition period, a weak conditioned response gradually increases in strength and frequency. Repeatedly pairing the tone with the food powder enabled Pavlov to produce much more frequent and profuse salivation in the dogs.

Aversive Conditioning

Pavlov also investigated aversive conditioning in dogs. He used electric shock to a paw as the unconditioned stimulus, leg withdrawal as the unconditioned response, and a variety of sounds and visual stimuli as conditioned stimuli. When the dog was strapped into a harness, the animal reacted not only with leg withdrawal but also with a generalized fear response. Thus any conditioned stimuli that preceded the unconditioned one regularly, such as a bell, a tone, or even the sight of a cat, came to elicit fear in the animal.

Aversive conditioning explains why people sometimes have irrational fears. Many fears do not make sense, such as a fear of harmless insects, small spaces, darkness, or hair. Not only physical events such as sounds, sights, and other phenomena are conditioned stimuli. Words or symbols associated with significant events can become substitutes for the events, producing the same reaction as the events themselves. Examples of such symbolic stimuli might be the flag or the national anthem of a country.

Generalization, Discrimination, and Higher-Order Conditioning

Generalization is an important principle in conditioning. A second stimulus similar to the first, presented to a subject after acquisition, will also produce a conditioned response. For example, if a man has learned to respond reflexively with a knee jerk to a particular musical tone, we would expect him to respond with a reflex-

> ## Spotlight 6.1.
> ## Classical Conditioning in the Church
>
> Classical conditioning theory can be used to determine the likely effects of church on people. For example, the Sunday school curriculum may be age-inappropriate. Many parents respond to restless children by punishing them, a pain-producing reaction that is soon associated with attending church. Likewise, fear-filled messages about the end times are likely to produce the same sort of conditioning. Classically conditioned reactions of boredom or fear may carry over into adolescence and adulthood resulting in avoidance of the conditioned stimulus, the church (Dobbins 1975). It is preferable to have separate children's services, geared to their developmental level, to avoid such unfortunate conditioning.
>
> Classical conditioning theory may explain the church's preference for certain songs or styles of music. Some styles may be appreciated more than others because of prior experience. If a certain song is associated with positive emotions in a revival context, those feelings may be elicited by that song at a future time. It may be that the response generalizes to other songs of the same style, even though the original conditioning context has long been forgotten. A style of music can be disliked, feared, or even hated because of negative associations from the past (Ratcliff 1983).

ive knee jerk to a tone an octave or so higher or lower than the initial tone. Usually, the more similar the second stimulus, the stronger the conditioned response to it will be. We can see how useful it might be for an organism to respond to all stimuli having potentially the same value. Yet an organism must also learn to discriminate between relevant and irrelevant conditioned stimuli, stopping its response to stimuli not directly associated with the unconditioned stimulus event. The more distinguishable the signal for a conditioned stimulus, the more quickly it will be identified and attended to.

Higher-order conditioning refers to a process by which a series of conditioned stimuli serves as a substitute for originally conditioned stimuli. For example, once a conditioned stimulus such as a bell is capable of eliciting a strong conditioned response such as a reflex knee jerk, the bell can in turn be paired with any other stimulus that the organism can perceive. That second conditioned stimulus will elicit the conditioned response in the absence of both the original conditioned stimulus and the unconditioned stimulus, and so on.

Extinction, Spontaneous Recovery, and Avoidance Conditioning

Once a conditioned stimulus no longer signals either danger or benefit, continued response is nonfunctional. When presentation of a conditioned stimulus is repeatedly not followed by the unconditioned stimulus, the conditioned response becomes weaker and eventually reaches zero in frequency. The response is then said to be extinguished.

During the period required to extinguish the conditioned response, an initial decrease in the response rate may be followed by sudden increased responding called spontaneous recovery. With further extinction trials, however, the conditioned response will become weaker and weaker.

Why do intense irrational fears linger so long after the unconditioned stimulus has gone away? One answer is that people tend to avoid situations where whatever they have learned to fear, such as snakes, mice, or tests, might appear (avoidance conditioning). If people flee as soon as the feared object or situation is presented or threatened, they never have a chance to learn that in fact the situation does not necessarily signal harm. Individuals who have had embarrassing failures in school as children may be afraid they could never do well in a college classroom. To extinguish such a fear response, conditions must be arranged so that the conditioned stimulus is not followed by danger or the threat of harm. Better yet, if the stimulus is followed by a pleasant event, counter-conditioning can take place.

Advertisers make use of some classical conditioning in attempting to sell products to the public. They know that the sight of a juicy hamburger or pizza, displayed in vivid color, is likely to produce hunger pangs. The sound of a soft drink being poured produces a conditioned response of thirst.

Watson's Investigations

American psychologist John Watson used some of Pavlov's ideas in working with a little boy named Albert (Watson and Rayner 1920). Watson found that loud noises, such as banging a gong, produced fear in the little boy. Thus the noise was an unconditioned stimulus (US) and the fear reaction was an unconditioned response (UR).

Watson then attempted to condition the boy. When he presented a rat to Albert; the boy was curious about the animal. Watson then sounded a loud gong, which produced fear. The rat became a conditioned stimulus (CS) that the psychologist assumed would then produce a conditioned response (CR) of fear. Watson later presented the rat to Albert and, as he had predicted, the little boy became fearful. Furthermore, the response generalized so that other furry objects, such as a rabbit, beard, or fur coat, produced the same fear response.

Watson intended to extinguish the conditioned reaction of fear, but Albert and his family moved. If Albert never had the fear response extinguished, we can assume that he went through life with a phobia of rats and perhaps other furry objects as well. Later experiments with other children, however, proved that such conditioned responses could be extinguished, as Watson had predicted (Jones 1924).

Counseling Applications

Psychologists have used the concepts of classical conditioning not only to extinguish irrational fears, but also to condition new fears. For example, alcoholics may be taken to a barlike setting and given a glass of beer. When they begin to drink, an electrical shock is applied, thus conditioning a fear response to the alcohol. Eventually the taste of alcohol, and perhaps even the smell, will produce a fear and avoidance response (Walen, Hauserman, and Lavin 1977, 132–44).

This approach works well for those who truly want to stop drinking, but those who do not have a genuine desire to quit can obviously extinguish the fear response. The same principle is applied in antabuse programs in which a medication is taken that will make individuals ill if they begin to drink. Some programs help people stop smoking through the combination of tobacco and a noxious substance. An individual can, however, subvert the program by smoking or drinking and within a short time the conditioned fear will extinguish. Strong motivation to quit is necessary for the success of such programs.

The conditioning and avoidance approach has also been used with pedophiles. Here the approach is a bit more complex but can be quite effective. Slides of naked children are shown to the molester. If the molester has an erection at the sight of the child, a mild electrical shock is applied. Eventually the man can observe children without feeling sexually aroused, and thus the basis for the molestation (sexual arousal) is eliminated.

Addiction to food can be thought of in terms of classical conditioning. Obese persons have learned to eat even when not hungry. The sight or smell of food, pictures of food, the sight of other people eating, and even the environments in which they normally eat become conditioned stimuli for overweight persons. Such addiction is currently being treated with some success by decreasing the conditioned associations. That is why restricting eating to just one place and to predetermined times, or breaking up learned eating patterns, can be an effective treatment.

Discipline Applications

Children naturally have an avoidance reaction to spanking because of the pain involved, not unlike the avoidance reaction described by Pavlov and Watson. If the parent precedes a spanking with a reprimand, the reprimand should become a conditioned stimulus. The child is then likely to avoid undesirable behavior when reprimanded.

However, some children obey the reprimands of a parent but will not obey teachers or other adults. What might account for this difference? Classical conditioning theory would suggest that perhaps stimulus discrimination has occurred. In other words, the effect of the reprimand did not generalize from the home to the school, because the CS-US-UR acquisition did not equally apply to school and home. Parents who follow up discipline problems at school with appropriate consequences at home are more likely to increase the effects of a teacher's reprimand. Of course, there can be other reasons for unruly behavior at school, such as lack of positive consequences for desired behavior, boredom, or unrealistic expectations.

Operant Conditioning

Learning which events in the environment are predictably related (conditional) is beneficial for adaptation and survival. In general, though, an organism must also learn what relationships can be expected between its own actions and subsequent events in the environment. In particular, it needs to learn what changes it can achieve or prevent.

An early figure in American psychology concerned with learning based on these kinds of relationships was Edward L. Thorndike (1874–1949). Thorndike (1932) did laboratory research on animal intelligence by putting cats into puzzle boxes. If a cat could figure out how to unlatch the box's door, it escaped and was often given a bit of food as a reward. At first the animals showed what Thorndike called random behavior, such as scratching, licking themselves, meowing, or crying. They tried to squeeze through the bars or bite the bars. Then, apparently by accident, a cat would bump into the latch; the door would open, and the cat would escape from the box. The next time the cat was put into the box, it performed many random behaviors but, again, it eventually hit the latch and got out. After several trials, the cat would spend more and more time in the vicinity of the latch and would get out of the box sooner. Finally the cat seemed to learn what was required, and the moment it was put in the box, it would hit the latch.

Thorndike's graph of the amount of time it took cats to learn how to exit the box is an example of a learning curve. Research since that time demonstrates that human learning curves have the same shape. Thorndike theorized that animals learn to escape from puzzle boxes by trial and error; that is, they perform various responses in merely mechanical ways until some action is effective in securing their release. Much initial behavior is thought to occur at an instinctual or reflexive level. On succeeding trials the animals learn that certain types of behavior (roaming around the apparatus, licking themselves, biting the bars, scratching the door) may help them get out. Ineffectual responses, such as licking themselves or meowing, tend to drop out of the animals' behavioral repertoire, or hierarchy of behaviors. Actions that gain release and secure a reward are most satisfying, so these responses become more and more effectively connected to the stimuli—and hence are more likely to occur the next time the animal is put in the box. From his observations of such trial-and-error learning, Thorndike began the study of what has come to be known as instrumental conditioning. Through conditioning, the organism learns which of its behavioral operations will be instrumental in gaining benefit.

In classical conditioning, the experimenter produced the response whenever desired by presenting the unconditioned stimulus to form a new association between the conditioned stimulus and the conditioned response. In instrumental conditioning, the experimenter takes a response that the subject has already been making and strengthens it by reinforcing it every time it occurs.

On the basis of his observations Thorndike formulated the law of effect, which states that the stimulus-response bond, or learning, is strengthened by reward or satisfaction. Thorndike's law of effect was essentially a modern restatement of a doctrine of hedonism advanced by the founder of utilitarianism, English philosopher Jeremy Bentham (1748–1832). In short, we do what gives us pleasure and avoids pain.

Behaviorism

B. F. Skinner (1904–1990), a well-known behavioral psychologist in America, based his work on the principles of operant conditioning. A number of Christians have been critical of Skinner, confusing his philosophy (which is generally considered incompatible with Christianity) and his techniques. Yet the theory of behaviorism is quite compatible with Christian thought in general and the writings of Schaeffer in particular (Ratcliff 1988). Several evangelical writers have emphasized the value of Skinner's psychology in child rearing, counseling, and the church (Dobson 1970; Bufford 1981; Cosgrove 1982; Ratcliff 1978, 1981a, 1981b, 1982a, 1982b, 1982c, 1982d, 1983).

What is it about Skinner's philosophy that Christians find so objectionable? In *Beyond Freedom and Dignity* he states that people do not have genuine freedom, but

---

Spotlight 6.2.
Reinforcement, the Bible,
and the Church

Reinforcement can be used in the church setting. For example, children could be given rewards for learning memory verses. Unfortunately, extinction is quite likely as soon as such rewards are removed, so it is important that children receive other benefits in addition to material rewards. It is better to focus on the social-emotional rewards of being with fellow believers rather than relying on the exclusive use of external rewards (see spotlight 6.5). Ultimately the goal should be enjoyment of the activity and people rather than the extrinsic rewards. This goal is more likely to be accomplished if the external rewards are gradually phased out.

As will be noted later in this chapter, it is often necessary to break down skills into smaller, manageable ones. To expect perfect performance in choir, for example, is to require something most unlikely for amateurs. It may be useful to incorporate some ideas from Maslow's hierarchy (see chap. 5) in helping motivate people to join such groups, appealing to the level of greatest need.

The use of reinforcement in the church is consistent with the teaching of the Bible. Throughout the Bible positive consequences of desired behavior are described. For example, the Book of Proverbs repeatedly emphasizes the positive results of following God's law, including natural consequences and eternal rewards. The sense of fellowship with other Christians, a personal relationship with God, and a sound foundation for life are all positive consequences of the Christian life.

---

are controlled by their environment. With a fuller understanding of reality, as provided by operant conditioning, the concepts of freedom and dignity are no longer useful. Utopia, as exemplified in Skinner's early novel *Walden Two*, is achievable if society will make use of the principles of conditioning in a systematic manner for the betterment of humanity. Skinner's assumption is that operant conditioning is capable of explaining all human behavior in naturalistic terms, leaving no room for choices and no room for God.

Unique to Skinner's concept of learning is that consequences determine the conditioning. An experimenter can study learning by allowing a subject to make a response initially and as often as the subject likes. The experimenter then observes the rate of responding; that is, how many times the response occurs over a unit of time (sometimes called a baseline). The response is rewarded each time it occurs by a reinforcer or reinforcing stimulus. A reinforcer is defined as any stimulus that follows a response and increases the probability of its occurrence. If getting food as a result of opening a latch makes the latch-opening response more probable next time, then getting food is a reinforcer.

The terms "instrumental" and "operant" are used interchangeably by many psychologists, though "operant" remains Skinner's preferred term. The rate at which a freely available response occurs when its consequences are neither positive nor negative is called the operant level of that response. Each free response has an operant level for a given individual. Psychologists study the change in response rate resulting from various kinds, intensities, and timings of reinforcement.

Few things are reinforcers for everyone in every situation. People have distinct preferences. A factor in determining if something is reinforcing is how much the item is desired. Satiation describes the condition in which a previously desired item is no longer desired because so much has already been acquired. For example, a bowl of ice cream may be a great reinforcer for children, but if ice cream is served for dessert every day it will probably no longer function as a reinforcer.

Spotlight 6.3.
Shaping and the Christian Life

Many applications of shaping are relevant to the Christian life. Ratcliff (1978), for example, applies shaping to the development of personal evangelism programs in churches. Griffin (1976) uses similar ideas in the context of reinforcing evangelistic efforts.

In his *Straight Talk to Men and Their Wives* (1980) Dobson describes how the process of shaping can lead to an extramarital affair. The affair usually begins with an innocent gesture of friendship, such as a lunch that lasts too long or a harmless touch. This initial step is enjoyable (reinforcing), and so the action is repeated. The next day, or perhaps the next week, the touch or lunch is extended further with more pleasant outcomes. The relationship begins to increase in frequency and intensity. Romantic feelings are powerfully reinforcing and before long the two people are involved in a sexual relationship. Dobson suggests that we need to guard against this process by ending it at stage 1. Pastors are especially vulnerable to affairs because of the number of dependent women who come to them for counseling.

Shaping is mentioned in the Bible, both in negative and positive terms. In Jeremiah 18:1–6 God is described as shaping Israel as a potter shapes a vessel. We can be shaped into what God wants of us when we are open and receptive to his teaching and correction. Gradually, God brings us closer and closer to what he desires. Of course, he may do his shaping of us through methods other than positive reinforcement and systematic approximation.

Reading the Bible is a task that can be behaviorally influenced. Many of us struggle to read difficult books like Job, Jeremiah, and Leviticus. To motivate study of these books, people should be encouraged to read only small portions at first, following each difficult reading with one or more less difficult selections from the New Testament. The easier reading thus serves as a reinforcer while the small sections of difficult books function as steps in a shaping sequence. Gradually, over time, the Old Testament sections read could be lengthened. External reinforcers such as pizza and soft drinks or social reinforcers such as sharing insights from reading in a group Bible study might help.

Is a reward the same thing as a reinforcer? Usually the terms are interchangeable, but technically there is a distinction. A reward is any positive consequence of a behavior. But a reward is only a reinforcer when it increases that behavior. Therefore a medal given for valor in war is a reinforcer only if the rewarded behavior is more likely to occur. This is why behavioral psychologists prefer the term "reinforcer" to "reward." Reinforcers actually affect behavior, while rewards may or may not.

Shaping and Chaining

Operant conditioning is a process by which behavior is modified. More specifically, the rate of occurrence of an operant response is controlled through environmental manipulations. If an operant response is followed by a positive reinforcing stimulus, the probability that the response will occur again is increased. For this shaping process to take place, a behavior must be reinforced that at least vaguely resembles the behavior ultimately desired. After this initial behavior becomes established through reinforcement, a different behavior is required, something closer to what is desired as an end product. By reinforcing approximations of the target behavior, the learner gradually learns the final behavior.

Let us consider a classroom situation. Frequently, a professor feels uncomfortable the first day of classes. A student's smile or nod may help the professor relax, and thus may be a reinforcer. If every time the professor tells a story, the students smile and nod, the probability of the professor telling stories increases. After several lectures, the professor may well be telling stories most of the time. The students have shaped the professor's behavior.

While shaping refers to the development of a single behavior by using a succession of steps, chaining refers to acquiring a series of behaviors, one step at a time. One of the most effective ways to change an organism's behavior is to begin at the end of the response and work backward. Such backward chaining has been found to be the most effective in training humans in a variety of complex tasks. In teaching a child to tie a shoe, for example, most parents begin with the initial step of crossing the laces. Crossing the laces is just one of approximately fifteen complex steps before the final bows are pulled into the knot. It is the final achievement of tying the shoe that provides reinforcement, however. Using an operant-conditioning learning model, a parent would therefore begin with backward chaining, first helping the child learn to pull the bows.

Discriminative Stimuli and Secondary Reinforcers

In the process of learning, a person comes to identify (discriminate) those par-

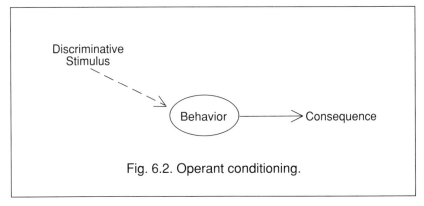

Fig. 6.2. Operant conditioning.

ticular cues (stimuli) that indicate a rein-forcer will follow an operant response. Such signals, called discriminative stimuli, let the organism know when a behavior will or will not be followed by a payoff. A discriminative stimulus sets the stage or provides the occasion for the organism to emit a voluntary operant response. It does not elicit the response in the sense that a bright light elicits an eye blink. It simply signals, in effect, "if you do it now you get a reinforcer." Shortly before the curtain opens for a play, for example, the lights are dimmed. Dimming the lights produces a notable decrease in the audience's talk-ing and focuses attention on the main stage. By controlling the reinforcing stim-ulus, the operant conditioner can control the rate or probability of the response. An organism is said to be under stimulus con-trol when it responds consistently in the presence of a discriminative stimulus and not in its absence.

Another feature of operant conditioning is the importance of conditioning rein-forcers, or secondary reinforcers. Anything consistently associated with a reinforcer can in time itself become reinforcing, that is, it can increase the rate of behavior it follows. Smiles, nods, and pats on the back represent generalized conditioned re-inforcers which can be used to control a wide range of responding. Such rein-forcers bridge the gap of social interaction.

Although conditioned reinforcers are more variable than primary reinforcers in their effect on learning, they are often more effective. They can be dispensed more rapidly, they are portable, and al-most any available stimulus event can be used as a conditioned reinforcer. For ex-ample, a teacher might use tokens instead of simply saying, "That's a good job," to help students complete assignments. The tokens could be exchanged at the end of the class period for some kind of reward,

such as listening to a special tape; or they could be exchanged at the end of a longer period for something like a trip. Tokens, usable only in the classroom situation, cannot be spent the way money could be for other things.

Another important concept is behav-ioral contingency. By setting up different contingencies (that is, different relation-ships between responses and reinforcers) those who use the operant conditioning approach can induce a given response. The timing and frequency of reinforcers can be changed, making them available after the desired response but not at other times. When a reinforcer is made contin-gent on a desired response, that response becomes more probable. The operant con-ditioner must first study what conse-quences currently follow an undesirable response (the payoff for certain behavior). Then new payoff relationships can be ar-ranged, making the payoff contingent on desired behavior and preventing payoff from being achieved by the behavior that is to be eliminated. For example, instead of giving in to a whining child (thus rein-forcing and maintaining the whining) a parent can learn to reinforce desirable be-havior by paying attention only when the child is not whining.

Schedules of Reinforcement and Superstitious Behavior

Once a response is learned, it can be maintained by intermittent reinforcement. Four schedules of intermittent reinforce-ment are possible: (1) fixed ratio, where a response is rewarded after it occurs x times; (2) variable ratio, where a variable number of responses occur between each reinforcement; (3) fixed interval, where a reinforcer follows the first response after a certain amount of time has elapsed; and (4) variable interval, where the reinforcer

---

Spotlight 6.4. Little Lisa

A number of years ago I accepted the task of teaching a second-grade Sunday school class. It was during one of the first years that I taught introductory psychology, and I thought it might be a nice break from college-level teaching.

Within a couple of weeks I began hearing about a little girl we will call Lisa. Everyone told me she would be my worst problem all year. She was only seven years old but already she had a well-known record of disturbing classes and starting conflict. Former teachers warned me of the hurricane that would hit as soon as she was in my class. I thought their comments were exaggerated.

When Lisa entered the room, the first thing she did was to scatter crayons all over the table. Before I had time to fully collect my wits, she had emptied a box of scissors and threw a number of other materials on the table; she then paused briefly to punch the boy next to her. The stories I had thought to be exaggerated were indeed true. The hurricane had struck!

The next week I decided to apply behavioral techniques and Proverbs 16:21 with Lisa. Behaviorism and the Bible both told me that teaching would be most effective if it was a rewarding experience for the student.

As I thought about Lisa's behavior it occurred to me that her uncontrolled behavior had probably been reinforced. Her family, a large one, probably gave her attention only when she was disruptive (this suspicion was later confirmed when I visited her home). She soon discovered that Sunday school teachers would give her a lot of attention when she acted in an extreme, uncontrolled manner. My job was to reverse the process so that she would be rewarded for quiet, cooperative behavior and not receive a reward when disrupting the class.

The following week I handed out five coupons to each child in class and told them that if they had four coupons left by the end of class, they would receive a penny sucker. Very carefully I explained how they might lose a coupon: for disruptive behavior such as run-

---

follows the first response after a variable amount of time.

Each reinforcement pattern or schedule induces a characteristic pattern of responding. The more prompt and specific the reinforcement, the more effective it will be in increasing the rate of responding. Fixed-ratio schedules of reinforcement have been found to be the most effective in learning a behavior. Variable-interval schedules have been found to be best for maintaining behavior already learned. Whatever the schedule of reinforcement, reinforcers, to be effective, must be prompt. If too much time elapses between the response and its reinforcement, the reward will not be as effective. Teachers should make use of this simple principle to help students perform better in the classroom. Frequently, studying for an exam is rewarded anywhere from five to ten days after the exam is taken. Obviously, if a student who studied very hard for an exam could be told of positive rening around, beginning fights, talking loudly, and so on (I basically itemized Lisa's behaviors). The children liked the idea because it was a game, and of course the suckers added to their interest.

We began the Sunday school lesson. Almost immediately Lisa dashed for the crayon box without permission. I quietly walked over to the place where she had been sitting and stated loudly enough for everyone to hear, "I see that someone has already lost a coupon for getting up without permission." I took a coupon and Lisa quickly returned to her seat. She was perfect for the rest of class; she saw by my following through with the threat that I was serious.

Few of the other teachers believed me, but I had no real problem with her after that point.* The investment of a couple of dollars for suckers and coupons did the trick. A few weeks later I informed the children that the sucker game was over, but that those who still acted as they should could sit by me in church. That privilege was as effective as the suckers, but less tangible. I also began to ride with the children on the church bus, giving a little extra attention to Lisa for her quiet, controlled behavior. I eventually phased out all of the reinforcements through a more or less variable schedule of reinforcement, and the behavior was thus maintained by occasional attention on a more informal basis.

I doubt if the behavior generalized to Lisa's home or school environment, but I did get reports that Lisa remained controlled when she was promoted into the third-grade Sunday school classroom. The key, I believe, was not only the behavioral intervention, but also the care taken in phasing out the program. Sometimes behavior modification (another term for operant conditioning) has gotten a bad reputation because the programs are not ended in a proper manner.

*Experiences with other children indicate that it may take several "testings" of the rules before they change behavior (see Ratcliff 1982c).

sults within an hour of the exam's completion, appropriate study habits would be reinforced.

Reinforcement schedules have other predictable results. The fixed interval is particularly interesting in that the reinforced behavior tends to dramatically increase shortly before the interval is completed. Thus if a rat is on a five-minute fixed-interval schedule, the rat soon learns to wait until shortly before the five minutes are completed and then fervently be-

gins performing the desired behavior. This process is called scalloping. Students have been known to scallop by waiting until the night before a test to begin studying, for example. Perhaps rat behavior is not all that different from its human counterpart!

Superstitious behavior is defined by behavioral psychologists as behavior that is accidentally reinforced and as a result later reoccurs, even though the behavior was not actually related to the reinforcement. People may avoid walking on the

---

Spotlight 6.5.
When Is Reinforcement
Inappropriate?

While reinforcement and other behavioral ideas can be very useful, there are also times when they are inappropriate. For example, while there is a place for material reinforcements in working with children, motivating adults in such a manner can be quite inappropriate.

Behavioral concepts should not be substitutes for good teaching. The emphasis in Christian education should be on good teaching methods and an interesting curriculum rather than external rewards. A limited use of incentives may encourage children to finish their lessons, for example, but what we teach should be reward in itself.

Operant conditioning must not be used to *manipulate*. Some highly emotional revivals make use of rather extreme forms of influence to get people to respond. These people may eventually realize they were manipulated and end up rejecting the gospel. Christians need to influence people but allow them the freedom to choose (Griffin 1976, 40).

Bolt and Myers (1984, 75) consider some other situations in which reinforcers may be inappropriate for churches. While Bufford (1981, 174–93) extols the use of reinforcements for such things as memorizing Bible verses and completing Bible lessons, Bolt and Myers fear that the general use of reinforcers will foster a self-oriented faith that militates against the biblical teaching that we must not be self-centered. God may be viewed as One who exists to give us things rather than One we should try to please. While external rewards might be useful in the initial process of motivation, they may not be the best general motivators.

Curiously, Green and Lepper (1974) have found that external rewards may actually undermine intrinsic interest in activities when such interest already exists. Bolt and Myers point to the fact that the

---

cracks of a sidewalk, for example, because they had a better day one time when they avoided cracks. The superstitious individual believes a relationship exists between an event and certain consequences even when it actually does not.[1]

Contingencies

Thus far nearly all of our comments about operant conditioning have centered on the idea of positive reinforcement.

1. For a detailed analysis of superstitious behavior within a Christian framework, see Myers 1978.

While much of the research in this area has focused on this important concept, there are other possible consequences of behavior that should also be considered. Actually five kinds of contingencies are possible between responses and reinforcers, three that increase the rate of an operant response and two that decrease it. Response rates increase when responding is followed by: (1) a positive reinforcing stimulus, (2) escape from an aversive stimulus, or (3) avoidance of an aversive stimulus. The rate decreases when the re-effect of rewards tends to evaporate once the intervention ends, although the use of a variable schedule of reinforcement can reduce this tendency.

There is an even more serious problem in using rewards in that they can communicate to people that the behavior is not inherently worth doing. The desire for the consequence may make the target behavior peripheral.

Bolt and Myers conclude that using rewards may indeed be the best route if we desire only short-term influence or if we are convinced the behavior is basically boring. In contrast, if we want to increase *intrinsic* interest in the behavior, we should use reinforcers cautiously and avoid them when possible. On the other hand, they cite research that external rewards may even *increase* intrinsic interest. If rewards are used to give information on how well individuals are doing rather than to control what they do, intrinsic interest is more likely. The issue is how rewards are presented. If they are unanticipated, then people tend to perceive them as a source of feedback rather than as a means of control. Thus Bolt and Myers recommend that teachers use reinforcers occasionally as an unanticipated bonus rather than emphasizing rewards from the beginning.

Bolt and Meyers' suggestions are well worth noting, but we should also endeavor to make the general atmosphere of the church more rewarding. We must not overlook a basic fact: people attend church because they think they will in some way gain or profit from the experience. Perhaps the distinction we need to make is not reward versus nonreward, but rather long-term and lasting rewards rather than immediate rewards.

sponding is followed by (4) an aversive stimulus (punishment) or (5) absence of any reinforcer (extinction). "Time out" procedures, such as sending children to their room, are an example of extinction because all normal reinforcers are removed from the general environment. Punishment is the presentation of an aversive stimulus that decreases the probability of a response. Although it can be effective under some circumstances, punishment must be used carefully to avoid undesirable consequences. It must be made clear, for example, that the response and not the person is the object of the punishment.

Escape from an aversive stimulus is sometimes referred to as negative reinforcement. Although this concept is often equated with punishment, they are quite different. While punishment is the delivery of an aversive or unpleasant consequence as a result of behavior, negative reinforcement is the *removal* of an unpleasant or aversive situation as a result of behavior. Thus negative reinforcement makes a

Spotlight 6.6. Superstition and Prayer

Myers and Jeeves (1987, 89–96) and Myers (1978, 157–75) have proposed that the prayers of Christians are sometimes related to superstitious behavior. There is a strong tendency for us to perceive an order in random events because we have prayed and then seek evidence that will confirm our expectations. Myers and Jeeves decry those who view God as a celestial Santa Claus, an image which fosters a preoccupation with the person praying rather than with the God of the Bible.

Through prayer God offers us a new perspective on events rather than magical changes. We must not conclude that God changes natural events in a verifiable manner in response to our prayers. Instead, *prayer changes us;* prayer is an effect rather than a cause.

We can appreciate Myers and Jeeves' concern that we not be superstitious in our responses to prayer, but we should also question whether their approach might not be too naturalistic. Their conclusions seem to imply what Schaeffer (1976, 142) calls a "closed universe" in which God does not supernaturally intervene. But what, then, are we to do with biblical accounts of prayer followed by miracles? Are these also to be explained by an appeal to superstition? When Christ prayed for healing, was he being superstitious? Was he mistaken about the nature of the universe? Or do we have an errant Bible at this point?

While admitting that some Christians are superstitious in their perception of answers to prayer, being convinced that God has answered when actually the results were random, Christians also need to affirm that God sometimes does intervene in human affairs, rather than just changing our perceptions. Myers and Jeeves overlook the impact of the faith (or lack thereof). They also ignore the possibility that God might answer prayers in a manner that those praying do not desire. It is also possible to attribute natural causes to divine activity. There are verified accounts of supernatural intervention by God (Grazier 1989).

We need to follow Christ's example in praying for God's intervention, yet trust the results to him. We should also be cautious about criticizing people simply because they believe God has answered their prayers. The Bible says we should pray in faith while acknowledging God's sovereignty.

given behavior more likely to occur while punishment makes it less likely to occur.

Consider, for example, a child who acts up in a class that he hates, and is dismissed to see a counselor. The child gets out of the unpleasant situation, and as a result is more likely to act up in the future.

Negative reinforcement assumes an already existing negative situation which no longer exists after the performance of the behavior.

Punishment, in contrast, is perhaps the most powerful way of suppressing behavior. Yet psychologists are often hesitant to recommend its use (although many psychologists are less permissive than they used to be). If punishment is so powerful, why should it not be used routinely?

There are a number of dangers associated with the regular, exclusive use of punishment. It may teach aggression. A punished child might imitate the punishing parent or teacher and become even more aggressive, particularly with smaller and weaker children. The child may begin to see hitting as a solution to problems. Behavior learned by punishment tends to be temporary; good behavior occurs only

Spotlight 6.7.
Using Other Aspects of Operant Conditioning

In spotlight 6.2 we considered some of the positive reinforcers in the church and the Bible. There are other kinds of contingencies. For example, the Christian escapes from the meaninglessness of life without Christ (negative reinforcement) and avoids eternal punishment.

These other contingencies also influence behavior in the church. Many people, for example, prefer to sit near the back of the church, yet these same people may attend a baseball game and sit in the front row. The baseball game is reinforcing whereas what happens in the pulpit at church may be less reinforcing (at least for those who sit in the rear).

There are several reinforcers for sitting near the back of the church. On Sunday morning, those near the back can more quickly get to their cars. Young people may be able to meet friends outside more quickly. Misbehaving children are less noticeable at the rear of the sanctuary. For some, sitting near the back may be an avoidance technique because of past aversive stimuli originating from the pulpit. Extinction can help change this behavior. Regular exposure to a warm, loving pastor, both in church and in members' homes, will encourage people to sit near the front of church.

Positive transfer of learning refers to the greater ease of learning a new behavior if it is similar to behavior learned in the past. Positive transfer is especially helpful to those preparing for some kind of future ministry. Christian service assignments allow students to practice what is learned in the classroom. Learning concepts without application is like trying to learn to drive a car by reading books. Books are invaluable aids, but practice is the only way to make ideas work.

Positive transfer is also useful for future pastors who cannot bring themselves to call on others. Christian service assignments could help seminarians develop skills which can positively transfer to whatever future Christian work they plan to pursue.

Shaping can be used to develop regular devotional habits. An individual might start by reading a few verses and praying for only a minute or two. These commitments can gradually be expanded until a quarter-hour or more might be spent reading the Bible, with another quarter-hour or more spent in prayer. The Bible might be left in a conspicuous place so that it will serve as a discriminative stimulus.

The same principles could be used to encourage family devotions. Parents should strive to make such a routine interesting to children. They can also include some of the principles of learning. One approach is to send children to bed with the option of a short time of prayer and Bible reading as an alternative to immediately going to sleep. This makes staying up a reinforcer for devotions. In contrast, if the child sees television as the alternative to devotions, the special family time will come to be viewed as something to be avoided.

Spotlight 6.8. Punishment of Children

That only "the rod" and "reproof" are specified in the Bible does not mean that other forms of discipline should not be exercised. It does imply that spanking and verbal reproofs should be the parent's primary disciplinary tools. Further, the "sentence for a crime" should be quickly executed. For a mother to tell a disobedient son that when his father gets home he will be spanked for what he just did is unwise, both scripturally and psychologically.

From the psychological standpoint, it is wrong for two reasons. First, by the time his father gets home and spanks him, he may have forgotten what it was he did wrong. Even if the father reminds him of what it was, the spanking may have lost much of its effectiveness.

Second, delaying punishment until the father comes home tends to alienate the child from his father. Some mothers, unconsciously or even consciously, use this technique to win the child's undivided affection. A neurotic relationship is set up and the child comes to think of the father solely as a disciplinarian. Some adults have a very legalistic view of God because, no matter how much they read the

Bible, their overall view of God is to a large degree colored by how they viewed their own father during childhood.

Parents must stand together in disciplining children. Discipline should be carried out immediately by whomever saw the disobedience. A verbal reproof is frequently all that is necessary, especially for a first offense. Children may be reproved verbally and then be sent to their room for a period of five minutes. Isolating children for long periods of time falls into the category of provoking them to anger, since after about fifteen minutes they will either forget or misunderstand why they are being punished. Spanking is immediate in effect, and after ten or fifteen minutes, children usually get over any anger toward the parent.

Parents should allow children to tell them that they are angry. But if children hit a parent, throw something, or show disrespect, they should be spanked again. Parents who do not demand respect when children are young will not get any respect—or deserve any, for that matter—when their children become teen-agers.

---

when the parent is looking. For some children the attention they receive during punishment can be reinforcing. Thus they misbehave to get attention. This is most likely with children who are neglected and receive attention only when they are naughty. Finally, there is the avoidance of the stimulus. Whatever is associated with the punishment becomes a conditioned stimulus for pain and is thus avoided. For this reason some parents believe spanking should be done with an object rather than the hand, although it should be pointed out that just the sight of the parent could serve as a conditioned stimulus.

While there are definite dangers to avoid, there is a place for punishment in

To punish or not to punish, that is the question!

An excellent book on disciplining children is Dobson's *Dare to Discipline* (1970). Dobson emphasizes demanding respect, recommends spanking for willful acts of disobedience, and recognizes that every child is different. Some children want parental approval so much that a look of scorn will bring repentance. Such a child requires very few spankings. Others are born with more spirit and less concern for parental approval. For such children, many spankings for the same offense may be necessary before they finally decide that a particular behavior is unprofitable.

Although parents frequently claim that spanking simply does not work for their child, it will work for any child who is not severely mentally retarded. No one advocates bruising a child; in fact, slapping a child's face or punching a child comes under the categories of child abuse and provoking to wrath. Solomon's words, "if you punish him with the rod, he will not die" (Prov. 23:13), seem almost to be mocking us for being afraid to spank. Parents whose love is selfish and imma- ture tend either to be weak disciplinarians ("sparing the rod") or physical abusers ("provoking them to wrath"). But God's Word assures us that diligent discipline is an important aspect of parental love.

A child with at least average intelligence and an adequate education will begin to reason abstractly at about ten to twelve years of age. Reasoning with a younger child about abstract concepts, such as the morality of certain behavior patterns, is a relative waste of time. Simple, concrete reasoning can sometimes be quite effective with young children. As children get older, the emphasis should be on natural consequences rather than punishment. They should come to experience the negative consequences that result from undesirable or immature actions, which can be understood at a concrete level. By the time children are eleven or twelve years old, parents should try to do away with spankings. Reasoning and trying to communicate on an adult level should become the pattern.

child rearing. What is most important is to supplement punishment with other kinds of disciplinary techniques, such as extinction and positive reinforcement for desired behavior. As much as possible it is preferable to reinforce behavior that is not compatible with undesirable behavior. If a child tends to run around the room uncontrollably, one could reinforce his sitting quietly.

One of the best contingencies is praise, which serves as a positive reinforcer. However, praise is not always appropriate. Praise should only be used if something has actually been accomplished; if the motive is genuine; and if it is not overused. While many people like the idea of praise rather than punishment, it must be admitted that it is easier to see the bad than the good. Most important, though, is consistency; knowing what is to be expected is crucial in producing desired behavior.

Learned Helplessness

Seligman (1975) is famous for his studies on "learned helplessness." He placed one group of dogs in restraints and administered shocks, from which they could not escape. A second group received the same shock, but could easily escape. Each dog was then placed in a box from which it could escape by simply jumping a hurdle. The dog was then given an electrical shock. The dogs who had been shocked in restraints earlier did not jump out; they had learned to be helpless.

People can learn to be helpless. Some individuals fail to take advantage of opportunities because in the past they have had painful events that they had no control over; they become resigned to a helpless state. Rodin (1986) found that elderly persons are happier and more alert when they believe they have some degree of control over their environment.

Christians can also acquire "learned helplessness." Some do not speak out on current issues because they feel they have no influence. Some Christians have given up on a local church because they believe it is beyond help. Extreme Calvinists fit this category. Some believers point to the Bible and assert that decline is inevitable. Revival is unlikely, however, unless individuals believe things can be changed for the better.

Operant versus Classical Conditioning

The distinction between operant and classical conditioning should be kept clearly in mind. Operant conditioning focuses on what occurs *after* the behavior (the consequences) while classical condi-

"How shall we handle this? Punishment, positive reinforcement, or... extinction?"

tioning is more concerned with what occurs *before* the behavior (the antecedents). Skinnerian psychologists study voluntarily emitted behavior which is then reinforced rather than the involuntary behavior elicited automatically by a preceding stimulus, as in Pavlovian conditioning.

Yet both types of conditioning may occur simultaneously and even overlap to some extent. Pavlov's dogs were reinforced by receiving the meat powder; and in operant conditioning the discriminative stimulus is similar to a conditioned stimulus (cs).

Observational Learning (Modeling)

Bandura (1969) proposes that much of the behavior we display has been learned or modified by watching models engage in those actions. Such models include parents, teachers, peers, and television performers.

According to Bandura, the influence of modeling is determined by four interrelated processes. The first is the attentional process. People will learn from a model only if they are attending to the critical features of the model's behaviors. Specifically, models who are attractive or perceived as similar to the observer and who

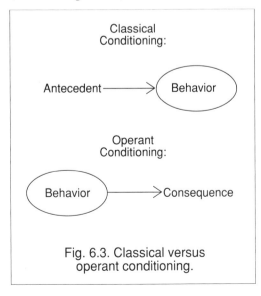

Fig. 6.3. Classical versus operant conditioning.

Spotlight 6.9. Modeling in the Church

Observational learning is useful in the church. A pastor can certainly be an effective model, demonstrating to the congregation how to witness to others, how to visit the sick, and how to help those who are in need. The pastor also models hermeneutical skills (biblical interpretation) in his sermons. People are more likely to imitate what is done than follow verbal instructions alone.

Teen-agers are likely to imitate an attractive and interesting leader. A young person who receives Christ and whose life changes as a result may influence others. Missionaries speak of tribes in which no one responds to the presentation of the message of salvation until the leader does so.

The Bible presents many descriptions of godly men and women. We must strive to model their positive attributes. Even Christ was an example by his life among us. By modeling the descriptions of great men and women of God we can more concretely visualize what God wants of us.

are repeatedly available and are engaging in important functional behaviors are more likely to be influential. Some models, such as those seen on television, are so effective in capturing attention that viewers learn the modeled activities even in the absence of special incentives to do so. A second factor, the retention process, refers to the ability to remember the model's actions after the model has disappeared from the scene. The third factor is the motoric reproduction process. Even if individuals learn new behaviors by observing a model, they cannot show evidence of such learning unless they can perform the modeled activities. Deficiencies in certain skills can render them unable to do what they have seen. The fourth and final factor is reinforcement in motivational processes. Performance of learned behavior depends on whether it will be rewarded or punished. If there are positive incentives,

model behavior will be given more attention, will be learned better, and will be performed more often. Modeling, or observational learning, has been found to be a rapid form of learning. Frequently, modeling can reduce learning trials dramatically. Modeling may also be responsible for the learning of irrational or fearful responses. It is thought that many children become frightened of dogs or other animals not because they have had an aversive experience with an animal, but because they have observed their parents' frightened behavior.

References

Bandura, A. 1969. *Principles of behavior modification.* New York: Rinehart and Winston.

Bolt, M., and D. Myers. 1984. *The human connection.* Downers Grove: Inter-Varsity.

Bufford, R. 1981. *The human reflex.* San Francisco: Harper and Row.

Cosgrove, M. 1982. *B. F. Skinner's behaviorism.* Grand Rapids: Zondervan.

Dobbins, R. 1975. Too much too soon. *Christianity Today* (Oct. 24): 99–100.

Dobson, J. 1970. *Dare to discipline.* Wheaton, Ill.: Tyndale.

———. 1978. *The strong-willed child.* Wheaton, Ill.: Tyndale.

———.1980. *Straight talk to men and their wives.* Waco: Word.

Grazier, J. 1989. *The power beyond.* New York: Macmillan.

Green, D., and M. Lepper. 1974. How to turn play into work. *Psychology Today* 8 (Sept.): 49–53.

Griffin, E. 1976. *The mind changers.* Wheaton, Ill.: Tyndale.

Jones, M. 1924. The elimination of children's fears. *Journal of Experimental Psychology* 7: 383–90.

Meier, P. 1977. *Christian child-rearing and personality development.* Grand Rapids: Baker.

Myers, D. 1978. *The human puzzle.* San Francisco: Harper and Row.

Myers, D., and M. Jeeves. 1987. *Psychology through eyes of faith.* San Francisco: Harper and Row.

Pavlov, I. 1927. *Conditioned reflexes: An investigation of the physiological activity of the cerebral cortex.* New York: Dover.

Ratcliff, D. 1978. Using behavioral psychology to encourage personal evangelism. *Journal of Psychology and Theology* 6: 219–24.

———. 1981a. Christian behavioural counselling. *Christian Counsellor's Journal* 2: 20–27.

———. 1981b. Basic concepts of behavioural counselling. *Christian Counsellor's Journal* 3: 11–15.

———. 1982a. Behaviorism in the sanctuary. *Journal of the American Scientific Affiliation* 34 (Mar.): 47–49.

———. 1982b. Behaviorism and the new worship groups. *Journal of the American Scientific Affiliation* 34 (Sept.): 169–71.

———. 1982c. Behavioral discipline in Sunday school. *Journal of Psychology and Christianity* 1 (Summer): 26–29.

———. 1982d. Behavioral psychology in the Sunday school classroom. *Journal of the American Scientific Affiliation* 34 (Dec.): 241–43.

———. 1983. Music, God and psychology. *Journal of the American Scientific Affiliation* 35 (June): 102–4.

———. 1988. Francis Schaeffer and B. F. Skinner. *Creation Social Science and Humanities Quarterly* 10 (Summer): 21–25.

Rodin, J. 1986. Aging and health. *Science* 233: 1271–76.

Schaeffer, F. 1976. *How should we then live?* Old Tappan, N.J.: Revell.

Seligman, M. 1975. *Learned helplessness and depression in animals and humans.* Morristown, N.J.: General Learning.

Skinner, B. 1971. *Beyond freedom and dignity.* New York: Knopf.

Thorndike, E. 1932. *The fundamentals of learning.* New York: Teachers' College.

Walen, S., N. Hauserman, and P. Lavin. 1977. *Clinical guide to behavior therapy.* Baltimore: Williams and Wilkins.

Watson, J., and R. Rayner. 1920. Conditioned emotional reactions. *Journal of Experimental Psychology* 3: 1–14.

Memory, Cognition, and Self-Esteem

Almost every task requires the processing of stored information. Think of all the complex information you may have processed so far in reading this book, including information about the brain, anatomy, and aspects of psychology and theology. Other information inputs come from school, parents, and other significant people in our environment. Some of the things we learn come easily and naturally, while other information is difficult to retain.

Memory

Memory, which plays a significant role in physical as well as intellectual activity, is a basic component of human wholeness. How memory works is still something of a mystery, although scientists have identified several parts of the brain that seem to participate in the storage of information and have distinguished two separate storage processes: short-term and long-term memory.

In human beings, far more than in any other species, the processing of information goes beyond simply receiving and coding input information. Human information processing involves selection, reorganization, and transformation of input into a storage area (see chap. 3).

Such a coding or selectivity operation is necessary because there is too much input for us to be able to process each item separately. Our processing and storage capacities would become overloaded if we lacked mechanisms for selective organization and coding of those stimuli. Learning in humans is dependent to a great degree on the ability to process information and to retain new knowledge.

Sensory Storage

Information seems to be processed by human beings in several stages. The first is the sensory-information storage stage (step 3 in fig. 7.1). For example, when you hear a musical tone, that informa-

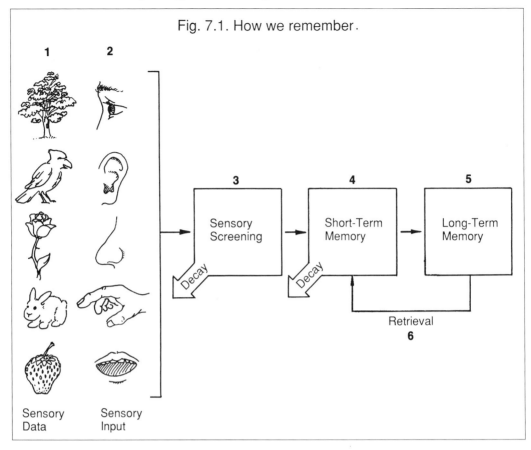

Fig. 7.1. How we remember.

1   2

3 Sensory Screening
Decay

4 Short-Term Memory
Decay

5 Long-Term Memory

Retrieval
6

Sensory Data   Sensory Input

tion is briefly stored much as a tape recorder would store the sound on tape. When the sound reaches your brain you become aware that you have heard a tone. Although the receptors in the ear heard the tone externally (the original stimulus), what is presented to the brain is a coding of that tone. The brain immediately begins to process that information for significance. The sensory-information storage stage usually lasts no more than one second (Sperling 1960). The reticular system of the brain screens the input and either allows the stimulus to pass through to the next stage or blocks it.

Short-Term Memory

After the reticular system has judged the importance of incoming messages (resulting in either attention or inattention), the message may be held briefly in the short-term memory. Short-term memory holds limited amounts of information for a short time period. For example, you may look up a phone number and then dial that number. Less than five minutes later, however, you may have to look up that number again in order to dial it correctly.

The delimitation of time is somewhat relative. There is about 80 percent recall after three seconds, 40 percent after six seconds, and 20 to 25 percent after nine seconds (Murdock 1961; fig. 7.2).

The short-term memory system typically cannot hold more than seven items at a given time (plus or minus two). As new information passes through the short-term memory, previously stored items are apparently pushed out.

Short-term memory has often been tested using digit memorization and recall experiments (Murdock 1961). Thus the

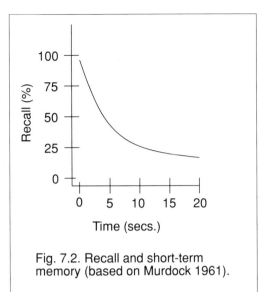

Fig. 7.2. Recall and short-term memory (based on Murdock 1961).

upon how meaningful the material is. Obviously highly meaningful material may increase the amount of information that can be stored at any given time because large quantities of information may be "chunked" or grouped together. Regardless, we can still speak of the limitation of seven bits of information if we assume that each bit actually consists of chunked material that may, in turn, consist of several other pieces of information. The related information may be recalled with the assistance of another stage of memory called long-term memory. Anderson (1985, 148) notes that the seven refers to material that is the central focus of attention, not all the related information that might be recalled.

limitations of this form of memory, cited above, refer largely to how digits are stored. Is other information stored in a similar manner? This depends in part

It is a good idea to keep in mind the limitations of short-term memory in learning information. Try to organize the infor-

---

Spotlight 7.1. Using Short-Term Memory in Teaching

Applications of memory theory are relevant not only to college- and seminary-level study but also to learning and teaching in the church. In Bible memorization, for example, it is best to break down the words of a verse to be learned into groups of seven or less. Learn a phrase of seven or fewer words, then go on to the next phrase of seven or fewer words. Verses should be divided into conceptually related sections.

In relation to children, it is important to choose memory verses that they can understand. Too often well-meaning teachers require children to learn verses that they cannot understand. Religion becomes incomprehensible and may later be set aside as irrelevant. Use verses that are meaningful and applicable. Perhaps some class time can be spent discussing how memory verses may be used every day. As noted in the text, it is crucial for good recall to relate information to things already learned.

The repetitive processes (rehearsal) that aid memorization are quite compatible with certain computer programs. A phrase of seven or fewer words can be flashed on the screen. The screen then goes blank, and the person is required to type in the phrase from memory. In the next frame of the program, a second phrase of seven or fewer words is presented, followed by a pause with a blank screen, and then both phrases are typed. If an error is made, the phrase with the mistake is displayed again and a second chance to type it is given. Thus the cognitive procedure of rehearsal is used in combination with the behavioral concept of shaping.

The limits of short-term memory often surface indirectly when the congregation reads Scripture as a body. The extended pauses between phrases are not physically required (a breath does not have to be taken that often), but the pauses punctuate the span of short-term memory.

mation into groups of seven or less. If you have more than seven items to recall, try to organize them into two or more larger categories so that each large category will have seven or fewer items of information. If there are more than seven larger categories, topics, subtopics, and even sub-subtopics can be developed. Obviously this process can be extended to additional levels.

While it may be possible for information to get to long-term memory immediately from short-term memory, more often this transfer requires a step called "rehearsal" (see fig. 7.3). This involves the repetition of the information in short-term memory which aids the transfer of information to long-term memory.

Rehearsal may involve the simple repetition of information. In studying for an examination, a student may decide to read the text or lecture notes several times. But is sheer repetition the best way to place information in long-term memory (so it will be recalled for a test, for example)? The best research to date indicates that this is not the case. Rather than simply repeating information, it is better to do something to it in a variety of ways. For example, you can read a textbook, outline it, underline it, and summarize it. You can do much the same with lecture notes. They can be reorganized, summarized, outlined, and underlined. You may also take the material from lectures or books and recite the material aloud or even try to regive the lecture. You might develop questions and then study with other students, answering questions you have written.

It is important to find as many different ways to rehearse the information as you can. You may think of the different ways of rehearsing as making more and more connections in the brain. The more connections you have, the more likely you will be able to recall information because you will have more cues by which to associate the questions on the test.

Two ways of rehearsing information have been identified: massed-time and distributed-time rehearsal. In massed-time rehearsal, a large segment of concentrated time is involved in going over information. In distributed-time rehearsal, the same amount of time going over information is spread out over several days. Research to date indicates that distributed-time rehearsal is the best for most college classes (Reynolds and Glaser 1964), and is even

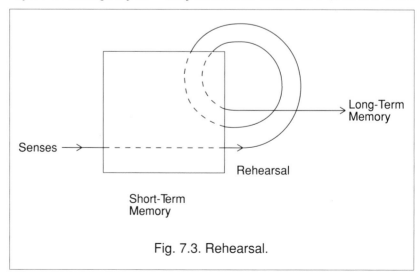

Fig. 7.3. Rehearsal.

Spotlight 7.2. Memory Theory and Sermon Delivery

Memory theory can be applied to sermon delivery. Memorizing the outline of a sermon helps the pastor concentrate on sermon delivery. Instead of using sheer memorization, it may be better to practice giving a sermon several times prior to actual delivery, preferably before a mirror or in front of a video camera.

Some pastors begin each point of the sermon with the same sound or letter. Although alliteration has some merit because of association value, it is easily overdone and may not provide enough association to aid memory. The pastor might try spelling out a word with the first letters of the main points, but this technique is also likely to get old quickly. On the other hand, using an overhead projector, showing a movie, or even acting out a skit may accentuate the major ideas in a more effective way. Objects might be brought to the pulpit to illustrate the sermon. Unusual and unexpected events often increase memory, as can a joke or vivid story.

It is a good idea to present the main points at the beginning and end of the sermon, not only because first and last things tend to be remembered best, but also so the congregation will get three exposures and three rehearsals. Major points and subpoints should number less than seven. Shorter sermons with fewer main points are more likely to be recalled than longer sermons with many complex ideas.

Pargament and DeRosa (1985) suggest that only a modest amount of information from a sermon will be retained. More details from a sermon were recalled when the listeners had higher verbal ability, were interested in the topic, were actively engaged in private and public expressions of religion, and held prior beliefs consistent with the content of the message.

Perhaps the most vivid finding in the study was distortion of sermon content. Although the sermon heard lasted only a minute or less, 18 percent of the content was distorted and only one-third to one-half of the content was recalled. This was in spite of the fact that most of the people studied had a significant level of religious involvement and were encouraged to listen closely, the messages were straightforward, and the participants were evaluated immediately after hearing the message. In contrast, in an earlier study (Johnson 1970) more than 50 percent of the material was retained from a fifteen-minute sermon that was read rather than heard, and which participants were exposed to twice rather than once.

Pargament and DeRosa also note that the most distorted messages were those which had unusual content and challenged the listeners' assumptions. This may explain why many laypeople are unaffected by sermons: they distort the content so that it fits their ideas.

Myers and Jeeves (1987, 75–81) cite studies that indicate a low level of comprehension, with only 10 percent recalling the sermon from the week before and 30 percent denying that they had even heard a sermon on that topic. Myers and Jeeves recommend that pastors use sermons that get attention, are understandable, persuade people, and compel people to action. They emphasize the importance of vivid, concrete examples rather than abstract information. The pastor must use ideas that relate to what people have experienced and already know, using repetition that is spaced out over time. Congregational members should take sermon notes and then discuss the sermon, perhaps in a Sunday school class. A time for questions, answers, and comments at the end of sermons should be provided. Offering plates might be passed to pick up questions that people want answered.

more important in learning skills than in learning facts.

It is also possible to use overlearning during the rehearsal process. Information is rehearsed to the extent that it can be recalled, and is then rehearsed several more times. Overlearning results in even greater retrieval from long-term memory than rehearsing to the point that the information can just barely be recalled.

Long-Term Memory

Long-term memory is the next step in the progression, although it should be noted that loss of information is possible due to decay at any of the previous stages. Whether information can decay from long-term memory is debatable. Some believe that if information is known well enough to actually enter long-term memory it may be there permanently (unless it is lost through physical brain damage). An individual may not be able to recall (retrieve) that information, but under the right conditions it might be accessible.

What is the relationship between brain activity and memory? As noted in chapter 2, the hippocampus is directly related to memory recall, but does not actually store memories. So where is memory in the brain? Neuroscientists are not in full agreement, but some research (Lynch and Baudry 1984) suggests that memory is associated with the brain's synapses.

Long-term memory can be divided into two portions: relatively permanent long-term storage and active memory (Anderson 1985, 140; fig. 7.4). Active memory is memory from which information is easily retrieved; it generally lasts about forty-eight hours. Thus when you have studied something within the last forty-eight hours and then study it again, the information is much more easily recalled. Thus some review of previously learned material is probably good prior to an exam.

Information stored in long-term memory may be lifelong and the storage capacity is essentially unlimited. Long-term memory is like a huge library with billions of books on its shelves. Even the largest computer system cannot match the complexity of the brain's memory banks.

The library analogy is helpful because information stored in a library's card file is coded under a central-index retrieval system. To retrieve what is in a book, a library user must be able to find the proper call number, or code, for that book. Similarly, long-term memory may be indexed in several different ways to make available a great number of facts. People who can-

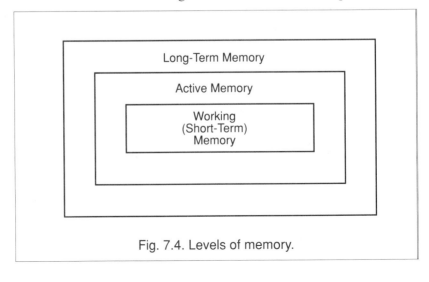

Fig. 7.4. Levels of memory.

not remember an event in an ordinary situation frequently can recall that event when a certain type of stimulus presents itself. For example, a person who has not seen a friend for many years but observes the kind of car the friend used to drive may immediately recall the image of that friend's face and many details of pleasant encounters with that person.

One possibility for indexing long-term memory is the use of verbal coding. If what is filed away in storage is a code based on the verbal description of an experience, the use of a word may recall a whole scene. For example, the word "dog" might cause someone to think of a pet, while "Skippy" might evoke memories of a particular kind of pet that once had that name. Other types of memory coding may also occur. Visual coding, based on visual perceptual processes, has sometimes been called an eidetic memory coding system. It is important to note that memory is active and often changes over time, so the library file analogy does not fit perfectly. But within limits, it can aid our understanding of how memory is stored.

Associations are an important way to code information in long-term memory. For example, some of us learned the five points of Calvinism using the acrostic TULIP.

> Total depravity
> Unconditional election
> Limited atonement
> Irresistible grace
> Perseverance of the saints

Other kinds of associations may be more helpful. For example, you can reflect on the concepts you are trying to learn and attempt to relate them to prior events in your life or to things that have happened to other people. You may be able to relate the material to ideas in other classes (although it is important to maintain dis-tinct differences when dealing with similar ideas, as we will see later). Not only should rehearsal take place in different ways, but there is some evidence that rehearsing information in different locations may also help. Ideally, information should be rehearsed in a location similar to the context in which the material is to be recalled (Anderson 1985, 193).

Long-term memories may be elicited by hypnosis or psychoanalysis. But if memory occurs through so many well-coordinated processes, how is it that we are always forgetting things? As already mentioned, each new sense impression in short-term memory destroys the information of the impression before it. The brain must therefore take in each new stimulus pattern, scan it quickly, and then either store it or reject it. If the information being processed is of an emotionally threatening or disturbing character, it may be difficult to remember later. That is why individuals who have been through an experience such as an automobile accident or natural disaster may not remember accurately the sequence of events. Since the coding acts like an indexing system, the influx of new material interferes with the ability to retrieve stored material. In that process, sometimes referred to as retroactive inhibition, the more similar the new material is to old material the more it will interfere. Sometimes, however, in a process called proactive inhibition, material already in the memory interferes with new material learned. Sometimes when trying to memorize a group of Bible verses, individuals will begin to associate them with other memory verses and find themselves quoting two different Bible passages yet simultaneously integrating the two. Thus forgetting is not information loss but an inability to access information (Nelson 1971).

Periodic review of material to be re-

Spotlight 7.3. Other Applications of Memory Theory

Similar ideas must be distinguished or interference will result. For example, there are two definitions of church: the church as all true believers, and the church as a building or organizational structure. If these concepts are not distinguished, confusion will ensue.

Topics such as holiness, sin, and sanctification may be understood in a very different manner by different denominations. Interference can be minimized by noting the differences in definition among denominations. For example, when the holiness Christian says that certain Christians do not sin and the Baptist says all Christians sin every day, they are not using the same meaning of the word "sin." There is a tendency to forget the unaccepted definition due to interference.

Interference is a problem in evangelistic presentations. People often use different definitions for terms such as "fundamentalist" or "born again." For example, a man shares his faith with a woman on the street, who is receptive yet looks confused when he states that she needs to confess her sins to become a Christian. She has heard a television preacher say people cannot do anything to merit salvation, that only God can do it. Such interference may cause a forgetting of what the evangelist is trying to say because the television message interferes with the new presentation. The man at this point should clearly distinguish between confession as admission of guilt and doing "good works" to merit becoming a Christian.

Finally, it should be noted that in recent years some Christians have emphasized the importance of the "healing of memories." This approach is based not upon the memory theory detailed in this chapter, but on the Freudian idea that forgetting is due to the repression of painful memories. This certainly can occur and in the process of counseling these memories may need to be revived and dealt with consciously (Seamands 1985).

The healing of memories demands that early memories be reexperienced consciously, followed by either forgiveness of others or self. God is then asked to heal the pain associated with the memory. Sometimes God is visualized as being there and assuming the pain himself.

While memory healing can be very helpful, not everyone is in need of such healing. This approach seems most appropriate for those who have suffered very traumatic events. It should also be noted that some Christians writers in this area add unhealthy concepts such as erasing or substituting memories, which is actually a form of repression. Also, the trauma and pain of the reliving of such experiences probably require the intervention of a professional counselor rather than someone who has only read some materials on the subject.

---

membered can aid recall. A book read at the beginning of a course should be reviewed before a final examination. Reading out loud encourages active attention, which not only affects the index and long-term memory but also alerts the perceptual processes to focus on the stimuli, in essence duplicating the whole process of learning the material originally. Another strategy is to discover significant aspects of the material to be learned and to group these aspects into some kind of coding. Poetry is generally easier to remember than prose because poetry has built-in codes, such as meter, rhyme, and alliteration.

Psalm 119 is a familiar example of poetic coding. In the original Hebrew the psalm forms an elaborate acrostic, with each line in a particular stanza beginning with the same letter, and with the stanzas arranged to spell out the entire Hebrew alphabet. Many performers of amazing feats of memory use some form of association of what is to be remembered with items on a coding framework they have memorized.

From this description it would be tempting to conclude that long-term memory is fixed and unchanging. This is far from the case, however. We have all heard people recall events and embellish them considerably. An old memory may be contradicted by a newly found photograph or the recall of another person. Long-term memory is not passively stored, but can actively change—particularly in the process of recall—to better fit the present understanding of situations. A new perspective changes how we perceive what has occurred previously.

Cognition

Thinking has been defined as the ability to manipulate and organize elements in the environment by means of symbols instead of physical acts. Symbols include gestures, words, pictures, diagrams, and abstract entities such as numbers. Thinking takes on many forms, from pragmatic reasoning to daydreaming. Creativity is a remarkable form of thinking in which mental activity at almost a fantasy level is used in the service of reality.

Adult thinking ranges across a whole spectrum of relationships to the external world. At one end of the continuum an individual may be coping realistically with the environment through reasoning and creative effort to change the environment or adapt to it. At the opposite end, autistic thinking may focus on the inner person—on fantasies, daydreams, and responses to the need for self-gratification.

Cognitive psychology, concerned with the process of knowing in the broadest sense, includes perception, memory, judgment, language, and other factors. Cognition refers to both the process of knowing and to the product of the act of knowing. The branch of philosophy that deals with knowing is called epistemology. The ability to know by combining perception with thinking is what has enabled human beings to transcend the immediate environment through the development of theology, science, literature, history, and other scholarly disciplines.

Cognition includes images and words. Images are mental pictures of actual sensory experiences. Imagery is not essential to thought processes, but some people ex-

"No, Ma! I forgot to take out the trash."

"Rats! I thought sure she would understand short-term memory."

perience strong visual imagery. Imagery has the capacity of being as clear and accurate as the original perception. Thinking is not carried out in a machinelike brain isolated from the environment, however. Feedback from the environment in a kind of intermediate trial-and-error process seems to be a necessary factor in thinking and learning. Individuals respond to their environment in a variety of ways. Realistic thinking, or reasoning (in contrast to autistic thinking), helps us adjust to reality.

Three different processes are generally considered to be part of reasoning. Deductive reasoning describes a process in which data are combined and conclusions are drawn from those "facts." Inductive reasoning is a process in which inferences about the unknown are formulated on the basis of what is already known. Finally, evaluative reasoning is a process of judging the appropriateness of a new idea or concept.

Individuals blocked from reaching some goal or confronted by some obstacle have a problem to solve. Human problem solving appears to require a combination of insight and trial-and-error learning. We generally begin with some insights about how to solve a problem and try one solution after another, perhaps only in our minds. Finally we come up with a workable solution.

Concepts

An important cognitive issue is the specific nature of the concepts we use. Two basic theories have been suggested: the classical theory and the exemplar theory.

The classical theory, originally suggested by the ancient Greeks, is that different concepts have certain critical features which are used in the process of associating a particular object with a concept (Smith and Medin 1981). Critical features are the most obvious features of an object, action, or idea.

For example, the critical features of the concept "bowl" are that it is concave, used for food, and lacks a handle. Thus a bowl can be distinguished from a cup because the cup has a handle and is made for liquids. We ignore many features that are irrelevant and emphasize the critical features in trying to associate an object, action, or idea with a particular concept.

While this theory has been predominant throughout history and may well reflect the nature of certain adult concepts, does it account for all concepts for people at all ages? The best research to date indicates that it does not (Rosch 1975). The classical theory appears to be an artificial theory that is more the result of abstract philosophical analysis than observing how people naturally use concepts every day. Young children, in particular, do not use critical features in identifying objects, but a process more consistent with exemplar theory (Ratcliff 1988).

It could be pointed out from the above example of a bowl that each of the critical features could be violated and still the object could be recognized as a bowl. One could think of a square bowl with handles used to hold nuts and bolts. True, it would be an odd bowl perhaps, but a bowl nonetheless!

From her research with children Rosch concludes that best examples are crucial to identifying concepts (thus the exemplar theory). Certain examples of a concept are more representative than others. For example, a robin is a better example of the concept "bird" than a chicken or a bat. We use the best example of a concept in evaluating a new object to determine if that object belongs to the conceptual category. The new object must not only resemble the best example of a given concept, but also be sufficiently unlike the best example of all alternative concepts. We are more

Spotlight 7.4. Biblical Prototypes

The Bible contains many prototypes of Christian concepts. For example, the Old Testament tabernacle and temple are prototypes of heaven. Certainly Christ and the great biblical saints are prototypes. They stand out as examples of righteousness, faith, and other spiritual qualities. God provides us with personal accounts of both saints and sinners. He wants us to develop a "family resemblance" to people with godly characters and to shun those people who are not of the faith. We as Christians already have some family resemblance in that we are created in God's image, but we are to have an ever more perfect resemblance through the process of spiritual growth.

likely to compare a flying object with a robin to determine if it is a bird, rather than comparing it to a chicken or bat. Likewise the flying object must also be sufficiently different from an airplane and other flying objects. The similarity between the best example and a new example of a concept is called "family resemblance."

The best example (or prototype) of a concept is more quickly identified with the concept than are other examples and tends to be the first example learned when the concept is initially acquired. The prototype is more likely to be the first example cited when the person is asked for an example and is more likely to be the reference point for comparing nontypical members of a concept (Smith and Medin 1981). Clearly the exemplar or prototype theory of concepts is the best approach to understanding children's concepts and may well be the principal way that adults identify concepts as well.

Problem Solving and Decision Making

How do people solve problems? Two methods often described by cognitive psychologists are algorithms and heuristics. An algorithm is a set of procedures that guarantees the solving of a problem. For example, the answer to a subtraction problem can be checked by adding the answer and the number to the right of the subtraction sign; if the problem has been done correctly, the sum should equal the first number. A heuristic is not as certain. It is a rule of thumb that generally leads to the best answer, but there are exceptions. For example, a common way of finding a person's address is to look in the telephone book, but this does not always work because some people are not listed.

Other ways of solving problems include attempting to minimize the difference between the end result and current state. New problems can often be solved if they can be simplified or converted into a form with which we are familiar. Another method of problem solving is to start at the goal and work backward in reasoning to the initial state. Sometimes using an analogy can help in problem solving. If there are not too many options, trial and error can be used to find solutions to a problem. Sometimes a sudden flash of insight may provide the needed answer.

Wheeler and Janis (1980) researched the question of how good and poor decisions are made, and found five steps that make wise decisions more likely: (1) take on the challenge; (2) seek answers; (3) evaluate alternatives, giving both positive and negative aspects of each; (4) make a commitment; and (5) stick with the decision and deal with the difficulties.[1]

Language and Thinking

Is cognition related to language, and if so, exactly what is the relationship? This question has been long debated by psychologists and is still a source of considerable disagreement.

At one extreme is Whorf (1956), who believes that language powerfully affects thought. Arguing that the distinctives of every culture are transmitted through language, Whorf emphasizes that cognition is shaped by the language we use. Whorf notes that Eskimos have many words for snow and thus make finer distinctions in reference to that substance; English-speaking people have only one word for it. Vocabulary and grammar come from a culture's interpretation of the world.

While language does influence our perceptions and vocabulary is socially acquired, there is evidence that grammar is partly innate. Chomsky (1975) provides evidence that there is a deep structure to human language, a universal grammar common to all languages. He points out that certain arrangements of words in sentences are quite common across languages, while other combinations are rare or nonexistent. Chomsky maintains, therefore, that many grammatical components are more the product of maturation than culture. Indeed, as children acquire the complexities of grammar, each rule is not explicitly taught, suggesting that people are "wired" for acquiring many of the rules of language.

Piaget (1926) disagrees with Whorf, claiming that thought precedes language. From early infancy the child is thinking and trying to understand the world. The

1. See spotlight 4.4 on impressions and decision making.

initial development of language at about age two is an indication of a new kind of thinking, preoperational thought (see chap. 10).

Vygotsky (1962) takes issue with Piaget, believing that thought is simply language that has been internalized. During early life, speech and thought develop separately. When the child begins speaking there is a joining of language and thought. Disagreeing with Chomsky, Vygotsky holds that grammar is entirely learned (not innate) and eventually influences logic (Piaget, in contrast, holds that logic develops first).

Behaviorists such as Skinner (1957) argue that all of the above theories are too mysterious and complicated. Language is nothing more than behavior that has been reinforced. Those who hold to observational learning theory would emphasize imitation of what we have heard as a basis for language.

Which theory is correct? There is some evidence for each, and a clear consensus has not yet been reached. For the time being, it is probably best to admit that culture does powerfully influence us, and that one of the ways culture is transmitted is through language. The exact relationship between language and thought is unclear at present. Probably cognition affects language and vice versa, but it is difficult to determine which is primary. From the biblical account of the tower of Babel (and the development of different languages as a result), we might conclude that the reason for certain deep structures in all languages is because at one time all humanity spoke the same language; there is a common source for them all. But this is not to rule out some genetic linkage to deep structures. In spite of the confusion of languages at Babel, there may still be a common pattern in the speech center of the brain preprogrammed for certain grammatical structures and reflecting God's original intent: unbroken humanity with a common language.

Language and Communication

In the broadest sense communication is the process by which individuals give and receive cognitive and other information. Information—which may include facts, ideas, or feelings—can be transmitted in a number of ways, such as speech, gestures, and pictorial or written symbols. An important means of communication for human adults is verbal communication (although nonverbal language may be even more important, as noted in chap. 4). The use of a highly complex linguistic system is one of the most distinctive and curious accomplishments of human beings.

The psychological study of language and speech is called psycholinguistics. Linguistic analysis takes place on three levels. The phonological level is concerned with phonemes, or the basic sound units of a language. The grammatical level has two components: morphology is the study of words and meaningful word segments, while syntax deals with rules for combining words and phrases into sentences. Finally, the semantic level is concerned with meanings. Those who translate the Bible from one language into another must have a good understanding of psycholinguistics, the broad principles of which apply to any language.

The acquisition of language has been researched in detail within developmental psychology.[2] Language production during the first year of human life is limited to very basic forms of crying and babbling. By the end of the first year, certain recognizable words appear and speech begins. After that children continue to increase their vocabulary and develop their use of grammar, beginning with single words and progressing to two-word sentences. The average year-old child has a vocabulary of two to three words; this increases to about fifty words by age two and to one thousand words by age three. It has been shown that the IQ of deprived children exposed to highly verbal environments during their first three years of life increases (Ramey, Yeates, and Short 1984); these children are probably more verbal and language-oriented than those who have not participated in a verbal enrichment program. The stimulation provided by daily exposure to television programs such as "Sesame Street" can have a significant impact on language development (although television is not a substitute for a systematic reading program). Acquisition of words and language skills ordinarily continues as the child matures. Within North American culture, success is directly related to acquisition of language skills.

Self-Talk

Instead of mere stimulus-response (S-R), many of our actions are stimulus-*organization*-response (S-O-R). But what kind of organizing goes on between the stimuli we receive and the responses we make?

Some psychologists have described the cognitive activity in which we give ourselves certain messages as "self-talk" (Meichenbaum 1977). Statements made to the self may be self-defeating thoughts, beliefs, and expectations that reflect automatic and illogical assumptions (Beck 1976). Self-talk tends to overemphasize painful events and the significance of others' comments. Cognitive behaviorists emphasize the need to get more information before reaching conclusions about what others may think, thus allowing for disconfirmation of those harsh conclusions. This often involves the monitoring and challenging of thought content.

---

2. See Hall, Lamb, and Perlmutter 1986, for an excellent summary.

Ellis has identified a number of irrational assumptions that often are a part of self-talk (Ellis and Grieger 1977). These commonly held statements need to be identified and confronted when they occur:

1. I need to be loved by everyone.
2. It is terrible when things are not precisely the way I want them.
3. Painful things which happen to me are due to circumstances or other people outside of my control.
4. I need to get upset about threatening things and focus all my attention on them.
5. It is better to avoid my problems than to face them.
6. I must be totally competent in every situation.
7. If something at one time has affected my life, it will always affect me.
8. I must be completely self-controlled.
9. Doing little or nothing about a situation will make me happy.
10. I cannot control my emotions and need not assume responsibility for how I feel.
11. There is always a right and perfect solution; there will be a catastrophe if I cannot identify it.

While the Christian can certainly agree that the above self-statements are irrational, Ellis adds two others about which the Christian should have some reservations. One of these statements focuses on the fact that some actions and people are wicked and thus deserve punishment. Certainly this statement is not as irrational as Ellis would like to believe, as it is quite compatible with the teaching of the Bible. No one, of course, is beyond hope and prayer, but it is certainly not irrational to identify individuals and actions as wicked when they clearly are.

A final irrational statement Ellis emphasizes is the need to depend upon someone more powerful and stronger than the self. Christians affirm that people need to depend upon God. Yet, paradoxically, relying upon God increases our internal strength; it is the Holy Spirit within us who enables us to face the world and the problems we encounter. What Ellis seems

Spotlight 7.5. Sources of Self-Talk

Several Christian writers have investigated self-talk and rational thinking. Perhaps best known is the work of William Backus (Backus and Chapian 1980). While Backus's approach is somewhat simplistic, there are some good things to be gained by using what he calls "misbelief therapy." The book has been popular with the public and Backus has published several followup volumes that apply the ideas in a number of contexts. Much of what Backus describes can be considered a Christian application of cognitive therapy.

Schmidt, a clinical psychologist, has written an equally practical and readable book entitled *Do You Hear What You're Thinking* (1983). Crabb's earlier work (1977) not only critically considers Ellis's theory but also develops the whole idea of self-talk within a Christian framework.

to be speaking against is the continual reliance upon other people, a problem often encountered in counseling situations. We should encourage others to rely upon God and the strength he gives, rather than allowing them to become emotional parasites.

Developing Healthy Self-Esteem

Cognitive self-talk often derives from the more generalized concept of the self that a person has. One's self-concept begins to develop in early childhood and becomes more elaborated and stable during adolescence and adulthood (see chap. 11). Yet the self-concept may become less than optimal as a result of feelings of inferiority or poor self-esteem (Meier 1977, 4–41).

Most people have been told in many ways, throughout their lives, that they are inferior. These messages are both verbal and nonverbal, intentional and unintentional. They threaten the development of a strong sense of self-worth. Without such a sense of self-worth individuals will not only have a miserable life, but also will be unable to reach the potential to which God has called them.

It is easy to impress on young children that they are inferior because they are physically smaller than the adults around them, and more clumsy, ignorant, and naive. Parents and older siblings dictate their every move. When they go to school, attention always seems to focus on what they have done wrong. These factors make the development of a healthy self-concept extremely difficult.

Parental Value Systems

A major factor in the development of self-worth is the influence of parental value systems. No matter what parents say, their actual focus may be on materialism, athletics, good looks, intelligence, or humanitarianism rather than godly character.

MATERIALISM

Parents who focus on material gain in their daily life and conversations do have an influence on children. Even if eventually successful in a worthwhile profession that pays decent wages, these children may as adults have conscious (or unconscious) inferiority feelings because they have not lived up to their parents' materialistic expectations. In turn their children detect their inner dissatisfaction and frustrations about not having more money and material possessions. Seeing those frustrations eat away at their parents' self-worth, step by step, the children learn to measure their own self-worth by material possessions: motorcycles, clothes, ten-speed racing bikes, and spending money. If they do not have these things, they feel worthless. And even if they do have them, they compare themselves with peers who have more, and still feel inferior. Thus a faulty value system can be passed on from generation to generation.

It is a sin to base our self-worth on riches. Although some of the godliest people in the Bible were also the richest men on earth in material terms—such as Abraham, Isaac, Jacob, Joseph, Job, and David—their self-worth was based on their faith in God.

Other servants of God had similar virtues but they lived in poverty. Take, for example, the disciples or Paul. Paul said he had experienced both riches and poverty, both popularity and abasement; but Paul based his self-worth on his relationship with God and could therefore say, "I have learned to be content whatever the circumstances" (Phil. 4:11). Likewise, Christ said, "But seek first his kingdom and his righteousness, and all these things will be given to you as well" (Matt. 6:33). Life on earth is a temporary pilgrimage.

Developing a godly character is more important than devotion to money.

EDUCATION

Some parents emphasize good grades and perfect scores on tests. An emphasis on education, although important, can get out of hand in some families. One young man whose parents had taught him that anything less than an A was a dishonor to the entire family made As in all but one course in college. When that happened, his uncle flew in from out of state to talk to him about it. Years later, as a brilliant scholar with a doctorate in economics from Harvard, he still carried around bad feelings about that one course. Children whose parents have unrealistic expectations for them will feel like failures, no matter how much they succeed in the world's eyes.

ATHLETICS

Young people's self-worth is influenced considerably by how they are regarded by their peers. Being average or better than average in some sport is one way children and adolescents can gain the respect of others their age. Sports teach teamwork, enthusiasm, how to compete with oneself, how to compete with others, how to win graciously, and how to accept defeat and frustrations. Children and teens can see themselves improving with practice and can apply such concepts to the "game of life." Sports can help youngsters gain self-confidence as their ability increases. Being on an athletic team can help them develop close friendships and learn to relate to others.

Athletics can, however, destroy self-worth and even teach sociopathic values. When a father plays baseball with his children, does he praise them when they do something right, or does he remain silent when they hit or catch the ball and criticize them when they miss it? Is he continually correcting and showing them how

they *should* have done it? What they really need is his acceptance, companionship, and genuine praise for what they do right.

An emotionally healthy coach helps develop character in youngsters. There are also emotionally disturbed or spiritually depraved coaches who need to win so badly that they teach their athletes to cheat, to injure other players, and to do whatever else is necessary to win. A child who accepts a "win at any cost" philosophy in sports will apply it to other areas of life as well. An intense desire to win is healthy, but not at any cost. Children should learn to be assertive and competitive, but not sociopathic.

Children with poor athletic ability may get some social benefits from compensating rather than trying to excel in areas where they lack basic abilities. Many parents expect their children to succeed in areas that they were weak in when they were growing up. It is far more important for children to meet personal and spiritual needs, than to feel obligated to make up for the deficiencies of their parents.

APPEARANCE

Millions of Americans experience inferiority feelings from comparing their real or imagined physical defects with the physical attributes of others. Common in both men and women, this faulty value system is perpetuated whenever a little girl is praised over and over again for how pretty she is, or a little boy for how handsome he is, but they are never praised for anything else. There is nothing wrong with praising children occasionally for how nice they look but it is psychologically unhealthy to praise good looks at the expense of other more important things, like godly character traits. Some parents even brag to others about their child's good looks in the child's presence.

Well-meaning parents can unconsciously teach their young daughter to measure her self-worth on the basis of her physical attractiveness or sex appeal. Especially during her teens she will compare herself with others who have a prettier face, a better figure, or less knobby knees. She will seldom acknowledge physical attributes that are satisfactory. Often the more attractive the girl, the more inferior she feels, partly because her parents probably placed excessive emphasis on her looks.

What a difference it would make if parents would praise a child's good character and behavior! Character and behavior defects are correctable; physical defects seldom are. Therefore, parents who value and praise good character will help their children learn to behave properly while developing the feelings of self-worth that are vital to good mental health.

Many people carry hidden resentment toward God for not designing them the way they would have designed themselves. Yet God lovingly designed us the way he did because he wants to develop within each of us a Christlike character so that we can experience life abundantly.

> For you created my inmost being;
>> you knit me together in my mother's
>> womb.
> I praise you because I am fearfully and
>> wonderfully made;
>> your works are wonderful,
>> I know that full well.
> My frame was not hidden from you
>> when I was made in the secret place.
> When I was woven together in the depths
>> of the earth,
>> your eyes saw my unformed body.
> All the days ordained for me
>> were written in your book
>> before one of them came to be.
>> (Ps. 139:13–16)

While our bodies were being formed within our mothers' wombs, each "inward part" was designed exactly as God intended—including both our strengths and weaknesses. We have the responsibility of living up to our potential, correcting any correctable defects. Our self-worth as well as our Christian witness will benefit from praising God for designing us the way we are.

Consider Paul. Paul made himself available to God. Although many Christians seem to think they can run their own lives better than God can, Paul writes:

> To keep me from becoming conceited because of these surpassingly great revelations, there was given me a thorn in my flesh, a messenger of Satan, to torment me. Three times I pleaded with the Lord to take it away from me. But he said to me, "My grace is sufficient for you, for my power is made perfect in weakness." Therefore I will boast all the more gladly about my weaknesses, so that Christ's power may rest on me. That is why, for Christ's sake, I delight in weaknesses, in insults, in hardships, in persecutions, in difficulties. For when I am weak, then I am strong. (2 Cor. 12:7–10)

Even though God gave Paul the gift of healing, he said no to Paul when Paul requested the power to heal himself. God answers every one of our prayers, but to expect him to answer them only affirmatively is a naive attempt to usurp God's omniscience and omnipotence. Paul's uncorrectable defect was for his own good and for God's glory.

Solomon said, "Remove the dross from the silver, and out comes material for the silversmith" (Prov. 25:4). Each person, however endowed, is a vessel made according to God's divine plan. Each person is also covered, to some extent, by the dross of human error, including parental error. Underneath that dross, none is inferior to any other, though each may have a unique design. Christians should strive for spiritual and emotional maturity, placing

Spotlight 7.6. Legalism and Self-Esteem

Many Christians have been brought up in churches where they were taught that self-hatred is a virtue rather than a sin. They generally take what transactional analysts call the "I'm not OK but you're OK" position or (even worse) the "I'm not OK and you're not OK" position. The latter is the most emotionally harmful position a person can have (see Harris 1976). Withdrawn from others and having neither self-worth nor genuine love relationships with others, many of these unfortunate people become depressed or psychotic because reality—or at least reality as they see it—becomes too painful to bear.

It is not surprising that many non-Christian psychiatrists regard all religion with suspicion. After all, many of their mentally disturbed patients are hysterically trying to play God, telling him what to do and how to do it. The more inferior people feel, the more superior they will probably act to compensate for their feelings of inadequacy. If those feelings reach psychotic proportions, people sometimes make up, and actually believe, grandiose delusions about themselves. Paranoid delusions make people feel more important.

A negativistic or legalistic local church can make matters even worse for persons with an abundance of inferiority feelings who are so buffeted by legalistic teaching that their self-worth finally hits bottom.

Children's self-worth can be permanently damaged when they grow up in a negativistic, legalistic church that neglects God's grace. Many children who could otherwise live abundant lives and further the cause of Christ never reach that potential because they are ruined by rigid churches that stand for the wrong things.

Each human being is extremely important to God. Christ said, "Are not two sparrows sold for a penny? Yet not one of them will fall to the ground apart from the will of your Father. And even the very hairs of your head are all numbered. So don't be afraid; you are worth more than many sparrows" (Matt. 10:29–31). Christ also showed how important we are to him when he said, "My sheep listen to my voice; I know them, and they follow me. I give them eternal life, and they shall never perish; no one can snatch them out of my hand. My Father, who has given them to me, is greater than all; no one can snatch them out of my Father's hand. I and the Father are one" (John 10:27–30).

Some churches convey the unhealthy idea that God is waiting for Christians to dare to break one of his rules so he can punish or reject them. The God of the Bible is a God of perfect love and perfect justice who sent his Son, Jesus Christ, to die on a cross in order to save us from hell. He is a God who loves us so much that he gave us his Word, with the principles for us to live by if we want abundant life. Christ says that those who put their faith in him are in the palm of his hand, already possessing life. The Father puts his loving hand around Christ's hand, so that our position is fully secured by his grace. "For it is by grace you have been saved, through faith—and this not from yourselves, it is the gift of God—not by works, so that no one can boast" (Eph. 2:8–9).

themselves in God's hands so he can remove that dross and produce a vessel of honor rather than of dishonor.

Healthy Self-Esteem

Is it really God's plan for us to love ourselves? If love of self means vanity and pride, the answer is "definitely not!" When God lists sins he hates, the "I'm OK, but you're not OK" position is included (see spotlight 7.6).

Sinful pride and vanity have nothing to do with loving ourselves in a healthy way—in the way that pleases God because he loves us and wants us to experience the abundant life. True self-love makes us more useful to God.

A legal expert asked Jesus which of the commandments was most important. "'The most important one,' answered Jesus, 'is this: "Hear, O Israel, the Lord our God, the Lord is one. Love the Lord your God with all your heart and with all your soul and with all your mind and with all your strength." The second is this: *"Love your neighbor as yourself."* There is no commandment greater than these'" (Mark 12:29–31, emphasis added). Paul writes, "In this same way, husbands ought to love their wives as their own bodies. He who loves his wife *loves himself*" (Eph. 5:28, emphasis added). Individuals who have a negative self-image will also be critical of others. Individuals who do not love themselves in a healthy way will find it impossible to develop genuine love relationships with others. Psychiatric practice bears out Scripture on two important points: (1) you cannot truly love others until you learn to love yourself in a healthy way; (2) lack of self-worth is the basis of most psychological problems.

TAKING CARE OF GOD'S TEMPLE

Loving self in a way that will please God includes taking care of our bodies. Parents who want their children to take proper care of their bodies need to take care of their own. "Don't you know that you yourselves are God's temple and that God's Spirit lives in you?" (1 Cor. 3:16). "Do you not know that your body is a temple of the Holy Spirit, who is in you, whom you have received from God? You are not your own; you were bought with a price. Therefore honor God with your body" (1 Cor. 6:19–20). Our bodies, "the temple of the living God" (2 Cor. 6:16), are obviously important to God.

As God's temples, we must develop healthy eating and sleeping habits, plus adequate exercise and recreation. A person may become more and more irritable and get angry over trifles because of psychological depression or from anemia. Anemia, which can be due to menstrual bleeding, fad eating, or crash dieting, can be corrected by restoring protein to the diet or taking iron supplements. Overeating can obviously be detrimental to both physical and emotional health. The incidence of heart attacks and other fatal illnesses rises sharply in people who are 20 percent overweight. It is somewhat contradictory for parents to preach self-control to their children if they themselves are exercising poor self-control.

Healthy sleeping habits are sometimes ignored by zealous Christians, who eventually "burn out." Individuals who continually get less sleep than they need are headed for trouble. Adults need about eight hours of sleep a night; some can get by on six while others require ten hours. Most adolescents need about nine hours a night, elementary school children about ten, preschoolers about twelve, and babies about sixteen to eighteen. Sleep, intended by God for the healing of both bodies and minds, is actually more important for mental health than for physical rest.

Recreation is another aspect of taking care of ourselves that Christians often neglect. It is wrong to think of watching a football game, hiking in the mountains, or playing games with friends as a waste of time. Of course, some kinds of recreation are healthier than others. And if Christians spent all of their time in recreation, they would accomplish little for the Lord. God intends a happy balance. Jesus himself spent quite a bit of his three-year ministry in the mountains, sometimes with his disciples (especially Peter and John), sometimes alone. There he could get away from the demanding crowds, relax, meditate, commune with the Father, enjoy the natural beauty he had created, and share intimately with his chosen disciples.

These physical aspects of loving the self God made are best taught to children by example. Good nutrition and healthful sleep, exercise, and recreation habits should be regarded as a heritage to pass on to children.

SPIRITUAL ASPECTS OF SELF-WORTH

A person who becomes a Christian is a new creation (2 Cor. 5:17), but is still far from sinless perfection. Sanctification, the process of becoming more and more like Christ, is almost always gradual. The new Christian is like a spiritual infant. Peter admonishes new believers: "Like newborn babies, crave pure spiritual milk, so that by it you may grow up in your salvation" (1 Pet. 2:2). Daily devotions are a must for spiritual and emotional maturity.

When his disciples were about to chase some children away so Jesus would not have to bother with them, Jesus said, "Let the little children come to me, and do not hinder them, for the kingdom of God belongs to such as these" (Mark 10:14). We can be sure that God desires to be in communion with children, and that their meditations on his Word will help them overcome temptations. Prayer and Bible study are especially important during the traumatic years between ages twelve and sixteen, when sons and daughters grow into

Spotlight 7.7.
Christian Sources on Self-Esteem

Dobson (1979) considers some of the false values associated with poor self-esteem as well as unfruitful ways people try to cope with inferiority feelings. Coping strategies include withdrawing, fighting, being the clown, denying reality, conforming, and compensating. While compensation is probably the best of these strategies, Dobson outlines several other ways parents can help their children overcome poor self-esteem. Dobson's book is very readable, even for young teen-agers.

A more advanced approach to the topic is found in *Your Better Self*, edited by Ellison (1983). Psychologists and theologians combine their efforts in developing a more distinctively Christian approach to self-worth. Of particular value are several chapters on church ministry and self-worth.

Clark (1985) considers the question of whether self-love is really a source of pride and thus contrary to Christianity. He distinguishes between being worthy of salvation and being worthful. We are worth saving although we are not deserving of salvation. Being worthful is compatible with the lack of pride the Bible commands. If we are worthy of salvation, then grace is unnecessary. Of course, the biblical record indicates that we are not worthy, yet because we are made in the image of God we are worthful. The doctrine of total depravity implies that every area of our lives is depraved; but this does not mean that we are depraved to the worst possible degree in each area. We are not worms lacking value, but people important enough that Christ died to forgive us.

> ## Spotlight 7.8. Family Devotions
>
> Families need to seriously consider having regular devotions. Billy Graham states that the divorce rate in families who have daily devotions is only one in five hundred.
>
> Parents can read small children a Bible story and have a short time of prayer. School children still like being read to. A Bible storybook with pictures in a comic strip format is quite appropriate for children of this age. It may also be good to include a time when each family member can share personal concerns and experiences. With adolescents, the sharing of experiences and difficulties is critical.
>
> Family devotions are most useful when they are practical. Rather than long-winded, boring lectures or readings, it may be better to read a short section of the Bible and then, as a family, summarize the key ideas. Each family member could also develop applications for their own lives as well as for other family members. Even parents may benefit from the applications their children suggest.

men and women, with all the associated hormone changes, impulses, cravings, and feelings of guilt and inadequacy.

Paul's assurance that God will help believers overcome temptation (1 Cor. 10:13) can be of tremendous comfort to young teen-agers. God will supply all our needs (Phil. 4:19). Human beings have a multitude of needs through which Satan continually tempts us. Christians may be called on by God to deny some of their *wants*, but God has promised to supply all of our *needs* (Phil. 4:9). He wants to supply them in his way, according to his principles of love. Satan keeps offering to supply our needs in his way, according to his principles of selfishness, greed, and hate. Needs are not temptations; it is Satan's way of meeting them that constitutes temptation. Our fallen human tendency is to meet our needs in Satan's way. With the new birth and spiritual insights, we see how to meet these natural needs in God's way, producing much greater ultimate joy and satisfaction.

Children should neither deny their natural needs nor meet them in Satan's way. These methods of dealing with needs serve only to create more intense temptations. To meet all our needs, including our sexual needs, in God's way, takes away Satan's power to tempt us. Children should be taught that God loves them and is concerned about their everyday needs. Parents with accepting attitudes show children, at least on a subconscious level, that God also is understanding and accepting of the struggles and temptations we go through.

Self-worth comes from doing what we know is right and not doing those things we believe are wrong. When we do things we know are selfish and sinful, we inevitably lose self-worth. Emotional problems are sure to follow as our self-worth continues to depreciate in value.

God refers to those who are called by his name as his own sons and daughters whom he created for his glory (Isa. 43:7). Even the vast complexities of our human bodies teach that we are of great importance to the Creator.

References

Anderson, J. 1985. *Cognitive psychology*. 2d ed. New York: W. H. Freeman.

Backus, W., and M. Chapian. 1980. *Telling yourself the truth*. Minneapolis: Bethany.

Beck, A. 1976. *Cognitive therapy and emotional disorders*. New York: International University Press.

Brown, J., and C. Brown. 1977. *Systematic counseling*. Champaign, Ill.: Research.

Chomsky, N. 1975. *Reflections on language*. New York: Pantheon.

Clark, D. 1985. Philosophical reflections on self-worth and self-love. *Journal of Psychology and Theology* 13: 3–11.

Coleman, J., J. Butcher, and R. Carson. 1984. *Abnormal psychology and modern life*. 7th ed. Glenview, Ill.: Scott, Foresman.

Crabb, L. 1977. *Effective biblical counseling*. Grand Rapids: Zondervan.

Dobson, J. 1979. *Hide or seek*. 2d ed. Old Tappan, N.J.: Revell.

Ellis, A., and R. Grieger. 1977. *RET*. New York: Springer.

Ellison, C., ed. 1983. *Your better self*. San Francisco: Harper and Row.

Hall, E., M. Lamb, and M. Perlmutter. 1986. *Child psychology today*. 2d ed. New York: Random.

Harris, T. 1976. *I'm ok, you're ok*. New York: Harper and Row.

Johnson, R. 1970. Recall of prose. *Journal of Verbal Learning and Verbal Behavior* 9: 12–20.

Lynch, G., and M. Baudry. 1984. The biochemistry of memory. *Science* 224: 1057–64.

Meichenbaum, D. 1977. *Cognitive behavior modification*. New York: Plenum.

Meier, P. 1977. *Christian child rearing and personality development*. Grand Rapids: Baker.

Murdock, B. 1961. The retention of individual items. *Journal of Experimental Psychology* 62: 618–25.

Myers, D., and M. Jeeves. 1987. *Psychology through the eyes of faith*. San Francisco: Harper and Row.

Nelson, T. 1971. Savings and forgetting from long term memory. *Journal of Verbal Learning and Verbal Behavior* 10: 568–76.

Pargament, K., and D. DeRosa. 1985. What was that sermon about? *Journal for the Scientific Study of Religion* 24: 180–93.

Piaget, J. 1926. *The language and thought of the child*. New York: Harcourt Brace.

Ramey, C., K. Yeates, and E. Short. 1984. The plasticity of intellectual development. *Child Development* 55: 1913–26.

Ratcliff, D. 1988. The cognitive development of preschoolers. In *Handbook of preschool religious education*, ed. D. Ratcliff. Birmingham, Ala.: Religious Education.

Restak, R. 1988. *The mind*. New York: Bantam.

Reynolds, J., and R. Glaser. 1964. Effects of repetition and spaced recall upon retention. *Journal of Educational Psychology* 55: 297–308.

Rosch, E. 1975. Cognitive representations of semantic categories. *Journal of Experimental Psychology* 104: 192–233.

Schmidt, J. 1983. *Do you hear what you're thinking?* Wheaton, Ill.: Victor.

Seamands, D. 1985. *Healing of memories*. Wheaton, Ill.: Victor.

Skinner, B. 1957. *Verbal behavior*. New York: Appleton-Century-Crofts.

Smith, E., and D. Medin. 1981. *Categories and concepts*. Cambridge, Mass.: Harvard University Press.

Sperling, G. 1960. The information available in brief visual presentation. *Psychological Monographs* 74.

Vygotsky, L. 1962. *Thought and language*. Cambridge, Mass.: MIT.

Whorf, B. 1956. *Language, thought and reality*. Cambridge, Mass.: MIT.

Wheeler, D., and I. Janis. 1980. *A practical guide for making decisions*. New York: Free.

Intelligence

Nearly everyone has heard of an IQ or "intelligence quotient," a measure of intellect derived from scores on an intelligence test. Some believe that an IQ score is a measure of innate intelligence or mental potential. Most everyone is also familiar with the term "mental retardation," which refers to a deficit in intelligence. People also talk about "senile" individuals. Sometimes those at the other end of the intelligence spectrum, the "gifted," receive special attention in advanced classes or programs. All of these categories in one way or another relate to the general concept of intelligence.

What does intelligence mean, how do psychologists measure it, and what are people like at each end of the spectrum of intelligence? These are the issues to be considered in this chapter.

What Is Intelligence?

Intelligence is a difficult concept for psychologists to define and describe. The ability to learn is often emphasized as part of intelligence. But an intelligent person has already learned many facts and skills. Furthermore, a "street-smart" teen-ager may be very clever but do poorly on an IQ test because he lacks the middle-class vocabulary used in the test. What is intelligence?

Sternberg et al. (1981) asked a number of people on the street what they thought the characteristics of intelligence were. Their conclusions were surprisingly similar to those of experts in the area: intelligence includes a good vocabulary, making wise decisions, planning ahead, and displaying interest in the world at large. This would suggest that the psychological views of intelligence are not that far removed from popular views.

Perhaps the best way to examine intelligence is by considering the various approaches to the topic used by psychologists and others. Some researchers, such as Piaget, speak of intelligence in terms of species differences. Thus the issue is not which person is more or less intelligent than others, but rather ways in which people are more intelligent than animals. The principal concern, then, is how species adapt to the environment. Some who hold this position have attempted to rank species in order of intelligence (Griffin 1976). In comparison with such distinctions, the differences *within* species (including the human species) are slight.

Most psychologists, however, prefer to emphasize the individual differences among human beings. Here a basic question is whether there is a general overall intelligence, or only different specific abilities. An IQ score on an intelligence test seems to presuppose a general intelligence, yet the best IQ tests break down this score into several subscores that indicate areas of strength and weakness. But how many abilities can be combined to produce general intelligence? Estimates have varied from two to well over one hundred. Guilford (1973) maintains that intellect is comprised of five intellectual operations, each of which can be performed on four kinds of content. Each of these combinations may result in six possible products. He places these three dimensions on the three faces of a cube. By adding all the potential combinations, he calculates 120 possible aspects of intelligence. In contrast, Cattell (1968) believes there are only two aspects of intelligence: crystallized (which is culturally acquired) and fluid (which is not significantly affected by culture). Cattell then subdivides each of these further.

Using Cattell's two aspects, we would expect a test that measures crystallized intelligence to discriminate between those who have acquired the test maker's culture and those who have not. In contrast, a test that measures only fluid intelligence would not be influenced by culture and consequently would be "culture fair." Unfortunately "culture fair" tests are impossible to construct because every test requires language (for instructions if nothing else) and language is powerfully influenced by culture.

This means that the results of intelligence tests are significantly affected by an individual's social class. Some psychologists, finding a general IQ difference among various races, have suggested that genetic differences account for IQ differences. But this argument overlooks the economic and cultural differences that go with differences in race in the United States. The best evidence to date indicates that racial differences in IQ are best accounted for by social and economic factors rather than by innate ability. For example, if the instructions for a test are in standard English, individuals who are fluent in that language will have no trouble. But how can people be expected to do well if their primary language is nonstandard English? In addition, different cultures (and even subcultures) value different kinds of intelligence, and what is valued may not be what is tested.

Theories of Intelligence

A number of theories of intelligence have been suggested. Structuralism emphasizes problem-solving abilities. Piaget, for example, believes that these abilities are wrapped up in mental structures and logic. As an individual interacts with the environment, intelligence develops.[1] This interaction is necessarily related to biological development. Mental structures are the result of experience combined with the physical maturation of the brain.

The information-processing theory holds that the way people process information is crucial. Leaning heavily upon memory and cognitive perspectives (see chap. 7), this theory focuses on the speed,

---

1. See chap. 10 for a detailed discussion of this developmental process in children.

capacity, and efficiency with which the person processes information (Carroll 1976). Other information-processing proponents attempt to break down problem solving into its components and then relate these to intelligence (Sternberg 1984).

A third theory is the psychometric approach. Individual differences are all-important in this perspective, and testing procedures are the focus of attention. Unlike the other two perspectives, the psychometric approach does not emphasize developmental theory or specific aspects of the processing of information. Instead the concern is practical: What tasks on an IQ test predict accomplishment? How do the IQ test scores of various children compare?

Intelligence: Inherited, Learned, or Unique?

Mental abilities vary widely among the adults of any particular culture. Is this primarily because of heredity or because of differences in early childhood environments? In spite of many studies, the relative contribution of heredity and environment to mental development is still debated (the "nature versus nurture" controversy). A famous study by Goddard (1912) traced the history of an American family (given the fictitious name of Kallikak) back to a Revolutionary War soldier who fathered two families, one illegitimate and one legitimate. The illegitimate family was begun with a tavern maid who was reportedly mentally defective. Later on, Kallikak married a young woman of better stock. Following the descendants of both unions, Goddard found that only a few of the nearly 500 legal descendants could be classified as undesirables. In contrast, the descendants of the tavern maid included a long line of mentally defective or socially deviant persons. Of 480 descendants, 143 were reported to be feebleminded, 33 were sexually immoral, 24

were alcoholics, and many others died in infancy. This high percentage of problems suggested to Goddard that the problems were genetically inherited rather than learned. Yet such a conclusion is unwarranted because each generation was reared by a prior generation of Kallikaks. Perhaps the problems developed because of poor parenting techniques passed on from generation to generation.

We might expect to obtain some insight into the heritability of intelligence by testing the intelligence of identical twins. Such studies have shown higher correlations of intelligence between genetically identical twins (Rowe and Plomin 1978). Questions, however, have been raised about both the soundness of much research based on intelligence testing and the interpretation of such studies. The best evidence to date from studies of children in foster homes who were moved to a more stimulating environment indicates that environment plays a crucial role in the development of intellectual functioning (Skeels 1966). Current evidence suggests that intellectual ability results from an interaction between heredity and environment (Bouchard and McGue 1981), with heredity setting the limits and environment determining the exact level reached.

"Hey, don't blame me, lady! I had low IQ parents!"

The stability of intellectual functioning over a period of years has also been investigated. Research seems to indicate that changes in mental ability may occur through the preschool period and in later childhood (Honzik, Mcfarlane, and Allen 1948). During their early years individual children seem to show differences in their intellectual growth patterns, with both spurts and plateaus. Boys and girls also seem to exhibit different courses of cognitive development. Further, individuals show marked differences in various mental abilities.

Why is there such variation in intellectual and cognitive development? Again, heredity and environment play a major role, but the rate of brain maturation is also a factor. IQ scores vary widely during early childhood because the tertiary parietal area of the brain matures at different rates in different children (see chap. 3). When we consider the wide variations in brain maturation, heredity and environment, and intellectual abilities, it is little wonder that we are as unique and different from one another as snowflakes.

Psychological Testing

There are a number of tests that psychologists use to better understand people. In chapter 11 we will consider personality testing, which is used by many counselors to assess counselees. This chapter will concentrate upon intelligence and ability tests, although many of our introductory comments can apply to other kinds of tests as well.

Basically, the purpose of psychological testing is to measure differences among individuals or among the reactions of the same individual to different situations. Historically, the first problem to prompt the use of such tests was detection of intellectual deficiency for school placement. Psychological tests are now used not only

---

Spotlight 8.1.
IQ Testing in the Church?

A teacher has a particular child in both her church school class and in her classroom at school. The child's school records indicate that he has a low IQ and thus cannot be expected to learn much in Sunday school. Another Sunday school teacher suggests that it might be a good idea to give all of the youngsters in her class an IQ test to find out how intelligent they are.

Since IQ is not a good measure of overall intelligence, the child in the first situation might be highly talented in the skills required in Sunday school. In fact, he might even do quite well because of greater knowledge of biblical content. There might be a danger, however, that the teacher's low expectations (from seeing the student's record) could adversely affect his performance in both Sunday school and his regular classroom.

Giving IQ tests is not appropriate for Sunday schools. While school grades may be predicted from IQ scores, there is no evidence that performance in Sunday school is correlated with IQ. On the other hand, a test has been developed to measure the religious concepts of children (Peatling 1973). The considerable research behind this instrument indicates that it may possibly be useful in evaluating children's concepts about the Bible.

to predict the probability of success in many situations but also to determine educational or therapeutic experiences for remediation of problems. Tests are also an important research tool for refining our concepts of how people function.

A psychological test is intended to be an objective, standardized measure of a sample of behavior. Observations are made on a small but carefully delineated sample of an individual's behavior. The diagnostic or predictive value of a test depends on the degree to which it serves as an indicator of a relatively broad, significant area of human behavior. A good test does that even if the test items do not resemble closely the behavior the test is to predict.

The predictive power of a psychological test is related to a number of factors. Validity refers to the extent to which an instrument (i.e., the test) actually measures what it is intended to measure. A test of ability to multiply should predict success in multiplication. Reliability refers to the degree to which people obtain the same relative scores each time they are measured. Reliability is usually determined by having individuals retake the same test. Although a test cannot be valid unless it is reliable, re-

liability does not guarantee validity. Objectivity refers to the degree to which different persons scoring the test obtain the same results using the same scoring methods. Standardization refers to administration of the same test under the same conditions to a large group of persons representative of the groups for which the test is intended. The standardization procedure yields "norms" (standards), so that any individual's score can be compared with the scores of a defined group. Tests should always be administered to all subjects under the same conditions.

It is reasonable to expect that people who develop psychological tests have followed accepted procedures in standardizing their tests. Those who use such tests, however, should thoroughly familiarize themselves with any test to be sure it measures what they want it to measure, regardless of the claims made for it. Psychological tests are reviewed periodically in the *Mental Measurements Yearbook* (1985).

The intelligence test is probably the most common testing instrument associated with psychology. The intellectual ability of human beings—the ability to use

Performance tests as well as verbal tests help to evaluate intelligence.

VERBAL

General Information
What day of the year is Independence Day?

Similarities
In what way are *wool* and *cotton* alike?

Arithmetic Reasoning
If eggs cost 60 cents a dozen, what does 1 egg cost?

Vocabulary
Tell me the meaning of corrupt.

Comprehension
Why do people buy fire insurance?

Digit Span
Listen carefully, and when I am through, say the numbers right after me.

7   3   4   1   8   6

Now I am going to say some more numbers, but I want you to say them backward.

3   8   4   1   6

PERFORMANCE

Picture Completion
I am going to show you a picture with an important part missing. Tell me what is missing.

'85

SUN	MON	TUE	WED	THU	FRI	SAT
1	2	3	4	5	6	7
8	9	10	11	12	13	14
15	16	17	18	19	20	21
22	23	24	25	26	27	28
29	30					

Fig. 8.1. Sample items from Wechsler Adult Intelligence Scale (WAIS) subtests.

reason—is one of the things that differentiates us from other creatures.

In 1905, Alfred Binet, a French psychologist, developed a measure of intelligence for the minister of public instruction in France. Binet and a colleague, Theodore Simon, developed a test that would reflect judgment and reasoning ability rather than mere rote memory. Binet expressed his results with reference to the age at which normal children could accomplish the tasks. That age was identified as the mental age of the child. Thus a child who completed the tasks for a five-year-old was said to have a mental age of five regardless of chronological age.

Picture Arrangement

The pictures below tell a story. Put them in the right order to tell the story.

Block Design

Using the four blocks, make one just like this.

Object Assembly

If these pieces are put together correctly, they will make something. Go ahead and put them together as quickly as you can.

Digit-Symbol Substitution

Code

△	○	⟋	✕	8
1	2	3	4	5

Test

△	8	✕	○	△	⟋	8	✕	△	8

Adapted from David G. Myers, *Psychology*, 2d ed. (New York: Worth, 1989), p. 321.

The Binet test was later revised and standardized by Lewis M. Terman of Stanford University. That test is today called the Stanford–Binet Test and is used as a standard measure of intelligence in children. Terman expresses the relationship between mental age (MA) and chronological age (CA) as a ratio. That ratio, called the intelligence quotient (IQ), is computed as follows:

$$IQ = \frac{MA}{CA} \times 100$$

The Wechsler Adult Intelligence Scale (see fig. 8.1) and the Wechsler Intelligence Scale for Children are other commonly used intelligence tests. They are administered individually and combine verbal and performance tests. The verbal tests require abstract verbal reasoning (Example: "In what way are a ball and a balloon alike?" Answer: "They are both round"). The performance tests require abstract motor reasoning and reaction (such as the assembly of a block design or puzzle).

Group intelligence tests combined with achievement tests have also been developed to permit more rapid testing of a larger group. The disadvantages are that an individual in a group testing situation may suffer from anxiety or depersonalization. Most school systems presently use some form of group testing such as the Otis–Lennon Mental Ability Test or the Metropolitan Achievement Test for class placement of students.

It should be noted that IQ tests only measure certain aspects of intelligence, not general intelligence (if such an entity even exists). Thus it would be inaccurate to conclude that a person with an IQ of 110 is necessarily smarter than a person with an IQ of 100. Not only do scores randomly vary by as much as five points or more for the same person, but also the testing situation, the personality of the tester, and the mood or attitude of the person being tested can affect the results. In addition, significant knowledge and ability may be completely overlooked. Cultural and ethnic minorities often receive lower

---

Spotlight 8.2.
Christianity and Intelligence

A note of caution must be sounded about placing undue emphasis on IQ scores. Our culture places a premium on intelligence. Children and adults with high IQs are often given privileged places in school and society. Yet from a Christian perspective there are matters much more important than intelligence, such as morality and a right relationship with God. Certainly intelligence is fine as long as it is not elevated to supreme importance in life.

Christians should also be aware of the danger of pride. Frequently, individuals with high IQs tend to be prideful. Intelligence is a complex entity, and intellectual ability is undoubtedly influenced by both inherited traits and environmental influences. Although some persons are born with a greater intellectual capacity than others, early childhood stimulation and opportunities for cultural development (schools, modeling, and verbal interaction) can also influence the development of measurable intellectual capacity. Christians who have a high IQ should avoid pride and humbly acknowledge a greater responsibility to use their intelligence to God's glory. Christians with an average IQ should not feel second-class or cheated, but should take advantage of all alternatives to utilize their abilities to God's glory. God recognizes no difference between rich or poor, smart or mentally handicapped, since all Christians are his children through faith in Jesus Christ (Gal. 3:26–28).

Collins (1985, 128–29) reminds us that intelligence is always relative to an absolute standard—that absolute being God. The most intelligent of us does not begin to approximate God's intelligence!

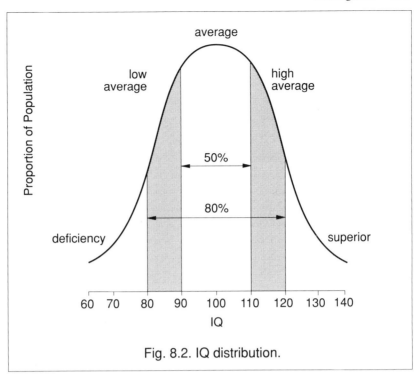

Fig. 8.2. IQ distribution.

IQ scores, while middle-class white Americans tend to get higher scores.

Because of the built-in bias of tests, some have called for the wholesale elimination of intelligence testing. This position might be justified if the purpose of such testing is to assess global intelligence; any test can only examine selected aspects of ability and knowledge. However, most school psychologists use intelligence tests for one of two reasons: to project future grades in school or to identify mental retardation. While intelligence tests have been helpful in making placement decisions, they are generally inadequate for evaluating intelligence in a comprehensive manner.

Mental Retardation

Mental retardation was referred to in ancient religious and medical writings less extensively than the purely psychological disorders, but like them was attributed to various causes. Some writers considered it a natural phenomenon, others a manifestation of demonic forces. Until the time of English philosopher and physician John Locke (1632–1704), mental retardation was usually considered a form of insanity. From the eighteenth century on it has been viewed as a separate entity, though it was treated by society in much the same manner as insanity until the twentieth century. A radical change in views of mental retardation was brought about by the study of genetic principles. However, only 5 percent of the cases have known hereditary factors. In 30 to 40 percent of cases, the specific cause remains unknown (DSM III-R 1987, 30).

Mental retardation is a condition in which below-normal general intellectual functioning begins before age eighteen and is associated with impairment in adaptive behavior. One percent of the general population is mentally retarded. General intellectual functioning is properly assessed by determining IQ with a standard intelligence test such as the Stanford-Binet

---

Spotlight 8.3. Bill

After Bill, a mildly retarded man, became a Christian, he asked if he could attend a church in the nearby community. The church was called and they said they would send a bus to the developmental center where Bill lived the next Sunday. Unfortunately, the staff at the center was not informed; as a result the bus had to wait for Bill to finish getting ready. When the bus arrived late at the church, everyone blamed Bill for the delay. Bill sensed their rejection and demanded to be taken back to the developmental center even before the church service began. He was taken back, and the church let it be known that the retarded were no longer welcome there.

While it is easy to be critical of the church in this situation, there is a deeper issue involved. A church that is genuinely interested in helping the retarded needs to prepare itself before taking on such a ministry. It is not enough to let the retarded join the current program; they require special attention and provision (see spotlight 8.4).

Intelligence Scale or the Wechsler Intelligence Scale for Children. Adaptive behavior is assessed by clinical observation of the individual's effectiveness in achieving personal independence and social responsibility appropriate for that individual's age and cultural group.

Causes

Some of the causes of mental retardation are definitely biological, but psychosocial factors can also play a role. Certain causes can be determined by a physician before a child reaches the age of two. For example, a routine test for phenylalanine (an amino acid essential to the human diet) in every infant's urine is required in most states to check for possible phenylketonuria (PKU), an enzyme deficiency that leads to mental retardation if not treated with a special diet beginning in infancy.

Certain disorders of fat and carbohydrate metabolism also lead to mental retardation. Down's syndrome (mongolism) is one of many genetic problems associated with mental retardation that can be recognized by a skilled physician at the time of birth.

Psychiatric disorders, ranging from aggressive behavior to schizophrenia, are three to four times more frequent in mentally retarded individuals than in the general population. Although not every mentally retarded individual has an emotional disorder, the lower the intelligence the greater the chance of an accompanying emotional disorder. Depending on the specific etiology, mentally retarded individuals often have seizures or problems with vision, hearing, or motor functions.

Much is being learned about prenatal factors, such as the mother's nutrition, that affect the development of a baby's central nervous system. Alcohol consumption during pregnancy can produce fetal alcohol syndrome, a condition manifested by retarded growth, mental retardation, and head, face, and limb deformities.

Because the majority of mentally retarded individuals are only mildly retarded, diagnosis is seldom made until children enter school. Many cases of mental retardation develop as a direct result of psychosocial deprivation. Lack of love and intellectual stimulation, malnutrition, physical abuse, and social isolation in

Table 8.1
Levels of Moral Development

Level	IQ	Mental Age (Yrs.)	Moral Stage
Mild	50–55 to 70	5–10	about 1 or 2
Moderate	35–40 to 50–55	3–5	0–1
Severe	20–25 to 35–40	2–3	0
Profound	Below 20–25	below 2	0

early life are all believed to be factors that can lead to mental retardation.

Classification

Psychologists classify the mentally retarded according to level of intelligence assessed from intelligence tests. DSM III-R (1987, 32–33) recognizes four categories: mildly retarded, moderately retarded, severely retarded, and profoundly retarded. Ratcliff (1985, 1987) has identified the levels of moral development (using Kohlberg's stages; see chap. 9) of retarded adults in each of these categories, summarized by level of retardation and approximate mental age (see tab. 8.1).

Mental retardation is more commonly found in males (1.5 males to every female), and more individuals are found at the higher level of intelligence (85 percent are mildly retarded; 10 percent are moderately retarded; 3 to 4 percent are severely retarded; 1 to 2 percent are profoundly retarded) (DSM III-R 1987, 32–33). In addition, DSM III-R also proposes a category of intelligence termed "borderline intellectual functioning," which includes people who have IQs between 71 and 84 (DSM III-R, 359–60). These individuals are not considered retarded.

Stigma and Placement

Over the years many retarded individuals have been stigmatized. Jobs have been denied to those willing and able to work on the basis of the label "retarded." Not long ago, institutionalization of the re- tarded was routine. With increased public awareness of the deplorable conditions of many such institutions, many retarded people have been transferred to group homes or private homes, or even discharged. While this has often had positive consequences, in many cases those who are discharged have joined the ranks of the homeless. On the other hand, those who remain in institutions may suffer from neglect and abuse by those who "care" for them, while being shunned by outsiders.

Thus far family placement and group homes have the best track record for helping the retarded, although some of these are deficient as well. New training methods, based upon the principles of learning (see chap. 4), have been used with the retarded with considerable success. Basic self-care, social, and job skills have been learned through shaping and reinforcement. While such skills do not constitute a "cure" for retardation, retarded individuals can often reach higher levels of adjustment than was once thought possible.

There is a genuine ministry available for those who wish to help the retarded. Whatever is done for the least of the brothers is done for Jesus (Matt. 25:40). There are opportunities for both companionship and Christian witness. Such activities produce definite benefits for the caregiver. Koop and Schaeffer (1983, 30) note that care for the disabled can produce "stronger character, compassion, deeper

Spotlight 8.4. Ministering to the Retarded

What specific guidelines are needed to minister to the mentally retarded? Can they be saved? Is reaching the retarded compatible with church growth?

Tasks must be simplified and powerfully reinforced for learning to occur. Shaping, chaining, and reinforcement (see chap. 4) are necessary in teaching the retarded. It is important not to talk down to retarded individuals, as they may perceive the speaker's condescending attitude. It is possible to simplify the cognitive content of material to comport with mental age, yet keep the form adult (for example, using adult figures in teaching Bible stories with the flannelgraph). Other suggestions for teaching the retarded are available (Ratcliff 1985).

The issue of salvation may depend upon the mental level of the retarded. If elementary school children can be won to the Lord, so may mildly retarded adults. On the other hand, the moderately retarded are less likely to have the cognitive capacity to understand salvation, as is often the case with normal preschoolers. The severely and profoundly retarded are even more doubtful candidates for evangelistic efforts.

Often the retarded and their families feel excluded by churches, and may avoid attendance. If the most conservative estimate of the number of retarded is considered, this would mean that one hundred retarded individuals live in a community of ten thousand. Add their families and this would total three to five hundred potentially reachable people. Not only is church growth compatible with ministry for the retarded, it can itself be a means to church growth.

---

understanding of another's burden, creativity, and deeper family bonds."

Several contexts for helping can be identified, including visiting the retarded in institutions, providing special Sunday school classes either in church or at the facility where the retarded live, and even developing live-in facilities (usually for mildly retarded individuals). Retarded individuals who are on the streets need help meeting physical and material needs, as well as training in self-care, which government agencies may fail to provide.

The intelligence deficiency in retardation must by definition be noted before the age of eighteen. What, then, is the diagnostic category of the person whose IQ decreases after age eighteen? If the decrease is significant and not just the result of random error, it is assumed to be due to some kind of brain damage or deterioration. The most likely diagnostic category would be "dementia." It is also possible for someone under age eighteen to have dementia (for example, a fifteen-year-old who is of normal intelligence prior to a major accident, but who meets the criteria of retardation afterward). Alzheimer's disease is one form of dementia.

Giftedness

We would be remiss in emphasizing deficiencies in intelligence without at least briefly looking at the other extreme in intelligence. Perhaps 3 to 5 percent of children are "gifted," with IQs near the top end of the scale. Often these individuals have been forced to stay with their peers, which results in boredom, frustration, and even failure.

Traditionally such children have sometimes been allowed to skip one or more grades because of their accelerated pace of learning. Yet these children can have social difficulties as a result; advancement in

Spotlight 8.5. Helping the Families of the Retarded

Christians have the opportunity to help both the retarded and their families (Ratcliff 1990). For example, it is often difficult, if not impossible, to obtain babysitters for the retarded (particularly for retarded adults). Because of this parents may never get a break from the family routine. Some retarded persons require extensive care and church members can show Christian love by volunteering to help.

Consider the plight of one mother with a retarded ten-year-old daughter (Dear Abby 1988):

> Maria is physically abusive. Babysitters quit after one day. If I try to get her to do something she doesn't want to do, it turns into a wrestling match. Abby, I love her. She is my child, but I can't understand why God did this to me. I used to go to church, but I can't take Maria, and no one will stay with her. . . . If I ever kill myself I will take Maria with me. She has already suffered enough on this earth. . . . I love her, Abby, but caring for her is killing me.

How badly this mother needs Christian help!

It is useful to understand the stages that parents of a retarded child customarily go through (Wolfensburger 1967). First, there is the awareness of some kind of problem. At this stage parents try to find some physical cause. As they begin to get professional help, the suggestion of retardation will be made which the parents will initially deny (the second stage). Often they go from specialist to specialist trying to find some diagnosis other than retardation.

A third stage is when parents recognize that their child is actually retarded. This recognition is usually accompanied by shock, grief, and withdrawal. Parents may blame themselves at this time. At this stage it is important for others to listen to the parents and explain that retardation should not be confused with insanity.

The search for a cause predominates in the fourth stage. This search is actually the parents' attempt to relieve themselves of guilt and self-blame. Parents often recall minor accidents from the past that are easily forgotten with a normal child. Sometimes at this stage they see mental retardation as a punishment from God for past wrongdoing. Most of the time the cause is not found, but even if it is this does not help the parents cope. What helps most is for them to meet other families of retarded people for mutual support.

The fifth stage is a search for a cure, again prompting parents to go from specialist to specialist. They need to realize that the mentally retarded can be trained and given skills, but not cured. The sixth and final stage is acceptance, which few parents achieve. Ideally the parents come to be proud of their child's assets and learn to accept weaknesses. Parents who are well adjusted in other areas are most likely to accept thier retarded child. Parents with low IQs tend to accept a retarded child more easily, perhaps because they are less likely to have high expectations. There is also evidence that those who are very religious are more likely to accept their retarded child.

Those who try to help the parents of the retarded need to realize that parents will tend to reject any statement that is inconsistent with their current stage, even distorting what is said to fit the present stage. There is also the tendency for parents to make the child a permanent infant.

Other problem areas include lack of finances, interference with social activities, unrealistic goals, and disintegration of the marriage.* Clearly the church can help families with these problems.

*See Schild 1976; Ratcliff 1990, for additional discussion on the problems of families of the retarded.

social skills and maturity does not automatically accompany academic promotion. Some schools have provided special classrooms for these children, often emphasizing creativity and individuality. Such isolation from the mainstream of students, however, can create a stigma of its own. Separate classes can also deprive average students of the stimulating presence of more gifted children. Admittedly there is no easy answer to the dilemma of what is best for the gifted, but it seems a shame to not take greater advantage of these talented students.

Of course the term "gifted" can have a second meaning as well. Myers and Jeeves (1987, 106–7) have noted that the Christian concept of giftedness refers to the specific place each believer has in the body of Christ. Every Christian is gifted in this sense. Paul identifies a number of gifts in his letters, such as teaching, administration, discernment, pastoring, service, and prophecy.

There is overlap between the two meanings of "gifted," however. Spiritual gifts imply an excellence that each Christian has and may develop further, yet the presence of specific gifts acknowledges the fact that not everyone has the same gifts. As Myers and Jeeves note, excellence requires different priorities for different people. Yet the goal in the body of Christ, the church, is the exercise of the various gifts in harmony and with excellence. Absolute equality in giftedness is not implied in Scripture, and it is incumbent upon us all to encourage the use of spiritual gifts and not resent those who have different gifts. We are all gifted, even if that giftedness is not an intellectual giftedness!

References

Bouchard, T., and M. McGue. 1981. Familial studies of intelligence. *Science* 212: 1055–59.

Buros, O. 1985. *Mental measurements yearbook.* 9th ed. Lincoln: University of Nebraska Press.

Carroll, J. 1976. Psychometric tests as cognitive tests. In *The nature of intelligence*, ed. L. Resnick. Hillsdale, N.J.: Erlbaum.

Cattell, R. 1968. Are IQ tests intelligent? *Psychology Today* 1: 56–62.

Collins, G. 1985. *The magnificent mind.* Waco: Word.

Dear Abby. 1988. *Atlanta Journal* (Nov. 26): 4C.

Diagnostic and statistical manual of mental disorders. 3d rev. ed. 1987. Washington, D.C.: American Psychiatric Association.

Dobson, J. 1976. The origins of intelligence. In *The mentally retarded child and his family*, eds. R. Koch and J. Dobson. Rev. ed. New York: Brunner/Mazel.

Goddard, H. 1912. *The Kallikak family.* New York: Macmillan.

Griffin, D. 1976. *The question of animal awareness.* New York: Rockefeller University Press.

Guilford, J. 1973. Theories of intelligence. In *Handbook of general psychology*, ed. B. Wolman. Englewood Cliffs, N.J.: Prentice-Hall.

Honzik, M., J. Macfarlane, and L. Allen. 1948. The stability of mental test performance. *Journal of Experimental Education* 17: 309–24.

Koop, C., and F. Schaeffer. 1983. *Whatever happened to the human race?* 2d ed. Westchester, Ill.: Crossway.

Myers, D., and M. Jeeves. 1987. *Psychology through eyes of faith.* San Francisco: Harper and Row.

Peatling, J. 1973. *The incidence of concrete and abstract religious thinking.* Ann Arbor, Mich.: University Microfilms.

Ratcliff, D. 1980. Toward a Christian perspective of developmental disability. *Journal of Psychology and Theology* 8: 328–35.

———. 1985. Ministering to the retarded. *Christian Education Journal* 6: 24–30.

———. 1987. Predicting the moral development of the mentally retarded. *Journal of Psychology and Christianity* 6: 65–67.

————. 1990. Counseling families of the mentally retarded. *Journal of Psychology and Theology* 18: 318–25.

Rowe, D., and R. Plomin. 1978. The Burt controversy. *Behavior Genetics* 8: 81–84.

Schild, S. 1976. The family of the retarded child. In *The mentally retarded child and his family,* eds. R. Koch and J. Dobson. Rev. ed. New York: Brunner/Mazel.

Skeels, H. 1966. Adult status of children with contrasting life experiences. *Monographs of the Society for Research in Child Development* 31.

Sternberg, R. 1984. Mechanisms of cognitive development. In *Mechanisms of cognitive development,* ed. R. Sternberg. New York: Freeman.

Sternberg, R., et al. 1981. People's conceptions of intelligence. *Journal of Personality and Social Psychology* 41: 37–55.

Wolfensburger, W. 1967. Counseling the parents of the retarded. In *Mental retardation,* ed. A. Baumeister. Chicago: Aldine.

Social Psychology

Social psychology is concerned with social influences upon the individual. Because it emphasizes the individual, it qualifies as psychology, yet because of its focus on the social situation it has much in common with sociology. Thus the general area where sociology and psychology overlap is called social psychology, although the topic involves far more than simply trying to find common ground between the two disciplines.

In his excellent introduction to social psychology, Myers (1987) has identified three areas of consideration in social psychology: the way people think about one another, how they influence one another, and how they relate to each other. These three topics comprise the content of the present chapter.

Attitudes

Social psychologists are concerned not only with the formation of attitudes but also with how attitudes can be influenced and changed. An attitude is made up of thought, feeling, and a predisposition to act upon that thought and feeling. Sheer thought is the basis of an opinion. While thought and feeling may technically make up an attitude, a third factor, behavior, is likely to result.

The credibility of the person attempting to change attitudes is an important factor in determining success. The perceived intentions of the communicator are especially important. If intentions are seen as positive, influence will tend to be greater.

Some have debated whether one- or two-sided presentations are the most effective. Is it better to just present one side of an issue or to give both sides? Research to date indicates that the one-sided approach is more effective if the audience is unintelligent, authoritarian, or already in agreement with the stated position. Generally, however, the two-sided approach works better because the presenter sounds more objective. The latter is particularly effective if the audience disagrees with the speaker or is likely to hear another side eventually (Jones and Brehm 1970).

To illustrate, you may have noticed that some advertisers have begun to say something like, "This may not be for everyone, but it sure works for me." This approach is more likely to work with more intelligent people who are not authoritarian and are not completely convinced of the product's value. This would tend to increase the attractiveness of the product with such people.

Cognitive Dissonance

Cognitive dissonance is an inner tension resulting from the attempt to hold two contrasting thoughts at the same time (Festinger 1957). One of those thoughts may result from behavior. Therefore, if an attitude contradicts action, dissonance results. When dissonance occurs, the individual tries to relieve that tension by changing opinions, changing actions, or adding new ideas to thinking. Any of these will tend to nullify the cognitive dissonance and reduce tension over the issue.

Festinger demonstrated this concept by having people perform an extremely boring task (turning knobs a quarter-turn on a board). He then asked each participant to convince another person, supposedly waiting to take part in the experiment, that it was an interesting task. At this point he offered either one or twenty dollars to the participant for convincing the other person the task would be interesting. Afterward he evaluated those who were paid to see whether they had enjoyed the knob-turning task.

While behavioral psychology might suggest that the bigger reward would produce the greatest change, just the opposite occurred. Those who received one dollar for lying were the most positive about the boring task while those who received twenty

dollars changed the least in their attitudes. Festinger concluded that the results were best explained by noting the dissonance between the task and what was told to the waiting person. When participants were paid twenty dollars there was not as much dissonance or tension between the genuine view that the task was boring and telling the other person it was interesting because they could rationalize that the lie was worth twenty dollars. On the other hand, those who only got one dollar did not have much justification for the lie, and thus changed their attitude from boredom to some degree of liking in order to relieve the dissonance.

Dissonance is a part of daily life. Consider the young woman who needs to decide which of two men she wants to marry. If both men have an equal number of good qualities and an equal number of deficits, she will have what psychologists call an "approach-avoidance conflict." This is because two contradictory opinions are held at the same time. She will probably make a decision, and then feel dissonance because of the positive qualities of the man she did not choose. To relieve dissonance, she will probably come up with additional reasons for making her choice, such as accentuating the positive qualities of the man she chose and emphasizing the negative qualities of the man she rejected. New information is sought (or perhaps self-generated) to convince herself that she made the right decision.

Self-Fulfilling Prophecy

Simply expecting something to occur in our relations with others makes the expected more likely to happen. We are also more likely to see evidence for what we expect.

When we interact socially, we often go through a process of labeling. We may consider other people to be rigid, relaxed,

Spotlight 9.1.
Applying Dissonance Research

Cognitive dissonance theory can be used to understand church members better. Consider Frank, who is firmly convinced that he is a Christian yet gives little evidence of this fact in his life. Furthermore, he is unable to recall a point in time when he made a decision to become a Christian.

At one time Frank may have felt dissonance due to the conflict between what the Bible requires and his lifestyle. He has probably convinced himself he is a Christian by *saying* he is a Christian. He probably has added new ideas to silence any doubts he might have about his salvation, so that dissonance will be minimized. For example, he might agree with the pastor's statement that a person needs salvation, yet not see how this fact affects him.

Could dissonance theory be used to influence Frank to accept the gospel? Perhaps the best approach would be to create dissonance requiring small amounts of change in behavior, since modification of opinion is more likely that way. Direct confrontation and condemnation may not be the best way to help Frank see his error.

Perhaps the best answer would be to emphasize the need to change one's ways as a Christian and to specifically detail what the differences are between the Christian's behavior and the non-Christian's behavior. These obvious statements are likely to arouse some dissonance, as Frank sees the difference between the views presented and his own behavior. He may choose to relieve dissonance by changing his behavior, by ignoring the advice, or perhaps even by leaving the church. This is his choice, but the possibility of a negative response should not discourage an attempt to help him.

indifferent, or lazy, and as a result of our expectations they are likely to become just that. The other person in the interaction is likely to fulfill the prophecy (expectation). If a number of people label an individual in the same way over an extended period of time, this is likely to influence the self-concept and behavior of that person.

Social Influence

Whether we like it or not, we influence others and, in turn, are influenced by them. Americans, highly individualistic, often overlook the powerful influences of others; in contrast, cultures that are very group-oriented are more likely to affirm the power of the group. The Bible clearly gives social influence proper credit. Repeatedly in the Old Testament believers are told to avoid the evil influences of the world, yet influence others to enter the kingdom of God.

Conformity

Asch (1951) undertook a series of experiments to investigate the effects of group pressure. A subject entered a room with six other people, presumably fellow participants in the research project. The group was told that the subject of the study was perception. Group members were instructed to compare three lines drawn on a card with a line drawn on another card. Then each person was asked which of the

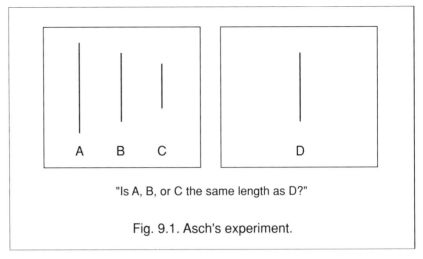

"Is A, B, or C the same length as D?"

Fig. 9.1. Asch's experiment.

three lines was the same length as the line on the second card.

While one of the three lines was clearly the same length as the line on the second card, six people in the group gave the wrong answer (they had been previously told to do so, without the seventh person's knowledge). Would the seventh person agree with the others, or give the correct answer?

About one-third of naive individuals conformed to the other six. If the task was given seven different times, 80 percent conformed at least once. With additional experiments it was found that if the decision of the seventh subject was anonymous or if at least one other person gave the right answer, there was far less conformity on the part of the seventh person.

The Putneys (1964, 1–12) describe conformity as a form of normal neurosis, a psychological problem that is socially acceptable. They point out that the costs are very high for not conforming while the rewards are often slim; thus people tend not to question the assumptions of their culture. The Putneys emphasize that Americans believe "adjustment" is the highest ideal—merely another word for conformity. While such neurosis is socially acceptable, the Putneys call for living above conformity by expressing our true feelings rather than staying at a superficial level of communication.

Groupthink

Social influence is also manifest in a phenomenon called groupthink, an extreme concern within a group that everyone reach full agreement. As a result the group fails to evaluate ideas adequately because of the desire for agreement. This is most likely to occur in groups that are closely knit, where members feel the group cannot make a mistake, and when group members place too much confidence in leaders. The sense of agreement is only an illusion, however, because ideas are never really evaluated; no one openly disagrees, and agreement is based upon lack of complete analysis.

For example, one of the authors once attended a small country church where the congregation was evaluating a pastoral candidate. A congregational meeting was called to discuss the candidate. The meeting opened with a strong call for unity from one of the elders. In this "family church," one of the oldest members, related to nearly everyone, voiced his approval of the candidate (in spite of rather questionable credentials). The vote was unanimous. Unfortunately, the negative effects of the groupthink decision became apparent when the new pastor preached an explicitly detailed series of sermons on sexual perversions.

Janis (1982) suggests several ways to discourage groupthink. First, leaders need to encourage discussion and be reluctant to give their own opinions. Second, the group may want to occasionally split into subgroups to discuss problems. Third, reviewing decisions and considering new information should be included on the agenda of some meetings. Fourth, outsiders should be asked to give their views on topics. Finally, members of the group should be encouraged to take different positions on topics and examine alternatives carefully.

Inoculation

Just as a vaccine, composed of a weakened form of a virus, can render a person physically immune to the full-strength virus, so too a person can be given a weakened form of an idea and be encouraged to formulate a strong refutation of that same point of view (McGuire 1964). Inoculation is basically a variation of the two-sided approach mentioned earlier, the distinction being that the two sides are not given equal time and the person to be convinced does the refutation.

There is evidence that inoculation can influence opinions significantly. Batson (1975), for example, made a presentation in which the beliefs of Christian teen-agers were attacked; because of their reaction the teens developed stronger beliefs.

Young people could be convinced not to consume alcoholic beverages using inoculation techniques. First, a weakened case for drinking could be presented (it is enjoyable, at least for awhile). The teen-agers could then be asked to make a strong case against it (you may become an alcoholic; it is expensive; it dulls the senses; it tastes bad; it can produce birth defects and brain damage, etc.). As a result, the young people will be less likely to drink and more likely to resist those who promote it. This, of course, assumes that the arguments against drinking are genuine and the case for drinking is not so weak that there is no real case at all (what is sometimes called a "straw man").

Spotlight 9.2.
Conformity in Evangelism

Many evangelists ask people to indicate their desire to become Christians by raising their hands during the invitation. Judging from Asch's research, if the evangelist wants to avoid conformity and obtain genuine decisions, probably the public raising of hands should be avoided. People conform less if responses are anonymous; thus having the audience close their eyes before a show of hands would be more appropriate.

Billy Graham has been criticized for having his counselors come forward at the invitation. Does this add to the conformity factor by prompting people to "follow the flow" of those going forward? Yet we can just as easily make the opposite argument: people will stay in their seats if most people are doing so. Thus having counselors go forward at the invitation actually reduces conformity and makes the option of responding to the invitation a genuine alternative.

Spotlight 9.3.
Inoculation, Fear, and Christianity

Francis Schaeffer encouraged Christians to teach their children secular philosophy early in life. He felt that this would prepare them to deal with secular viewpoints later in life. This is quite consistent with inoculation theory. Early presentations of secular philosophy would probably not involve a rigorous study of the field, but a more popular level of study (like Schaeffer's own writing). As a result of teaching children in this manner, they would perhaps be more likely to reject anti-Christian philosophy because of the strong refutation they could give in response to the weakened criticism. (Note that inoculation is most likely to occur if the student makes the refutation.)

Inoculation could also be used in evangelistic presentations. One could make a weak case for not becoming a Christian, and then have members of the congregation give a strong case for becoming a Christian.

The idea of inoculation has much in common with the two-sided versus one-sided approaches to making presentations. In many situations, Christians need to begin using more two-sided approaches. A two-sided approach to the gospel may result in more converts to the faith.

What role should fear have in evangelistic presentations? For example, is preaching about hell the best way to convince people to become Christians? Probably not unless the audience sees hell as a real possibility. Even then, vivid sermons on eternal judgment will probably cause most non-Christians to reject the church and the message of salvation. A positive approach would probably be more effective. In fact, nearly all references by Christ to the subject of judgment were in the context of speaking to the religious leaders and his disciples; fear was not used when attempting to evangelize.

Other Methods of Influence

Is the use of fear a good way to influence people? Fear seems to be effective only if the feared consequences are perceived as realistic by the listeners; there is enough fear to make them concerned; and the fear is not so intense that listeners avoid the issue. Mild, realistic threats seem to be the most effective (Aronson and Carlsmith 1963). Otherwise, other methods of persuasion appear to be more effective. Fear involves compliance. Compliance is when an individual does what is desired because of the possibility of obtaining a reward or avoiding punishment.

Using heaven as a reward or hell as a punishment in evangelism would be an example of this method.

A second method of influence is identification. Here the influencer is a model. Youth leaders who use the terminology and adopt the dress of young people exemplify this kind of influence.

A third method, and the method that is usually the most permanent and effective, is that of internalization. Here the credibility of the influencer is most important; influence occurs because the person is a trustworthy expert. The knowledgeable pastor who knows the Bible thoroughly and is able to apply it practically would be an example of this kind of influence.

Power and Obedience

In order to study the effects of power on obedience to an authority, Milgram (1974) told experimental subjects that they were participating in a study of learning using a shocking device. The supposed point of the research was to see if learning would be more likely as a result of receiving punishment. Each learner was supposedly given a shock by the participant whenever a response was incorrect. The strength of the shock could supposedly be increased from 15 volts to 450 volts.

Actually the "learner" was a trained actor who did not receive any shock at all. He merely *pretended* to receive shock, complaining that it hurt at lower voltages, screaming at 270 volts, later pounding on the wall, and finally not responding at all near the highest voltages. The question being studied obviously had nothing to do with learning, but rather with how long the subject supposedly administering the

shocks would continue doing so. If the subject protested, the researcher emphasized repeatedly that the experiment had to continue.

About 65 percent of participants completed the experiment all the way to the highest voltages. Sometimes they became very emotional in the process, crying and laughing. But they would still continue to "administer" shocks.

The fact that people could hurt and possibly even kill someone else for simply making some mistakes on an academic task underscores something of the darker side of human nature. This may offer an explanation for the cruelty in the German concentration camps during World War II: those who were cruel were responding to intense pressure from authority. What is most frightening is that it appears that the majority of people would participate in senseless murder, given the right circumstances.

People have a potential for evil that needs to be transformed by Christ. While many of the participants did not see them-

---

Spotlight 9.4. Credibility and Methods of Influence

Credibility is an important factor in influencing people. In recent years several television evangelists have lost credibility because of immoral behavior and/or excessive lifestyles. Specifically the credibility of religious communicators has been thrown open to question; if listeners see a preacher wanting to line his pockets with money, his appeals for money are likely to be ineffective.

When it comes to influencing people, compliance, identification, and internalization are not mutually exclusive (Griffin 1982, 180). Often a combination of two or all three methods of influence work within a group, or one can move from one method to another. While internalization is most likely to produce lasting change, one can make use of one or both of the other two methods to effect internalization. For example, offering Sunday dinner or free books to get college students to attend church (as one suburban Chicago church does) might work provided internalization is fostered through the church service and Sunday school once they get there.

selves as evil, clearly what they thought they were doing was inhuman and brutal. When pressured to take part in evil, it is the unusual person who can stand apart from the crowd and say "no." We must not "follow the crowd in doing wrong" (Exod. 23:2).

Altruism

We sometimes read newspaper accounts of unprovoked murder in public; bystanders do not even call the police for help. How can this be? In contrast, Jesus describes the Good Samaritan (Luke 10:30–35), who not only took notice of but even went to considerable expense to help the man who was robbed, beaten, and left for dead.

What causes people to be altruistic, to help others in need? Darley and Batson (1973) conducted an experiment they entitled "From Jerusalem to Jericho" (taken from Jesus' parable) at a prominent theo-logical seminary. The students were told to give a brief talk in a nearby building. On their way they passed a man groaning and coughing, lying face-down on the floor. When the theological students were told (prior to going to the nearby building) that they were late, only 10 percent stopped to help the man. Even students who planned to speak on the Good Samaritan parable failed to stop and help! In contrast, when students were told they had plenty of time, nearly two-thirds attempted to assist the man. Perhaps the problem the priest and Levite had in the parable was that they were in too much of a hurry!

The original experiment took place at Princeton Theological Seminary; it was then repeated at Wheaton College (Radant et al. 1985). This time a jogger, moaning and holding his ankle, was encountered. Students who were told that their destination was not very important and that they

---

Spotlight 9.5. Christian Sources on Social Psychology

A key Christian writer in social psychology is David Myers. He has written a major textbook in the area (1990). Myers has also coauthored a book on applying social psychology to Christian groups, entitled *The Human Connection* (Bolt and Myers 1984). There are chapters on the topics of conformity, groupthink, attraction, and altruism.

Another key writer in this area is Em Griffin, a communications professor at Wheaton College. His *Mind Changers* (1976) deals at length with the topic of persuasion as it relates to the church. He considers the roles of guilt, fear, incentives, credibility, and conformity within the context of persuasion. These issues are extremely important in evangelistic endeavors.

Two other books by Griffin also deserve mention. *Making Friends* (1987) considers attracting friends, our opinions of others, keeping friends, and other topics related to this important area of social psychology. He also considers motivation, self-concept, perception, language, and nonverbal communication.

Finally, Griffin's *Getting Together* (1982) addresses many practical issues related to group leadership and participation. Chapter 10 deals specifically with self-fulfilling prophecy.

need not be in a hurry were the most likely to help the supposed victim. The experimenters also found that the importance of the destination was as influential as the time factor in predicting the degree of altruistic response. Those who had read the parable before making the "journey" to another building were more likely to give aid. Curiously the experimenters did not find the drastic differences the original study indicated. Although the average amount of helping behavior differed between the hurried and nonhurried situations, it was not statistically significant. While these differences might suggest that students at Wheaton are different from those at Princeton, the degree of religiosity and social values of the students did not account for different responses.

Why do people help others? The costs and benefits of helping may play a factor in the decision to help. Some have even suggested that altruism is self-interest in disguise (the anxiety produced by seeing the situation is relieved by helping). Others argue that people are genuinely altruistic because they empathize with the person in need. Actually people are most likely to help others when they are the only bystanders, whereas they are less likely to help when others also see what is happening (Latane and Darley 1970). In addition, we are more likely to help others when we have observed others doing so.

Social Loafing

People tend to exert less effort when working with others and more effort when working alone. This is most likely to occur when the individual's contribution is not obvious, as in the game of tug of war. Yet if others are made aware of what each person contributes, such as football players in a game, individual performance may be even greater in the group than when alone.

As has been seen throughout this chapter, the individual is powerfully affected by others. Social psychology underscores the great importance groups have in our lives. That influence is pervasive and must not be overlooked as we examine all of the other areas of psychology.

References

Aronson, E., and J. Carlsmith. 1963. Effect of the severity of threat. *Journal of Abnormal and Social Psychology* 66: 584–88.

Aronson, E., B. Willerman, and J. Floyd. 1966. The effect of a pratfall in increasing interpersonal attractiveness. *Psychonomic Science* 4: 227–28.

Asch, S. 1951. Effects of group pressure upon the modification and distortion of judgement. In *Groups, leadership and men*, ed. H. Guetzkow. Pittsburgh: Carnegie.

Batson, C. 1975. Rational processing or rationalization? *Journal of Personality and Social Psychology* 32: 176–84.

Bolt, M., and D. Myers. 1984. *The human connection*. Downers Grove: Inter-Varsity.

Darley, J., and C. Batson. 1973. From Jerusalem to Jericho. *Journal of Personality and Social Psychology* 27: 100–108.

Festinger, L. 1957. *A theory of cognitive dissonance*. Stanford: Stanford University Press.

Golden, J., and P. Olczak. 1976. Psychosocial maturity and interpersonal attraction. *Journal of Research in Personality* 10: 146–54.

Griffin, E. 1976. *The mind changers*. Wheaton, Ill.: Tyndale.

———. 1982. *Getting together*. Downers Grove: Inter-Varsity.

———. 1987. *Making friends*. Downers Grove: Inter-Varsity.

Janis, I. 1982. *Groupthink*. 2d ed. Boston: Houghton Mifflin.

Jones, R., and J. Brehm. 1970. Persuasiveness of one- and two-sided communications. *Journal of Experimental Social Psychology* 6: 47–56.

Kalick, S., and T. Hamilton. 1987. The matching hypothesis reexamined. *Journal of Personality and Social Psychology* 51: 673–82.

Latane, B., and J. Darley. 1970. *The unresponsive bystander.* New York: Appleton-Century-Crofts.

McGuire, W. 1964. Inducing resistance to persuasion. In *Advances in experimental psychology,* ed. L. Berkowitz. New York: Academic.

Milgram, S. 1974. Obedience to authority. New York: Harper and Row.

Myers, D. 1990. *Social psychology.* 3d ed. New York: McGraw-Hill.

Putney, S., and G. Putney. 1964. *The adjusted American.* New York: Harper and Row.

Radant, N., et al. 1985. From Jerusalem to Jericho revisited. *Journal of Psychology and Christianity* 4: 48–55.

Rogers, C. 1970. *Carl Rogers on encounter groups.* New York: Harper and Row.

Rook, K. 1987. Social support versus companionship. *Journal of Personality and Social Psychology* 52: 1132–47.

10

Child Development

Theories of Child Development

Theories of child development help organize the pattern of development from conception to adolescence, the topic of this chapter. Each of the five theories discussed in this chapter relates to a different aspect of the child's life. They overlap to some extent, however, thus underscoring the holistic nature of the person.

Before considering these theories, we need to discern whether patterns of child development occur in stages. Strictly speaking, stages refer to differences in children that roughly correspond with age. These stages are generally held to be discrete (clearly separated from one another), sequential, cumulative (the characteristics of a given stage build upon those of the previous stage), and uniform (all children go through the same stages). The underlying assumption is that certain abilities exist at the same time, and this clustering of abilities is designated as a particular stage.

As we examine a given child, it is unlikely that major changes will be observed from one day to the next. In other words, there is continuity in development. Yet as we compare the behavior of the child at age five and at age ten, major changes can be observed. But do these changes fall within clear-cut phases? The stage theorists believe they do, and present considerable evidence for those phases. Yet it is often difficult to label a specific child as definitely in or out of a particular stage because he or she may be in a stage in some respects and not in it in other respects. This has led some psychologists to dismiss the idea of stages altogether.

Why is there a lack of uniformity among children? Moods and environmental influences affect the performance of children, so they may seem to be in one stage one day, and the previous stage the next. In addition, children may seem to be in two stages at once because of faulty ways of measuring stages. On the other hand, perhaps the theories do not adequately describe stages; they may need to be refined.

At present, perhaps the safest conclusion is that the concept of stages is helpful in understanding how children grow and develop, but the concept should be used flexibly. Changes with age may not be as uniform as some stage theorists would have us think due to differences in education and perhaps maturation. We need to allow for considerable variation in the age at which children reach a certain stage; and a particular child may not be uniformly in a particular stage. Stages better describe the differences between four- and eight-year-olds than they do the differences between four- and five-year-olds. They provide at least general guidelines for understanding child development.

In summary, we can say that a child's development is orderly and in sequences; uneven (it occurs in spurts); unique (no two children develop at exactly the same rate); and the result of both maturation and learning.

After a brief analysis of five stage theories, we will consider in depth the characteristics of the child at specific ages. The five theories are those of Freud, Erikson, Piaget, Kohlberg, and Fowler.

Freud's Psychosexual Theory

Freud (1905) developed what was once the standard psychological approach to understanding children. Freud did not work directly with children, but based his theory of child development on a reconstruction of childhood experiences narrated by the adults he treated. He concluded that children go through five major stages of "psychosexual" development. These stages (oral, anal, phallic, latency, and genital) are organized around sexual maturation and involve the child's search for pleasure which focuses on different parts of the body at different ages, body

areas Freud termed "erogenous zones." While many psychologists now question aspects of his theory, there can be no question that it has significantly affected Western society. Thus, even though we may dismiss parts of his theory (particularly in light of the fact that it was developed from studying abnormal rather than normal individuals), it is still worth understanding as other theories of child development have often been formed as a reaction or revision of his famous approach.

Freud believed that the infant is mouth-centered until about eighteen months of age. This he termed the oral stage. Certainly the baby *is* very mouth-oriented, exploring any new object by popping it in the mouth. Freud concluded that the mouth is the center for gratification at this age and frustration is likely to result in mouth-centered problems later in life, such as overeating or compulsive talking.

During the toddler years (eighteen months to about age three), Freud saw toilet training as the most important issue. He termed this the anal stage. Mothers and fathers who are tired of changing diapers would probably agree! The control of bowel and bladder functions are important accomplishments that usually take place at this time, although occasional

wetting of the bed is still considered normal up to age five (American Psychiatric Association 1987, 84–85).

Freud believed that frustration and trauma at this age, particularly if associated with toilet training, are likely to produce lifelong problems with obstinacy, frugality, or compulsiveness. He arrived at these conclusions because the struggle between the parent, who wants the child to eliminate in the socially approved way, and the child, who wants to eliminate at will, is manifested in later personality. Thus the child who refuses to eliminate on the potty chair becomes the adult who is obstinate, while the child who learns to be compulsively clean in the process of toilet training carries these compulsions into adult life.

While many psychologists now question these conclusions, most would agree that a great deal of punishment is probably not best during toilet training. Rewards should be given when the child is successful, while lack of success might be met with mild scolding or having the child clean up the mess. Most children are not ready for toilet training until about age two and sometimes not until later.

The third stage for Freud was the phallic stage, which lasts from ages three to six. "Phallus" is the technical term for the male sex organ, which is the center of attention for the child at this time. The child's center of gratification is no longer eliminatory functions but rather the opposite sex parent. Little boys, Freud said, are romantically and sexually attracted to their mothers (the Oedipus complex). Preschool girls, on the other hand, are attracted to their fathers (the Electra complex). Since boys realize they are now competitors with their fathers for the mother's attention, they begin to develop castration anxiety, which is only resolved when they eventually identify with the fa-

ther. Girls feel deprived and thus develop penis envy, but eventually they resolve this by identification with the mother.

This is perhaps the most controversial part of Freud's theory, but parents do acknowledge that children may at times talk of marrying the opposite sex parent at about this age. While this does not prove Freud's theory, he may have identified a trend at this age. This is probably not the most important feature of the preschool years, however!

Assuming all goes well, the school-aged child enters the latency stage, when sexual interests decline. The child becomes more interested in same sex peers than in the opposite sex. Children who suffer from trauma or excessive frustration at this time may be fixated at this stage (not move beyond it) and thus in adulthood avoid opposite sex relationships.

Was Freud's emphasis on same sex peers in the elementary school years accurate? Some reservations are certainly in order. Antipathy for the opposite sex, for example, does not occur in some cultures, thus indicating that this is not a basic characteristic of human personality. The dislike of the opposite sex at this age is probably more the result of cultural influences than something inherent.

Assuming there has been no major previous trauma, the adolescent enters the genital stage of sexuality. During this time the teen-ager develops a mature, adult-level sexuality in which the genitals become the primary source of excitation.

Most people begin, at this stage, to act on heterosexual impulses by taking interest in members of the opposite sex. Why do some become sexually attracted to members of the same sex? The evidence is far from clear, but it appears that homosexuality is due to a number of possible causes. Some homosexuals, for example, are not secure in their sex role identification, which is traceable to difficulties in the preschool years. Others have had homosexual experiences in their adolescent years and thus convince themselves they are not attracted to the opposite sex. For still others the problem seems to be more behavioral; they have been conditioned. There may be biological factors in some cases (see chap. 14). The Christian would emphasize the sinful nature of homosexual behavior, identifying it as rebellion against God and his moral law. The results of cross-cultural research are helpful. There are cultures in which homosexuality is virtually nonexistent because sex roles are distinct and a close father (or father substitute) is provided for every boy (Blitchington 1980; Rekers 1982, 37–50).

Erikson's Social-Emotional Theory

At each stage of Erikson's social-emotional theory of child development, the individual is confronted with two possible choices. While the positive is clearly preferable to the negative, Erikson believes that the ideal is for the psychologically mature individual to achieve a preponderance of the first quality, but also some degree of the second.

Erikson emphasizes that the key issue in infancy is trust versus mistrust. If children become attached to the mother and are thus assured of her presence and care, they will tend to develop a strong tie that makes them secure and outgoing later. If the mother is not found to be dependable, children later become overdependent and do not trust those around them. While all children cling occasionally, those who cling excessively into the preschool years, particularly if they cling to *anyone*, probably did not have a secure attachment in infancy. More recent research underscores the importance of attachment to the development of trust, although attachment can be made to a mother substitute and per-

haps even to several persons (Clarke-Stewart and Fein 1983).

During the toddler years the development of either autonomy or shame is the focus. The two- and three-year-old wants independence (some regard this as a first adolescence of sorts), and some degree of freedom should be given to the child. The tendency for some parents is to react to the desire for autonomy by overcontrol, which is likely to produce excessive shame in the child. This may carry over into adult life in the form of excessive concern for what others think.

Erikson sees initiative versus guilt to be the most important issue during the preschool years. Guilt refers to the violation of internal standards as opposed to shame which is the violation of external standards. Erikson emphasizes that we should encourage initiative in the child at this age and avoid making the child feel excessively guilty, which can carry over into adult life.

The school-aged child is marked by the development of either industry or inferiority. The child should receive feedback on productiveness through encouragement or occasional tangible rewards, rather than being made to feel inferior.[1]

Piaget's Theory of Cognitive Development

According to Piaget, cognitive development occurs as children discover and learn to apply rules that govern interaction with the environment. As children perceive discrepancies between their simple concepts and environmental events, they form new concepts to account for them. Piaget has outlined various stages in the process, which begins at a very primary level.

1. See Linn, Fabricant, and Linn 1988, for a discussion of prayer and Erikson's stages. Blazer 1989 relates the first of Erikson's stages to faith.

Fig. 10.1. Piaget's stages of cognitive development.

Sensorimotor (birth–18 months)	**Preoperational (18 months–6 yrs.)**

Most development is *sensory* (interpreting environmental stimuli) and *motor* (rapidly developing motor [movement] skills).	Gaining vocabulary and basic facts about environment rapidly.
Concrete Operations (6–11 yrs.)	**Formal Operations (begins 11–12 yrs.)**

Gaining rapidly in reasoning ability but reasoning is still quite black and white; learning is concrete	Continual improvement, if educated properly, in ability to *reason abstractly* (understanding analogies, parables, proverbs, abstract concepts, and generally deeper thoughts).

In the sensorimotor period (birth to age two), automatic reflexes and responses are important. At first these reflexes are of limited duration and do not seem to be purposeful. As infants mature, however, their reflexes and responses appear to be organized and consolidated into patterns. Thus infants initially wave their hands through the air purposelessly. Eventually their hands come in contact with various aspects of their environment, such as crib rails. Reflex responses of the hand then cause infants to grasp the rail of the crib or to grab and hold on to objects such as a rattle. Purposeful grabbing between the twelfth and the eighteenth months seems

to turn an infant into a seeker of knowledge or an explorer. The infant learns self-identification and develops an ability to recognize some cause-and-effect relationships. Identification of the self requires parallel development of a concept of reality as consisting of a larger environment in which the baby is differentiated from external objects. Separation of the figure from the ground is an important cognitive event basic to developing the sense of self as distinct from all that is not associated with self. For example, being able to play peek-a-boo is an important part of a child's development.

The development of causal thinking is

also very important. A baby begins to develop awareness of antecedent events that can be causes of other events, and of the connection between them. A game of fetch with an adult, where a baby throws a rattle off the high chair, the adult picks it up, the baby throws it down, the adult picks it up, and so on, is more than just a game; the child is learning physical causality.

In Piaget's scheme, assimilation and accommodation are important aspects of adapting to various environmental demands. Assimilation is a process of altering new perceptual cognitive elements to make them more similar to already familiar elements. Accommodation is a process of modifying previously developed cognitive structures on the basis of new experiences. Thus for Piaget cognitive development consists of a succession of changes by assimilation and accommodation. These changes exert a guiding or controlling influence over a child.

In Piaget's stage 2, the period of preoperational thought (ages two to seven), the principal achievement is development of the capacity to represent the external environment internally. It is in this period that symbols come to stand for objects. Symbolic functioning enables a child to represent not only those environmental events taking place at the moment, but also past and future events. During this stage children are egocentric; they are unable to imagine any other perspective but their own.

During stage 3, concrete operations (ages seven to eleven), children develop an organizational system for environmental events, including logical structures. They master mathematical operations, measurement, language, and spatial concepts. Also developed is the knowledge that the amount of a substance is unchanged even though its appearance may be changed by transferring it to a container of a different

size or shape. The concept of conservation requires a child to respond to two or more dimensions of a stimulus simultaneously. For example, if two equal amounts of water are poured into two identical glasses, a child of age five, six, or seven will generally report that the glasses contain the same amount. If the water from one of the glasses is poured into a taller and thinner glass, however, most five-year-old children will be convinced that there is more in the taller glass, whereas older children will probably see that there is still the same amount of water in the glasses. The concrete operational child has come to understand that the concept of amount depends on both height and width.

Piaget's stage 4, the period of formal operations, extends from about age twelve through adulthood. During this final stage of cognitive development, reasoning may proceed entirely from verbal abstracts. The ability to think in symbols dramatically alters children's comprehension of the environment around them as well as their ability to deal with it. They are now able to draw meaningful conclusions from purely abstract or hypothetical data. It is during this stage of formal operations that children gain enough experience and language ability to be able to create a personal theory of knowledge.

Of several variables influencing cognitive development, certainly a significant one is culture. In the advanced urban cultures of Western society, for example, schooling seems to provide a rather individualistic orientation to cognitive development. That orientation encourages individual initiative, promoting individual self-consciousness and mastery over the physical world. Thus a separation of self from the external environment is characteristic of cognitive development in Western societies and urban cultures. In contrast, many cultures emphasize collective

Spotlight 10.1 Church Applications of Piaget's Theory

Piaget notes that young children, particularly preschoolers, live in a magical world. The stories of Jesus' miracles and resurrection are likely to be accepted without question; if everything is magical, then miracles are to be expected. Children do not see death as permanent at this age (Tamminen et al. 1988); thus the story of the resurrection is not questioned. Some supernatural events may be discounted later, however, when children come to realize that the world is not magical; perhaps teaching such things should be reserved for the time when children will see them as clearly supernatural.

Young children can learn certain roles performed in church services (Ratcliff 1986). Likewise they can learn the biblically prescribed aspects of other roles, such as that of mother and father. Stories from the Bible can be enacted by young children (Ratcliff 1988b); children learn by *doing*. Through role playing children can begin to understand what a Pharisee was and who Pharaoh was.

Some have wondered at what age a child can accept Christ. This is unlikely to happen during the preschool years because of the child's inability to look back on life globally ("reversibility" as Piaget describes it) and commit everything to the Lord. Yet Christ rebuked his disciples for trying to keep children away. It is best not to discourage children's interest in serving God but to encourage them to confess their sins to God. Most children raised in godly homes have a natural curiosity and interest in becoming Christians, but parents probably should not expect a decision for Christ until later.

Many churches try to teach children concepts that they are incapable of understanding. Children become easily confused, like the child who reported hearing the congregation sing "Gladly, the cross-eyed bear"! If children cannot understand a concept, they certainly cannot apply it to their lives. The end result may be a separation of religious knowledge from everyday life—a real problem for many adult Christians. How many of *us* sing songs in church without thinking of the words? Perhaps we learned to do so as small children and the habit has carried over into adulthood.

Can children understand abstract metaphors? The best research to date indicates that children use metaphors as early as seven to nine years of age with comprehension, but cannot explain metaphors until later (Hyde 1991). Metaphors and parables that use very familiar ideas and objects may be understood earlier, as are those that make use of sensory terminology. Often, however, the child is unable to relate one general class of concepts to another in an abstract manner until age eleven or twelve. Thus the best way to teach evangelism to children this age would be the concrete and tangible account of Andrew bringing Peter; they are less likely to understand the parable of the sower and the seed. Most young children learn to sing, "I will make you fishers of men," which involves more abstract thinking than they are capable of. Unfortunately most children learn this phrase early; then in adolescence when they are able to understand the abstract nature of the concept, it is considered childish and is not appreciated for its rich metaphorical value.

Standard church services should be waived for children in favor of junior church experiences with much singing, story telling, role playing, and crafts. While attending a brief section of the church service is acceptable, children also need to be gradually shaped into full participation in regular services during the early adolescent years.

experience and provide less encouragement of individual initiative.

Is Piaget's theory accurate? While much of his research and study is brilliant and his insights are amazing, more recent evidence points to his tendency to oversimplify. For example, the divisions between the preoperational and concrete operational stages are not as well defined as he thought (Ratcliff 1988). Some concrete operational tasks are actually composites of several simpler tasks that can be completed individually by preschoolers. Also, the precise wording of instructions for a task (even a mechanical task) makes a considerable difference in whether it will be successfully completed. Some measures of conservation may not be realized until a child is well into the school years. The child's development is more of a continuous process than Piaget's stage theory—with its sudden major changes—would suggest.

Likewise, cross-cultural study of the formal operational stage has led some to conclude that certain cultures never reach this stage (Dansen 1972). However, this conclusion is based on tasks that require formal schooling; the use of other tests of formal operations (such as use of symbolism and allegory) reveal that other cultures do indeed reach this stage (Mitchell 1986; McCarron 1987).

Kohlberg's Stages of Moral Development

Beginning with Piaget's theory, Kohlberg (1983) has developed a theory of how children develop moral reasoning abilities. It is important to note that Kohlberg does not concern himself with the *content* of moral thinking (the decisions people make), but with the *structure* of their reasoning (the way people arrive at those decisions).

Kohlberg believes that children lack consistent moral reasoning until the preschool years, when they begin to reason from a punishment orientation. Power and the likelihood of punishment influence the child's reasons about why particular acts are good or bad. While some adults continue to function at this stage, most individuals advance to the next stage where the desire to fulfill needs is central. Reciprocity (fair exchange) marks this stage, the reasoning being that "I'll scratch your back if you'll scratch mine." This stage may develop as early as age seven (Wilcox 1979, 96). Politicians often make use of this style of reasoning.

Although an individual may remain at

Spotlight 10.2.
Using Kohlberg's Theory

Kohlberg's theory could aid in the analysis of discussions in the church. For example, Kohlberg found that people could understand only one stage above what they characteristically used in their own reasoning. Thus if a member of a Sunday school class begins to describe fairness using stage 3 reasoning (that of being a good person), another member who emphasizes reciprocity (stage 2) will still be likely to understand that argument.

People do not always reason at one stage consistently; an individual may move from stage to stage depending on the topic. Kohlberg identifies a given individual's stage as the *highest* stage used. Therefore we should be careful in assuming a given individual is necessarily stuck in a certain stage. He or she may in fact be capable of reasoning at a much higher stage on some topics.

Consider another situation. A church meets in small groups for Wednesday evening prayer. When someone discovers a local ordinance that forbids such groups from assembling in private homes, a meeting is called to discuss the matter. Jones says the church must stop meeting in homes because "we must be law-abiding citizens." Smith adds, "and besides, we don't want to pay any fines." Using Kohlberg's theory, we might conclude that Jones is using stage-4 reasoning (law and order) while Smith is at stage 1 (avoiding punishment).

Kohlberg's theory deals with structure rather than content, so using his theory alone would not provide an answer as to what is the *right* thing to do in this situation. While Kohlberg emphasizes a more relativistic style of thinking in his higher stages (not described in the text), the Christian position would suggest that God's law and principles are higher than man's law. Thus for the Christian the structure of Kohlberg's fourth stage must be supplemented by God's direction through his revelation.

---

this stage even into adulthood, most children progress to the good girl-good boy approach to moral reasoning, where the approval of others becomes paramount. Being nice is the child's main concern in reasoning about right and wrong. Wilcox (1979, 96) indicates that this form of reasoning can develop as early as age ten. By the teen-age years the person is capable of Kohlberg's fourth stage, which consists of an orientation toward law and authority. Doing one's duty and maintaining social order are considered important.

Kohlberg believes that individuals can go beyond the fourth stage (conventional thinking) to an emphasis on principles. Since the adult stages of moral development lack consistent research findings (Wolterstorff 1980, 91) and imply a more relativistic moral stand (Joy 1983, 91; Clouse 1985), they will not be considered here.

Christians have expressed concern that Kohlberg's theory elevates the structure of moral thinking over the content of moral decisions. Is there any room for moral absolutes if structure is the only concern? We can in fact point to Kohlberg's own life. Kohlberg apparently committed suicide because of excruciating pain from a disease he contracted in Central America (Niebuhr 1987). This act was certainly consistent with his content-less moral theory, but what an irony that the top expert in moral development would end his life in such a manner! In contrast, the Christian would maintain the value of human life, even in the midst of intense suffering, as a biblical absolute.

Fowler's Stages of Faith

Fowler, building upon the work of Piaget, Erikson, and Kohlberg, has developed a theory of how faith develops. It is important to note that Fowler's definition of faith does not necessarily mean religious faith; for Fowler, faith is a process of relating to what is most important in life. For the Christian this would be God, but for other people this could be something else. Like Kohlberg, Fowler is concerned with structure rather than content.

Infancy is characterized by primal faith, which emphasizes the trust described by Erikson. Trust is the precursor to faith as children begin to separate themselves from objects in the outside world, particularly the mother (Moseley and Brockenbrough 1988; Mahler, Pine, and Bergman 1975). In the preschool years the first real stage develops, intuitive-projective faith, which is imaginative and not controlled by logic. The child forms images of protecting and threatening powers in life, including God and Satan.

A second stage, mythic-literal faith, begins during the school years. Here the meaning of life is primarily represented in stories, with facts clearly being separated from fantasy and speculation. Fowler incorporates some of Kohlberg's thinking by describing God as punishing bad behavior and rewarding good behavior. During adolescence synthetic-conventional faith may begin, which integrates the different images of self to produce a coherent identity. The young person does not reflect upon the facts and thus appeals to authority when the facts conflict. During the young adult years the person enters the individuative-reflective stage, where beliefs and values are critically evaluated.

Two other stages are posited by Fowler, which ultimately move the person toward a more universalizing faith. Fowler admits that the highest stages of his theory, like that of Kohlberg's, are more the result of the theorist's convictions than hard data (Lawrence 1983). While affirming that conversion is a change in content rather than a stage change, he allows little room for the supernatural. Others would also suggest that conversion is more than a change in content; the Bible speaks of Christians becoming new creatures, a process affecting the totality of life.

Patterns of Child Development

Prenatal Development

Although we can observe the family environment shaping a child's personality almost immediately from birth, development actually begins at conception. Personality is built on the physical and mental equipment with which we are endowed by our parents—and ultimately by God. Consider the development of a child's intelligence, for example. In spite of the fact that some geniuses have weighed only a few pounds at birth and some mentally retarded persons have weighed much more at birth, research suggests a positive correlation between birth weight and IQ. Obviously, good nutrition during pregnancy (daily protein, calcium, and iron) can contribute to sound mental development in the newborn. Research has also shown that certain drugs, alcohol, and cigarettes can have deleterious effects on the baby in the womb (Hall, Lamb, and Perlmutter 1986, 97–98).

Another area of concern during pregnancy is the emotional state of the mother. Pregnancy, especially a first pregnancy, can be an anxiety-producing experience. It is normal for women to have ambivalent feelings about pregnancy. It is dangerous, however, for a woman to feel guilty about those ambivalent feelings, or to try to convince herself that she does not have them. If she represses them, they will cause physiological changes in her body chemistry which could not only damage her own health but also have deleterious effects on the physical and emotional development of the fetus.

A pregnant woman should talk about ambivalent feelings with her husband and other significant people in her life. It is especially helpful for her to talk to other women who have gone through the same experience. A pregnant woman's emotional and spiritual needs should be met in normal ways to insure a healthy emotional climate in the family when the baby is born. The father's emotional and spiritual needs should not be neglected in the process. A healthy baby born into a healthy family is God's ideal.

The Newborn

Birth can be a good or bad experience for the delivering mother. Although labor is quite painful, a woman's expectations can greatly influence the actual experience.

BREAST FEEDING

Most physicians agree that breast feeding is far superior to bottle feeding, especially during the first few months of life (Ziai 1969, 193).

Modern hospitals bring mothers and babies together for breast feeding if the mothers request it. During the first few hours babies do not get much milk from their mothers (they do not need it) but they do get fluid containing maternal antibodies which protect them against infections. Mother's milk is superior to cow's milk in the quality of its protein and its sterility. It is also inexpensive. Moreover, something about breast feeding brings emotional warmth to both mother and baby. Certain hormones released in the mother by breast feeding not only cause her hips to return to their normal shape but also serve as a natural tranquilizer, producing feelings of contentment and acceptance of the baby (Wilson, Beecham, and Carrington 1966, 613).

Some methods of breast feeding are more rewarding than others. McGrade's study (1968) of thirty newborn babies' responses to breast feeding was continued until the babies were eight months old. Newborns who cried and thrashed when they were taken off the breast nipple were tense at eight months, as measured by their withdrawal from strange adults and new situations. Babies who were satisfied during breast feeding as newborns, as measured by high but unstressful activity after breast nipple withdrawal, were more active, happier, and less tense at eight months.

MATERNAL REACTIONS

In an interesting study by Formby (1967), tape recordings of thirty-one newborns were played for eight new mothers forty-eight hours after delivery. All eight were able to select the cry of their own infant. A second group of ten mothers in multibed hospital wards following delivery was observed to see if they woke up at night upon hearing their own baby or any other baby cry. During the first three nights, fifteen out of twenty-six waking episodes were caused by the mother's own baby crying. After the third night, twenty-two out of twenty-three waking episodes were in response to their own babies.

Robson attempted to analyze the development of feelings of attachment in fifty-four mothers during the first three months of their first child's life. During the first six

Spotlight 10.3. Birth Defects

Some births present serious problems to families, especially when a baby has a birth defect. God has arranged female physiology in such a way that most abnormal fetuses end up as miscarriages in the first three or four months of pregnancy. Approximately one miscarriage occurs for every four or five pregnancies. Some defective babies, including those suffering from Down's syndrome (formerly called mongoloids) are born. Without entering into a theological debate over God's directive or permissive will, we can recognize that God allows such things to happen. Psalm 139 says that we were designed by God in our mother's womb and that the blueprint for this design was made before we were even conceived. No one should claim to know the mind of God (see Deut. 29:29), but we can proclaim that God is love, and that "God works for the good of those who love him, who have been called according to his purpose" (Rom. 8:28). The parents of a defective newborn often go through the same stages of grief experienced over the death of a loved one: (1) denial; (2) anger toward others and toward God; (3) anger turned inward; (4) genuine grief; and (5) resolution. A family may eventually have to decide whether to put a severely retarded youngster in a special home, or to keep the child in the home even though the entire family's life may be disrupted. There are no clear-cut answers to such a dilemma. Some parents put their mentally handicapped youngsters in homes and are glad they did; others are thankful they kept such children in their own homes. Sometimes it may be better for severely retarded children to live in a home where they can receive special training, with the parents visiting as needed. In other situations it may be better for children to remain in the parents' home. (See also spotlight 8.5.)

weeks, "the model mother experienced impersonal feelings of affection toward her infant, whom she tended to perceive as an anonymous nonsocial object" (Robson et al. 1970, 976). In the second month, when the infants began to smile and look at things longer, "maternal feelings intensified and the infant was now viewed as a person with unique characteristics who recognized his mother." After three months had passed, "maternal attachments were sufficiently strong to make the infant's absence unpleasant and his imagined loss an intolerable prospect." According to Robson, "mothers who developed an attachment late in time or not at all either did not want infants or had babies with deviant behavior" (p. 976). Clearly, events occurring in the first three months of life will affect the eventual emotional feelings of the mother.

Postpartum depression may begin soon after delivery and occasionally can become quite serious. Affected women may need antidepressants initially, followed by long-term counseling to help them accept motherhood. The letdown most women feel after delivery is to be expected. After all, the mother has lost blood, is anemic, and is now faced with getting up at night to change and feed a baby. The situation usually takes care of itself if the mother gets some help, eats right, and catches up on her sleep. Also, the baby usually settles down to a regular schedule within a few weeks. A pediatrician can help a weary mother put a demanding baby on a regular schedule after a month or two.[2]

Infancy: The First Fifteen Months

According to Theodore Lidz of the department of psychiatry at Yale University School of Medicine, "during no other period of life is the person so transformed both physically and developmentally" as during infancy. Further, "no part of his life experience will be as solidly incorporated in the individual, become so irrevocably a part of him, as his infancy" (Lidz 1968, 117). Just as lack of physical care can lead to poor health or even death, lack of social nurturing produces distorted emotional development and stunted intellectual growth.

Malnutrition can influence an infant's ultimate intellectual ability (Cravioto and Robles 1965) since all of the nerve and brain cells a person will ever have are produced by six months of age. After six months, brain cells may continue to enlarge and make new connections, but no more new cells will be formed. That is a major reason an infant needs plenty of protein, primarily from milk, during the first six months of life. Many poor mothers who have been induced to give up breast feeding for bottle feeding cannot afford to buy enough milk; hence they dilute the milk or put things like sugar-water into their babies' bottles. Poor nutrition during infancy has permanent effects. Even early enrichment programs usually come too late to make up for the loss. During the first six months an infant's physical needs predominate. From then on socialization and affection are just as important as physical needs.

STIMULATION AND EXPERIENCE

The drive for stimulation and activity is basic to the infant. Spitz (1945, 53–74) described what happened to a number of infants placed in a European foundling home during World War II. Their mothers were allowed to stay with them for the first three months of life, during which time the infants developed normally. Then, apart from their mothers, they were cared for by nurses at a ratio of one nurse per eight to twelve infants. The infants received adequate medical attention and food, but very little stimulation by way of being handled by the busy nurses. As a result of that lack of stimulation, 30 percent of them died of malnutrition within the first year. Most of the survivors could not stand, walk, or talk by the age of four, and had become mentally retarded.

The condition described by Spitz in which an infant refuses to eat and becomes more and more emaciated is known as marasmus. It is also called failure to thrive, and occurs frequently—even in America (Evans, Reinhart, and Succop 1972). Many of the parents of infants suffering from marasmus are physically abusive, and many of the fathers are alcoholics. Often such infants have to be legally removed from their homes and reared in foster homes. If rescued soon enough and given a lot of physical stimulation, some infants recover and may live relatively normal lives thereafter.

The importance of stimulation, and of the right kinds of stimulation, has also been demonstrated in various animals. Dogs restricted as puppies by being raised in cages, for instance, developed striking abnormalities of behavior by the time they reached maturity (Melzack 1969). When the dogs were allowed to leave their cages as young adults, they showed excessive behavioral arousal. They went into violent whirling fits and ran around the room from one object to another, rarely showing sustained attention to any single object. They did not get along well with normally reared dogs. In another study, Solomon

---

2. Two excellent books on pregnancy, birth, and early childhood are Davis 1986 and Dobbins 1985.

"I THINK YOU HAVE AN OVERACHIEVER HERE. WE CHANGED HER DIAPER EIGHT TIMES IN ONE HOUR!"

(1969) showed that rats which were handled daily, early in life, had a much more vigorous antibody response to infections than did rats deprived of physical handling early in life.

MOTHERS AND MOTHER SUBSTITUTES

Kaufman et al. indicate that "the loss of mother is disturbing to an infant and produces a searching, agitated response. Substitute mothering serves to relieve the distress, the extent depending in part on the degree of mothering provided and in part on the specific nature of the tie to mother." If the loss of the infant's mother is not relieved, "the infant soon lapses into a state of severe depression and withdrawal that appears to conserve his resources and minimize the danger of injury" (1969, 681–95).

Erikson's studies indicate that good mother substitutes are adequate for the first six months of life or so, but that after that, close contact with the mother is essential.

McDanald (1967, 74) states that "the mother's unconditional acceptance of the infant is the precursor to healthy self-acceptance which enables him to make the most of himself within the framework of his personal strengths and limitations, both physical and mental." Further, "the child who has been unconditionally loved has a good conscience, experiences normal anxiety, and is relatively free in his choice of action." On the other hand, an infant who has been conditionally loved, as he grows older, "has a restrictive or a 'bad' conscience and experiences undue quantities of anxiety, hostility, and guilt which engender various forms of compulsive behavior of a social or antisocial character." Many believe that by the time children are old enough to go to school, most of their character structure has already been established. An emotionally healthy, reflective child will be greatly enriched by contact with peers, teachers, and information. An anxiety-laden child who fears the unknown, however, will feel threatened by the new interpersonal and environmental relationships. McDanald (1967, 69) concludes that "the person who reaches adulthood with the feeling that life has been kind to him wants to give something of himself back to life."

Although some mothers obviously have to work outside the home, it might be better to deprive children of material things in order to give them something more important. Handicapped or retarded children, even more than nonhandicapped children, need their mother's unconditional love and acceptance to prepare them for what they will have to face when they become old enough to go to school. Another group of children who especially need their mothers are children who have to be hospitalized. Studies have shown that young children whose mothers fail to come and spend a lot of time with them in the hospital have a significantly higher mortality rate.

Harry and Margaret Harlow (1965), a husband-and-wife research team, took a group of young monkeys away from their mothers and put them in a situation with two imitation mothers. One "mother" was made of wire; a feeding device (a baby bottle full of milk) was attached. The other "mother" was made of soft terry-cloth; no feeding device was attached. The young monkeys would go for milk from the wire mother but would run to the soft terry-cloth mother whenever they were frightened. Both groups of monkeys, when they grew up, had problems mating and abused their offspring due to their own lack of mothering.

DEVELOPMENTAL ADAPTATION

Although human infants are perhaps the most dependent of God's creatures, they must develop responses to environmental stimuli; learn to control normal body functions such as eating, elimination, and sleeping; adapt to physical illnesses and major behavioral changes such as weaning; live up to increased social expectations imposed by parents; and cope with rapidly developing modes of mobility (crawling, standing, walking).

Collins (1971, 4) notes that typical problem areas of infants and their mothers center around "feeding, weaning, sleeping, thumbsucking, excessive crying and, later, toilet training." He mentions that "in years gone by, the mother gained support, encouragement and advice on these matters from experienced and sympathetic relatives, but this has all changed with the current mobility of families. In the United States approximately one family in every four moves each year. Relatives are now often far away, and the young parents who reside in relatively unfamiliar communities must depend more on books and articles—some of which give conflicting and confusing advice."

An infant's development may be complicated by parents who worry excessively about things that are absolutely normal— especially with their first child. For instance, thumbsucking, genital play, and "security blankets" are normal ways for infants to gain comfort. An infant deprived of such gratification may become frustrated and increasingly insecure.

Parents may also be concerned that various minor psychological stresses will injure the mental health of their infants, when in reality a degree of stress is beneficial to an infant. Lidz (1968, 88) states that "over protection or development in an extremely stable and homogeneous setting is likely to produce colorless individuals. As everyday experience often shows, difficulty can strengthen one; trauma can produce defenses that can serve well in later emergencies; deprivations can harden."

During the first month of life, infants learn by repeating innate reflexes, such as sucking, crying, blinking, and breathing. In the second month, infants learn that they have voluntary control over some of those automatic responses. They stick their thumbs in their mouths, stare, suck, and make noises at will. During the next six or seven months they learn to play, show emotion, imitate, and spend longer periods of time investigating various objects by sticking them in their mouths and rubbing them. Toward the end of the first year, they are able to crawl around and may even begin to walk. Infants try to experience everything available, which means that parents must make the house childproof. The average American home contains a number of poisonous substances or medications that an exploring infant could get into, such as furniture polish, aspirin, insecticides, and prescription medications. A major cause of death in infancy is accidents, especially household accidents and overdoses. Yet parents should be aware that infants who constantly have their hands slapped for getting into things may become adults who are rigid in their thinking and fearful of exploring new ideas.

The average one-year-old can say one or two words, like "dada" and "mama," al-

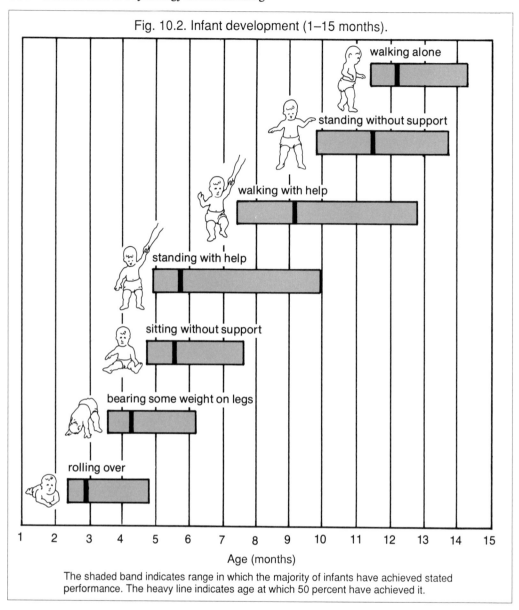

Fig. 10.2. Infant development (1–15 months).

The shaded band indicates range in which the majority of infants have achieved stated performance. The heavy line indicates age at which 50 percent have achieved it.

though some can say quite a few more and others have not yet started speaking. The rate of speech development, unless it is extremely slow, is no predictor of ultimate IQ. A fear of strangers and animals usually develops toward the end of the first year. Some children may be frightened by an expanse of water, like the ocean, when they see it for the first time. A fear of heights is often learned after falling off the couch a couple of times.

The Toddler:
Fifteen to Thirty-six Months

During the toddler stage the need for discipline increases dramatically. The period from fifteen to about thirty-six months is perhaps the most trying for the parents of any child. Their toddler has acquired amazing new motor skills but still has meager mental capacities. The chief mental capacity seems to be insatiable curiosity about everything that parents call a

Spotlight 10.4.
Heredity, Environment, and Discipline

The environment versus heredity debate has gone on for years, with the pendulum of opinion swinging back and forth. Two generations ago, heredity was overemphasized. Such erroneous thinking continues today in some circles. The next generation tended to blame nearly everything on environment and ignored the influence of heredity. As volumes of research data continue to pour in, scientists are now taking a new look at both heredity and environment. Most aspects of the human body and mind are influenced by both hereditary and environmental factors.

The Bible is entirely realistic about a child's nature. Children are not born morally "good," but with a built-in propensity to sin, to rebel against God. Of course, their parents were born the same way, yet by God's saving grace some parents are able to set good examples for their children. Children must be taught to be good. God's Word tells us that "folly is bound up in the heart of a child, but the rod of discipline will drive it far from him" (Prov. 22:15). Although we inherit a sinful nature, through discipline we learn to be good. Kaplan and Saddock (1975, 580) acknowledge that "typically the child learns to say no before he learns to say yes. He knows what he doesn't want long before he is able to formulate what he does want." Piaget's studies confirm that moral behavior is learned, and that children are not born with good morals. Young children try to imitate and please their parents to avoid punishment for being bad, and to gain approval for being good.

Many references in the Book of Proverbs stress discipline as a necessary part of the child's environment.

"no-no." Of course, by removing many of these "no-nos," parents can allow and even encourage toddlers to follow their natural bent toward exploration.

DISCIPLINE

Parents need to encourage independence in their children. Yet at the same time they must teach their toddlers to respect limits and renounce immediate gratification. In these crucial months, a domineering, overly demanding, overly protective mother can prevent a toddler from developing self-trust, self-worth, and initiative. A sense of worthlessness may result from constantly not living up to parental expectations.

In disciplining a child and setting firm limits, parents must be realistic as to what can be expected of a child this age. A first-born child with inexperienced parents who do not know what can realistically be expected usually has a more difficult time than siblings. Many such children become perfectionists, as perhaps seen from the fact that fifteen of America's first sixteen astronauts were firstborn sons. Counseling can help inexperienced parents know what to expect, for example, with regard to toilet training. Some mothers try to toilet train their infants by the time they reach their first birthday, although the average child is not neurologically ready until anywhere from eighteen months to more than four years of age.

Spotlight 10.5. Common Problems in the Toddler Years

Problem	Suggestions
Food refusal	May be manipulative behavior or genuine dislike. If a food item is particularly important to the child, the parent might give only that food to the child for a few days. Rather than getting angry, parents should simply remove the food if the child becomes negativistic or dawdles. Missing a meal or two will not hurt the child. Snacks between meals should not be permitted unless the child eats a reasonable amount at mealtime.
Pacifiers	A pacifier should not be tied around the neck, as there is a chance of choking if the child falls. Worn pacifiers should be replaced, since the rubber end might break loose and choke the child. Pacifiers help provide the oral gratification a child needs.
Thumb sucking	Children who have pacifiers during their first two years may not suck their thumbs as much later. Thumb sucking should be ignored, as children usually stop the behavior by the time they begin school. Some believe that sucking the thumb after age four may indicate too little affection during infancy. Protruding teeth are seldom the result of thumb sucking.
Genital play	Parents should ignore genital play unless it occurs in public. Children who are disciplined for doing this may develop poor sexual concepts later. Genital play is a natural part of exploring the body at this age. If children ask questions about their genitals, parents should give truthful answers using proper terms (such as vagina, penis, urine, etc.).
Selfishness	The foundations for sharing behavior must be taught during the toddler years. Parents should praise a child for unselfish behavior, as well as set good examples. Parents should also teach children the results of stealing, perhaps through stories on the topic.

Prior to thirty-six months of age, any attempts to reason on an abstract level with a child are simply a waste of time. Verbal reproofs are sometimes adequate, but if a child is openly rebellious, spanking seems to be the most effective form of discipline. Spanking should be used only for intentional breaking of a known rule or open rebellion. Yet parents are frequently disappointed when after spanking a child for blatant disobedience, they find the child repeating the same behavior five minutes later. The right thing to do is to patiently spank the child again, rather than to give up. Children at the toddler stage have very short attention spans and memories. Parents aware of these age characteristics realize that instructional dos and don'ts need to be repeated many times before a toddler understands them. Although a toddler's behavior may be exasperating, especially when it involves the destruction of some precious object or results in a mess that is hard to clean up, what children need most at this stage of life is calm parents.

Some parents threaten children with punishment but rarely follow through. Such children may go through life trying all the wrong things without fearing any punishment. In real life, they will not receive numerous warnings and may get caught after the first, second, or third violation.

SOCIALIZATION

At about two years of age, toddlers should have enough basic trust to develop relationships with other children, including the freedom to express and assert themselves, even in immature ways. The presence of other children after age two is very important, because children are neurologically and emotionally ready to learn social skills.

At about fifteen months, when most children are using single words to name a few familiar persons or things, like "mama," "dada," "dog," and "eat," they are also using a lot of nonsense words. Finally they start putting two or more words together, so that the average child can talk in sentences fairly well by age three, the end of the toddler stage. Language development depends on how much the parents talk to a child, as well as on the presence of older brothers and sisters. Thinking out loud and talking to themselves are perfectly normal toddler behaviors.

It is also normal for toddlers to have imaginary friends, which helps them practice talking. Their fantasy life helps them deal with the developmental conflicts they are experiencing in ways that are less threatening than real life. It may be good to affirm both reality and fantasy by saying, "It's fun to pretend, isn't it?"

Any prolonged separation from the mother during the toddler years can be detrimental. Many children in America today are being farmed out to day-care centers, some of which are harmful to a child's ultimate mental health and outlook on life. The day-care centers that are worthwhile have adequate staff to provide programming beneficial to children. Without government or other subsidies, however, they are usually too expensive for most working mothers. An adequate day-care center should have at least one well-adjusted, warm, loving staff member for every four or five toddlers.

The Preschooler: Ages Three to Six

Preschoolers' emotions are freely expressed. At about age three, children have many fears–of animals, of monsters, and perhaps even of "the big bad wolf." Since they have trouble differentiating between fact and fantasy, they need to be reassured over and over by their parents. Preschoolers also feel anxiety, jealousy, curiosity, joy, and love.

Parents should expose their preschoolers to children their own age. At age three, children seldom interact with other children playing in the same area. Such parallel playing soon ends, however, as children begin to interact. Eventually preschoolers become less self-centered and learn to feel empathy with others. At this stage, an adequately staffed nursery school can facilitate social development. Two or three mornings a week away from mother will do a child good and give the mother a needed break. Collins (1971, 50) states that childhood playing permits discharge of energy; provides needed stimulation; helps children develop motor skills; and enables children to act out and learn to understand adult roles.

Between the ages of three and six, children add thousands of words to their vocabulary and begin to reason concretely. They continue to live in a small world, however. They still think most events center in some way around them, and that almost all people see things the same way they do.

During these crucial years, children take great strides in becoming more self-sufficient. They learn to feed themselves and to cut up most of the food on their

Spotlight 10.6 Single Parents

A mother and father, each with self-worth, character, and genuine love, showing respect for each other and acknowledging Christ as the head of the home, tend to produce mentally healthy children with self-worth, character, and genuine love for others.

Although by God's grace mentally healthy offspring can also come from single-parent families, these children may have special problems of separation anxiety, grief, anger, depression, loneliness, and poor sexual self-identity. Tragically, millions of children in the United States today are living in fatherless homes.

Research indicates that there is a greater likelihood of serious problems among children who do not have a father. Boys who lose their fathers early in life are less oriented toward the masculine role and tend to be less competent in making moral judgments. McCandless and Trotter (1977, 173) showed that "boys whose fathers have been away for extended periods during their runabout-preschool years report more antisocial behavior than those whose fathers have been consistently present." Girls are either more shy or overly eager in heterosexual relationships once they become adolescents (McCandless and Evans 1973, 81, 170, 239; see also Blitchington 1981).

Increasingly, children in America come from broken homes. Such children have seen one or both parents being selfish and proud. Often the easy way out has been for a couple with marital and psychological conflicts to divorce and remarry, producing two families with marital and psychological conflicts instead of one, with the children torn between them. One study (Cline and Westman 1971) of 105 families that experienced divorce showed that 52 percent continued to have hostile interactions even after the divorce, and 31 percent required from two to ten court interventions during a two-year follow-up period. The study also showed that alliances between one parent and child against the other parent were especially common.

More recent research conducted by Wallerstein and Blakeslee (1989) indicates that only 34 percent of children of a divorce adjust adequately; 29 percent were coping but had not recovered; another 37 percent had severe problems. These influences continue even ten years after the divorce. A significant number of children continue to experience loneliness and general unhappiness even in the "adjust adequately" category.

The high divorce rate in America is separating many children from their fathers. Since divorced mothers are often forced to go to work, the children are also deprived of a stable relationship with their mothers. No wonder God's Word says, "Therefore what God has joined together, let man not separate" (Mark 10:9).

Sometimes a death in the family deprives young toddlers of one or both parents. At this time grandparents, other close relatives, or close friends must help the toddler reestablish a close parental relationship as soon as possible, even if the close relative or friend does not live in the same house.

plates. They begin to dress themselves, usually with some parental guidance on what to wear rather than how to put it on. They become completely toilet trained, using the bathroom when they need to and cleaning themselves afterward. They rely less on their mother socially as they begin to make friends.

The preschool years are the years in which sexual identities become solidified. Children need a parent of the same sex to identify with and to model themselves after. Time spent with preschoolers should be both quantitative and qualitative. Although parents should avoid stereotyping chores, having boys help their father with household chores and girls help their mother will facilitate the sexual identification process.

During these years most children go through a stage of thinking that they will eventually replace the parent of the same sex by marrying the parent of the opposite sex.

Parents should give children of both sexes warmth and affection, but should try to avoid overly stimulating preschoolers. Younger children can follow parents around when parents dress, use the restroom, or take a bath, and perhaps even sleep in the same bed, but parents must politely, yet matter-of-factly wean them off these activities. Preschoolers usually will not object a great deal, and will demand privacy themselves.

THE PRESCHOOLER IN THE FAMILY

The roles children have in the family greatly influence the development of their personalities. There are advantages and disadvantages to being the oldest, a middle, or the youngest child, and special disadvantages to being an only child. We have already noted that demands placed on the oldest child may produce an adult who is a perfectionist. Second children, especially if teased by the firstborn, are sometimes more shy and polite, trying to please everybody. From the third child on, children are frequently less inhibited, are more outgoing and extroverted, and generally enjoy life more than the firstborn, even though they may be less successful financially. The youngest child has a greater chance of being spoiled, more dependent, and less mature, depending on the maturity of parents. Children of older parents tend to be more serious-minded than children of young parents. Of course, there are exceptions to every rule.

The Chinese have special terms of address for persons of each position within a family, with special status and roles for each position. A study by Zajonc, Markus, and Markus (1979) revealed that the first-born had the highest IQ scores, and that IQ scores decreased slightly but definitely as birth order progressed. Another study has shown that menarche occurs later in girls from large families than in girls from small families (James 1973).

Regardless of birth order, children may have various special roles within the family, such as scapegoat, baby, pet, miniature spouse, or peacemaker. Handicapped children sometimes become scapegoats, and are made fun of and rejected by other children in the family—especially if the other children feel inadequate themselves.

The roles parents play in the family also influence the personality of each child. One research study on the roots of personality disorders was carried out over a seventeen-year period on sixty-four young adults. Rousell and Edwards (1971) found that permissive home atmospheres tended to produce neurotic (including hypochondriacal) and psychotic disturbances, especially in female offspring. Cold, permissive home atmospheres tended to produce sociopathic personality disorders in male offspring. Cold, punitive homes tended to produce phobic and psychotic males. Excessively warm, permissive homes tended to produce strong anxiety and psychotic reactions in males.

TELEVISION

Psychologists at the University of Georgia conducted a study on young children's emotional reactions to television violence (Osborn and Endsley 1971). They showed three brief violent television episodes to four- and five-year-olds while continuously measuring their perspiration (galvonic skin response). The children were also shown two nonviolent films. The children responded more emotionally to the violent

Spotlight 10.7.
Common Problems in the Preschool Years

Problem	Suggestions
Tantrums	Many preschoolers express anger in the form of temper tantrums. It is especially important for parents not to give children what they want as a result of a tantrum, as this will be a reward. Parents should try to ignore the first tantrum. If this attempt at extinction does not work, it may help to speak sternly. Spanking may be necessary in some cases.
Handicaps	Parental attitudes and childhood development in general can be greatly affected by a handicap (Bentovim 1972). Handicapped children may become overly dependent and withdrawn. Parents and others who feel sorry for handicapped children may let them have their own way, which may cause behavior problems. Handicapped children should be encouraged to be as independent as possible, without denying the handicap.
Obesity	Obesity destroys a child's self-image and incurs teasing by other children, so parents should prevent the problem at all costs. Giving children too much food to eat, then demanding that they "clean the plate" may lead to obesity.
Bed wetting	This problem is common in the preschool years, but becomes a major concern only if it persists into the school years. About 16 percent of children still wet the bed occasionally after age five (Rae-Grant, Carr, and Berman 1983, 181). Parents should not shame the bed-wetting child, but rather have the child clean up the bed each time an accident occurs.
Soiling	Encopresis, like bedwetting, is also normal in the preschool years. If it persists after age four, a psychologist should be consulted. Sometimes bed wetting or soiling is a medical problem, which can be treated with certain drugs.
Nail biting	A moderate amount of nail biting at this age is normal. Rewards may be used to discourage nail biting, but punishment is not suggested.

episodes and remembered them better one week later. When asked which of the five episodes (three violent and two nonviolent) they liked best, they chose the two cartoons they were shown, one of which was violent and the other nonviolent. The emotion evoked by the violent scenes was primarily fear. Violent scenes with human characters aroused more fear than violent scenes with cartoon characters. The children were able to recall twice as many details about the human violence as about anything else they saw, implying a relationship between emotionality and information storage and retrieval. Television can be useful or a great hindrance to children's emotional and spiritual maturation, depending on how it is used.

TWINS

Approximately one out of eighty-six births produces twins, about one-third of which are identical. Parents typically treat twins alike. Studies have shown, however, that it is better psychologically for twins to be treated as distinct individuals (Freed-

Problem	Suggestions
Tics	Such behaviors as inappropriate jerky motions, squinting of the eyes, and constant clearing of the throat are considered tics. Counseling may be indicated as these behaviors are usually due to underlying emotional conflicts. Tics usually go away after removing such conflicts (Freedman, Kaplan, and Saddock 1975, 1398–99). Medication may also be used for temporary relief.
Stuttering	Stuttering in preschool children is considered normal and usually goes away by age six. Stuttering is usually due to neurological immaturity. Parents should ignore stuttering unless it persists into the school years; the more attention paid to it, the worse it often becomes.
Fears and sleep problems	Fears of animals are common during these years, and are nothing to worry about. The parents should reassure the child. Nightmares and night terrors may be the result of emotional conflicts. In some cases medication is needed, particularly with night terrors where the child cries and thrashes about but does not wake up. A night light may help. Children should be encouraged to return to their own room rather than sleep with the parents. Sleep walking is common in young children. In persistent cases, medication may be needed.
Depression	Depression is common following the loss of a parent or loved object. Depression often takes the form of withdrawal, prolonged sadness, and a marked increase or decrease in activity level. Counseling may be needed; sometimes a low dosage of antidepressant medication is suggested.
Stress	Sunday school, moving to a new home, trips to the dentist or doctor, or the birth of a sibling may produce considerable stress for a child. The parent may prepare the child by talking about the event in a truthful manner. Parents should tell children when a babysitter is coming to minimize stress.

man, Kaplan, and Sadock 1975, 1494). Parents should not reward, praise, or punish twins at the same time, but do so individually as the situation warrants. It is better if twins wear different styles of clothing, depending on their own tastes, and even attend different classes in school.

Elementary School Years: Ages Six to Twelve

SEXUAL DEVELOPMENT

It is vitally important for school-age boys to identify with males and for girls to identify with females. Without such identification, children may later suffer sexual maladjustments in marriage or be inclined toward homosexuality.

Elementary school boys generally develop a contemptuous attitude toward girls and girlish things. Nearly all boys and girls have some wishes at times of being the opposite sex, so they develop contempt to repress those wishes during these years. Both sexes need to develop gratitude for being what they are, and need to see that each sex has its own distinct advantages.

Spotlight 10.8. Adjusting to School

Areas of the brain responsible for reading and writing may mature later in some children. As a consequence many boys, and some girls, will have minor learning disabilities, such as seeing or writing letters backward, until the nerves associated with these activities have fully developed. A critical teacher can make such children feel stupid, even though they may have average or better-than-average intelligence. Once a child is labeled stupid, it is hard to live that label down. First-grade teachers are extremely important because of the effect they will have on the child's attitude toward education in general. Good teachers are loving and understanding but at the same time are firm disciplinarians.

A child may be afraid to go to school and stay there all day. School phobia can develop due to a number of reasons.

First, it may be a matter of overdependence upon the mother, as was mentioned earlier in this chapter. Second, this problem can be due to a lack of exposure to other children. Children need to develop social skills like cooperation before they begin school. Third, the child may react with fear because of unfortunate conditioning. For example, one child became phobic of Sunday school because two older children were allowed to torment other students in the class.

Another possible reason for school phobia is immaturity; the child may not be mentally or emotionally ready for formal schooling. As noted in an earlier chapter, up to 40 percent of children are not ready for formal education by age five or six. Finally, children who are indulged by the parents may try to manipulate the parents through the phobic behavior.

What can a parent do about this problem? It is essential to determine the reason for the phobia. If it is a matter of manipulation, the parent must simply force the child to go to school. On the other hand, if it is a matter of immaturity, the child might need to stay home for another year or two (most states allow for home schooling in such cases). If the problem is lack of experience with other children, the child may need to be gradually introduced to other children through progressively longer times of planned interaction, either in the home or in a preschool setting.

Overdependence should probably be dealt with in a similar manner; the overprotective parent needs to seek counseling. Finally, if the problem is prior conditioning, it may be helpful to attend school with the child a few times so that the fear can extinguish. In severe cases, psychotherapy may be needed.

Sex education is important during these years. It should be done gradually by answering questions that a child asks, and nothing more. By answering questions truthfully and matter-of-factly, parents can help their children know all the facts of life by the time they are ten or eleven years old. Menstruation should be explained early to elementary school girls because the normal range for onset of menses is from nine to sixteen years old, with the average being about thirteen years in the United States (Malina 1979). Onset of puberty in boys is generally a little later, usually around ages thirteen to fifteen. That is why seventh-grade girls are frequently larger than boys.

SOCIAL DEVELOPMENT

Elementary school children develop a sense of belonging by participating in groups and a real sense of responsibility by sharing chores with older brothers and sisters. Belonging and responsibility are prerequisites to the development of leadership potential. Children must learn to obey before they can learn to lead effectively. Their self-concept continues to develop as they see themselves through the eyes of peers, parents, and authority figures. Interaction with other adults and children becomes increasingly important.

Play among children of this age group—be it baseball or dominoes—is characterized by poor organization, heated disputes over rules, lopsided

Spotlight 10.9. Missionary Children

Missionary children who are reared in foreign countries often have more problems than usual. Many of the special problems of foreign residence can be avoided, minimized, or resolved, however, according to a research study by Werkman (1972, 997). Werkman found that parents in foreign cultures often had to face unusual child-rearing practices and customs, problems with the caretakers of the children, aberrant sexuality, special fears, and a sense of alienation. Werkman concluded that parents should anticipate these potential problems, discuss them openly, make plans to avoid or minimize them, and act decisively on their children's behalf.

Often children on mission fields must be sent hundreds of miles away, nine months a year. Some may become bitter atheists as a reaction to parental rejection. Rearing children must be viewed as the first and utmost calling from God.

More missionaries should probably consider teaching their children at home. A substantial amount of research (Moore and Moore 1979, 101) indicates that home-schooled children adjust well to school when they eventually enter it; in fact, many excel academically and become leaders. Home schooling takes only two or three hours a day, and high-quality materials are available. For those who do not feel they can teach their children at home, correspondence courses are available.

There are definite advantages to rearing children overseas. Not only do nationals have the opportunity to see how Christian parents should rear their children, but the missionary children have the benefit of being exposed to a second culture, which tends to broaden their perspectives and simultaneously increase parental influence. Rearing children on the mission field appears to be good until the adolescent years, when perhaps the boarding school situation becomes more viable. Missionary children who do not leave home until they go to college have a hard time adjusting because of excessive dependence upon parents (Ratcliff 1983).

scores, and accusations of cheating. Children like to win, but must also learn teamwork—the ability to work in a common cause with others. They like to play marbles and exchange comic books. Parents should not assume that all comic books are the same. X-rated material circulates in comic book format alongside relatively innocent "funnies" and literary classics. At the other extreme are Christian comic books. It is not too early for the children of Christians to be set apart by higher standards as a witness to others.

Spotlight 10.10.
Common Problems in the School Years

Problem	Suggestions
Death	A death in the family can be a maturing experience for children if handled properly. Children generally go through the same stages of grief as adults when they learn of death or impending death in the family (see chap. 4). Younger children may become bitter or angry with the dying or dead parent, since they may believe that the parent has chosen to leave them. They may also feel guilty and blame themselves for the death of the parent. It is good for children to be allowed to attend the funeral of a loved one, if they so choose, and to express grief without repressing genuine feelings. If not allowed to express feelings, children may have unresolved conflicts in their adult lives.
Grandparents	Grandparents and other relatives should probably not live with the family, unless it is certain that there will be few conflicts as a result. Many have regretted letting grandparents move in, and it is difficult to back out of such a commitment. Yet some report that having grandparents in the home can be very meaningful. If the grandparents do not live with the family, it is generally desirable to live within driving distance. Children often have a special relationship with grandparents, and a strong relationship with the grandparent of the same sex may aid sex role acquisition. Parents should help take care of the grandparents, as this will give their children the opportunity to observe and teach them to do the same when their parents are elderly (1 Tim. 5:8).
Handicaps	Minde et al. (1972) discovered that handicapped elementary children recognize that the handicap will not disappear; depression usually follows that recognition. Parents need to help children accept their condition, see how God can use the handicap, and show them how to incorporate their problem into their life plans.

References

American Psychiatric Association. 1987. *Diagnostic and statistical manual of mental disorders.* 3d rev. ed. Washington, D.C.: American Psychiatric Association.

Bentovim, A. 1972. Handicapped pre-school children and their families—effects on the child's early emotional development. *British Medical Journal* 3: 634.

Blazer, D. 1989. *Faith development in early childhood.* Kansas City, Mo.: Sheed and Ward.

Blitchington, W. 1980. *Sex roles and the Christian family.* Wheaton, Ill.: Tyndale.

Clarke-Stewart, A., and G. Fein. 1983. Early childhood programs. In *Handbook of child psychology.* 4th ed. Vol. 2., ed. P. Mussen. New York: Wiley.

Cline, D., and J. Westman. 1971. The impact of divorce on the family. *Child Psychology and Human Development* 2: 78–83.

Clouse, B. 1985. *Moral development.* Grand Rapids: Baker.

Collins, G. 1971. *Man in transition.* Carol Stream, Ill.: Creation.

Cravioto, J., and B. Robles. 1965. Evolution of adaption and motor behavior during rehabilitation. *American Journal of Orthopsychiatry* 35: 449.

Dasen, P. 1972. Cross-cultural Piagetian research. *Journal of Cross-Cultural Psychology* 3: 23–39.

Davis, J. 1986. *The Christian's guide to pregnancy and childbirth.* Westchester, Ill.: Crossway.

Dobbins, R. 1985. *Venturing into a child's world.* Old Tappan, N.J.: Revell.

Dobson, J. 1970. *Dare to discipline.* Wheaton, Ill.: Tyndale.

———. 1978. *The strong-willed child.* Wheaton, Ill.: Tyndale.

Erikson, E. 1963. *Childhood and society.* 2d rev. ed. New York: Norton.

Evans, S., J. Reinhart, and R. Succop. 1972. Failure to thrive. *Journal of the American Academy of Child Psychology* 11: 440–57.

Formby, D. 1967. Maternal recognition of infant's cry. *Developmental Medicine and Child Neurology* 9: 293–98.

Fowler, J. 1981. *Stages of faith.* San Francisco: Harper and Row.

Freedman, A., H. Kaplan, and B. Saddock. 1975. *Comprehensive textbook of psychiatry.* Baltimore: Williams and Wilkins.

Freud, S. 1905 (repr. 1982). *Three essays on the theory of sexuality.* New York: Basic.

Hall, E., M. Lamb, and M. Perlmutter. 1986. *Child psychology today.* 2d ed. New York: Random.

Harlow, H., and M. Harlow. 1965. *The affectional systems in behavior of non-human primates,* eds. A. M. Schrier et al. Vol. 2. New York: Academic.

Hooper, D., et al. 1972. The health of young families in new housing. *Journal of Psychosomatic Research* 16: 367–74.

Houmes, D., and P. Meier. 1985. *Growing in step.* Richardson, Tex.: Today.

Hyde, K. 1991. *Religion in childhood and adolescence.* Birmingham, Ala.: Religious Education.

James, W. 1973. Age at menarche, family size and birth order. *American Journal of Obstetrics and Gynecology* 116: 292–93.

Joy, D. 1983. *Moral development foundations.* Nashville: Abingdon.

Kaufman, I., et al. 1969. Effects of separation from mother on the emotional behavior of infant monkeys. *Annals of the New York Academy of Science* 159: 681–95.

Kohlberg, L. 1983. *The psychology of moral development.* New York: Harper and Row.

Lawrence, L. 1983. Stages of faith. *Psychology Today* 17: 56–62.

Lidz, T. 1968. *The person.* New York: Basic.

———. 1972. The nature and origins of schizophrenic disorders. *Annals of Internal Medicine* 77: 639–45.

Linn, M., S. Fabricant, and D. Linn. 1988. *Healing the eight stages of life.* Mahwah, N.J.: Paulist.

McCandless, B., and E. Evans. 1973. *Children and youth.* Hinsdale, Ill.: Dryden.

McCandless, B., and R. Trotter. 1977. *Children: Behavior and development.* New York: Holt, Rinehart and Winston.

McCarron, M. 1987. Folktales as transmitters of values. *Religious Education* 82: 20–29.

McDanald, E. 1967. Emotional growth of the child. *Texas Medicine* 63: 73–79.

McGrade, B. 1968. Newborn activity and emotional response at eight months. *Child development* 39: 1247–52.

Mahler, M., F. Pine, and A. Bergman. 1975. *The psychology birth of the human infant.* New York: Basic.

Malina, R. 1979. Secular changes in size and maturity. *Monographs of the Society for Research in Child Development* 44: 59–102.

Meier, P. 1977. *Christian child-rearing and personality development.* Grand Rapids: Baker.

Melzack, R. 1969. The role of early experience in emotional arousal. *Annals of the New York Academy of Science* 159: 721–30.

Minde, K., et al. 1972. How they grow up. *American Journal of Psychiatry* 128: 1554–60.

Mitchell, E. 1986. Oral tradition. *Religious Education* 81: 93–112.

Moore, R., and D. Moore. 1979. *School can wait.* Provo: Brigham Young University Press.

Moseley, R., and K. Brockenbrough. 1988. Faith development in the preschool years. In *Handbook of preschool religious education,* ed. D. Ratcliff. Birmingham, Ala.: Religious Education.

Niebuhr, G. 1987. Philosopher of morality. *Atlanta Constitution* (Feb. 18): 1b–2b.

Osborn, D., and M. Endsley. 1971. Emotional reactions of young children to TV violence. *Child Development* 42: 321–31.

Piaget, J. 1950. *Psychology of intelligence.* Boston: Routledge and Keagan Paul.

———. 1954. *Construction of reality in the child.* New York: Basic.

Powell, J. 1988. Counseling missionaries overseas. Session at the International Congress on Christian Counseling, Atlanta, Ga.

Rae-Grant, Q., R. Carr, and G. Berman. 1983. Childhood developmental disorders. 2d ed., eds. P. Stienhauer and Q. Rae-Grant. In *Psychological problems of the child in the family.* New York: Basic.

Ratcliff, D. 1983. Letter to the editor. *Journal of Psychology and Theology* 11: 251.

———. 1986. The use of play in Christian education. *Christian Education Journal* 6: 26–33.

———. 1988. The cognitive development of preschoolers. In *Handbook of preschool religious education,* ed. D. Ratcliff. Birmingham, Ala.: Religious Education.

Rekers, G. 1982. *Shaping your child's sexual identity.* Grand Rapids: Baker.

Reppucci, N. 1971. Parental education, sex differences, and performance. *Developmental Psychology* 4: 248–53.

Robson, K., et al. 1970. Patterns and determinants of maternal attachments. *Journal of Pediatrics* 77: 976–85.

Rousell, C., and C. Edwards. 1971. Some developmental antecedents of psychopathology. *Journal of Personality* 39: 40–50.

Solomon, G. 1969. Emotions, stress, the central nervous system and immunity. *Annals of the New York Academy of Science* 164: 335–43.

Spitz, R. 1945. Hospitalism: An inquiry into the genesis of psychiatric conditions in early childhood. *The psychoanalytic study of the child.* Vol. 1. New York: International Universities Press.

Tamminen, K., et al. 1988. The religious concepts of preschoolers. In *The handbook of preschool religious education,* ed. D. Ratcliff. Birmingham, Ala.: Religious Education.

Wallerstein, J., and S. Blakeslee. 1989. *Second chances.* New York: Ticknor and Fields.

Werkman, S. 1972. Hazards of rearing children in foreign countries. *American Journal of Psychiatry* 128: 992–97.

Wilcox, M. 1979. *Developmental journey.* Nashville: Abingdon.

Wilson, J., C. Beecham, and E. Carrington. 1966. *Obstetrics and gynecology.* St. Louis: Mosby.

Wolterstorff, N. 1980. *Educating for responsible action.* Grand Rapids: Eerdmans.

Zajonc, R., H. Markus, and G. Markus. 1979. The birth order puzzle. *Journal of Personality and Social Psychology* 37: 1325–41.

Ziai, M. 1969. *Pediatrics.* Boston: Little, Brown.

11

Adolescent and Adult Development

Adolescent Development

Lidz (1968, 299) defines adolescence as "the period between pubescence and physical maturity . . . the transition from childhood, initiated by the prepubertal spurt of growth and impelled by the hormonal changes of puberty, to the attainment of adult prerogatives, responsibilities, and self-sufficiency." Many significant changes take place between the ages of twelve and sixteen.

At age twelve, a son or daughter is still considered a child. Four years later, that son or daughter has become a young man or young woman with an adult body, reproductive ability, and a desire for independence. These four years are probably the most difficult years of a person's life. The major adjustments that must be made in this period can be greatly facilitated by encouraging independent decision making and spiritual maturity during the first twelve years of life. Of course, parental guidance and discipline are necessary until children are on their own at age eighteen.

A major growth spurt, occurring at different ages in different individuals, initiates adolescence. That growth is accompanied by profound changes in social behavior. Consistent with Freud's theory (see chap. 10), a ten- or twelve-year-old may like other children of the same sex and hate those of the opposite sex, except, maybe, for a favorite or two. By age fourteen, most boys have decided that girls are not so bad after all. In fact, they may find it difficult to think about anything else. When boys begin spending more time with girls, old friendships may be broken up, especially with boys not yet interested in girls. Peer groups are rearranged, producing marked feelings of ambivalence toward individuals of both sexes. Children who were once friends can become competitors or even bitter enemies.

Theories of Adolescence

PIAGET'S FORMAL OPERATIONS

As noted in the previous chapter, Piaget describes the adolescent and adult years in terms of formal operations. The accomplishments of this stage include the discovery of the hypothetical in which all logical outcomes are considered, the creation of experiments to determine if hypotheses are correct, and the development of deductive reasoning and other more abstract forms of thought which reflect a new set of mental structures.

Piaget emphasizes that the early formal operations stage is characterized by an inflexible use of new mental abilities (Piaget 1967, 64). Although adolescents may be able to understand possibilities in a new situation, this understanding is not realistic. Teen-agers tend to be very idealistic, feeling they can change the world and solve its problems if only they adopt and pursue certain ideals. They may expect parents and church members to conform to *their* ideals. Piaget describes this as a second egocentrism due to the emphasis upon the adolescent's own idealistic perspectives. Even the reactionary words of many rock songs reflect an idealism—perhaps ideals that have been lost or destroyed, but ideals nonetheless. The adolescent's quest for love is also idealistic (Piaget 1967,64–67).

Later, as adolescents have experience thinking at a formal operational level, they become more flexible in the use of these mental abilities. This produces not a loss of ideals, but a more realistic approach to achieving those ideals. For some, this new realism is achieved in the mid- to late teen years; others may be in their twenties or thirties; some never achieve this realism.

Perhaps it is the development of formal operational abilities that accounts for the recommitment to Christ that many Christian teen-agers make. Adolescents gain the ability to think about thinking, and are now able to commit their thought life to Christ.

In the previous chapter it was emphasized that children should not be overwhelmed with content that is too much for them. Perhaps the opposite caution applies to teen-agers. This is not the time for warmed-over Sunday school material; lessons should be challenging and provocative. Teaching adolescents simplified philosophy and allowing them to participate in short-term missions experiences are likely to help them mature (Campolo and Ratcliff, 1991).

ERIKSON'S IDENTITY STAGE

During the adolescent years the teen-ager struggles with role confusion versus role identity (Erikson 1963). Adolescents question who they are and where they are going. In the process they develop their own self-concept as opposed to the self-concept acquired from others. This often involves a questioning of the basics of society, morality, and religion.

This time of questioning and searching is difficult for teen and parent alike, but it can be good. In the process adolescents develop their own faith rather than borrow a faith from others. Questioning foundations paves the way for laying better foundations. The parents and church need to guide young people, encouraging discussion and understanding of moral guidelines, nudging rather than forcing and pushing. Those who are pressured into religious practices at this age are likely to completely reject the church and the Christian faith, or accept it blindly as second-generation Christians. Either alternative falls far short of a mature faith. A healthy local church can be a positive influence on impressionable adolescents as they begin their struggle for identity and seek guidelines by which to live.

Spotlight 11.1.
First-Generation Christians

A second generation of believers typically loses the vitality of the first generation. The third and fourth generations observe their parents and grandparents (the second generation) and reject their lackluster faith. By the third and fourth generations, the "faith of the fathers" is lost.

This phenomenon can be observed in certain denominations where the founders have a vibrant faith; their children maintain that faith; and their grandchildren are embarrassed by the first generation's enthusiastic faith and dismayed by the empty faith of the second generation. The questioning of the third generation tends to produce a fourth generation that rejects the faith altogether.

Some teen-agers and college students have a shallow faith borrowed from parents or grandparents. Once away from home, they are attracted to the wrong crowd. They compromise what little faith they may have. Their faith has no deep roots and when tested, these young believers lose out spiritually.

The solution to spiritual decline is for each generation to be first-generation Christians. A vital faith is the result of a radical, personal commitment to Christ that goes beyond mere conformity. We must help adolescents develop a distinct faith of their own, the result of a genuine encounter with Christ. Such an encounter may come after intense questioning of the beliefs they grew up with, which often happens during adolescence.

OTHER THEORIES OF ADOLESCENCE

Blos (1962), building upon Freudian theory, describes adolescence as a psychological adaptation to biological maturity. The young person is psychologically adjusting to the fact of physical adulthood, or (probably less often) is waiting for biological maturity to catch up with psychological maturity. The rate of adaptation varies from person to person, since each individual has a biological clock that may be either ahead or behind the level of psychological maturity. Blos states that this adaptation occurs in three phases: early, middle, and late adolescence.

During early adolescence young people become involved with those of the opposite sex. Inconsistency and disorder may characterize the person at this age, due to the gap between biological and psychological maturity. Blos notes that the early adolescent is marked by defensiveness because of this gap.

With adolescence proper or middle adolescence, the teen-ager begins to withdraw from people who were significant during childhood. The adolescent reassesses goals, fears, and conflicts involved in earlier relationships, so that ultimately the energy from these earlier bonds can be invested in new relationships. Blos describes this process as a way of saying "good-bye" to those who were important in childhood, thus making possible new and deeper friendships as well as romantic involvements.

In late adolescence the teen-ager consolidates much of what has gone before. This consolidation involves the development of sexual identity, the emergence of a stable and distinct self (including interests and judgment), a decrease in self-preoccupation, and the development of a public self that is distinct from the private self. The basic identity of the person is formed, although an integrated sense of self must wait until adulthood.

Havighurst (1972) emphasizes the influence of society upon adolescent behavior. During adolescence young people learn the general tasks society requires of its members. The individual who learns these tasks becomes satisfied and is rewarded, while the one who fails to learn them is punished and is dissatisfied.

For Havighurst the learning of certain tasks in a specific order is crucial to adjustment. There are ages at which individuals are most likely to learn specific tasks ("teachable moments," or "sensitive periods"). If not learned at the most appropriate time, tasks are unlikely to be learned later. These tasks include:

1. Development of more mature relationships with peers
2. Development of appropriate sex roles
3. Acceptance of personal physique
4. Development of emotional independence from adults
5. Preparation for marriage and family
6. Preparation for a career
7. Development of values and ethics that constitute an ideology or guide to actions
8. Development of socially responsible behavior

Selman (1980) considers the social cognition of adolescents, or how they represent other people mentally and the inferences they make about others. How do teen-agers come to distinguish between their own perspectives and the views of other people? Selman, influenced significantly by Piaget's theory, identifies four stages in the development of interpersonal understanding.

Young children are extremely egocentric, but by the time they start school they realize that other people have different perspectives. However, the school-aged child believes that only one perspective can be correct. The feelings of others are judged by outward appearances, even though children at this age are aware that the genuine motives or reasoning of others may not be reflected in these outward appearances. Just before the adolescent years children begin to think about how their own actions might appear to others. The viewpoints and feelings of others may differ, yet both may be correct.

During early adolescence individuals take on the objective perspective of an outsider. Interpersonal relationships are understood to involve players, various alternatives, and certain consequences from any decision that might be made. In later adolescence and adulthood this position of an outsider, apart from the interaction, becomes more abstract so that individuals can perceive how society in general will understand their activities. They become aware that feelings and unconscious thoughts can influence their actions in ways they do not fully understand. They act in a manner that is aimed at impressing others in specific ways, and they become more adept at influencing others.

These theories of adolescence supplement the broader theories of Piaget and Erikson, giving us richer detail and a broader perspective on this important phase of life. What can be done to help the adolescent during these years of transition into adulthood? What guidelines will help other members of the family cope with the conflicts and struggles that occur?

Coping with the Adolescent

MAINTAINING COMMUNICATION

Keeping the lines of communication open is extremely important in families with teen-agers. Many families temporarily regress to earlier modes of behavior, as parents symbolically relive their own youth. A creative regression can be quite healthy, enabling family members to empathize with the adolescent's feelings. As a result, family members can grow together. It is important for parents to avoid being overly rigid; they must try to adjust to some extent while maintaining overall family stability.

The stereotype of a generation gap that produces high levels of conflict is now regarded as a myth (Peterson 1988). However, even in the best of families, there are often conflicts that disrupt family activities and communication. Fortunately, most of these conflicts are over relatively minor and even trivial issues (Montemayor 1982).

Why are there increased conflicts at this time of life? Some have suggested that hormonal changes play a part (Udry and Tolbert 1988), while others point to conflict as a mechanism for creating distance from the family, fostering the adolescent's later separation as an adult (Caine 1986). Kotesky (1981, 1987) emphasizes that conflicts result from the fact that adolescents are actually adults but are treated as children (see spotlight 11.3). What can be done to deal with conflicts and promote better communication?

A weekly family meeting may open lines of communication. Such meetings can be used to offer constructive criticism and suggestions. Solomon said, "Reliable communication permits progress" (Prov. 13:17 LB) and "Pride only breeds quarrels, but wisdom is found in those who take advice" (Prov. 13:10). The prophet Amos asked, "Do two walk together, unless they have agreed to do so?" (Amos 3:3). Parents who want to "walk together" with their teen-agers have to make a real effort to communicate.

Much has been learned about communication patterns in the families of adolescents. One study (McPherson et al. 1973) showed that in the families of aggressive, antisocial adolescents, the predominant pattern was for the father to pretend to be in authority if both parents were in public, but for the mother to disregard her husband on other occasions. The antisocial adolescent tended to tune out whenever both parents were present. With passive, negativistic teen-agers, the usual communication pattern was for the father to give the teen-ager wordy lectures, but to disregard whatever the teen-ager had to say. The mothers, who also ignored their teen-agers, at least asked them an occasional question. With introverted, withdrawn teen-agers, the usual communication pattern was for the mother to ignore the teenager's presence and to interrupt whenever the teen-ager spoke. The father generally let the mother dominate and was very attentive to her, while frequently interrupting his son or daughter. The introverted teen-agers paid close attention to both parents in spite of the fact that their parents ignored them.

Another family communication study had a number of families enter a room, one family at a time, to do individual and group interpretation of Rorschach ink-blot cards. The families had already been divided into two groups: those whose teenagers had good personality integration, and those whose teen-agers had made poor psychological adjustments. The purpose was to see if family communication patterns had made any difference in the psychological development of the teenagers. It was found that "families of children high in personality integration displayed more direct person-to-person communication, more efficient task orientation, more role clarity on the part of the parents, and less psychological distance than was true for families with lower adjustment children" (Odom, Seeman, and Newbrough 1971, 285).

In research carried out at the University of Utah, Alexander (1973) studied the families of twenty-two normal adolescents and twenty delinquent adolescents by videotaping each family during "resolution-of-differences" tasks. He found that the families of the juvenile delinquents were defensive in their communications and did not work at the tasks as a unified group. The families of the normal adolescents, who were very supportive of each other, were able to work together as a unit instead of as defensive individuals.

Parents can often eliminate nagging and other negative communications by reevaluating all family rules, chores, and punishments objectively. In a special family session, teen-agers can be asked to draw a line down the middle of a blank sheet of paper, putting specific rules and chores they think they should have on the left side of the line, and the punishments they think they should receive for breaking each of the rules on the right side. (Most teen-agers will be harder on themselves than their parents would have been. Wanting more controls, teen-agers frequently break rules so that parents will make them a little stricter.) The parents then go over each of the rules, chores, and punishments the teen-ager has listed and discuss them. The reasonable ones can be left as they are and changes negotiated in any that are either too strict or too lenient. The parents should have the ultimate say. Both parents and the teen-ager should sign and date the list, making it a contract between teen-ager and parents. The teen-agers should be specific about the day of the week on which they plan to do each chore. If they live up to their part of the contract, there will be no need to nag them. If they fail to keep their part of the bargain, the consequence is listed on the right side of the line. Such a contract should be made for about a two-month period, with weekly family meetings to discuss how things are going. During that period the parents should make an effort to show respect for their teen-agers as young adults, listening to what they have to say, even if the parents disagree.

When the two months are up, the contract can be renegotiated, with a little more freedom in the new contract if the teen-ager has done a good job. Poor performance may require a stricter contract. The goal is to keep the communications constructive and positive, and to compliment the teen-ager for showing responsibility. The contract technique helps reduce the power struggles and at the same time acknowledges teen-agers as persons by valuing their opinions on the rules they ought to have.

A special problem that needs to be mentioned at least briefly is the father-daughter communication problem. Young daughters enjoy sitting on their father's lap. Most fathers, however, feel very uncomfortable about the physical attractiveness of a teen-age daughter. Not realizing that such feelings are quite normal, some fathers withdraw from their daughters, perhaps even taking an extra job to avoid confrontation. The daughter, feeling rejected by a father she loves very much, may develop a variety of psychological problems. Later in life, for example, feelings of unworthiness may keep her from feeling accepted by God or by her husband. It is especially important for fathers to be available to both sons and daughters; even mother-child interaction increases when the father is present (Gjerde 1986).

Overcoming depression

Psychological depression in teen-agers is frequently disguised. Whereas a depressed adult will lose appetite or sex drive, wake up frequently at night, develop headaches, or have feelings of despair, teen-agers often manifest their depression in different ways. A teen-ager who has never been a problem may suddenly, over a period of a few weeks or months, become increasingly irritable, rebellious, and hostile, with intermittent guilt feelings. Such symptoms probably indicate depression. Depression generally is not seen in teen-agers who have been a problem all their lives.

Depressed, previously good teen-agers, are quite easy to treat. Sometimes putting

---

Spotlight 11.2. Christian Resources on Adolescence

There are several fine resources available that may help Christians better understand adolescence. Perhaps first on the list should be Kotesky's *Understanding Adolescence* (1987). Kotesky confronts a number of myths about the teen years and provides helpful guidelines for parents and others who work with youth.

The Lilly Endowment has funded two major studies of youth in the church. The first identifies the five most important concerns of teen-agers: (1) poor self-esteem and loneliness; (2) family difficulties; (3) the desire to help others and a social concern for injustice; (4) a dislike for closed-mindedness and prejudice; and (5) a desire to minister. These characteristics surfaced from a study of over seven thousand youths in a number of denominations, and the findings remained fairly consistent from the time of the initial study until a followup study seven years later. The findings of this research are summarized in Strommen's *Five Cries of Youth* (1988).

A second project funded by the Lilly Endowment produced *Religious Education Ministry with Youth* (Wyckoff and Richter 1982). The first chapter summarizes a large number of research projects with youth, while the remainder of the book cites several approaches to the topic.

Dobson wrote *Preparing for Adolescence* (1978) for preteens to read with their parents. Consistent with Dobson's emphasis on reaching the preadolescent, Strommen (1984) recommends that youth ministry begin prior to the adolescent years, even as early as the fifth and sixth grades (The Myth 1984). A number of evangelical writers have pooled their collective wisdom and practical experience in *Parents and Teenagers* (Kesler 1984). David Elkind, a religious child psychologist who has been featured on Dobson's radio program, has written *All Grown Up and No Place to Go* (1984; see spotlight 11.3). The work of Tony Campolo can be helpful in understanding teen-agers, including his popular film series and book *You Can Make a Difference* (1984). Youth leaders should find his *Sociology of Youth Ministry* (1989) helpful in broadening their understanding of this important stage of life.

them on antidepressant medications alone will dramatically lessen the problem in about ten to twenty days. Counseling sessions with the entire family are then necessary to reestablish communication patterns that have broken down.

If parents think a son or daughter is going through an adolescent depression, the first thing to do is to reestablish positive communication with a loving and accepting attitude. It may help to compare the family rules to those of other Christian families. Frequently, parents of depressed adolescents are either too strict or too lenient.

PEER PRESSURE

Young children's allegiance is to their parents. Because they want their parents to love them, they largely stay in line with parental wishes. But especially in early adolescence, allegiance is switched from parents to peers. To some extent, most adolescents adopt the morals of their peers. Conformity peaks at age eleven to thirteen and declines thereafter (Costanzo and Shaw 1966; Steinberg and Silverberg 1986).

If the parents have brought them up right, however, adolescents tend to choose peers who believe the same things as their parents. Although Sebald and White (1980) note that adolescents are more likely to conform to parents than peers when the issues are very important, in seeking popularity and social acceptance, conformity to peer-group ideologies, loyalties, and standards is paramount.

Parents have little control over the friends their adolescents choose to associate with away from the house. All parents can do is control whom is allowed in the home and instruct their teen-agers about whom they should and should not associate with elsewhere, hoping they will obey. If the lines of communication have been kept open, parents will find their opinions

respected when the time for such guidance arrives.

Interpersonal relationships developed during adolescence are often more important than what is learned scholastically. After reviewing the literature on adolescent socialization, Segal et al. (1967, 173) comment that "every major social psychiatry study in the past decade has called attention to the probability that an absence of satisfying interpersonal relationships is a cause, and not just a result, of emotional disturbance."

SEX

The onset of puberty brings problems of menstruation, masturbation, and wet dreams (nocturnal emissions).

If girls have been told ahead of time by their mothers about menstruation it is less likely to come as a traumatic shock. In mid-adolescence a girl's menstrual cycle becomes more regular. The estrogen predominating the first two weeks of each cycle influences her to want to share her love with others. During the next two weeks, when progesterone predominates, she may be less secure and needs to know that others love her. Then during the two days before menses start again, she may be more irritable or moody (Wilson, Beecham, and Carrington 1966, 59–71). It is best for parents not to pamper a daughter too much. Learning to cope with menstruation in adolescence will make it easier for her the rest of her life.

The sex drive is greatest in males at about age seventeen or eighteen, when androgens reach their peak level (in females the sex drive is greatest at about age thirty). According to the Kinsey reports (1948, 1953) about 90 percent of males and about 70 percent of females have had sexual intercourse by age twenty-one. Of course these statistics include sex within marriage, but the wide social acceptability of premarital sex in American society

Spotlight 11.3.
Growing Up Too Soon or Too Late?

Elkind (1981) believes that society expects children to grow up quickly, but fails to provide teen-agers with firm expectations. Unlike previous generations (and certain other cultures today), we prolong the irresponsibility associated with childhood into the late teens and even twenties. While the age of puberty has decreased, our society expects teen-agers to wait longer for marriage (Kotesky 1981, 1991).

One of the results of pressuring children to grow up and encouraging adolescents to be childishly irresponsible is the rise in immorality. Even from the early school years children are encouraged to have girlfriends and boyfriends and go out on "dates," yet when young people reach adolescence and are physically mature enough for marriage, society tells them to wait at the very least until leaving high school and preferably until college is completed.

In the Old Testament people commonly married by the age of twelve or thirteen. During the Roman era marriage was common at age thirteen (girls not married by age nineteen were considered "old maids"!) This explains why there is much more in the Bible about adultery than about premarital sex. It simply was not a major problem because young people were married before they had sexual desires, often even before puberty.

Kotesky (1981) suggests four guidelines to help adolescents with this problem. First, allow for special arrangements. Parents and those who minister to youth need to recognize our historically unique situation. While the Bible clearly forbids homosexuality and heterosexual intercourse before marriage, it has nothing to say about masturbation.

Second, provide counseling to help teen-agers deal with their feelings of guilt and to provide premarital sexual instruction.

Third, encourage young people to accept responsibilities, including the consequences when they misbehave.

Finally, early marriage with parental consent, perhaps even by age fifteen or sixteen, is seen by Kotesky as a possible Christian alternative. It is to be granted that high divorce rates exist for teenage couples at present. This may be due to the fact that some teen-agers marry in order to escape from a poor home situation—always an undesirable basis for marriage. In contrast, Kotesky emphasizes parental support of (not interference with) the newly married couple. He points to the biblical emphasis upon the role of the extended family in helping the newly married couple. While not a perfect solution, perhaps Kotesky's idea does merit consideration by Christians.

today undoubtedly puts pressure on Christian young people who want to save that experience for marriage. Although children should know the facts of life by the time they are six or seven, ongoing discussions with parents can help Christian teen-agers maintain a determination to live up to God's sexual standards. Such discussions should not be forced on teen-agers, but parents should look for natural opportunities to introduce it.

Attitudes toward masturbation have changed among many segments of the Christian community, although most would still discourage its regular practice. Sensitive adolescent boys may have to be reassured that wet dreams are normal or that occasional masturbation is not sinful.

Parents generally view a teen-age son or daughter in one of three ways. Some parents project their own sinful impulses onto their teen-agers, suspecting their teen-agers of doing things of which they are not guilty. Other parents automatically assume that their teen-agers are extensions of themselves. Both attitudes are unrealistic. The third, healthy, way is empathy. Parents who empathize with their teen-agers accept them as separate individuals and try to understand them and their struggles. Especially in discussing sexual matters with their teen-agers, parents should be sure they are not projecting unwarranted suspicion or assuming that their children think exactly as they do.

Teen-age pregnancies are a major social problem, and today's teen-agers generally have access to abortion clinics. In many localities abortions are granted to almost any pregnant teen-ager who thinks that having a baby would cause her to have emotional problems, even though studies have shown that the girls who have abortions are much more likely to have emotional problems as a result (Reardon 1987, 119–21). Another major social problem is venereal disease, epidemic among today's youth.

DATING

Dating is an important experience in the adolescent's life. Dating relationships can have a significant impact on future marital relationships. Christian teen-agers should not be allowed to date until they have reviewed the Scriptures and written a list of dating rules. A good rule is to limit dating to those who might be considered a potential spouse. Christians must always keep in mind Paul's warning not to be yoked with unbelievers (2 Cor. 6:14).

Parents frequently ask at what age teen-agers are old enough to date. This depends on the teen-ager's level of emotional and spiritual maturity. For adolescents of average or above-average maturity a fairly good rule of thumb is that they will probably be ready for group dating at age thirteen or fourteen, double dating at fifteen, and single dating at sixteen. Group dating includes activities such as a party where boys and girls pair off to sit together or participate in games. In early adolescence, boys and girls are primarily trying to figure out what the opposite sex is all about, but as they mature in late adolescence, genuine love for someone of the opposite sex becomes possible.

In the sexual area as in other areas, mid- and late adolescence is a time for the process of delimitation. In early adolescence the limits individuals set for themselves are vague and sometimes bendable. But toward the end of adolescence, individuals are searching for self-identity. Since this includes moral identity, they begin to fix or mark their moral limits. The individuals who stick to those limits will like themselves. Those who do not will experience guilt and a lowering of self-esteem.

Teen-agers beginning to date may be terribly self-conscious about their personal appearance. The acne and body odor that accompany the hormonal changes of puberty sometimes cause great concern. Encouraging teen-agers to improve their grooming habits usually takes care of pimples and body odor, but treatment by a dermatologist may be needed for severe cases of acne.

LATE ADOLESCENCE

In late adolescence many individuals are emotionally ready to make meaningful commitments to Christ. Late adolescence is also a time when young people begin thinking seriously about what career they want to go into, what they hope to accomplish in their lifetime, and the type of person with whom they want to spend the rest of their life.

Many late adolescents become critical of their parents. This is partly because their self-goals, which are frequently idealistic and unattainable, are projected onto and expected of others—particularly their parents. Teen-agers may see their parents not living up to the expectations they hope to attain some day. The older and wiser they get, however, the more accepting they will become of their parents.

By young adulthood individuals are less introspective and more goal-oriented. Glasser (1965), however, believes that youth today are much less goal-oriented than the youth of a generation ago. Today's youth generally seem to be more pleasure- and experience-oriented.

Of course adolescents today face problems that did not exist to any significant extent just one generation ago, such as drugs and the occult. Although political activism occupied many students in the late 1960s, today's adolescents are often characterized more by apathy than by any kind of activism. Sensing a void in their lives, they try to fill it with drugs or other wild experiences. Even many Christian teen-agers seem bored and apathetic, more concerned with narcissistic emotional experiences than with Christ. Evangelical groups like the Navigators, Fellowship of Christian Athletes, Campus Crusade, Inter-Varsity, and Young Life help many young people come to a personal acceptance of Christ. For the Christian, this commitment is critical to achieving proper self-identity (Campolo 1984, 13).

RUNNING AWAY

Running away is a common teen-age problem. Psychiatrists can determine a great deal about teen-agers and their families on the basis of running-away patterns. Spoiled, overly dependent teen-agers (usually girls) run away to punish the family for not letting them have their own way. Such dependent runaways generally see to it that they are caught, usually within twenty-four to forty-eight hours; they cannot bear to be away from their mothers longer than that.

Teen-agers who run away and stay away may be healthier than those who run away for only a day or two. Some teen-agers might mature more by running away than by staying in a mentally unstable home. Teen-agers who run away to make their parents feel guilty should not be rewarded when they return. If running away is a repeated problem, a family should seek counseling to figure out the family's psychodynamics. According to Stierlin (1973), between six hundred thousand and one million teen-agers run away from home each year in America. More than half of them are girls, mostly from the white suburbs. Stierlin (p. 59) notes that

> the more a binding (smothering) parent gratifies, indulges, and spoils his child, the more conflicted, insatiable, and monsterlike the child becomes. This interpersonal scenario—quick disillusionment with peers, heightened conflicts with parents—explains why a good many of these adolescents run away, yet return home quickly as abortive runaways.

The task of the therapist in such situations is to encourage the parent and child to become more independent of each other. In fact, "an offspring's successful running away can signal progress rather than a setback, as it reflects this adolescent's (and his parents') increasing ability to live apart from, and independently of each other" (p. 59).

ENCOURAGEMENT
FOR CHRISTIAN PARENTS

Perhaps the only thing more difficult than being an adolescent is being the parent of an adolescent. Many Christian parents become frightened as they lose control of their children, or disheartened at some of the choices their teen-agers make. Parents need encouragement, especially when they feel they have made serious mistakes. One approach is to remind them that Paul compares the Christian life to a race: "Do you not know that in a race all the runners run, but only one gets the prize? Run in such a way as to get the prize" (1 Cor. 9:24). Paul's competitive spirit may be a stimulus to Christian parents, who are in effect in competition with the world and its influences on their children. Parents strive to produce children who will become emotionally and spiritually healthy.

Each year the best college football players are selected for professional teams in the pro draft. What would happen if God had a "pro draft" each year to select the very best Christian parents to rear chil-

---

Spotlight 11.4. Letting Go

Many Christian parents do not know when to "let go." When a baby robin reaches a certain stage, its mother pushes it out of the nest and the young robin learns how to fly on its way down to the ground. Without adversity and independence, no teen-ager will grow up and "learn to fly." A psychiatrist sees many neurotic and inadequate patients who are still living with their parents at age thirty or even older. This is especially true of young adults who eventually become schizophrenic. It is also true of male alcoholics, many of whom marry several mother-types before divorcing for the last time and moving back to mother to live out their short lives.

It is wise for teen-agers who have graduated from high school to move several hundred miles away from home. At college or in some other situation they can develop their God-given talents and learn the hard lessons of life by making mistakes and then correcting them. If parents have reared their children by God's standards during those crucial first six years of life, when personality is primarily formed, most of them will do well.

Parents should trust their children. If they have not reared their children by God's principles, most attempts to teach eighteen-year-olds something they should have learned at age three will be futile. They need to learn from life; parents should pray that God will mature their children. The greatest freedom is to make a mistake and go on from there, having learned a valuable lesson from the experience. Parents should not kick their children when they are down. They will probably kick themselves enough when no one is looking. If they can learn to lose their fear of failure, they have learned an essential lesson.

dren? Paul says, "Run in such a way as to get the prize." Parents often feel they have made many mistakes. But there is no use in dwelling on the past. They should strive to become the very best parents their children could possibly have. Children can tolerate many parental mistakes. The general *pattern* of child rearing is more important than occasional errors (Kagan 1979).

Christian parents must dedicate themselves to God so he can accomplish what he wants to accomplish in their children. He has promised to help them be the kind of parents he has called them to be. Parents should confess their past mistakes to God, remembering his promise that "if we confess our sins, he is faithful and just and will forgive us our sins and purify us from all unrighteousness" (1 John 1:9). Parents should learn to forgive themselves and move on, "forgetting what is behind and straining toward what is ahead" (Phil. 3:13). God will reward parents richly for turning from the selfish ambitions of this world and totally committing themselves to his highest calling: being wise, strong, loving, and godly Christian parents.

Adult Development

The subject of adult development has only recently been investigated by psychologists. Thus many of the present conclusions in this area are tentative at best. The adult years can be divided into three periods: early adulthood (ages 20–30), middle adulthood (ages 40–65), and later adulthood (postretirement years).

Early Adulthood

Erikson describes the early adult years as the time when the individual chooses either the intimacy of close relationships and/or marriage, with the requisite sacrifices, or chooses the path to isolation because of the fear of such relationships (Papalia and Olds 1986, 399). A mutual and loving heterosexual relationship is the norm for these years of life. The intimacy of marriage and sexual relationships results in the formation of a new family.

LOVE, MARRIAGE, AND SEX

Characteristically American couples "fall in love" and marry for love. Americans are unusual, both historically and culturally, in marrying on the basis of feelings rather than carefully reflecting upon all the factors involved. Many considering divorce complain that they do not "feel anything anymore" and believe that this is an adequate reason for separation. The irrationality of "romantic love" has been documented by sociologists such as Campolo (1986, 148).

What is love, anyway? Is it a feeling? An action? A figment of our imagination? True love is real, even though the love people *think* they have is frequently illusory. Many people mistakenly think of love as an automatic sensation that comes and stays forever when a person performs some magical ritual like saying "I do." Love is more than mere emotion, even though it has a large emotional component.

God has designed us to share our love with others on three planes: spiritual, emotional, and physical. It is important for love relationships to develop in that order. In today's society, the physical "love" that comes first is often simply old-fashioned lust, cheapening the sexual communion created by God. God intended physical, sexual communion, which provides tremendous relief from sexual tensions, to be a regular part of married life. He warned that those who commit fornication, adultery, or homosexual acts will suffer the consequences.

Psychologists see numerous patients with sexual problems because of Victorian misconceptions about what the Bible really says concerning the sexual relationship in marriage. It is sad to see the effects of the Victorian ethic on the children of such husbands and wives. Christians often overlook the fact that Paul warned husbands and wives never to turn each other down for sexual relations, except during prayer (1 Cor. 7:3–5).

Marriage partners whose spouses are insensitive to their sexual needs or feelings about sex will be tempted to meet those needs in unscriptural and neurotic ways. In a Christian marriage, physical affection is beautiful in the eyes of God who created that couple for each other. Sexual union is the physical expression of true love existing on a spiritual and emotional level. It promotes good mental health in the entire family. Sadly, few people reach their true love potential in the marriage relationship.

An adolescent's new-found love, described in honest terms, frequently means something like this: "I want to use you to prove who I am, and to satisfy my physical and ego needs." A naive person feels flattered by this kind of love; an emotionally mature and realistic person, who may feel also physically flattered, knows that such love will not satisfy the soul and spirit. Mature love is patient. Mature love is kind. Mature love seeks the other person's benefit, expecting nothing in return, though appreciative when true love is returned (1 Cor. 13).

Most individuals have learned (and chosen) to love only on an infantile, childish, or adolescent level. Mature, intimate love is found in a few adults, adolescents, and exceptionally mature children. Such individuals have generally sought the help of the God of love in reaching that state: "Dear friends, let us love one another, for love comes from God. Everyone who loves has been born of God and knows God. Whoever does not love does not know God, because God is love" (1 John 4:7–8).

ROLES OF HUSBAND AND WIFE

Husbands and wives are equal, but they have different roles. The role of the husband is that of provider. A husband provides for the spiritual, psychological, and physical needs of his family as well as the sexual needs of his wife. In traditional marriages a husband is regarded as the final authority in the home, even though he consults his wife before making decisions. Finally, the husband is a leader (Blitchington 1980, 65–78).

Several biblical guidelines can help a husband carry out his role. A husband's priority must be loving his wife in the sacrificial and committed way that Christ loved the church (Eph. 5:25–33). Such love provides stability and security. Genuine love avoids harshness (Col. 3:19). Expressions of love, such as flowers, compliments, and phone calls, also underscore a husband's affection for his wife.

A husband should be polite and considerate, showing respect for his wife by opening doors or helping her be seated. Public praise is a positive recognition that will reinforce desired qualities. He should also privately and verbally tell his wife that he loves her and why. The wife should be reminded of her privileged position as a wife. Criticism needs to be private and should never be directed toward unchangeable qualities a wife has. Comparison with other women is certainly unwise, and the husband should not expect more of his wife than of other people. Finally, the husband should avoid going to bed angry (Eph. 4:26–27). Anger should be dealt with immediately and both partners should forgive each other, whether they agree on the issue or not, by the time they go to bed.

The wife's role, as noted earlier, is not inferior to the husband's, but different. While the Bible describes the wife's role as one of submission (Eph. 5:22), this does not demand that the wife become a slave or a brainless, speechless doormat. Submission is basically an attitude of respect for the husband and recognition of his leadership in the home.

Guidelines for the wife include showing her husband respect. A husband needs respect as much as his wife needs love. A wife should avoid discussing her husband's faults in public. A wife should love her husband by knowing what pleases him. Nagging, gossiping, and questioning her husband's decision-making abilities are definitely forbidden.

A wife should also realize that a man is usually more physical in his sexual response, while a woman's sexuality is often more emotional. A man becomes sexually aroused more quickly and tends to be more sexually assertive, sometimes desiring sexual relations more often than his wife. Both partners need to learn to satisfy one another sexually; for example, the husband should learn to lengthen the period of sexual foreplay so that his wife can reach orgasm. Many women fail to respond sexually because their husbands inconsiderately rush through love making (Wheat and Wheat 1981, 89–107).

The wife should be a good manager. Proverbs 31 describes the ideal wife as

"WHILE WE HAVE A LITTLE PEACE AND QUIET, LET'S WORK ON SOME OF YOUR FAULTS."

having good business sense. She should not be lazy, but rather be busy both inside (Titus 2:3–5) and outside the home (Prov. 31). Yet she should not be so involved in outside activities that her responsibilities in the home are short-changed.

THE CHALLENGE OF PARENTHOOD

A major aspect of young adulthood is parenthood. People today seem to be having fewer children later in life. Many couples wait until after age thirty to have their first child. Certainly there is wisdom in not having children immediately after marriage. A couple needs time to become adjusted to one another and to their new roles as husband and wife. There are certainly advantages and disadvantages to starting a family early, but the advantages generally outweigh the disadvantages (Olds 1983). While children can certainly be an emotional and financial strain, there is evidence that much of the research in this area takes an unfairly negative view of rearing children in the earlier years of marriage (Papalia and Olds 1986, 422).

God has given parents an awesome responsibility to "train a child in the way he should go" (Prov. 22:6). How parents train their children during the first six years of life will affect those lives for perhaps sixty or seventy years, and may determine how much enjoyment and success they experience.

God's concern for children is evident throughout Scripture. "People were bringing little children to Jesus to have him touch them, but the disciples rebuked them" (Mark 10:13). The disciples obviously thought Christ was too busy talking to adults to waste his time with children. But

when Jesus saw this, he was indignant. He said to them, "Let the little children come to me, and do not hinder them, for the kingdom of God belongs to such as

---

Spotlight 11.5.
Resources on Marriage and Parenting

Many books by Christians are available on the topics of marriage and parenting. Many of these are based upon personal experiences, while others make use of scholarly research.

Among the best resources on marriage and family (other than those mentioned in other chapters of this text) are Grunlan's *Marriage and Family* (1984), Balswicks' *The Family* (1989), and Rekers' *Family Building* (1985). The latter is a compilation of materials by twenty-three authors. The book centers on six qualities generally found in strong families: commitment, time spent together, good communication, the expression of appreciation for one another, spiritual commitment, and being able to deal with crisis situations. A fourth resource to consider is *Marital Counseling* (1981), written by well-known Christian counselor Norman Wright. Finally, James Dobson has written, at last count, twelve books that deal with marriage and parenting issues, all of which are very readable and entertaining. His practical perspectives are both psychologically sound and thoroughly Christian.

Recent writers tend to combine marital issues with the stages of adult development, such as Conways' *Your Marriage Can Survive Mid-Life Crisis* (1988), Wright's *Seasons of a Marriage* (1982), and Olthuis's *Keeping Our Troth* (1986).

---

these. I tell you the truth, anyone who will not receive the kingdom of God like a little child will never enter it." And he took the children in his arms, put his hands on them and blessed them. (Mark 10:14–16)

Childlike qualities are held up as examples for adults in a passage in Matthew, which also gives a warning about our attitudes toward children:

At that time the disciples came to Jesus and asked, "Who is the greatest in the kingdom of heaven?"

He called a little child and had him stand among them. And he said: "I tell you the truth, unless you change and become like little children, you will never enter the kingdom of heaven. Therefore, whoever humbles himself like this child is the greatest in the kingdom of heaven.

And whoever welcomes a little child like this in my name welcomes me. But if anyone causes one of these little ones who believe in me to sin, it would be better for him to have a large millstone hung around his neck and to be drowned in the depths of the sea.

Woe to the world because of the things that cause people to sin! Such things must come, but woe to the man through whom they come!" (Matt. 18:1–7)

Another warning God has given about children should make parents think soberly about their child-rearing responsibilities: "I, the LORD your God, am a jealous God, punishing the children for the sin of the fathers to the third and fourth generation of those who hate me, but showing love to a thousand generations of those who love me and keep my commandments" (Exod. 20:5–6).

Many people are troubled by this passage, not understanding how a loving God could punish three or four generations of children for the sins of their parents. This seems inconsistent with the passages about Christ's love for children as recorded in the Gospels. Yet a psychiatrist who sees mentally disturbed children every day and has to deal with their parents and grandparents can grasp the meaning of the passage immediately.

One of the main causes of neurotic parent-child relationships is a neurotic husband-wife relationship. Treatment for chil-

Spotlight 11.6.
Are Parents to Blame for Their Children's Behavior?

Myers and Jeeves (1987, 36–40) raise the intriguing question of how much credit or blame parents should receive for their children's behavior. Throughout the discussion of child psychology in the previous chapter and also in the adolescent section of this chapter, we have assumed that parents can powerfully influence their children. Yet should parents take complete credit for their children's behavior or assume full responsibility for their failures?

Dobson (1978b, 20) points out that certain children seem to be born with nasty temperaments. As he puts it, they enter the delivery room "smoking a cigar and yelling about the temperature." They are demanding, strong-willed youngsters whose defiance is a continual trial to their parents. Other children are more compliant and easy to get along with. Perhaps the majority are somewhere in between, although Dobson believes there are more in the defiant category than in other categories (1978b, 22).

While we can learn a great deal about parenting from available psychological research and literature, and we should give our children every possible advantage in this area, we must also realize that the outcome is not completely in our hands. There are normal adults who come out of very poor childhood environments, while some children from fine homes with good parents do not turn out well.

How can this be? As the Bible states, each of us has choices to make in our lives. God, in his wisdom, has permitted us a degree of freedom. We are not completely determined by our parents, but are a combination of inherited personality dispositions, parental influences, and personal choices.

Dobson (1987, 184–86) emphasizes that we must correctly interpret Proverbs 22:6: "Train a child in the way he should go, and when he is old he will not turn from it." This proverb, like most other proverbs, is probabilistic. The proverbs in the Bible are not absolute statements that never have any exceptions, but descriptions of *trends* in human behavior.

Consider Proverbs 10:27: "The fear of the LORD adds length to life, but the years of the wicked are cut short." While this is a general tendency, there are definite exceptions to the rule; some godly people die young and some wicked people live to old age. Likewise, Proverbs 22:6, correctly interpreted, indicates that properly reared children are *more likely* to not depart from the faith, but this certainly does not take away their freedom of choice. We as Christians should do out best to rear children according to biblical guidelines and valid psychological principles, but there comes a time when we must let them make their own decisions (see spotlight 11.3). Our responsibility is to do our best, but the final outcome is not entirely under our control.

dren's problems often requires helping the parents to learn better ways to live and love. Husbands and wives whose love needs are not being met by their mates often look elsewhere for satisfaction. A husband may get involved in an affair; a wife may develop a neurotic need for her child to love her. A neurotic mother may be so desperate for her children to love her that she is afraid to spank them when they need it; spanking would cause them to stop loving her for a few minutes or hours. Mothers or fathers may turn to their children for love, treating a child of the opposite sex like a little husband or wife.

Some mothers do not want their children to grow up because of an intense fear of being left alone eventually without the only relationship they have. Hence they smother their children, spoil them, make all their decisions for them, and discourage independence. By the time they are six, such children may be afraid to go to school because they are too neurotically involved with their mothers. In their teens, recognizing their inadequacies, they may turn to drugs or alcohol, hate their mothers, and fail to become emotionally mature. When her children eventually marry and have children of their own, the neurotic mother may extend her attempts to dominate into the new home, smothering the grandchildren and dividing their parents. Generations can be affected by a husband and wife who do not love each other as they should.

Parents who live sinful lives, lives that are not in accord with the health-producing principles of God's Word, will have a profound effect on their children and their children's children, to three or four generations. *God* is not punishing their offspring for their sins, but *parents* are—by not living according to his precepts.

Levinson's stages of adulthood

Levinson (1978) conducted in-depth interviews with men to determine how adults change as they grow older. He found that during the late teen-age years to about age twenty-four the man is in transition from preadult to adult status. In the process he generally moves out of his parents' home and becomes more independent.

Males enter the adult world between the ages of twenty-two and twenty-eight. However, there is a tentativeness about occupational commitments during these years. Some men are committed and stable, while others are dreamers who keep their options open. Often the male develops an especially close relationship with a mentor, an older person about eight to fifteen years his senior, who offers insight, inspiration, and support.

Between ages twenty-eight and thirty-three there is another time of transition in which the person takes a second look at his commitments and either concludes that he was premature or else recommits himself to his occupation and marriage. This transition phase can result in a crisis, and a high percentage of men begin a new job. There is also a peak in the divorce rate. Additional research by Sheehy (1976) indicates that many women experience a similar transition at about age thirty, often moving from a focus on career to a new emphasis upon home and child rearing.

Levinson notes that the individual then moves on to another phase in young adulthood, from ages thirty-two to forty, where there is a settling down and the development of a second structure of adult life (in contrast to the first structure developed in the twenties). People set new goals and try to establish their place in society, attempting to advance while also being committed to stability.

Near the end of this settling down phase the male often begins to feel the need for greater independence from constraint and oppression, but he also desires respect and affirmation. He may begin to be at odds with family, friends, and those at work. The mentor of an earlier phase of adulthood is generally lost by this time.

At this point the person tends to take one of five alternative ways of adjusting. Most individuals commit themselves to their chosen careers. Some experience serious failure—at least from their own perspective. Some believe that they need a radical change, and struggle to determine which direction their career should take. Some may receive a promotion. Finally, a small percentage are characterized by instability, usually an instability that continues throughout their thirties.

Women often follow a similar course, although they find themselves trying to deal with the conflict between the more traditional role of child rearing and home making, and the contrary social pressure to advance in an occupation outside the home. Even outside the home, however, such women are likely to describe their work in terms of relationships rather than specific achievements (Gilligan 1983).

Middle Adulthood

At about age forty, a person enters midlife. Erikson (1963) describes the issue at this stage as generativity versus stagnation; individuals can choose to help the next generation (guiding their own children or becoming mentors). While self-centeredness is to be avoided, some degree of inactivity is helpful.

Middle-age people who successfully adjust to life tend to make four necessary changes. First, they come to define themselves in terms of wisdom rather than physical strength, which is usually beginning to diminish by this time. Second, they value people for their unique personalities and for the companionship they provide. Emotional flexibility is important, as people begin to lose certain relationships through the death of parents or friends. Finally, while people have generally found answers to life, they keep an openness and flexibility in their evaluations.

Jung (1933, 278) suggests that during middle age there is a shift from an emphasis upon outer aspects of life (such as occupation and family) to inner aspects of life (searching for answers). Those over age forty generally are oriented toward spiritual issues. Midlife is often portrayed as a time of intense questioning and career change or divorce.

Spotlight 11.7.
Using Mentors in the Church

Most churches have "elders" who help the pastor deal with the needs of the congregation. Perhaps such people could be used as mentors for younger adults in the church, particularly those who are spiritually immature. Too often Christians try to go it alone when the Bible clearly tells us we belong to the *community* of believers. Joy (1988, 109–12) notes that Paul was Timothy's mentor. Often the pastor is somewhat removed from the congregation. A program of discipleship involving older, more mature Christian laypersons is needed. Not only could such mentors deal with problems younger people have, but there could also be periodic spiritual checkups to determine how younger adults are developing spiritually. Spiritual mentors should avoid dominating the relationship; there should be definite give and take.

Recent evidence, however, suggests that such a crisis is most likely in lower middle-class men, such as clerical workers and small businessmen (Farrell and Rosenberg 1981, 83–88). Such individuals appear to be well adjusted, but tend to project their problems upon others. A crisis may be precipitated by a wife who threatens to leave because of the facade. Twelve percent of people in this situation have a clear-cut crisis; 56 percent have a crisis but hide it or do not fully realize it is occurring; and the remainder do not have a crisis. In fact, the "midlife crisis" is often an expression of long-term feelings of insecurity. Perhaps this crisis has been conveniently used as an excuse for adultery and other irresponsible behaviors.

Levinson emphasizes that the forty- to forty-five-year-old is in transition, consistent with the supposed "midlife crisis," but by the mid-forties again settles down either using routines established earlier in life or new choices that have come out of the transitional crisis. Levinson notes that many people find this the most creative and fulfilling time of their lives.

From age fifty to fifty-five the male may again be in transition, but will probably not undergo another crisis unless he failed to do so earlier. From fifty-five to sixty he is again fulfilled; from sixty to sixty-five he begins a transition to retirement and late adulthood. During this phase of middle adulthood, women have to make adjustments to the "empty nest" when the children leave home, as well as the physical strain of menopause. However, researchers conclude that these adjustments are not as difficult as usually thought, although women at this time do report an intense struggle in making the transition from being home- and family-centered to taking on new roles outside the home (Baruch, Barnett, and Rivers 1983; Rubin 1979).

Later Adulthood

The later years of life are marked by a gradual decline in both physical and mental abilities. Although there is a tendency to stereotype elderly people as "old and senile," many maintain their mental abilities for decades, even though they are more likely to suffer from illness and physical impairment. Many of the elderly are faced with poor housing, loneliness, and a loss of social status as well as income (Peters 1985, 209–12).

Erikson (1963) notes that this time of life involves the crisis of ego integrity as opposed to despair. Older adults either accept or regret their past. Those who achieve ego integrity believe that they have done their best and accept their imperfections and shortcomings. In contrast, those who do not achieve ego integrity are reduced to despair, realizing that it is too late to start over. All elderly people have some degree of despair, Erikson points out. The elderly now have time to play—in a sense, experience a second childhood—and continue to be creative, sexual beings.

The years of later adulthood also involve the development of new family roles, including that of grandparent. Grandparents usually enjoy their grandchildren as much or more than their own children because they do not have the responsibilities or time pressures that go with having children. Sometimes there is also role reversal, as grown children begin to "parent" their elderly parents.

Older people suffer a loss of status in our society, unlike other societies where the elderly are valued for their wisdom. Many older adults are neglected or sent to nursing homes. A youth-oriented society such as ours can easily overlook the important contribution that the aged can provide.

Maloney (1986) maintains that older adults want to participate, not passively watch others. Older people tend to be

---

Spotlight 11.8. Resources on Adult Development and Death

There are several important books on the subject of adult development. Chic Sell, a Christian education professor at Trinity Evangelical Divinity School, has written *Transition* (1985). Stubblefield's *Church Ministering to Adults* (1986) makes use of adult developmental theory. Two religious education texts that are not always evangelical but nonetheless helpful are *The Religious Education of Adults* (McKenzie 1982) and *The Religious Education of Older Adults* (Vogel 1984). An older but still usable source is Collins' *Man in Transition* (1971).

Two excellent resources on death and dying are *Resources for Ministry in Death and Dying* (Platt and Branch 1988) and *When Someone You Love Is Dying* (Kopp 1980). *Death and the Caring Community* (Richards and Johnson 1980) and *Facing Death and the Life After* (Graham 1987) may also be helpful.

---

more intellectual, tolerant, and reflective; they may make decisions for Christ for the first time. Maloney concludes that as the baby boom generation moves toward old age, there will be an increased need for geriatric care in hospitals and other human service settings. There will also be more people to visit, with the number of hospitalized people from a typical congregation increasing from ten at present to twenty or thirty.

Another concern which the elderly face is death. In recent years there has been an increased interest in this area. A number of excellent resources are available that reflect both Christian and psychological insights on dying and bereavement.

Clearly human development does not end with childhood or adolescence. There is, in fact, a potential for continued emotional, spiritual, and mental growth throughout life.

References

Alexander, J. 1973. Defensive and supportive communications in normal and deviant families. *Journal of Consulting Clinical Psychiatry* 40: 223–31.

Balswick, J., and J. Balswick. 1989. *The family*. Grand Rapids: Baker.

Baruch, G., R. Barnett, and C. Rivers. 1983. *Lifeprints*. New York: McGraw-Hill.

Blitchington, W. 1980. *Sex roles and the Christian family*. Wheaton, Ill.: Tyndale.

Blos, P. 1962. *On adolescence*. New York: Free.

Caine, N. 1986. Behavior during puberty and adolescence. In *Comparative primate biology*, eds. G. Mitchell and J. Erwin. Vol. 2. New York: Liss.

Campolo, A. 1984. *You can make a difference*. Waco: Word.

———. 1986. *Who switched the price tags?* Waco: Word.

———. 1989. *A sociology of youth ministry*. Grand Rapids: Zondervan.

Campolo, A., and D. Ratcliff. 1991. Activist youth ministry. In *Handbook of Youth Ministry*, eds. D. Ratcliff and J. Davies. Birmingham, Ala.: Religious Education.

Collins, G. 1971. *Man in transition*. Carol Stream, Ill.: Creation.

Conway, J., and S. Conway. 1988. *Your marriage can survive mid-life crisis*. Nashville: Nelson.

Costanzo, P., and M. Shaw. 1966. Conformity as a function of age level. *Child Development* 37: 967–75.

Dobson, J. 1978a. *Preparing for adolescence.* Santa Ana, Calif.: Vision.

———. 1978b. *The strong-willed child.* Wheaton, Ill.: Tyndale.

———. 1980. *Emotions: Can you trust them?* Ventura, Calif.: Regal.

———. 1987. *Parenting isn't for cowards.* Waco: Word.

Elkind, D. 1981. *The hurried child.* Reading, Mass.: Addison-Wesley.

———. 1984. *All grown up and no place to go.* Reading, Mass.: Addison-Wesley.

Erikson, E. 1963. *Childhood and society.* 2d rev. ed. New York: Norton.

Farrell, M., and S. Rosenberg. 1981. *Men at midlife.* Boston: Auburn.

Gilligan, C. 1983. *In a different voice.* Cambridge, Mass.: Harvard University Press.

Gjerde, P. 1986. The interpersonal structure of family interaction settings. *Developmental Psychology* 22: 297–304.

Glasser, W. *Reality therapy.* New York: Harper and Row.

Graham, B. 1987. *Facing death and the life after.* Waco: Word.

Grunlan, S. 1984. *Marriage and the family.* Grand Rapids: Zondervan.

Havighurst, R. 1972. *Developmental tasks and education.* 3d ed. New York: David McKay.

Joy, D. 1988. *Walk on.* Wheaton, Ill.: Victor.

Jung, C. 1933. *Modern man in search of a soul.* New York: Harcourt, Brace.

Kagan, J. 1979. Family experience and the child's development. *American Psychologist* 34: 886–91.

Kesler, J., ed. 1984. *Parents and teenagers.* Wheaton, Ill.: Victor.

Kinsey, A., et al. 1948. *Sexual behavior in the human male.* Philadelphia: Saunders.

———. 1953. *Sexual behavior in the human female.* Philadelphia: Saunders.

Kopp, R. 1980. *When someone you love is dying.* Grand Rapids: Zondervan.

Kotesky, R. 1981. Growing up too late, too soon. *Christianity Today* (Mar. 13): 24–28.

———. 1987. *Understanding adolescence.* Wheaton, Ill.: Victor.

———. 1991. Adolescence as a cultural invention. In *Handbook of Youth Ministry,* eds. D. Ratcliff and J. Davies. Birmingham, Ala.: Religious Education.

Levinson, D. 1978. *Seasons of a man's life.* New York: Knopf.

Lidz, T. 1968. *The person.* New York: Basic.

McKenzie, L. 1982. *The religious education of adults.* Birmingham, Ala.: Religious Education.

McPherson, S., et al. 1973. Who listens? Who communicates? *Archives of General Psychiatry* 28: 393–99.

Maloney, H. 1986. The graying of America. *Christianity Today* (Jan. 17): 8.1–9.1.

Montemayor, R. 1982. The relationship between parent-adolescent conflict and the amount of time adolescents spend alone. *Child Development* 53: 1512–19.

The myth of the generation gap. 1984. *Christianity Today* (Oct. 19): 14–19.

Odom, L., J. Seeman, and J. Newbrough. 1971. A study of family communication patterns and personality integration in children. *Child Psychiatry and Human Development* 1: 285.

Olds, S. 1983. *The working parents' survival guide.* New York: Bantam.

Olthuis, J. 1986. *Keeping our troth.* San Francisco: Harper and Row.

Papalia, D., and S. Olds. 1986. *Human development.* New York: McGraw-Hill.

Peters, J. 1985. Youth and aging. In *Social problems: Christian perspectives,* eds. C. DeSanto and M. Poloma. Winston-Salem, N.C.: Hunter.

Peterson, A. 1988. Adolescent development. *Annual Review of Psychology* 39: 583–607.

Piaget, J. 1967. *Six psychological studies.* New York: Random.

Platt, L., and R. Branch. 1988. *Resources for ministry in death and dying.* Nashville: Broadman.

Reardon, D. 1987. *Aborted women.* Westchester, Ill.: Crossway.

Rekers, G. 1985. *Family building.* Ventura, Calif.: Regal.

Richards, L., and P. Johnson. 1980. *Death and the caring community.* Portland, Oreg.: Multnomah.

Rubin, C. 1979. *Women of a certain age.* New York: Harper.

Sebald, H., and B. White. 1980. Teenagers' divided reference groups. *Adolescence* 15: 979–89.

Segal, B., et al. 1967. Work, play and emotional disturbance. *Archives of General Psychiatry* 15: 173.

Sell, C. 1985. *Transition*. Chicago: Moody.

Selman, R. 1980. *The growth of interpersonal understanding*. New York: Academic.

Sheehy, G. 1976. *Passages*. New York: Dutton.

Steinberg, L., and S. Silverberg. 1986. The vicissitudes of autonomy in early adolescence. *Child Development* 57: 841–51.

Stierlin, H. 1973. A family perspective on adolescent runaways. *Archives of General Psychiatry* 29: 59.

Strommen, M. 1988. *Five cries of youth*. Rev. ed. San Francisco: Harper and Row.

Strommen, M., and A. Strommen. 1985. *Five cries of parents*. San Francisco: Harper and Row.

Stubblefield, J. 1986. *A church ministering to adults*. Nashville: Broadman.

Udry, R., and L. Tolbert. 1988. Sex hormone effects on personality at puberty. *Journal of Personality and Social Psychology* 54: 291–95.

Vogel, L. 1984. *The religious education of older adults*. Birmingham, Ala.: Religious Education.

Wheat, E., and G. Wheat. 1981. *Intended for pleasure*. Rev. ed. Old Tappan, N.J.: Revell.

Wilson, J., C. Beecham, and E. Carrington. 1966. *Obstetrics and gynecology*. St. Louis: Mosby.

Wright, H. 1981. *Marital counseling*. Denver, Colo.: Christian Marriage Enrichment.

———. 1982. *Seasons of a marriage*. Ventura, Calif.: Regal.

Wyckoff, D., and D. Richter. 1982. *Religious education ministry with youth*. Birmingham, Ala.: Religious Education.

12

Personality

Personality is the ingrained pattern of behavior, thoughts, and feelings consistent across situations and time. Although we tend to act differently depending upon whom we are talking to, there are certain tendencies in behavior and thinking which persist regardless of the situation or person.

Theories of Personality

While there are a number of theories of personality, four have become dominant in this century. One of the oldest theories of personality is the trait theory. The ancient Greeks categorized people as phlegmatic (emotionless), choleric (active and irritable), sanguine (happy), and melancholic (depressive). LaHaye (1971) attempted to incorporate these temperaments into a Christian framework, but most psychologists would agree that these categories are hopelessly dated.

Sheldon (1942) maintains that personality is linked to body type. The ectomorph is a thin, fragile, inhibited, and scholarly person; the endomorph is soft and round, sociable, and affectionate; the mesomorph is strong, muscular, and noted for courage, aggression, and activity. Sheldon's categories are considered little more than stereotypes by many psychologists, although Tucker (1983) provides evidence which supports Sheldon's ideas.

Allport (1937) holds that there are three kinds of traits: cardinal traits influence personality the most; central traits are more common but not all-consuming; and secondary traits are preferences in given situations.

How many traits are possible? Certainly thousands, in that a trait can be any characteristic of an individual. Cattell (1973) identifies sixteen traits based upon his research. The many traits possible in different coding systems account for the popularity of trait theories, but also makes this approach highly questionable. Traits are often oversimplified descriptions of people. We do not observe traits, but infer them from behavior. In addition, trait theories tend to overlook the influence of context upon behavior. Finally, there is the already noted problem of stereotyping. Traits do not always cluster together (for example, not all obese people are sociable like Sheldon suggests).

Somewhat similar to trait theory is Kelly's personal-construct theory. According to Kelly, people create their own constructs of opposite categories, such as kind-unkind and smart-dumb, which they then use to understand others and interpret events. In a particular situation, some of these constructs take on more importance than others. Thus the subjective perspective of the individual becomes all-important.

Freud (1900) saw personality as a matter of hidden, unconscious conflicts between the id (innate basic drives) and the superego (the socially acquired conscience). The negotiator between these unconscious components is the ego or self. Conflicts are central to personality, and can be dealt with in a number of ways, including defense mechanisms. Freud focused on the hidden, negative influences that he saw as most important to an individual's personality.

A third major theory of personality is that of the behaviorists, which we examined in depth in chapter 6. Patterns of behavior, thinking, and feeling are due to prior contingencies, such as reinforcements, punishments, and conditioned responses. If taken to its philosophical extreme, this would mean that people are basically neither good nor bad but rather amoral. Their personalities are strictly the result of prior conditioning. While a Christian would obviously have difficulty accepting the philosophical extreme of behaviorism, it is possible to accept the fact

of behavioral influences upon personality. A variation of the behavioral approach is Bandura's social learning theory.

A fourth major theory, that of humanistic or phenomenological psychology, emphasizes the basic goodness of humanity. Rogers (1959) states that people are *becoming*, naturally developing toward greater wholeness and self-understanding. The key to becoming is being accepted unconditionally. Another phenomenological psychologist, Maslow, emphasizes the importance of having needs fulfilled (see chap. 5); the culmination of this process is self-actualization. Although the Christian should question the humanist belief that goodness is the fundamental characteristic of humanity, this does not require a complete dismissal of phenomenological theory.

From a Christian perspective, we can find value in each of the four theories in their attempt to develop a holistic perspective on personality. The Freudian theory underscores the darker side of the human condition. As Heinroth notes, the id is the sin nature that we possess. There is something fundamentally distorted about human nature, and the biblical concept of innate sin is the best explanation for that distortion.

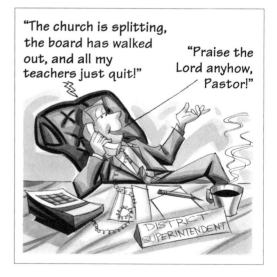

"The church is splitting, the board has walked out, and all my teachers just quit!"

"Praise the Lord anyhow, Pastor!"

Yet, as Darling (1969, 25) has so cogently stated, "theologians, it would seem, have told us the truth, but unfortunately they have not told us the *whole* truth." People also have something very good about them; they still bear the image of God from creation, though that image is seriously marred.

Behavioral theory can help us fill out the picture of personality more completely. Behaviorism helps explain why people act as they do by focusing on previous rewards and punishments. Behaviorism helps explain specific sinful behavior, but not the fact that people do sin. Combining these major theories of personality with each other and Christian doctrine provides a foundation for a Christian theory of personality.[1]

Personality Testing

Psychologists and other researchers sometimes make use of tests in their attempt to understand personality. There are both objective and projective personality tests. They differ in both form and underlying assumptions. Objective tests have been most influenced by trait theories, while projective tests developed largely through the influence of Freudian theory.

Objective tests are self-report inventories in which an individual is asked a number of questions, such as "Do you like to read mechanics magazines?" or "Do you get up most mornings feeling fresh and relaxed?" Through asking a number of questions related to a particular aspect of personality, certain trends in answers are found which are thought to reflect personality patterns. Objective personality tests are often used by colleges, employers, and mission boards to identify those who have major personality problems.

---

1. See also Burke 1987; VanLeeuwen 1985; Philipchalk 1988; and Kotesky 1980 for other ways of looking at personality from a Christian perspective.

The Taylor–Johnson and Minnesota Multiphasic Personality Inventory (MMPI) are commonly used objective personality tests. The MMPI is a standard tool of clinicians who treat or evaluate psychopathology. Its authors developed the test to reflect deviation from normality on ten clinical scales of psychiatric distress, such as depression, psychopathic deviance, and schizophrenia. The MMPI therefore can be an indicator of emotional disturbance, although it affords a relatively poor description of normal personality.

Projective tests present a standardized set of ambiguous or neutral stimuli, such as inkblots or drawings for an individual to respond to. The person administering the test then subjectively interprets the responses. Projective tests generally require individual administration and tend to be heavily influenced by the assumptions of the test authors and evaluators. The Rorschach Ink-Blot Test (see tab. 12.1) and the Thematic Apperception Test (TAT) are well-known projective tests. The assumption behind these tests is that the personality is deeply hidden in the unconsciousness of the person, which can be examined only indirectly. In general, projective personality tests have much lower reliability and validity than objective tests.

Why Are Personality Tests Used?

Personality tests can help a therapist make diagnostic decisions. Problems are not always clear from the onset of counseling, and personality tests can clarify what the basic problem really is. In some cases, clients are nonverbal or lack the ability to sufficiently describe the real problem.

Personality tests tend to assume the medical model of personality (Stuart 1970, 6–7), which states that outward behavioral difficulties are mere symptoms of a deeper underlying cause. Just as a virus is the cause of a cold, a presenting problem is the

Table 12.1
Sample Interpretations of Rorschach Responses

This is a butterfly. Here are the wings, feelers, and legs.

Using the whole blot in this way is considered fo reflect the subject's ability to organize and relate materials.

This is part of a chicken's leg.

Referring to only a part of this inkblot is usually interpreted as indicative of an interest in the concrete.

This could be a face.

The use of an unusual or tiny portion of this blot may suggest pedantic trends.

Source: Benjamin Kleinmuntz, *Essentials of Abnormal Psychology* (New York: Harper and Row, 1974), p. 78.

manifestation of a more basic problem. If we treat only the presenting problem, as many behaviorists do, some believe it is more likely that the underlying cause will make itself known through another outward problem ("symptom substitution").

Personality tests may be used as screening devices to identify those with psychological disturbances. Mission boards and employers often want to discover those with major difficulties before they are placed in important positions. Thousands of dollars and many months of preparation may be wasted if problems are not discovered early.

Personality tests can also be used as research tools. Certain personality traits may be associated with successful teaching; or patterns of test scores may relate to categories of abnormality.

The Value of Personality Testing

In recent years, psychologists have begun to question the use of personality testing. Perhaps the most complete critical review of personality testing is to be found in Mischel's *Personality and Assessment* (1968, 41–148). Mischel points out that most psychologists no longer use personality tests in counseling, and documents a number of reasons for that decline.

One of Mischel's objections is that many questions on personality tests are vague; the same question can be answered several different ways depending upon an individual's interpretation and mood. There is also evidence that test scores do not predict problem behavior as well as accounts of relevant past history. Personality tests make no allowance for cultural and ethnic distinctives. There is also the possibility of faking socially desirable answers. Mischel describes the problem of labeling: the categorizing of behavior makes it more likely that counselors will overlook contrary evidence and even create or encourage pathological behavior

---

Spotlight 12.1. The Ethics of Personality Testing

In recent years ethical issues in psychological testing have become a concern. Those who use such instruments have an obligation to do so in an ethical manner; people are not objects to be manipulated. The American Psychological Association (1981), in fact, has developed a number of ethical principles that relate to research, therapy, and testing.

Confidentiality and invasion of privacy are issues in personality testing. Not only might test results become common knowledge and thus unfairly prejudice others, but people might try to use test results without recognizing the limitations of such tests. Most counselors use tests as *possible* indicators of problems, not authoritative summaries of personality. Although test results may indicate certain trends, someone who is unfamiliar with the limitations of such testing may unfairly conclude that a definite defect is found just because a score is unusual.

For example, a student was given the popular Taylor–Johnson inventory. He received poor scores on every scale of the test. However, when he was interviewed by the examiner he admitted that he had been having an unusually bad day when he took the test. The student was encouraged to take the test later when he was in a better mood; the scores were normal on all the scales.

The effectiveness rate of personality tests should be a concern. Every measure can be described in terms of "hits" and "misses" (validity). If the number of times a measure is correct significantly exceeds the number of times it is mistaken, the measurement device is considered effective. Yet even a high ratio of hits to misses may not ethically justify the use of a personality test. For example, suppose a test was 90 percent accurate (which would be quite good for a personality test). That would mean that there would be nine accurate assessments for every one inaccurate assessment. But what about that other 10 percent? If one out of every ten people developed psychological problems not present previously because of taking a test, is that test not a menace to mental health?

Perhaps personality testing can be used with ethical integrity when results are used cautiously and without communicating them to the person taking the test. Personality tests should be given only when the person taking the test has willingly consented to the process and confidentiality is assured. Finally, the results of tests must be weighed against the even more important factors of relevant past experience and clinical observation. For example, in evaluating potential missionaries, a brief internship may provide better indications of potential problems than a test.

---

consistent with a given category. Finally, the medical model is an insufficient basis for understanding all problems, demonstrated by the lack of evidence for symptom substitution (Stuart 1970, 9, 103–17).

One particularly telling experiment may

help show why personality tests remain popular among some counselors:

> College students were administered personality tests and then given personality descriptions. . . . Although the interpretations supposedly were based on their psychological test results, in fact each of the fifty-seven students obtained the identical report. . . . The overwhelming majority of the students indicated the reports captured their personalities very well. Of the fifty-seven students, fifty-three rated the report as either excellent or good, only three giving it an average rating, one calling the interpretation poor, and none very poor. Their general enthusiasm was also reflected in open-ended comments of great praise and excitement. (Mischel 1968, 128–29)

Should Personality Tests Be Used?

Recent writers, such as Phares (1988, 62), continue to emphasize both the strengths and weaknesses of personality tests. Apparently some problems fit the medical model, and thus are more amenable to personality testing; other problems are habits resulting from faulty conditioning or other sources.

Personality tests are most likely to have value in evaluation of the nonverbal or inarticulate client, yet may prove to be misleading for problems best understood by conditioning models of learning. Psychologists stand on both sides of this issue. It is important to note that the position taken by a particular psychologist is in no way a reflection of competence. Perhaps the best conclusion is that personality tests should be given with caution, if they are used at all, because they are created by human beings and thus are less than perfect.

Defense Mechanisms

Freud and those who followed after him described a number of ways that an individual deals with unconscious anxiety. These mechanisms are defensive in the sense that they protect an individual from seeing unconscious conflicts, and from others seeing the problems. Defense mechanisms have several characteristics.

First, defense mechanisms are by definition unconscious, that is, they are not consciously chosen nor are they even aspects of mental functioning about which we can easily become aware.

Second, defense mechanisms are ways of protecting us from painful emotions and experiences. They are used to help us avoid anxiety from inner conflicts that we do not want to deal with. For example, being around people who have problems similar to our own may result in our condemnation or rejection of such people because they remind us unconsciously of ourselves. The overly critical parent can quickly see certain shortcomings in a child, for example, because the parent has those same weaknesses.

Third, defense mechanisms are self-deceptive. Because they involve deception, they are generally sinful. Mature Christians should occasionally analyze their behavior to see their own blind spots (although this can be overdone.)

Fourth, defense mechanisms are used by everyone, although some people use more of them more often. The only exception is Christ; he had no sinful motives and conflicts.

Fifth, defense mechanisms may prevent or delay psychological problems. Knowing all of our unconscious conflicts at one time might prove to be overwhelming; thus the mind uses defense mechanisms to avoid them. In contrast, allowing God to gradually reveal the truth about our unconscious mind can help us become genuinely free; Christ gives us a new heart and a new mind.

In examining defense mechanisms, we can begin to see the degree to which we have been affected by the sin nature. At the deepest levels of our existence, the unconscious mind, we are basically selfish, distorted, and destructive. Theologians term this condition "depravity" (Ryrie 1984, 312–13). Yet people are blind to their own basic sinfulness; there are sinful influences in our lives that we are not even aware of. Even good acts that we do may be the result of unconscious sinful motives; we can deceive others (and ourselves) into thinking we are basically good and do not need God. Repentance from sin involves more than consciously known acts of sin; we need to repent of hidden attitudes and inner dispositions of which we are not aware. These, too, need the healing of God.

Finding out the truth about our depravity is a painful process that brings temporary pain, partly because the more we learn about the depraved motives, desires, and defense mechanisms of humankind in general, the more we learn about our own. In the end, that knowledge can bring us joy and a greater acceptance of others. After all, who are we to condemn a person for being unrighteous when we are depraved ourselves? That would add hypocrisy to our already long list of conscious and unconscious sins.

Paul encourages Christians not only to examine themselves (2 Cor. 13:5), but also to faithfully confront other Christians in love (Eph. 4:15; 2 Tim. 4:1–5). God asks that we correct our neighbors as needed, though never in a hostile or vengeful spirit. We must love our neighbor as ourselves (Lev. 19:17–18).

Christians are to get rid of the sins in their lives and everything else that hinders them from serving God. This includes childhood conflicts, hangups, and defense mechanisms. God enables us to do this gradually, to spare us the pain of seeing ourselves as we really are all at once. Experienced psychiatrists know that patients have to be stripped of their defense mechanisms gradually; to do so rapidly might produce a psychotic break to escape overwhelming emotional pain.

There is a plethora of defense mechanisms (DSM III-R 1987, 393–95). Some of them are associated with severe psychological problems (see chaps. 14 and 15). Here we will consider the most common defense mechanisms.[2]

Repression

Lidz (1968, 256) defines repression as "the barring or banishment of memories, perceptions, or feelings that would arouse the forbidden." Lidz believes that "in order to prevent rearousal of some childhood sexual experiences or the discomfort of remembering sexual desires for a parent, the entire period of early childhood may be repressed."

Repression not only hides ideas and impulses from awareness, but the previously repressed content is also prevented from coming into conscious awareness. Repression is the primary defense mechanism on which all other defense mechanisms are based, and thus is the most commonly used defense mechanism.

Projection

Projection involves the attributing of one's own impulses or wishes to someone else. A boy who feels hostile toward his sister, but does not want the uncomfort-

---

2. For a description of defense mechanisms in the Book of James, see Nelson 1976.

able feelings that accompany hostile wishes, may convince himself that it is really his sister who is angry at him. Adults with little sense of self-worth often use projection, becoming very critical of others who have problems that unconsciously remind them of their own. Jesus addresses the use of projection in Matthew 7:1–5:

> Do not judge, or you too will be judged. For in the same way you judge others, you will be judged, and with the measure you use, it will be measured to you.
>
> Why do you look at the speck of sawdust in your brother's eye and pay no attention to the plank in your own eye? How can you say to your brother, "Let me take the speck out of your eye," when all the time there is a plank in your own eye? You hypocrite, first take the plank out of your own eye, and then you will see clearly to remove the speck from your brother's eye.

A man may have strong cravings for attention, for example, but is unaware of them because such awareness would hurt his false pride. Being around other attention-seeking persons arouses his anxiety (fear of finding out the truth) level, so that he self-righteously condemns the speck in his brother's eye instead of dealing with the plank in his own. Saul probably projected his hostility toward God onto David, while David may have projected his guilt over his sin with Bathsheba to a fictitious culprit who stole a neighbor's only pet lamb (see also Rom. 2:1–3; James 1:13–17).

Isolation

Various unacceptable emotions (such as jealousy, greed, and lust) may be split off from conscious thought and isolated from conscious awareness. This defense mechanism is commonly used by compulsive individuals whose consciences are so strict that they mistakenly think all anger is sin; in effect, they isolate their anger in order to relieve their own false guilt. In reality they are sinning by not experiencing the negative emotion of anger. God would prefer for them to be aware of their anger so they can deal with the problem maturely and forgive the other person "by sundown" (Eph. 4:26; Lev. 19:17–18).

Intellectualization

Individuals may avoid becoming aware of inferiority feelings and other unconscious conflicts by the excessive use of intellectual vocabulary, thinking, discussions, and philosophies. This is a very common defense mechanism.

For example, a boy grows up in a very critical, cold, upper-class family. Because of their unconscious inferiority feelings, his parents regard with disdain anyone whose tastes are not up to their level. The boy gets As and Bs in school, but this is not enough to satisfy his parents. In college he becomes a philosophy major, uses lots of long, rarely used words, talks only about philosophical issues (never about his own feelings), and looks down on people who are less intellectual than himself.

Rationalization

Individuals may justify unacceptable attitudes, beliefs, or behavior by the misapplication of viable reasons or by the invention of false reasons. A pastoral counselor might spend an inordinate amount of time with a female counselee, in spite of his own unconscious lustful thoughts about her, because he has convinced himself that his motives are pure. He rationalizes that he is seeing her out of Christian love, that she needs to spend time with a father figure to compensate for the father who ignored her as a child.

Spotlight 12.2. Defense Mechanisms in the Church, 1

The overemphasis on certain doctrines in the church may be due to threatening alternatives which produce anxiety at the unconscious level; it may be easier to overlook alternatives than to seriously consider them. The conflict produced between the accepted approach and legitimate alternatives is thus repressed and the status quo is emphasized.

Projection often occurs in churches. A particular point the pastor makes in his sermon may arouse inner conflicts in some church members. They may find it easier to think about others who have that particular problem than realize they have that problem as well. A pastor might unconsciously be thinking of committing adultery, and thus preaches on that subject several times within the space of a couple of months. A young woman may come to believe that God wants her to go overseas as a missionary when in fact she unconsciously wants to be near her missionary parents who are stationed in that part of the world.

The Putneys (1964, 49–51) describe an atheist and a Christian who spent hours arguing about which position was right. Since the Christian had been reared in an agnostic home, he was actually attempting to dispel unconscious doubts about his Christian faith by arguing vehemently with the atheist. The atheist, raised in a religious family, argued just as strongly, trying to rid himself of his unconscious doubts about his atheism. Clearly what the Putneys describe is projection. How much better it would be to deal with doubts at a conscious level and then influence people in less defensive ways (see chap. 9). The emotionally mature Christian shares Christ with others, yet allows them to hold contrary views. Jesus never forced faith on anyone.

Intellectualization is represented by the tendency of some pastors to use theological and religious jargon excessively. This can easily replace genuine expressions of the self, including the emotional self. A pastor may find himself interpreting problems in intellectual or theological terms rather than empathizing with the counselee. This is because he has conflicts that are deeply hidden at the unconscious level. It is emotionally taxing for a pastor to "feel with" the person or say "I don't know"; it is much easier to use cliches or technical terms. Christ listened and empathized as well as analyzed. We need to remember that the Holy Spirit works not only cognitively, but also affectively.

Reaction Formation

Attitudes and behavior contrary to an individual's true feelings or unconscious impulses may be adopted. This is known as reaction formation. To illustrate, a pastor crusades for sexual purity and integrity but is unconsciously seductive with female counselees. Separating his sexual feelings from his actions, he can thus consider himself faultless in the situation and is not consciously hypocritical. Another example would be a religious leader who harbors strong homosexual and/or heterosexual urges, yet preaches strongly against sexual promiscuity.

Displacement

Individuals may transfer an emotion from its original object to a more acceptable substitute. A man who is angry at his boss but afraid to express his anger at work comes home and criticizes his wife or spanks his son for behavior he normally would have ignored. A five-year-old girl with unconscious conflicts about her intense love for her father, including a desire

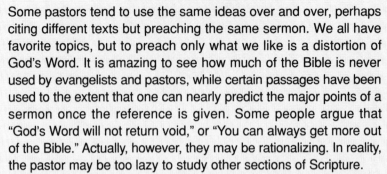

Spotlight 12.3. Defense Mechanisms in the Church, 2

Some pastors tend to use the same ideas over and over, perhaps citing different texts but preaching the same sermon. We all have favorite topics, but to preach only what we like is a distortion of God's Word. It is amazing to see how much of the Bible is never used by evangelists and pastors, while certain passages have been used to the extent that one can nearly predict the major points of a sermon once the reference is given. Some people argue that "God's Word will not return void," or "You can always get more out of the Bible." Actually, however, they may be rationalizing. In reality, the pastor may be too lazy to study other sections of Scripture.

Rationalization may also be behind arguments for keeping the King James Version as the main translation for study or worship. Advocates of this position may, for example, say that there are too many versions today or that the King James is the most accurate or most accepted. Perhaps the real reason is that leaders are afraid of upsetting rigid parishioners.

Even missionaries are not immune to defense mechanisms. For example, a missionary was friendly and cordial to nationals when they came to visit her, but would become very critical of them as soon as they left her house. This pattern could be identified as a form of reaction formation. Another missionary spoke out strongly against sexual immorality while raising funds in his homeland, but nationals described numerous affairs in which he had been involved. Church members may manipulate others by calling themselves servants in order to assert their own dominance—another form of reaction formation. How different from Christ, who not only suggested that we must be servants, but also provided an example by washing his disciples' feet.

---

to marry him when she grows up, displaces her love to her teddy bear and takes it everywhere she goes.

Saul may have displaced his anger at God onto David. Moses struck the rock for water and smashed the tablets of the law, thereby displacing the anger aroused by his people's sin.

Identification

Identification may be healthy, particularly if it is conscious (though technically it is not then a defense mechanism since by definition such a mechanism is an un-conscious process). Identification occurs when individuals model their values, attitudes, and behavior after another person's without knowing that they are doing so.

A child watching a violent hero on television, a teen-ager watching an erotic movie, or an employee observing the underhanded business methods of an employer are good illustrations of how this defense mechanism can influence people. Individuals can also identify with group values and attitudes, as in cults. A positive example of identification would be our identifying with Christ.

Regression

Some defense mechanisms, such as regression, are manifested in early childhood. Regression occurs when individuals faced with current conflicts return to an earlier stage of emotional immaturity where they felt more protected from life's stresses.

To illustrate, a four-year-old boy who is totally toilet trained and maturing satisfactorily is faced with the birth of a brother. He has unconscious conflicts about his mother being in the hospital for a week, then spending much of her time with the baby. He suddenly begins to wet the bed, use babytalk, soil his pants, have temper tantrums, and be hyperactive. Unconsciously he is returning to infancy in order to again receive his mother's undivided attention. This is a very common occurrence. Regression can occur in adults during times of stress such as a major move, a job change, the birth of a first child, physical illness, or the death of a loved one. Most hospital patients behave less maturely than they would when well and at home. Regression might be illustrated by Christians who move from spiritual "meat" to spiritual "milk," to use Paul's metaphor.

Fixation

Instead of returning to an earlier stage emotionally, the fixated person encounters trauma at some point in life and remains at that level of emotional development. Such individuals may act irresponsibly and childishly in adulthood. They may spend money on frivolous things, not thinking of the accumulation of unpaid bills. Or they may neglect the family in favor of watching ball games on television.

Spiritual development may produce unconscious conflicts because spiritual growth often requires sacrifice and humility. People resist correction for many reasons, and the need to develop spiritually can conflict with emotional struggles at an unconscious level, resulting in spiritual fixation. Churches often have dozens of spiritual infants who have not matured in the faith or taken their proper place in the

---

Spotlight 12.4. Defense Mechanisms in the Church, 3

The defense mechanism of displacement might be evoked by a sermon that speaks to a weak area in an individual's life, thus creating anxiety. At the door the pastor receives a smile and a handshake. At home that afternoon, however, the children are harshly spanked for minor misdeeds. The next week during a board meeting the guilty parishioner makes the color of the new carpet a major issue. He might even threaten to leave the church over the carpet.

While identification is normal in childhood, it occasionally surfaces in adulthood, when a member of the congregation begins to unconsciously imitate the pastor. An individual may imitate an aggressive person who arouses anxiety; an unconscious modeling then takes place. Psychologists sometimes call this "identification with the aggressor." Christians must be careful not to imitate the hostile approach taken by some of their opponents; a loving rebuke is far better than anger.

body of Christ. Growth in Christ, not spiritual fixation, is to be the norm. We must "put away childish things."

Undoing

Individuals may carry out unconscious acts or verbal communications in order to negate a previous mistake, as though the mistake never occurred.

On a date a young woman's declaration of love is warm but later she convinces herself that she was only joking and treats her date politely but coldly. Another example would be a Christian criticizing a fellow Christian, then feeling unconscious guilt the next day and going out of his way to compliment the person he criticized without remembering that he had been critical or knowing why he is being so complimentary. Another illustration would be a young man who feels a strong conviction to become a missionary but unconsciously struggles with the hardships of leaving his home country. He convinces himself that he never really wanted to become a missionary in the first place and ends up with a secular job, but heads up the missionary society of his local church.

Undoing is not to be confused with its healthy counterpart, a conscious restitution or apology for wrongs that have been done.

Compensation

Individuals may attempt to make up for real or imagined personal deficiencies in physique, performance, talents, or psychological attributes. This can become a healthy defense if the compensation is done consciously and with proper motives. Compensation here, however, refers to an unconscious striving to make up for inferiority feelings resulting from lack of acceptance of the way God made us. For example, a young woman becomes sexually promiscuous without realizing that she is

doing so to compensate for severe inferiority feelings over her (real or imagined) unattractiveness.

Overcompensation

While compensation is a socially acceptable way of making up for weaknesses, overcompensation is the attempt to make up for deficiencies in socially unacceptable ways. For example, a person may try to be the life of the party, and thus overcompensate for poor self-esteem, by telling jokes that no one finds funny. In spite of groans and other negative feedback from others, he perseveres in his joke telling, thus further alienating himself from others in the group and increasing his poor self-esteem.

In the church overcompensation might be represented by an individual who constantly asks the pastor to let her sing solos, in spite of an obvious lack of talent. While trying to make up for her poor interpersonal skills, she fails to realize that others distance themselves from her because of the aggressive desire to prove herself through her singing.

Perhaps the Pharisees, focusing on legalistic religious behavior rather than genuine spirituality, were overcompensating. Many Jews were attracted to Christ because they saw such legalism as undesirable and Jesus presented an alternative.

Sublimation

With unhealthy sublimation, consciously unacceptable drives (such as hostility or lust) are acceptably channeled without the individual ever becoming aware that the unacceptable drives exist. It would be healthier to become aware of such drives, pray about them, and then consciously redirect them. For example, an athlete might try to sublimate sexual impulses by putting that energy into his playing on the field. Or a girl might channel her anger by directing that energy constructively into painting.

Paul speaks of single people being able to put all their energy into spreading the gospel (1 Cor. 7:32–35). Certainly the evangelist or missionary *is* freer to travel and has more time for activities when single. Perhaps sublimating sexual energy is an option for some Christians who are so gifted (Campolo 1988, 64–68).

Substitution

While sublimation is the expression of an unacceptable drive by redirecting that drive through an unrelated channel, substitution occurs when individuals deceive themselves about their true desires and end up accepting partial or modified fulfillment of those desires.

To illustrate, a young man is not aware that he has much repressed hostility toward his mother and women in general.

Spotlight 12.5. Defense Mechanisms in the Church, 4

I once visited a church where the Sunday school class was taught by a teen-ager. The young man spoke at length of sexual thoughts he had about certain girls, even naming the individuals he had thought about! His talking may have been an attempt to make amends for thoughts which made him feel guilty.

In contrast to such undoing would be conscious restitution or apology. These need to take place in such a way that the circle of confession is the circle of commission. If a sin has been committed against God, it should be confessed to God. On the other hand, if an individual wrongs an entire congregation, the congregation should receive the confession. This is probably what James had in mind when he said, "Confess your sins one to each other" (James 5:16).

Compensation might be represented by a woman who spends a great deal of time at the church and is constantly involved in committees and other activities. She spends little time at home because her husband constantly criticizes her appearance and cooking. She thus compensates by doing what she believes she does well and avoiding other things. Ideally she should be made conscious of what she is doing, but as noted previously, the compensating then would no longer be a defense mechanism. As noted by Dobson (1979, 162–65), compensation can be healthy if it is a conscious way of coping with weaknesses.

Some church members may make sarcastic remarks about a pastor although these same people may generally like him. It may be that sarcasm is a partial expression of an unconscious hatred or resentment of him, particularly if the sarcasm is of the biting variety. This is an example of substitution. However, it should be noted that humor may also help release built-up tensions. Appropriate humor, even gentle sarcasm, during a difficult church business meeting may be the best thing to help calm the atmosphere and pave the way for genuine accomplishment.

He makes constant critical jokes about women being ignorant or inferior and then fails to understand why some individuals are offended. Another example would be a boy who grows up in a strict religious family. Being aware of his own strong hostile drives would hurt his pride and conscience, so he becomes an expert hunter as a boy, killing many "acceptable" animals. In high school and college he becomes an exceptional middle linebacker in football, noted for his "killer instinct." He eventually becomes a surgeon. All of those activities help him to express his hostile drives yet he never becomes aware of their existence.

Compartmentalization

Individuals may unconsciously experience their attitudes as though they were unconnected and unrelated—in separate compartments of their brains—to hide from their conscious awareness the conflicts between their real unacceptable feelings and motives and their idealized feelings and motives. For example, a severely anxious adult male starts to become aware of unconscious guilt feelings when he starts to see the relationship between his current fantasy and a recent conflict he

had. His unconscious immediately convinces him that the fantasy and conflict are unrelated, so he feels at ease temporarily and starts thinking about something else. The Book of James emphasizes the need to go beyond just talking about the gospel to actually *doing* it, thus overcoming compartmentalization of religion and life.

Denial

Denial is "the ability to deny the existence of something disturbing, such as one's own anger or sexual feelings" (Lidz 1968, 258). Thoughts, feelings, wishes, or motives are denied access to consciousness. It is the primary defense mechanism of histrionic personalities, who deny their own sinful thoughts, feelings, wishes, or motives even when they become obvious to those around them. For example, a woman might act seductively but is not consciously aware of doing so because of denial, then becomes angry at the man she is unconsciously seducing for making sexually suggestive responses. If what she was doing was pointed out to her, she would probably deny it vehemently (see also Prov. 14:15; 16:2; James 3:14).

Counselors often refrain from identifying their clients' obvious problems because of the likelihood they will deny those problems. Counselors should help such clients identify the problems themselves, confirming what clients suggest without fear of denial. Once a client denies a diagnosis, it is very difficult to later admit that a problem actually exists.

Alternatives to Defense Mechanisms

Freud believed that defense mechanisms could be eliminated through the use of psychoanalysis. Over time, the client would gradually express unconscious thoughts, sometimes aided by dream analysis or hypnosis. Unusual associations between topics and Freudian slips were also thought to re-

> ## Spotlight 12.6. Defense Mechanisms in the Church, 5
>
> Compartmentalization might be represented by someone who believes that psychology has no place in the church because psychology is psychology and the church is church. Such a person may have hidden unconscious conflicts produced by the study of psychology that illuminates areas that fail to meet certain ideals. The conflict is at the unconscious level, so the mind separates church and psychology into two separate compartments. It refuses to see any possible relationship between the two. Yet it is clear that principles which are valid in everyday life are also valid in church life.
>
> One of the most distressing problems pastors have are individuals who call themselves Christians, yet separate life into the sacred (Sunday in church) and the secular (the rest of the time). It is a sad fact that many attend church for years without discerning a connection between faith and everyday life. This situation, commonly found even in good churches, is an example of compartmentalization. All of us can apply the principles found in the Bible and church to our everyday lives. Indeed, this is a requirement if we are to be whole Christians. We need to see that all of life, not just church life, is sacred and belongs to God.
>
> Some people emphasize "possibility thinking" and "making a good confession" to the extreme of glossing over genuine problems in both themselves and others. A Christian may refuse to admit obvious difficulties and require a "praise the Lord" in all situations.
>
> The conflict between a no-sickness theology and the reality of disease may result in refusing to admit symptoms. Clearly the person is engaging in denial in such a situation. Some espouse a perfectionistic religion yet fail to recognize obvious sin in their pride and other attitudes. This vividly contrasts with Paul's open admission of his struggle with sin (Rom. 7) and John's realization that Christians can and do sin (1 John 2:1).

veal the unconsciousness. Freud assumed that if the unconscious is made conscious, problems will be more consciously resolved. Technically, when defense mechanisms are made conscious, they are no longer defense mechanisms by definition.

But is mere awareness enough to deal with the unconscious mind? Psychoanalysis emphasizes that individuals must "work through" conflicts. But is even this enough? The number of frustrating years people can spend in analysis suggests that Christians need more than what Freud recommends. As Benner (1988, 116) has noted, spiritual growth is closely tied to psychological growth.

As they grow toward Christlike maturity Christians should strive to become aware of and gradually do away with unconscious defense mechanisms. Self-deceiving defenses should be replaced with healthy defenses.

Forgiving others who have wronged us, or forgiving ourselves when we have made a mistake or committed a sin, is the primary healthy, scriptural, and psychological defense against unhappiness and depression. We may get angry—without sinning—but *never* have a grudge-holding, vengeful spirit (Lev. 19:17–18; Eph. 4:26).

The primary conscious defense against the emotional pain that comes from true guilt is confession of sin to God, followed by an attitude of forgiveness toward self (1 John 1:9). Christians are encouraged to confess their sins to each other and are promised that such confession will result in physical/spiritual healing (James 5:16).

Patience is an excellent conscious defense against the frequent minor frustrations of life. Selfish, immature individuals who give themselves too many rights are constantly plagued with anger, since so many of their "rights" are violated. Giving up those rights to God and expecting fewer things to be perfect will result in patience, greater humility, less anger, and greater joy in life.

Love is a conscious choice. The giving and accepting of genuine Christian love is the primary conscious defense against inferiority feelings and loneliness. The Great Commandment given by Christ (Luke 10:25–27) includes loving God, others, and self (an expression of godly self-worth).

Anxiety is due to lack of faith. Failure to recognize what we can do with God's help is a major cause of anxiety. Anticipating a difficult situation with a prayerful, trusting attitude can reduce anxiety. Solomon encourages God's children to have faith in God's principles ("sound wisdom and discretion"). "Then you will go on your way in safety, and your foot will not stumble; when you lie down, you will not be afraid; when you lie down, your sleep will be sweet" (Prov. 3:23–24; see also 3:5–7).

Awareness of personal deficiencies (correctable defects) allows us to ask for and expect God's help to overcome such defi- ciencies (Phil. 4:13). This not only increases our self-worth but also makes us more efficient in furthering the cause of Christ.

Altruism is basically doing good deeds to please the Lord and has many benefits. (1) It furthers the cause of Christ and is an act of obedience to God. (2) It increases self-worth (it is easier for us to like ourselves when we are worthwhile to others). (3) It enables us to get our minds off ourselves and worry less about minor personal frustrations. (4) It builds friendships, which are essential for mental health.

Very few conflicts go away by merely waiting them out. Taking conscious control means becoming responsible and making conscious choices for overcoming conflicts. Conscious control enables us to overcome many of the unconscious defense mechanisms which would control behavior if we remained passive.

Healthy identification means making conscious choices to develop some godly personality characteristics seen in other Christians we admire. God does not expect any Christian to try to become someone else; a Christian's primary identification should be with Jesus Christ (Rom. 8:29).

One of the fruits of the Spirit is joy. The ability to have fun and enjoy life and the ability to laugh at ourselves are definite signs of mental and spiritual health. Laughing at our own minor mistakes (like being forgetful) is much better than self-condemnation.

Redirection is the conscious, healthy counterpart of the unconscious defense mechanism of sublimation. The difference is that with redirection mature individuals can become aware of some unwanted psychological or spiritual conflict (such as repressed hostility) and consciously dissipate hostile energy while they are in the process of getting rid of repressed hostility through prayer, forgiveness, and other means.

When mature individuals offend someone, they show genuine humility and concern for the offended individual by making restitution. Restitution can be a verbal apology, or it may require financial compensation for damages done to someone else's possessions.

Suppressing the truth without first dealing with the problem is a sin. Obsession over a past failure without forgiving oneself is equally sinful, however. Mature individuals confess past errors to God, forgive themselves, and then suppress the past errors so they can concentrate on present or future concerns. Nor should we rest on past successes, with no motivation to accomplish future goals for God. Paul states, "Forgetting what is behind and straining toward what is ahead, I press on toward the goal to win the prize for which God has called me heavenward in Christ Jesus" (Phil. 3:13–14).

Dreams help us resolve unconscious conflicts, or at least dissipate some of the emotional pain tied to unconscious conflicts. A normal, spiritual, unmarried adult male, for example, will be relieved of his biological sexual tensions by having "wet dreams," perhaps several times a week. Newborn babies, facing the real world outside of the mother's womb for the first time, may spend ten hours dreaming each day. Christians should not deprive themselves of sleep. Sleeping and dreaming are gifts of God to maintain our mental health.

References

Allport, G. 1937. *Personality.* New York: Holt, Rinehart and Winston.

American Psychological Association. 1981. Ethical principles of psychologists. *American Psychologist* 36: 633–38.

Benner, D. 1988. *Psychotherapy and the spiritual quest.* Grand Rapids: Baker.

Burke, T. 1987. *Man and mind: A Christian theory of personality.* Hillsdale, Mich.: Hillsdale College Press.

Campolo, A. 1988. *Twenty hot potatoes.* Dallas: Word.

Cattell, R. 1973. *Personality and mood by questionnaire.* San Francisco: Jossey-Bass.

Darling, H. 1969. *Man in triumph.* Grand Rapids: Zondervan.

Diagnostic and statistical manual of mental disorders. 3d rev. ed. 1987. Washington, D.C.: American Psychiatric Association.

Dobson, J. 1979. *Hide or seek.* Rev. ed. Old Tappan, N.J.: Revell.

Freud, S. 1900. *The interpretation of dreams.* New York: Modern Library.

Hughes, P. 1984. Grace. In *Evangelical dictionary of theology,* ed. W. Elwell. Grand Rapids: Baker.

Kotesky, R. 1980. *Psychology from a Christian perspective.* Nashville: Abingdon.

LaHaye, T. 1971. *Transformed temperaments.* Wheaton, Ill.: Tyndale.

Lidz, T. 1968. *The person.* New York: Basic.

Mischel, W. 1968. *Personality and assessment.* New York: Wiley.

Nelson, M. 1976. The psychology of spiritual conflict. *Journal of Psychology and Theology* 4: 34–41.

Phares, E. 1988. *Introduction to personality.* 2d ed. Glenview, Ill.: Scott, Foresman.

Philipchalk, R. 1988. *Psychology and Christianity.* 2d ed. Lanham, Md.: University Press of America.

Putney, S., and G. Putney. 1964. *The adjusted American.* New York: Harper and Row.

Rogers, C. 1959. A theory of therapy, personality, and interpersonal relationships. In *Psychology,* ed. S. Koch. New York: McGraw-Hill.

Ryrie, C. 1984. Total depravity. In *Evangelical dictionary of theology,* ed. W. Elwell. Grand Rapids: Baker.

Sheldon, W. 1942. *The varieties of temperament.* New York: Harper and Row.

Stuart, R. 1970. *Trick or treatment.* Champaign, Ill.: Research.

Tucker, L. 1983. Muscular strength and mental health. *Journal of Personality and Social Psychology* 45: 1355–60.

VanLeeuwen, M. 1985. *The person in psychology.* Grand Rapids: Eerdmans.

13

The Psychology of Religion

In chapter 1 we considered a number of possible ways Christianity and psychology are related, including the psychology against theology position. This position attempts to apply psychological approaches to the understanding of religion, thus producing what is often called the psychology of religion. While this field stirred considerable interest among psychologists early in this century, it has generally been ignored for many years. Recently, however, there has been a resurgence of interest in this area among both Christian and non-Christian psychologists.

The psychology of religion attempts to find psychological factors in religious belief and practice. Thus it has historically tended to be critical of religious faith, although this has not always been the case. Several Christians have written books on this subject. We can gain insight from scholars in the field of the psychology of religion if we realize they often limit themselves to observable data and exclude theological considerations. We can gain a great deal from their findings if we realize those limits and use discernment in accepting their conclusions.

Freud's View of Religion

In his *Future of an Illusion* (1927), Freud vents much hostility toward religion, declaring that it can be compared with neurosis (mental illness). He expresses the hope that religion will soon come to an end. Freud maintains that the dependency fostered by religion causes an infantile regression. In *Totem and Taboo* (1913) Freud emphasizes the centrality of guilt in religion; the "dos and don'ts" undermine mental health. From Freud's perspective, religious faith produces a repression of impulses and thus keeps the personality secure at the expense of honesty. We overlook the actual drive-oriented nature of the person because this aspect of human nature has long been suppressed by religion. Freud suggests, however, that insecure people de-

Spotlight 13.1. True and False Guilt

We need to differentiate between true and false guilt. Freud seemed to think that all guilt is false guilt, and many psychiatrists today agree. Christians disagree that guilt is always an unhealthy thing. True guilt is the uncomfortable inner awareness that we have violated God's moral law. True guilt is produced partly by the conviction of God's Holy Spirit and partly by our own conscience.

Conscience is what Freud called the superego. It is molded by many influences in our environment: what our parents taught was right or wrong, what they practiced (not always the same as what they taught), what our church taught was right or wrong, what church members practiced, what our friends and teachers thought was right or wrong, and so on. A Christian's conscience is molded also by what the Bible says is right or wrong, but even that is influenced by individual interpretation. No two consciences are exactly alike. Although the Holy Spirit is always right, our consciences can overlook something we do that is wrong. An enlarged conscience, wrongly taught that everything is sin, will bother us even when we do things that God does not consider wrong. False guilt is feeling guilty for something that God and his Word in no way condemn.

True guilt is valuable. It can lead us to repentance. When we do what is right, our fellowship with God will be joyful and we will like ourselves more. Doing what is wrong lowers our self-worth. Generally when people tell a psychiatrist they feel guilty, they *are* guilty. Straightening out what they are doing wrong is sometimes all that is needed to straighten out their feelings of depression.

Christians from legalistic churches often express feelings of guilt for things that the Bible in no way condemns. They may feel guilty for being tempted, for example. It is no sin to be tempted; it *is* sin to dwell on that temptation and yield to it. Christ himself was tempted: "For we do not have a high priest who is unable to sympathize with our weaknesses, but we have one who has been tempted in every way, just as we are—yet was without sin" (Heb. 4:15).

Tournier calls true guilt "value guilt" and calls false guilt "functional guilt":

A feeling of "functional guilt" is one which results from social suggestion, fear of taboos or of losing the love of others. A feeling of "value guilt" is the genuine consciousness of having betrayed an authentic standard; it is a free judgment of the self by the self. On this assumption, there is a complete opposition between these two guilt-producing mechanisms, the one acting by social suggestion, the other by moral conviction. . . . "False guilt" is that which comes as a result of the judgments and suggestions of men. "True guilt" is that which results from divine judgment. . . . Therefore real guilt is often something quite different from that which constantly

---

sire a cosmic father figure to provide security.

Freud describes religious activities as rituals. Rituals are compulsive behaviors performed to temporarily ease the intense guilt feelings that are fostered by religion (Freud 1970). The mentally ill neurotic may compulsively wash his hands several times every hour, trying to symbolically wash away his unconscious feelings of guilt. Likewise Christians neurotically try to free themselves of guilt feelings by performing religious rituals.

Is there anything to Freud's thinking here? Certainly churches do develop rituals. The order of worship generally has singing first, followed by an offering and announcements, and concludes with a ser-

weighs us down, because of our fear of social judgment and the disapproval of men. We become independent of them in proportion as we depend on God. (Tournier 1962, 64–70)

Hyder states that

the causes of false guilt stem back to childhood upbringing. Too rigid a superego or conscience can only be developed by too rigid expectations or standards imposed by parents. For example, parents who excessively blame, condemn, judge, and accuse their children when they fail to match up to their expectations cause them to grow up with a warped idea of what appropriate standards are. Unforgiving parents who punish excessively increase guilt. Adequate and proper punishment given in love and with explanation removes guilt. Some parents give too little encouragement, praise, thanks, congratulations, or appreciation. Instead they are never satisfied. However well the child performs in any area of school, play, sports, or social behavior, the parents make him feel they are dissatisfied because he did not do even better. The child sees himself as a constant failure, and he is made to feel guilty because he failed. He does not realize at his young age what harm his parents are doing to his future feelings of self-worth. He grows up convinced that anything short of perfection is failure. However hard he tries, and even if he actually performs to the maximum that he is capable of, he grows up feeling guilty and inferior.

As an adult he suffers from neurotic or false guilt, low self-esteem, insecurity, and a self-depreciatory pessimistic outlook on all his endeavors and ambitions. He then blames himself and this leads to anger turned inward. He attempts to inflict punishment upon himself because of his feelings of unworthiness. His failures deserve to be judged and punished, and since no one else can do it for him, he punishes himself. This intropunitive retribution, part anger and part hostility, leads inevitably to depression. It can also cause psychosomatic complaints and inappropriate sorts of actions. (Hyder 1971, 121–22)

According to Hyder, the only treatment for false guilt is understanding it and evaluating it for what it really is. Feelings of bitterness and pride need to be separated from feelings of guilt. People can be helped to understand that they have no right to condemn themselves; only God has that right and Christians should leave judging and condemning to God alone. Then they need to set new goals for themselves that are realistically attainable, no longer comparing themselves to others more gifted than they are in specific areas. We should compare our performance with what we believe God expects of us. God does not expect his children to achieve sinless perfection in this life. But he does want us to seek his will in our lives to the best of our abilities.

mon. Once such a routine is established, departure from it is rare. The Lord's supper and baptism may also be considered rituals.

Yet we can just as easily argue that denying the reality of God's existence is neurotic. What is more neurotic than an atheist who persists in denying the reality of God in spite of the obvious evidence of His existence (see Rom. 1:20)? The existence of an omnipotent divine Being certainly would produce anxiety in the atheist, which produces in turn the defense mechanism of denial. The hostility and vehemence of some atheists would indicate the underlying turmoil of self-doubt.

Freud's linking of ritual and compulsive behavior is also to be questioned, as he overlooks some important differences between them (Darling, personal correspondence, spring 1971). First, ceremonial rituals tend to be public activities, while compulsions are largely private. Second, rituals are inherently meaningful, as they symbolize important aspects of doctrine and historical events, while compulsions are senseless (once a person comes to understand the conflicts behind a compulsion, it generally ceases). Third, religious rituals are reality-based. We usually take communion, for example, because we believe in the reality of Christ's atoning death for sin and use this ceremony to recall his great love. Compulsions, on the other hand, are a means of avoiding reality; the compulsive individual avoids dealing with the actual unconscious conflicts that are behind the compulsion. Finally, rituals can be a means of dealing with guilt. The pastor often asks the congregation to reflect prior to taking the Lord's supper, and if need be confess and repent of any sin in their lives. Compulsions, on the other hand, allow us to avoid dealing with the guilt that underlies the compulsive behavior. Clearly ceremonial ritual is not the same thing as compulsive behavior, as Freud believed.

Why was Freud so hostile to religion? In studying Freud's life, Vitz (1988) found considerable evidence for unconscious conflicts in the area of religion. Early in his life, Freud had a Roman Catholic nanny who influenced him even more than his own mother; the nanny may have baptized him secretly into the Catholic faith. This was a source of intense conflict for Freud later because he was raised in a nominally Jewish home. While Christians were considered adversaries by his family, he was attracted to the Christian faith of the woman he was most attached to in infancy. He may have attempted to resolve this conflict by resorting to atheism, yet Vitz documents the struggle Freud continued to have throughout his life with religion. Vitz concludes that Freud was powerfully influenced by Christianity, driven by an unconscious longing for a faith that he denied to the end of his life.

Jung's Archetypes

While Jung (1933) initially followed Freudian thought, he later broke away from Freud partly because he saw the unconscious mind as being in two parts rather than one as Freud did. In addition to the personal unconsciousness, Jung also posited a collective unconsciousness, an endowment which each person receives from experiences people have had throughout human history. In this collective unconsciousness are hidden symbols which Jung termed "archetypes."

Among these archetypes are the God image and the image of evil. Because these archetypes are preexistent in the collective unconsciousness, individuals are quick to acknowledge such ideas once exposed to them. Young children readily accept the idea of God or Satan because they already have archetypes that correspond to these ideas. Archetypes are "systems of preparedness" that help the individual organize experience. Jung did not believe in a transcendent God (a God "out there"), but saw the psyche as reaching back to a primitive past to find meaning in present existence.

While Christians believe in a transcendent God, it is also interesting to see the possible overlap between Jung's God archetype and biblical theology. Even Augustine spoke of a God vacuum that exists in every person, an emptiness that only God can fill. This emptiness can be denied and the person calloused (Isa. 6:9–10), but the hunger remains. We are indeed made for God and his law (Eccles. 3:11; Rom. 2:15).

Maslow's Peak Experiences

In chapter 5 we examined Maslow's hierarchy of needs. Each level of need requires some degree of fulfillment before the person can move on to the next higher level of need. The highest level is self-actualization, which is characterized by peak experiences. Maslow (1954) states that these subjective and somewhat mystical experiences are the core of religion, and are not dependent upon association with a given church body or possession of religious belief. William James also linked religious experience with self-acceptance, concern for others, and peak experiences.

A peak experience is marked by deep concentration and disorientation with respect to time and space (time seems to "stand still"). Those who have such experiences report seeing the universe as a whole and claim that such experiences make life seem more worthwhile. There is a lack of fear and a greater receptivity during these times which are also marked by an awesome, worshipful feeling. The person feels responsible yet free and spontaneous. There are also feelings of selflessness, love, and honesty. Finally, those having such experiences feel they do not deserve them, yet have a sense of transcending a worldly existence.

Do Christians have peak experiences? Certainly many accounts of conversion and moments of worship after salvation have some of the characteristics that Maslow describes. Such mystical and emotional experiences may be greatly appreciated by Christians, but it is difficult to accept Maslow's statement that they are the core of religion. The foundation of genuine faith must be the Word of God and the Word incarnate, Jesus Christ, and what he accomplished for us by dying on the cross. Peak experiences may be an interesting and enjoyable part of Christian faith, but they are not our foundation. Other religions have such experiences, and they can even be present without any religious faith at all. As Darling (1971) has stated, "It is not how high we jump inside, but how straight we walk outside that matters." Our faith must be based upon more than mystical and emotional experiences.

Allport's Theory of Religious Prejudice

Allport suggests that religious individuals are more prejudiced than nonreligious individuals (Allport and Kramer 1946). Religious people tend to justify their prejudice by appealing to religious sanctions, such as quoting verses of Scripture out of context. There is widespread prejudice against the Jews among Christians, in spite of the fact that Jesus was a Jew and that Christians accept the Jewish Scriptures (the Old Testament).

A more careful analysis (Allport and Ross 1967) reveals that there are actually two groups of religious people. Some individuals are *intrinsically* religious. These people attend church regularly and see their faith as being central in their lives. There are others who are *extrinsically* religious; they place less value on church attendance and tend to be socially acceptable. Their religion is peripheral to their lives. Extrinsically religious individuals are far more prejudiced than either intrinsic or nonreligious individuals. Because there are so many extrinsics in the church, the church appears to be extremely prejudiced. Intrinsically religious individuals are by far the least prejudiced. When the Christian faith is allowed to transform believers completely, they become more Christlike and thus less prejudiced.

Why Do People Become Christians?

One way of summarizing the above four theories, as well as introducing some other perspectives on the psychology of religion, is to consider the question of why people are converted to Christianity. Freud would emphasize the desire for a cosmic father figure, as well as excessive guilt instilled by preachers during sermons, guilt that is then only partially rectified through neurotic compulsive rituals. Jung, on the other hand, would say that people are converted because they are responding to the inherent archetype of God. Maslow might describe the act of becoming a Christian as a peak experience, possibly followed by others as a part of one's religion. Allport might emphasize that religion validates one's prejudices and that religion may involve a putting down of others in favor of one's own social group.

These views may be contrasted with the theological view that conversion is made up of three components. First, the person repents of sin, turning from it in response to conviction from the Holy Spirit. Second, there is forgiveness of sin through Christ's work on the cross. Third, there is a rebirth, a new life. Is the theological view compatible with the four psychological viewpoints? Freud's theory reminds us that we need to let the Holy Spirit convict sinners rather than manipulate people from the pulpit (Collins 1969, 144–58). Jung gives us a motivation for conversion: we lack wholeness apart from God. Maslow describes part of the emotional component of faith, even though it is not central to faith. Finally, Allport's research reminds us that genuine Christianity moves us away from prejudice.

The Development of Religious Concepts

How do religious concepts develop? A number of research studies have been con-

---

Spotlight 13.2. Sources on the Psychology of Religion

Evangelical Christians became interested in the psychology of religion at about the same time that they began writing about the relationship between psychology and Christianity. Two early writers contributed significantly to this area. Darling wrote *Man in Triumph* (1969), while Collins wrote *Search for Reality* (1969) which is an excellent supplement to a general psychology or psychology of religion class. More of a textbook approach was taken in Oates's *Psychology of Religion* (1973). A few years later this was followed by an anthology by Malony (1977).

Paloutzian's summary of the field (1983) has been widely used in both Christian and secular contexts. Fleck and Carter (1981) edited a book of readings, taken largely from Christian psychology journals. More recently the *Journal of Psychology and Christianity* published an entire issue (Summer 1986) which summarized the current status of the field from a Christian perspective. It should also be noted that the prestigious American Psychological Association has created division 26 for psychologists interested in religious issues. Clearly there is a strong interest in the psychology of religion both within and outside the Christian framework.

ducted in this area, most of which have to do with the concept of God. Until recent years researchers have focused on the development of religious concepts in school-aged children, but during the 1980s more interest was generated in the earliest foundations of religious concepts. Curiously, Piaget's theory of cognitive development has exerted the strongest influence upon research involving preschool and older children, while psychodynamic theory (Freud and his intellectual descendants) has had a stronger influence on investigating the religious thinking of infants and toddlers (Ratcliff, in press).

The Infant's Concept of God

Fowler (1989) has emphasized the development of RIGS—representations of interactions that are generalized—in infants. Borrowing the concept from Stern (1985), Fowler describes RIGS as models the child develops in the course of interactions with others; these eventually lead to "evoked companions"—the sense of self being with others which exists even when the infant is alone. The child acts as if an object or person is present even when it is not. Evoked companions provide a foundation for the concept of God.

Evoked companions exist beyond the immediate context, and may be related to everyday rituals like diaper changing and feeding. Such rituals involve a dependency upon the mother; and such feelings of dependency may be reiterated in adulthood through the traditions and rituals of religious faith (see Fowlkes 1989).

Fowler cites Rizzuto's (1979) research on the presence of transitional objects in the young child's life. Transitional objects are teddy bears, blankets, or other objects that help the child separate from the parents. The transitional object symbolizes the care and security provided by parents, and thus aids the development of the child

as an individual apart from the parents (Erikson's concept of autonomy described in chap. 10). God becomes a transitional Object for the child, but a unique transitional Object since he is not tangibly observed by the child.

Smith (1988) describes the development of the God concept in infancy by using object relations theory. Object relations theory emphasizes that objects are mental representations of the external world which exist even before object permanence develops (see Piaget's theory in chap. 10). Prior to object permanence, these mental representations ("background objects") help the infant sort out reality. A fully developed God concept, of course, requires object permanence; God is there even if he is not directly detected by the senses.

Smith postulates the existence of an ultimate background object (UBO)—a primitive experience of God during infancy. The UBO is related to interactions with the mother and thus eventually helps the child to trust or not trust God later when the concept of God is fully acquired. The degree of trust in God is, of course, related to the mother-child interaction. The mother in fact mediates God to the child. A positive UBO produces a sense of harmony and unity which is carried over into adult religious life by "feeling the love of God."

The Preschooler's Concept of God

Recent research in Italy and the Scandinavian countries has focused on the development of religious concepts in the preschool years (Tamminen et al. 1988). Young children project human qualities upon God. The characteristics of God are closely related to experiences the child has had with parents. Fairy tale images are sometimes present. Children may believe that God lives far away in a castle, but usually distinguish God from fantasy figures such as Santa Claus. Children from nonreligious homes are more likely to have concepts of God that are gloomy or frightening, but in general the mental picture of God is positive at this age.

While human characteristics predominate among preschoolers' concepts of God, five- or six-year-olds have a partial understanding of omnipotence and omniscience. God becomes more than a typical man, and becomes a magician, giant, or invisible man.

Belgian research (Tamminen et al. 1988) notes that up to about two and a half years of age the child may confuse Jesus with objects related to him (such as a cross), but after this point the two will be distinguished. The child may believe that God lives and sleeps in church. The pastor, an usher, or other church worker may be confused with God. By age three or so the child begins to realize that God is in heaven, but may initially resist this revelation. God is understood to come down from heaven to influence natural events, such as weather or situations in the home. God is thought to be exclusively concerned with the child's wishes and desires. By four or five years of age the child sees God as more transcendent.

Older Children's Concept of God

Ratcliff (1985) found that six- to eight-year-old children have God concepts that are relatively uniform across denominations. The God concept is generally more masculine for girls and more feminine for boys at this age, a trend that declines as they get older. In describing God, children emphasize outward physical appearance until age nine or ten. They describe God's view of a person as either all bad or all good. God is fundamentally a provider who has magical qualities and speaks in a physical manner.

By nine to ten years of age, the child de-scribes God in terms of his authority; doctrine is prominent in descriptions of God. God is seen as meting out concrete punishments and rewards.

By the time the child is eleven or twelve, God is understood as basically human but possessing supernatural abilities. God is thought to see people not as all good or all bad but rather with a mixture of these characteristics. God is understood to control and use nature to intervene in human affairs, rather than directly intervening. God is perceived to be more personal than at earlier ages; he is more of a friend and less parental. Boys tend to portray God as more personal and spontaneous, while girls perceive God in a more static fashion.

By the adolescent years God is understood to be the upholder of natural laws. He is thought to act out of concern for people rather than just judging them. The teen-ager realizes that God is beyond mere sensory experience; the individual's encounters with God are internal and mental rather than external. The adolescent characteristically feels unworthy before God and may realize that when God seems unfair it is because humans do not see the whole picture.

Facilitating Spiritual Growth

Young children can be guided in spiritual development when their parents follow God's commandments to teach them (Deut. 6:6–7), train them (Prov. 22:6), and bring them up in the instruction of the Lord (Eph. 6:4). Christian parents often fall short. Fathers especially may become so wrapped up in their own world that they neglect their highest calling, the spiritual development of their children.

The psalmist says that God "decreed statutes for Jacob and established the law in Israel, which he commanded our forefathers to teach their children, so the next generation would know them, even the children yet to be born, and they in turn would tell their children. Then they would put their trust in God and would not forget his deeds but would keep his commands" (Ps. 78:5–7). God said, "These commandments that I give you today are to be upon your hearts. Impress them on your children. Talk about them when you sit at home and when you walk along the road, when you lie down and when you get up" (Deut. 6:6–7). "He who fears the LORD has a secure fortress, and for his children it will be a refuge" (Prov. 14:26). With that kind of confidence, parents can seek opportunities to encourage spiritual development at each stage of their children's growth.

Infants

Some foundations for spiritual development can be laid during infancy. An infant certainly does not understand religious beliefs and concepts, but religious beliefs strongly influence the attitudes parents will have toward that infant. The child, sensing the overall home atmosphere, begins to respond to parental behavior and attitudes.

Toddlers

Young toddlers are acquiring language skills rapidly, grasping for new experiences, and observing everything that happens in the world around them. Children's experiences with their father lay the groundwork for future conceptions about what God is like. Parents may start by teaching children to say a memorized prayer; even at thirty-six months of age, children will be saying the words but thinking about what their earthly father is like. Harsh, critical fathers definitely influence children's conceptions of the Father to whom they are praying. If children are in a loving, secure, and accepting environ-

ment during their early years, they will develop a basic trust enabling them to have a more meaningful faith in God later. What parents let children watch on television and the music played in the home strongly influence personality development in ways that will either facilitate or hinder future spiritual development.

Preschoolers

Preschool children pick up thousands of words in their vocabularies but their knowledge of abstract concepts is still minimal. They reason concretely, but everything is either black or white. Without a stimulating environment or some formal education, many people never outgrow this dichotomous way of thinking.

Preschool children are very concrete in their thinking. Collins (1971, 48) notes that during the singing of the national anthem, young children frequently substitute words like "the grandpas we watched were so gallantly screaming."

Piaget's research on the neurological, social, and moral development of children was discussed in chapter 10. Piaget's studies show that three- to six-year-old children believe almost everything their parents tell them, and think that their parents have divine qualities (Piaget 1967, 67). Reasoning with them about misconduct is futile; a straight yes or no or a spanking is much more effective at this age. Parents obviously need to understand their children's level of reasoning in order to make spiritual teaching effective. For example, stories about Jesus and some of the little children in the Bible have a great deal of meaning to preschool children, but trying to teach abstract concepts like parable interpretation or agape love will only make them wish their parents would get it over with so they can get back to their toys. The more appropriate the spiritual training children have during these three years, the more they will rely on their Christian faith when they are older and have made their own commitment to Jesus Christ. Some children not yet six years old have a simple faith in Christ: they know that they are sinful, want God to forgive them, and want to live forever in heaven.

To help preschool children develop spiritually, we should keep in mind that the main sources of their learning are total life experiences rather than adult words. As Collins (1971, 53) says, "A 'loving heavenly Father' is foolishness if the child's views of God, Heaven, angels, and Hell are in terms of pictures he has seen." As noted earlier, children frequently pray as though God were a magician in the sky whose purpose is to grant their wishes. Of course many adults also pray this way, trying to play God or use God's magic to accomplish their will, instead of asking God to show them his will so they can act accordingly. As parents pray with their children, they should show by example that prayer is a means of merging their wills with the will of God. Preschool children derive their notions of what is right or wrong from what they see parents doing, not from what parents say is right or wrong.

Parents should encourage children to let them know when they feel angry. Children who hit a parent when they are angry or throw something at a parent should be spanked; but children who tell parents they are feeling angry toward them or someone else should be commended for their forthrightness and encouraged to talk about the situation. Parents can use such opportunities to suggest some appropriate ways to deal with the anger.

Parents must be careful to tell the truth to their children. Even for many Christian children, Santa Claus becomes a replacement for Jesus Christ. When six-year-olds go to school and find out that their parents have been lying to them about something that has become a major part of

their beliefs, they may begin to doubt everything else they have been taught—especially about God.

On the other hand, parents should not take all the fun out of Christmas. At a department store during the Christmas season, they can take the children to Santa's corner, telling them on the way: "Look! There's another man dressed up in a funny red suit and beard. Go climb on his lap and he'll give you some candy."

There is no one right way to celebrate Christmas, but there are a lot of wrong ways to celebrate the birth of Christ. Christmas presents can be reminders that the wise men brought presents to Jesus, and that Jesus is God's present to us. Children could also be told about Martin Luther, who said he put an evergreen tree in his home at Christmas because it was shaped like an arrow pointing up to God in heaven. Some Christians refuse to exchange presents at Christmas. They have their fun in other ways, and explain to their children why they do not buy presents for that particular day.

Christian parents should tell their children the Easter story in simple form—that Jesus died and came back to life again because he is God, that he is still alive and helps us every day, and that some day Christians will go up to heaven to live with him forever. But this need not preclude taking children to a neighborhood Easter egg hunt or coloring eggs as a family project.

Parents can be an example of truthfulness by letting their children know when they are telling them a fairy tale and when they are telling a true story. Young children have difficulty separating the two. Some of the traditional fairy tales can have detrimental effects on young children. Violent stories of witches and people cutting off other people's heads create tremendous fears in preschoolers, who may see mean giants hiding in their closets at night. Parents should be somewhat selective even about which Bible stories to tell their children. Children should learn Bible stories, but only as they are ready to comprehend the significance of the story.[1]

Elementary School Years

As young children who have accepted Christ grow older, their salvation experience will take on new meaning. At this age children no longer project divine qualities on their parents; God is clearly distinct from parents (Piaget 1967, 67).

Children of about age eleven can begin to understand many of the abstract concepts of the Christian faith. It is important for Christian parents to create a devotional atmosphere in their home, which means more than having prayer and Bible study. Primarily it means loving, communicating, and exhibiting the fruit of the Spirit. Life cannot be separated into secular and sacred. Every part of family life is sacred— even going to a baseball game and eating hot dogs!

Family devotions are essential but should be kept short. Devotions should not be something to endure but a happy time of sharing Christ with each other. Mealtimes are good times for family devotions. Parents should be creative, buying Christian storybooks to supplement good secular reading; rewarding children for memorizing short, meaningful Bible verses; taking advantage of outings to talk about serious topics that do not come up at home; helping people in need as a family project. The goal is to use natural opportunities to focus attention on the Lord and to create special opportunities for devotional exercises.[2]

Christian camps can provide special op-

portunities for the spiritual development of children. At some Christian camps children spend so much time in Bible study that they become alienated. Other camps are expertly planned to draw children to Christ and to help them grow in faith.

The church that parents choose for their family is extremely important. The characteristics of a psychologically and spiritually healthy church have been described in the writings of Gene Getz, Ray Stedman, and Watchman Nee. A healthy church has the Bible as its firm foundation and has practical Christianity as its way of life. A healthy church stands on three legs, like a tripod: a sound doctrinal leg; an evangelical leg; and a relational leg, with genuine sharing and love among the members.

In a series of experiments on the moral development of children, Hartshorne and May (1930, 607–19) found that although children learn more about what is right and wrong as they grow older, they also grow increasingly deceptive. Children who were honest in certain situations were dishonest in others. Children with lower intelligence, emotional instability, and from lower socioeconomic environments also lagged behind in moral development. One of the most significant findings was that children enrolled in Sunday schools showed honesty, cooperation, persistence, and inhibition of undesirable behavior.

Piaget's (1948) studies of moral development in children leave no doubt that moral behavior is learned. Although some psychiatrists and theologians insist that children are born good but society teaches them how to be bad, the truth is that we are all born with a sinful nature. Christian parents have the responsibility of teaching their children to deny their selfish impulses and to be good, using both rewards and punishments. According to Solomon, "Folly is bound up in the heart of a child,

---

1. For a comprehensive source on helping preschoolers develop spiritually, see Ratcliff 1988.
2. For more on teaching the Bible to children, see Ratcliff 1987.

but the rod of discipline will drive it far from him" (Prov. 22:15).

The Teen-Age Years

Teen-agers develop strong interests in ideals and ideologies as they search for personal identity. While in this stage of development, they are ready to make serious spiritual commitments, even though Christianity may have bored them previously. They have a powerful need to strengthen their consciences and seek the meaning of life. They begin to integrate faith into their life system, making a pact with God (Piaget 1967, 67).

The importance of creating a spiritual atmosphere in the family, with emphasis on positive communication between parents and teen-agers, has already been stressed. Perhaps a closer look should be taken at the way many Jewish people maintain religious traditions in their homes, especially through the Bar Mitzvah ceremony. On a boy's thirteenth birthday, relatives and close friends are invited to a religious ceremony at which he is declared a young adult, with increased responsibilities and freedoms. The parents make a verbal contract with the boy. In some Conservative and Reformed Jewish congregations, families have an analogous ceremony for their thirteen-year-old girls.

As described in chapter 11, Christian parents could write out a contract with their children, giving them new freedoms along with new responsibilities. Parents should agree not to spank young adolescents, recognizing that spanking, which is generally effective with younger children, is degrading for teen-agers. Parents should also remind young adults of their responsibilities before the Lord, and encourage them to make some commitments to the Lord, perhaps in the form of personal devotions. Such commitments must be made

by the young people themselves, however, without parental pressure.

Relatives and close friends of the family could be invited to this "covenant" ceremony, plus friends the teen-ager wants to include. Guests should not be allowed to bring gifts. Passage into adulthood has many emotional and spiritual implications which should not be confused with materialistic gain.

A Christian ceremony of this nature would have the additional value of reminding the parents that their children are growing up. Parents frequently treat their teen-agers as though they are children. Teen-agers can reason like adults, even though they are less mature. Communication with them should show not only love but also respect.

Some consistent spiritual developments typically take place in the late teen-age years or early twenties. Although young children generally accept everything their parents say as truth and adopt as their own beliefs the religious beliefs of their parents, individuals in their late teens or early twenties have a great need to feel independent of their parents. Tournier, in *The Whole Person in a Broken World* (1964), describes this stage in life as taking off the "coat" of parental morality and "knitting" a personal coat. Tournier says that

> this crisis is necessary and normal. Before he attains adult maturity the young man must go through this time of storm and stress when he has to subject everything to question. The day will come when he will discover again many of the treasures of his childhood, when he will return to the faith in which he grew up and the principles which were inculcated in him. For they were true, and life sees to it that he rediscovers them. But then he will give them a quite personal turn; he will profess them as his own convictions, based upon his innermost experi-

ence. In psychology, this is called integration. (p. 2)

Tournier's observation helps us understand what Solomon was saying when he was inspired to write, "Train a child in the way he should go, and when he is old he will not turn from it" (Prov. 22:6). Solomon is not saying that individuals will never go through doubts, but that eventually they are likely to return to what they have been taught.

In *The God Who Is There* (1968), Schaeffer emphasizes the need to ground young children in the Word of God and teach them why we believe what we believe. We must "communicate Christianity in a way that any given generation can understand" (p. 139). If parents, as well as youth leaders of local churches, communicate a living Christianity to teen-agers, along with clear statements about why they believe the Bible, they will greatly facilitate the normal maturation process.

Spiritual Development

The acquisition of religious concepts must be distinguished from spiritual development. The latter may take place at any age, although it tends to assume adult or at least adolescent abilities. Exactly how religious concepts and other developmental characteristics relate to spiritual development is a relatively undeveloped area.[3]

Fundamental to the concept of spiritual development is the idea of a beginning distinctive from other areas of development. This beginning is often described by Christians as conversion or spiritual birth. Price (1981) considers supernatural truth as more crucial than supernatural experience in the initial phase of Christian life, while

3. But see Benner 1988; Helminiac 1987; McDonald 1983 for some interesting explorations in this area.

Oakland (1974) parallels subsequent spiritual growth (theologically termed "sanctification") with Maslow's self-actualization.

In terms of human development, however, birth is not the beginning of life. An unborn baby goes through the germinal period (fertilization to two weeks after conception), the embryonic period (two to eight weeks), and the fetal period (eight weeks to birth). Might spiritual development have some corollary to this prebirth development?

Engel and Norton (1975, 45) describe eight stages of spiritual development prior to the new birth experience. First, the individual is aware of the existence of a Supreme Being but has no real knowledge of the gospel. With proclamation of the gospel come conviction and an embryonic awareness of the message of Christ. This initial awareness comes to include the fundamentals of that message in the third stage. The implications of the gospel come to be understood (stage 4), followed by an increasingly positive attitude toward Christ and the gospel (stage 5). In stage 6 the person comes to recognize the presence of a problem—the lack of salvation, sometimes in connection with other personal problems. Stage 7 involves the decision to accept or reject the gospel, while stage 8 involves repentance and faith in Christ.

Theologians have long debated exactly how spiritual growth should be diagrammed following salvation. The predominant viewpoint, held by most Baptists, Presbyterians, and others of Reformed persuasion, is that following salvation there is a gradual growth in Christ. Some would hold that there are many works of grace in addition to salvation, but that development is usually in small increments rather than major stages.

An alternative view is held by those of the holiness and Pentecostal persuasions.

Those who follow in the tradition of Wesley generally distinguish two works of grace, that of initial salvation and a later crisis which involves an additional cleansing. A few of this persuasion claim to obtain "entire sanctification" in which the bent toward sin is taken away and the person lives without sinning in daily life. Variations on the Wesleyan perspective include certain Pentecostals and charismatics who believe that the second crisis involves a baptism of the Holy Spirit accompanied by speaking in tongues. A few even posit this baptism as a *third* work of grace in addition to salvation and entire sanctification.

Which of these theological views is correct? Darling (1969, 142–47) has attempted to combine the Wesleyan and Reformed perspectives into a broad stage theory of spiritual growth, relying heavily upon biblical terminology. Spiritual growth parallels general development in Darling's view, and thus the stages of birth, childhood, adolescence, and adulthood can be identified. More precisely, these stages are actually two phases and two transitions, generally marked by gradual change. While day-to-day changes are rarely noted, the individual may look back over the years of being a Christian and note a definite progression.

In Darling's model, spiritual development begins with salvation or spiritual birth. There is a distinctive and sometimes dramatic change in direction at this point: "all things have become new." This is followed by spiritual childhood, marked by both security and immaturity. New Christians are often narrow and rely upon others to do their thinking for them. Because of their immaturity, they need discipleship.

Eventually the Christian comes to spiritual adolescence, marked by uncertainty

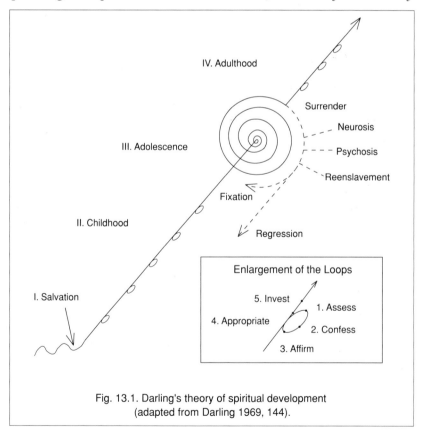

Fig. 13.1. Darling's theory of spiritual development
(adapted from Darling 1969, 144).

Spotlight 13.3. Benner's Model of Spiritual Development

Benner (1988, 130–32) has suggested eight milestones in spiritual development. In some respects these parallel Darling's stages. These milestones involve three general phases: preparation (stages 1–4), justification (stage 5), and sanctification (stages 6–8).

An individual is initially characterized by an openness and trust (milestone 1). This is followed by self-transcendence through surrender of the self and finding one's place in the universe (milestone 2). The previous longing is next understood as a seeking of God and the realization that God is calling (milestone 3). The fourth milestone is an awareness of God's standards (the law) yet inability to meet these standards. Milestone 5 involves receiving the grace and forgiveness of God.

Following justification, the Christian moves toward greater freedom from sin through participation in spiritual warfare (milestone 6). Milestones 7 and 8 are enjoyment of the fruit of the Spirit and a deepening of faith and mystical communion with God producing greater union and fellowship with other believers.

and conflict. The turbulence of this adolescent experience causes a reexamination of one's spiritual life as well as a consideration of several alternatives. The individual may choose to become a spiritual neurotic, anxious and worried about losing faith, or spiritually psychotic, adopting an escapist religion that is completely separated from reality. Another alternative is reenslavement to sin and a life marked by spiritual defeat or possibly rebellion. The individual may choose spiritual regression, returning to the immaturity of a childish faith. Spiritual fixation is another alternative, in which the person adopts the continual rebellion, confusion, and uncertainty of spiritual adolescence as a way of life (thus what is intended to be a transition becomes a stage). There is, however, another possibility—surrender to Christ, producing a mature faith marked by abundance, service, and affirmation. In biblical terms the person has gone from being a babe in Christ to spiritual adulthood; from the milk to the meat of the Word; from

being a servant to a son or daughter of God (Seamands 1988, 22–23).

Along the way there are loops in the progression. These loops are steps that insure continual progress in spiritual growth. Each loop involves an assessment of weaknesses and inadequacies; confession of sin or failure; affirmation of God's love and forgiveness; appropriation of God's resources; and investment of those resources in the lives of others.

The Spiritual Basis of Emotional Problems

We began this chapter by examining some of the criticisms of religion made by Freud. Are there religious reasons for certain problems people have? Here we wish to examine not the problems caused by religion, but rather problems that are spiritually based.

Lack of Intimacy with God

A major source of emotional pain is lack of intimacy with God. Alienation from the love of God is a basic human problem. Reconciliation to God along with restoration of his love and acceptance is the only complete answer. People develop a true sense of identity when they realize that God loves them unconditionally. People who find their identity in a loving relationship with God do not have to depend on others to establish their self-identity. Trusting in God and relating to his Word meet three basic needs. First, we know we are accepted unconditionally and feel a sense of belongingness: "For it is by grace you have been saved, through faith—and this not from yourselves, it is the gift of God—not by works, so that no one can boast" (Eph. 2:8–9). Second, we know that we have been forgiven: "If we confess our sins, he is faithful and just and will forgive us our sins and purify us from all unrighteousness" (1 John 1:9). Third, we know that we are not inferior or inadequate because God is with us at all times: "Never will I leave you; never will I forsake you" (Heb. 13:5).

To be complete persons we must know ourselves and be glad about what we know, and then commit ourselves completely to God: "Love the Lord your God with all your heart and with all your soul and with all your mind" (Matt. 22:37). Loving God with all the heart means to love him with all our affection; loving God with all the soul means to love him with all our will according to our knowledge of him; loving God with all the mind means to love with a total commitment of ourselves to him. With that type of loving relationship with God, emotional pain can be conquered.

The Need to Deal with a Specific Sin

Many people need to deal with materialism, sexual misconduct, or personal ambition and selfish desires, all of which preclude mental health. Such prideful lusts come "not from the Father but from the world" (1 John 2:16), and many specific sins grow out of them. Peter says that sinful desires "war against your soul" (1 Pet. 2:11). Sin produces emotional instability, weak wills, and sick minds. Much depression and grief can be avoided simply by refusing to engage in sinful behavior. Among women, for example, having an abortion or premarital or extramarital affair can cause great anxiety. Sometimes people with mental problems react by engaging in even more sinful behavior in an attempt to relieve their emotional pain.

Sin produces guilt. True guilt with resulting mental anguish is (and should be) the normal response of those who sin and do not turn to Christ. In fact, those who sin without sensing true guilt should question their salvation. Many godly individuals have suffered from mental stress because of sin and true guilt including David, who wrote that his bones were crushed (Ps. 51:8).

Self-control is encouraged in many Bible passages. The Book of Titus commends the ability to be "sober" (KJV), "sensible" (NASB), or "self-controlled" (NIV). Lack of self-control, sin, and depression is the sorry sequence of events in the lives of many Christians.

Anyone who habitually chooses and willfully practices a known sin is not a Christian. Many need to be reminded of the strong warnings about sin's lawlessness in such passages as 2 Timothy 3:1–7 and 1 John 3:4–10. Yet Christians sin daily, and continually need to claim God's promise to forgive their sins. The promise of 1 John 1:9 was written specifically for Christians. No true Christian can willfully practice a known sin without developing deep guilt and depression. The key word is *practice*. Christians do not make a practice of sin—of living in sin—because

Christ lives within them. When Christians do sin, they should be admonished to stop the sin and turn to God for forgiveness, using such encouraging passages as 1 John 1:9; Psalm 103:12–14; and Lamentations 3:21–23.

Demonic Influence

The last category of spiritual problems is that of demon possession and demon oppression. With an upsurge of interest in demon possession today, much confusion exists. That was also true in the fifteenth century when the *Malleus Maleficarum* was written to help in the diagnosis of witchcraft and demon possession.

Demons are referred to about sixty-five times in the New Testament but only a few times in the Old Testament. In Scripture, bizarre and violent behavior, extraordinary strength, and strong opposition to the name of Christ are common symptoms of demon possession. Other symptoms suggested have included a change in voice, various looks of the eyes, and allegedly supernatural acts.

On the basis of such symptoms it would be difficult to distinguish demon possession from ordinary psychological problems. Demon-possessed people usually react strongly to the name of Jesus. Many individuals with mental disorders, even if they are not Christians, seem to react warmly to the name of Jesus. In Scripture, demon-possessed individuals spoke in a logical manner. In many mental disorders (such as schizophrenia) affected individuals are confused and do not speak logically. Clear evidence of supernatural power would perhaps be indicative of demon possession.

Individuals with certain mental disorders are less likely to be falsely diagnosed as demon-possessed in our culture than in some less-developed countries where Satan may be worshiped. Missionaries have sometimes given rather convincing reports of what they regard as demon possession. Of course, individuals in America who experiment with Satan worship would certainly be prone to demon possession.

Impressionable individuals can easily become convinced (after reading a book or seeing a movie on the subject) that they are demon-possessed. They begin to act accordingly, perhaps speaking in a different voice or going into seizures. Some individuals actually develop a second personality.

People with schizophrenia (see chap. 14) have also sometimes been diagnosed as being demon-possessed, because of their bizarre behavior and hallucinations. But the bizarre behavior is a reflection of disturbed brain chemistry and confusion, and the hallucinations are their own "tapes" playing in their heads. Hearing their own confused thoughts, they are out of contact with reality. In contrast, the demons in Scripture carried on sensible conversations with others.

Individuals with personality disorders may be thought to be demon-possessed. Having much repressed anxiety from their past, they displace that anxiety to some thought they do not want to think (such as fear of committing the unpardonable sin) but repeatedly *do* think. John Bunyan, who wrote *Pilgrim's Progress*, said the following about himself:

> The tempter came upon me again, and that with a more grievous and dreadful temptation than before: and that was, to sell and part with this most blessed Christ—to exchange him for the things of this life, for any thing. The temptation lay upon me for the space of a year, and did follow me so continually that I was not rid of it one day in a month; no, not sometimes one hour in many days together, unless when I was asleep. . . .

Spotlight 13.4. Symptoms of Demon Possession

It is often difficult to distinguish psychological problems from demon possession, in part because neither psychologists nor theologians have studied the area to any extent. Several cases of demon possession in the Bible resemble multiple personality disorder (see chap. 14) or epilepsy (see chap. 2). In the Old Testament only one or two cases are mentioned and even these are doubtful (Bufford 1988, 35–44). Most of the cases occurred during the ministry of Christ and the early church. Perhaps demon possession was more common during the life of Christ because Satan brought all the demons to Palestine to defeat the work of Christ. Regardless, the biblical record indicates that demon possession is quite rare.

It is possible that at least sometimes the symptoms of demon possession are learned phenomena (Ratcliff 1982); supposed "deliverance" services are more the result of psychological suggestion than demonic activity (biblical accounts of demonic activity do not take place within church services!). Yet in clinical counseling the presence of the demonic clearly stands out from other abnormal behavior (Peck 1983, 190–99). Perhaps the best descriptions of demon possession are found in Collins (1969, 63–71), Johnson (1982), and Sall (1976).

Demon possession can be distinguished from psychological problems:

1. The demon-possessed have extrahuman strength.
2. The demon-possessed react negatively to the name of Jesus Christ, while those with psychological problems usually respond positively.
3. There is a change of voice when the demon speaks.
4. Demon-possessed people can perform supernatural acts.
5. Demons speak logically while individuals with psychological problems sometimes do not.
6. Those possessed often have a past history of occult activities such as participating in seances or Satan worship.
7. Demon-possessed individuals do not respond to therapy.
8. Many writers in this area have concluded that a genuinely born again Christian cannot be demon-possessed (see 2 Cor. 6:14), although Christians can certainly be tempted and even oppressed by Satan.

It was neither my dislike of the thought, nor yet any desire and endeavor to resist it, that in the least did shake or abate the continuation or force and strength thereof; for it did always , in almost whatever I thought, intermix itself therewith in such sort that I could neither eat my food, stoop for a pin, chop a stick, or cast mine eyes to look on this or that, but still the temptation would come, Sell Christ for this, or sell Christ for that; sell him, sell him. Sometimes it would run in my thoughts not so little as a hundred times together, Sell him, sell him, sell him; against which I may say, for whole hours together I have been forced to stand as continually leaning and forcing my spirit against it, lest haply before I was aware some wicked thought might arise in my heart that might consent thereto. . . .

These blasphemous thoughts were such as stirred up questions in me against the very being of God and of his only beloved Son, as whether there were in truth a God or Christ, and whether the holy Scriptures were not rather a fable and cunning story, than the holy and pure word of God. . . . Could I think that so many ten thousands in so many countries and kingdoms should be without the knowledge of the right way to heaven, if there were indeed a heaven, and that we only, who live in a corner of the earth, should alone be blessed therewith? Every one doth think his own religion rightest, Jews and Moors and Pagans; and how if all our faith and Christ and Scriptures should be but a think-so too? . . .

These suggestions, with many others which at this time I may not and dare not utter, neither by word nor pen, did make such a seizure upon my spirit, and did so overweigh my heart both with their number, continuance, and fiery force, that I felt as if there were nothing else but these from morning to night within me, and as though indeed there could be room for nothing else. (Bunyan 1978, 53–54, 40–41)

Although Bunyan had thoughts he did not want and urges to irrational actions, he was not demon-possessed. Anxiety, not a demon, is behind obsessions and compulsions (see chap. 14). As the underlying anxiety is dealt with, obsessions and compulsions decrease.

Individuals with Tourette's syndrome have sometimes been thought to be demon-possessed. They may have facial tics, grimacing, involuntary or explosive movements, vocal expressions such as a barking noise, and the sudden utterance of obscenities. The onset of the disorder is usually in boys of ages seven to fifteen. Over 50 percent of the brain-wave readings will be abnormal. Haldol, one of the major tranquilizers, often helps.

Whenever demon involvement is suspected, a counselor should: (1) be sure the individual knows Christ as personal Savior; (2) encourage the individual to stop paying attention to the "demon" or "voice"; (3) suggest that Christ is greater than any demon (1 John 4:4); and (4) help the individual grow in Christ through the Word, prayer, and fellowship with stable Christians.

Much more common than demon possession is demon oppression. Satan likes nothing better than to oppress Christians. Christ once told Peter that Satan desired to have him so that he could sift him like wheat. Peter later wrote: "Be self-controlled and alert. Your enemy the devil prowls around like a roaring lion looking for someone to devour" (1 Pet. 5:8). Satan seems to know the weak points of each individual. He tempts us over and over at our weak point, whether it is a problem with lust, worry, greed, or something else. We should be alert to both our vulnerable points and the enemy's devices. We should make use of God's armor against Satan, as Paul urges in Ephesians 6:12–18:

For our struggle is not against flesh and blood, but against the rulers, against the authorities, against the powers of this dark world and against the spiritual forces of evil in the heavenly realms. Therefore put on the full armor of God, so that when the day of evil comes, you may be able to stand your ground, and after you have done everything, to stand.

References

Allport, G., and B. Kramer. 1946. Some roots of prejudice. *Journal of Psychology* 22: 9–39.

Allport, G., and J. Ross. 1967. Personal religious orientation and prejudice. *Journal of Personality and Social Psychology* 5: 432–43.

Benner, D. 1987. *Readings in psychology of religion.* Grand Rapids: Baker.

———. 1988. *Psychotherapy and the spiritual quest.* Grand Rapids: Baker.

Bufford, R. 1988. *Counseling and the demonic.* Dallas: Word.

Bunyan, J. 1978. *Grace abounding to the chief of sinners.* Grand Rapids: Baker.

Collins, G. 1969. *Search for reality.* Santa Ana, Calif.: Vision.

———. 1971. *Man in transition.* Carol Stream, Ill.: Creation.

———. 1988. *Can you trust psychology?* Downers Grove: Inter-Varsity.

Darling, H. 1969. *Man in triumph.* Grand Rapids: Zondervan.

Diagnostic and statistical manual of mental disorders. 3d rev. ed. 1987. Washington, D.C.: American Psychiatric Association.

Engel, J., and H. Norton. 1975. *What's gone wrong with the harvest?* Grand Rapids: Zondervan.

Fleck, J., and J. Carter. 1981. *Psychology and Christianity: Integrative readings.* Nashville: Abingdon.

Fowler, J. 1989. Strength for the journey. In *Faith development in early childhood,* ed. D. Blazer. Kansas City, Mo.: Sheed and Ward.

Fowlkes, M. 1989. Roots of ritual in social interactive episodes. *Religious Education* 84: 338–47.

Freud, S. 1913. *Totem and taboo.* London: Hogarth.

———. 1927 (repr. 1961). *The future of an illusion.* New York: Norton.

———. 1970. Obsessive actions and religious practices. In *Personality and religion,* ed. W. Sadler. New York: Harper and Row.

Hartshorne, H., and M. May. 1930. A summary of the work of the character education inquiry. *Religious Education* 25: 607–19, 754–62.

Helminiak, D. 1987. *Spiritual development: An interdisciplinary study.* Chicago: Loyola University Press.

Hyder, O. 1971. *The Christian's handbook of psychiatry.* Old Tappan, N.J.: Revell.

Johnson, W. 1982. Demon possession and mental illness. *Journal of the American Scientific Affiliation* 34 (Sept.): 149–54.

Jung, C. 1933. *Modern man in search of a soul.* New York: Harcourt, Brace.

McDonald, R. 1983. *The how of spiritual growth.* South Plainfield, N.J.: Bridge.

Malony, H. 1977. *Current perspectives in the psychology of religion.* Grand Rapids: Eerdmans.

Maslow, A. 1954. *Motivation and personality.* New York: Harper and Brothers.

Oakland, J. 1974. Self-actualization and sanctification. *Journal of Psychology and Theology* 2: 202–9.

Oates, W. 1973. *The psychology of religion.* Waco: Word.

Paloutzian, R. 1983. *Invitation to the psychology of religion.* Glenview, Ill.: Scott, Foresman.

Peck, S. 1983. *People of the lie.* New York: Simon and Schuster.

Piaget, J. 1948. *The moral judgement of the child.* Glencoe, Ill.: Free.

———. 1967. *Six psychological studies.* New York: Random.

Price, R. 1981. The centrality and scope of conversion. *Journal of Psychology and Theology* 9: 26–35.

Ratcliff, D. 1982. Behaviorism and the new worship groups. *Journal of the American Scientific Affiliation* 34 (Sept.): 169–71.

———. 1985. The development of children's religious concepts. *Journal of Psychology and Christianity* 4: 35–43.

———. 1987. Teaching the Bible developmentally. *Christian Education Journal* 7: 21–32.

———, ed. 1988. *Handbook of preschool religious education.* Birmingham, Ala.: Religious Education.

———. In press. Baby faith: Infants, toddlers, and religion. *Religious Education.*

Rizzuto, A. 1979. *The birth of the living God.* Chicago: University of Chicago Press.

Sall, M. 1976. Demon possession or psychopathology? *Journal of Psychology and Theology* 4: 286–90.

Schaeffer, F. 1968. *The God who is there.* Downers Grove: Inter-Varsity.

Seamands, D. 1988. *Healing grace.* Wheaton, Ill.: Victor.

Smith, N. 1988. *God, the Ultimate Background Object.* International Congress on Christian Counseling, Atlanta, Ga., Nov. 12.

Stern, D. 1985. *The interpersonal world of the infant.* New York: Basic.

Tamminen, K., et al. 1988. The religious concepts of preschoolers. In *Handbook of preschool religious education,* ed. D. Ratcliff. Birmingham, Ala.: Religious Education.

Tournier, P. 1962. *Guilt and grace.* New York: Harper and Row.

———. 1964. *The whole person in a broken world.* New York: Harper and Row.

Vitz, P. 1988. *Sigmund Freud's Christian unconscious.* New York: Guildford.

14

Abnormal Psychology

Defining Abnormality

How, precisely, can we distinguish between abnormal and normal? The standard guide used by psychologists is the *Diagnostic and Statistical Manual of Mental Disorders*, which is now in a revised third edition (1987). DSM III-R offers the following definition of abnormality:

> a clinically significant behavioral or psychological syndrome or pattern that occurs in a person and that is associated with present distress (a painful symptom) or disability (impairment in one or more important areas of functioning) or with a significantly increased risk of suffering, death, pain, disability, or an important loss of freedom. In addition, this syndrome or pattern must not be merely an expectable response to a particular event, e.g., the death of a loved one. Whatever its original cause, it must currently be considered a manifestation of a behavioral, psychological, or biological dysfunction in the person.

DSM III-R emphasizes that this definition does not include deviance or conflicts with others unless these characteristics are the result of a more basic dysfunction.

The emphasis on dysfunction in the above definition implies that psychological problems are the result of inadequate inner functioning. We could thus speak of the normal person's thinking being "functional" (achieving a purpose) because the mental activity accomplishes what it should, while the abnormal person is "dysfunctional" because thinking is inadequate.

In contrast, the term "abnormal" literally means "not normal" or "deviant." The DSM III-R definition explicitly states that deviance is not a sufficient definition because people can be unusual and different and yet not have dysfunctional thinking. Deviance involves not meeting the expectations of society. Yet societies can be quite different, so that what is normal in one society can be abnormal in another. This definition lacks any ultimate standard for normality, and thus the Christian should question its adequacy. Indeed, we can look at many spiritual people in the Bible, including the prophets, Christ, and Paul, and observe that they were clearly different from the norm, yet their thinking was clearly functional (actually more functional than the thinking of those around them). As Christians become more Christlike, they will become more abnormal in some respects, but their thinking will be more functional (achieving God's purpose) in the process.

Other psychologists have proposed that those with psychological problems should be considered maladjusted. To be normal, according to this perspective, is to adapt to the environment. Unlike the deviance perspective, the emphasis upon adjustment states that a person has normal behavior if what he or she does enhances what is best for the individual and the group. Thus the conforming person could be abnormal in the sense that conforming may not be what is best for the group. This viewpoint could be considered consistent with Christianity if one defines what is best for everyone as the Bible describes it.

Another approach to understanding abnormality is to see those who have severe problems as being disordered. DSM III-R is careful to emphasize that people are not disordered, but rather *have* disorders. A person is not an alcoholic but rather has alcohol dependence. This perspective is

---

Spotlight 14.1. Iatrogenic Illness

There is a danger that as we study psychological problems, we may come to doubt our own sanity and observe some of the symptoms described in ourselves (Stuart 1970).

There are at least two reasons why this occurs. Many people fall prey to the power of suggestion. It is easy to study something and begin to see what we read about in ourselves. This sometimes occurs in medical school where students begin to manifest the symptoms of each disease they study.

The second reason for iatrogenic illness is that many abnormal people manifest an unusual form of normal behavior. For example, abnormal behavior may be an extreme form of normal behavior or it may be normal behavior in inappropriate situations. Many things may be perfectly acceptable when done in private that are quite abnormal when done publicly. It should be noted that abnormal behavior, by definition, must interfere significantly with one's occupation or social life or cause considerable distress to the person.

If, during the process of reading this chapter, you find yourself wondering if you have a particular disorder, remember this warning. It is important to carefully read the description of each disorder and not overlook those aspects of a problem you do not have. It may also help to talk with friends who are reading this book or taking this class. They may very well be asking the same questions you are. Finally, if you believe you actually have a problem, consult a counselor and talk it over. It is far better to be rid of the questioning than to let the problem fester.

prevalent among psychologists today, but a Christian must question this separation of the disorder from the person. Does this imply a complete lack of personal responsibility? Certainly we can observe clusters of symptoms and describe them as a disorder, but a holistic approach would suggest that the individual is both influenced by circumstances and influences those circumstances in turn.

A final perspective on abnormality views it as a disease. This viewpoint takes the idea of lack of responsibility a step further: an individual cannot be blamed for acquiring an illness. The disease model of abnormality implies the medical model of personality (described in chap. 12) which many psychologists have rejected. However, it should be noted that certain psychological problems may fit this category, particularly those which result from physical brain damage or hormonal problems.

Thus, as defined above, abnormality is perhaps best understood as a dysfunction, maladjustment, and—when caused by physical impairment—disease. Collins (1973, 10–12) emphasizes that the abnormal individual experiences internal conflicts that lead to intense and prolonged feelings of insecurity, anxiety, or unhappiness (the dysfunctional aspect) or the individual is troubled by conscious or unconscious alienation from God. The latter extends the concept of abnormality far beyond what the typical psychologist would, thus including the majority of humanity. From God's perspective this is entirely correct. We are not how God intended us to be from the beginning, and a right relationship with him is the first step toward ultimate normality—normality as God intended from the beginning.

Some psychologists think that all categories of mental illness should be abolished. Szasz (1970) argues that labels for abnormal behavior are inherently destructive. Adams (1977) presents much the same argument, concluding that emotional problems should be categorized as either physical or due to a lack of responsibility. Certainly labels can be dangerous and should be used with extreme caution. But to throw out all systems of classification would not be sensible because we think in categories. Using only two categories for psychological problems is simplistic and overlooks the important environmental influences that affect the individual. Clearly the drug abuser, the depressive person, and the schizophrenic are very distinct from one another and require very different classifications.

Mental Health

Another way to understand mental illness is to examine its opposite—mental health. Total health in a whole person demands healthy relationships in three directions—inward toward self, outward toward others, and upward toward God. Individuals may be considered mentally healthy if they are in contact with reality and sufficiently free of anxiety so that they are not significantly incapacitated functionally, socially, or biologically for any extended period of time.

What characteristics are found in a person who is mentally healthy? The first is obviously an ability to function at full capacity physically, intellectually, and emotionally. Maintaining a balance in life leads to mental health.

A second important characteristic is an ability to adapt to changing situations with self-control and discipline. A person with a strong ego has an ability to tolerate stress and to cope with a wide variety of environmental situations. Healthy persons show that they are in contact with reality by reacting to all situations in a realistic way. Although we all face stress and change from time to time, mentally

Spotlight 14.2.
Guidelines for Mental Health

Dempsey and Zimbardo (1978, 414–15) provide seven guidelines for staying mentally healthy. First, we must *know our weaknesses.* We need to improve in areas where we can, or compensate if improvement is impossible.

Second, we should *use stress to develop problem-solving skills.* For example, the stress of an upcoming test may be used as motivation to study.

Third, we should *analyze what leads up to a personal crisis.* For example, if you have problems with normal depression, knowing what causes that temporary imbalance in your life can help you cope better.

Fourth, *negative thoughts should be replaced by positive thoughts.* As noted in chapter 7, we are more affected by "self-talk"—the interpretation we give to events—than by the events themselves. As we will see in chapter 15, irrational thoughts are at the root of many problems.

A fifth guideline is to *know when and where to go for help.* Bottling up feelings makes things worse in the long run. Five priorities in seeking help can be identified: (1) Talk to God about it first. God, in his power, is able to conquer any problem. But God, in his wisdom, may choose to use human resources to heal. (2) Family and friends are important resources. (3) Pastors are contacted for emotional problems even more frequently than psychologists. (4) A doctor may be needed. A good counselor will first attempt to rule out possible medical problems. (5) Most people can benefit from counseling at some time in their lives. Colleges and seminaries usually provide such services free of charge or at reduced rates.

A sixth guideline is to *develop our potential.* It is easy to get into routines and miss the real vitality of life. Develop a new hobby, read a good book, try something new!

Finally, *develop and maintain close relationships.* We need other people for feedback and recognition.

---

healthy individuals react appropriately by exercising self-control. Able to accept what is unchangeable, they are free from excessive, prolonged anxiety in the face of change.

A third characteristic of a mentally healthy individual is an attitude of confidence, usually accompanied by a sense of humor. Such confidence, of course, must stem from faith in God.

Another characteristic found in mentally healthy persons is an unwavering purpose in life. Living for God and for his principles gives meaning and direction to life.

Mentally healthy persons relate well to a variety of people. Because they can accept the legitimate authority of individuals and institutions, they perform well on the job. They can make and keep friends, love and be loved. A capacity for intimacy in close interpersonal relationships is a clue to mental health.

An important characteristic of mental health is balance. Capacity to function in both dependent and independent roles, to be taken care of or to take care of oneself, to follow or to lead (depending on the circumstances) is a sign of health. Other signs are a balance between competition and compromise, between ability to pursue objectives alone and to work effectively with others. Healthy persons know how to strike a balance between being organized and being creative. Organizing their knowledge and experience so as to draw meaningful conclusions, they ap-

---

Spotlight 14.3. The Spiritually Healthy Christian

Darling (1969, 129–42) identifies seven characteristics of the mentally and spiritually healthy Christian. Though some of these characteristics are idealistic, they are certainly worthy goals to pursue.

First, the healthy Christian is marked by *confident surrender*. This confidence is a sense of belonging to God because of surrender to Christ, a definite decision without any thought of turning back.

Second, the Christian should be *transparently spontaneous*. Transparency is the honesty and openness that should mark Christians; there is no need for masks because God knows us as we are. We can also be spontaneous because we are made in the image of God and a fundamental characteristic of God is creativity. Christians need not settle for mediocrity.

Third, we should have *purposeful integration* in life. Our purpose comes from having real meaning in life through Christ, while integration refers to our holistic nature. There is a harmony, a unity, a wholeness to the spiritually healthy Christian.

Fourth, healthy Christians are marked by *adjusting tension*. There is a tension between the ideal and real in the Christian life (Rom. 7). We strive to integrate what we ought to be and what we are, which is basically a creative process. Yet we must also be able to accept that we will be less than absolutely perfect. God will perfect us by, as the Bible says, "pruning" us to bear more fruit. We need to accept our strengths and weaknesses, realizing that suffering, temptation, and other problems in the Christian life are opportunities for growth (Rom. 8:28). And we have unlimited growth potential!

Fifth, the Christian is to be characterized by *wholehearted affirmation*. This includes a self-affirmation in which we are set free by Christ to be fully creative. All of life is sacred to the Christian; we must not dichotomize life into the religious and secular. God empowers us to live a great life (Phil. 4:13). God's strength compensates for our weakness (2 Cor. 12:9). Self-love is possible because we are sons and daughters of God, coheirs with Christ. Not only are healthy Christians self-affirming, but they are also affirming of others. Love for others is the badge of the Christian (1 John 4:7–8); we are to love others as we love ourselves (Matt. 22:39). We need to accept others as they are, unique and yet having the potential to change for the better.

Sixth, healthy Christians *appropriate resources from God*. We need to realize he has resources beyond our comprehension, and then ask for and use those resources. This underscores the value of prayer, Bible reading, and the spiritual gifts. We must let God fill our vessels with "new wine."

Finally, the healthy Christian *invests resources*. We must not let the "new wine" stagnate, but rather share it with others through discipleship, evangelism, and social concern ("good works"). Giving our whole lives for others and for the kingdom of God must be a priority; we must share what God has given us.

proach tasks and problems systematically but without oversystematizing. Too much organization can destroy creativity, so the individuals who are most effective generally have a healthy balance of both.

Spiritual balance is also an indication of mental health. There should be a balance between reading the Word of God, prayer, witnessing, and Christian fellowship. Churches or individual Christians who overemphasize prayer often seem too emotional. Those who overemphasize doctrine may seem cold. Those who overemphasize witnessing may at times offend others unnecessarily. Those who overemphasize fellowship and neglect the other basics of the Christian life may lack depth. Christians should seek a balance within themselves and within the body of Christ.

Another mark of mental health and maturity is dependability. Christians should be trustworthy. Others should not find any evidence of corruption or negligence in our lives. Our personal standards should enable us to resist pressures to sin or to act impulsively.

Another criterion of mental health is the capacity to be other-centered. Individuals who are wrapped up in their own selfish desires, anger, jealousy, suspicions, and problems have little to give to others.

The ability to express and control emotion is an important aspect of mental health. Persons who can tolerate strong emotions have good ego strength. Healthy persons neither avoid situations that arouse strong emotions nor use the mechanisms of isolation and dissociation to keep from feeling. Their emotions are not repressed but their behavior is under control.

Mentally healthy persons are usually satisfied with their maleness or femaleness. They are relatively free from fears and complexes involving sexuality and if married are able to enjoy an active and satisfactory sex life.

A final characteristic of mental health from a Christian perspective is a positive relationship with the Lord. The fact that Christians generally read the Bible daily is not only an indication of their mental health but also a major reason for it. The Word of God produces peace, joy, and contentment, and prevents anxiety, depression, defensiveness, and immaturity.

Causes of Psychological Problems

Few psychological problems develop suddenly without a "history," although many of the factors leading to a given problem may have gone unnoticed. Minirth (1977, 111–12) outlines the three major causes of psychological problems:

> Mental illness . . . often is not caused by one factor. A spiritual problem may be the cause of the emotional problem, but other factors often come into play or are responsible.
>
> For example, the genetic background is important when examining a mental problem. I have seen one mental problem in particular, *manic-depressive psychosis*, where an unusually high proportion of the relatives had also had the problem. And, as stated elsewhere in other chapters, scientific studies have documented that children of schizophrenic parents develop schizophrenia significantly more often than other children, even when they are raised away from the parents. Furthermore, one does not have to look far to see that personality traits run in families. Just as dogs pass on personality traits (German shepherd—aggressive, St. Bernard—friendly), so do humans.
>
> Secondly, the importance of environmental background has probably been overstated through the past several years. However, there is no doubt that this factor is of much importance in forming a personality. Children are taught to be

humble, aggressive, polite, or rude. I have seen parents who wonder why their sixteen-year-old Johnny is rude, rebellious, and disobedient. Yet, the parents have never disciplined him. Physical health could also be included in this category. Children or adults who are physically ill usually have less capacity to withstand emotional stress.

Usually, a third factor is necessary for a psychological problem to develop. This third factor is a precipitating stress. Although one may have hereditary factors present and may have had a difficult early environment, a psychological disorder may never develop unless he is in an acutely stressful situation.

Truly, the genetic and environmental background are factors of major importance. To deny this is naive. However, it is equally naive to use these as excuses for present conduct. Many problems are brought about through irresponsible behavior. What Apostle Paul said many years ago is still true: ". . . whatsoever a man soweth, that shall he also reap" (Galatians 6:7). Many times emotional problems are brought about through irresponsible behavior, sins, or just not knowing, or failing to rely on the resources that a Christian has at his disposal.

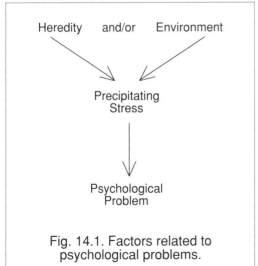

Fig. 14.1. Factors related to psychological problems.

The above three factors—heredity, environment, and precipitating stress—have been elaborated into the diathesis-stress model. "Diathesis" refers to the predisposition or vulnerability an individual may have for a particular disorder due to either biological influences or some aspect of the past or present environment. Having a predisposing cause for a disorder does not mean that an individual will automatically have a particular psychological problem; rather it means that the problem will probably surface *if* the person comes into contact with a certain precipitating stress. If the person does not encounter the precipitating stress, a disorder is not likely. (It is thought that the majority of people with a diathesis for a disorder will not have that disorder; only those who meet with very potent stressors will.)

Other factors can also influence whether a person will have a given disorder. Sometimes there is a primary cause; that is, a specific condition must be present for that disorder to occur. An example is organic brain disorders, which are always due to a specific physical problem (such as a tumor or stroke). Psychologists also emphasize reinforcing causes—getting attention or avoiding undesired activities due to the psychological problem. Reinforcing causes tend to perpetuate psychological problems (see chap. 5).

Yet we must be careful in assigning causation for a particular form of mental illness. There are often several predisposing influences that combine with precipitating stress to cause a problem, rather than one cause producing the problem. Indeed, one cause can produce an effect that in turn is causative of other effects. Sometimes effects will feed back on causes; thus the effects make the causes more likely to be repeated. For example, could a nagging wife cause her husband to become an alcoholic, or does the alcoholism precipitate the nagging?

Biological Causes

Biological causes include chromosomal abnormalities, genetic influences, and other biological factors. An example of chromosomal abnormality is Down's syndrome which results from an extra twenty-first chromosome. Chromosomal abnormalities are quite rare, however, occurring in only about one-half of one percent of newborns (Sergovich et al. 1969).

Genes on specific chromosomes can also play a part in causing mental problems. Unlike chromosomal abnormalities, these defects cannot be directly observed and thus it is harder to predict who will have certain disorders. Generally several genes must be present in a certain combination to produce a predisposition for a problem. This combining is inferred from the fact that certain psychological problems are more likely to run in families, even when children are reared apart from their parents. Perhaps the best example of a genetic psychological problem is schizophrenia.

Some have suggested a genetic influence may be present with alcoholism and homosexuality as well. At present this is more speculation than the product of good research. Even if such an influence could be proven, it would be a mistake to blame sinful behavior on "bad genes." While our genetic makeup does have a powerful effect upon us, we are not determined solely by our genes. The best research to date, summarized by Jones and Workman (1989), indicates that often (but not always) prenatal hormones influence gender orientation. When combined with certain socialization experiences, homosexuality becomes more likely; however, such influences do not force an individual to engage in homosexual behavior. People's choices

add to the many other influences that exist. Genes may predispose some people to develop clinical depression under stress through chemical imbalances, but genes do not program people to hold grudges. A Christian can conclude that the genetic potentials and predispositions of each individual are part of the plan of God. They produce strengths and weaknesses that can ultimately bring glory to him (Ps. 139:13–14; Isa. 43:7).

Other physical factors may also influence psychological problems. There is evidence, for example, that males may be inherently more likely to be aggressive and react emotionally to frustration, while females may be inherently more likely to be fearful and dependent (Pervin 1978). These tendencies, however, say little about a particular male or female. Personal choice and the environment combine with gender to influence a particular individual.

As mentioned previously, organic disorders are clearly the result of biological factors. Older individuals are more likely to have such organic disorders; 17 percent of those over the age of sixty-five have brain damage that significantly affects behavior (Kolata 1981). A number of psychological problems can result, but the best-known organic disorder is Alzheimer's disease.

Environmental Influences

Biological influences are sometimes related to environmental factors. Perhaps the best example would be deprivation of basic needs, such as sleep and food. In previous chapters we have observed that basic needs that go unmet can produce problems such as personality changes and lowered intelligence.

Other psychosocial aspects of the environment also powerfully influence us, although our knowledge of exactly how these affect abnormal behavior is less precise than the understanding of biological influences. Throughout this book, and particularly in chapter 10, the important role of the individual's early environment has been underscored. For example, emotional deprivation or trauma in childhood can carry over into later life. Children who are institutionalized early in life are severely impaired in their interpersonal relationships as early as one year of age (Provence and Lipton 1962). Parental rejection and neglect likewise can produce negative outcomes, the former producing more impulsive, aggressive behavior (Patterson 1979).

Traumatic events in childhood can also produce problems that may remain dormant until later stress reactivates their emotional component (though the adult may not recall the specific childhood event that causes a certain exaggerated reaction). Single traumas are unlikely to predispose an individual to adult pathology (psychological problems), but recurrent trauma in early childhood is more damaging.

Meier (1977, 45–79) has documented several linkages between child-rearing practices and adult pathology. Children with strict and harsh parents are more likely to be overly perfectionistic and depressive as adults. Children who have been subjected to incestuous relationships are likely to have personality disturbances (cf. Owens 1984). Children reared with little or no discipline are likely to lack a conscience and be uncontrolled. Research indicates that overly indulged children are more likely to be antisocial and aggressive later in life (Sears 1961).

Meier also indicates that children reared in a church where the pastor stresses conditional acceptance by God will probably feel insecure in their relation to God. A child from a home where the father is overly passive and the mother overly dominant is more likely to have one of a wide variety of psychological problems in adulthood. Unrealistically high or low parental demands may also produce lifelong difficulties. Finally, research indicates that overprotection fosters dependency, anxiety, and excessive fear (Jenkins 1968; Poznanski 1973).

Other general family influences have been determined to cause psychological problems. Parents who are continually fighting produce an atmosphere that is hardly conducive to mental health. Communication patterns in such a home may be severely disrupted. The absence of a parent, either through divorce, separation or death, can predispose children to abnormality. For example, absence of a father negatively influences gender identity for both boys and girls (Hetherington, Camara, and Feathermore 1983), while divorce can produce long-range emotional problems for children (Wallerstein and Blakeslee 1989).

The above trends, it should be emphasized, are statistical probabilities rather than absolute certainties, as is true of all scientific research. Although there is no doubt that early environmental factors influence mental health, it must be stressed again that these factors should not be used as excuses for irresponsible behavior. Through Christ, and the healing body of believers (which might include Christian counselors), individuals can learn to cope with even the most difficult early environmental factors.

Precipitating Stresses

If individuals have a potential genetic weakness, a difficult early environment, and do not turn to Christ and fellow Christians for help, then during times of stress they are likely to develop a mental disorder. The precipitating stress is often the complaint presented by a person seeking help from a counselor. Such things as marital trouble, financial problems, or job difficulties may constitute the third factor necessary for a psychological problem to develop.

It would be naive and unwise to assume, as Adams (1977), that all stresses are brought on by personal sins and irresponsibility. A counselor must genuinely grieve with a mother who comes seeking advice and consolation because her child is dying of leukemia. She should be helped to see that this is in no way the result of sin in her life, but that disease and death are as much a part of human life as are birth and falling in love. Parents often assume that the death of their child must be punishment for some sin that they have committed. Such an assumption is basically self-centered, implying that all of life's events somehow revolve around the parents.

On the other hand, a battered wife who seeks advice and consolation because her husband has beaten her must be confronted about her share of the responsibility for his attacks. She may be provoking (usually unconsciously) her explosive husband until he reaches the boiling point. Of course, her actions in no way diminish her husband's responsibility for attacking her.

Many people think they are in control of their lives but are, in reality, allowing themselves to be dominated by their own unconscious drives, conflicts, and motives. Such persons generally emphasize the precipitating stresses in their environment that are making their lives unbearable. A wise counselor will try to look into an individual's heart, to see unconscious thoughts and emotions and to help that individual avoid bringing on precipitating stresses, if possible.

Psychological Disorders

In the remainder of this chapter we will examine six broad categories of psychological disorders. These are the most common and significant disorders, but by no means do they exhaust the types of psychological problems people can have.

Anxiety Disorders

This group of disorders, in which anxiety is the predominant feature, includes phobic disorder, panic disorder, obsessive-compulsive disorder, and generalized anxiety disorder. It has been estimated that 8 to 15 percent of the population has an anxiety disorder (NIMH 1985).

How an individual handles anxiety determines the type of anxiety disorder that develops. For example, if anxiety from a past or present stress is displaced onto a neutral object, the individual has a phobic disorder. Anxiety displaced to thought or worry produces an obsessive-compulsive disorder. Anxiety left free-floating so that the individual feels panic produces a panic disorder.

Anxious individuals may be hyperalert, irritable, fidgety, and overdependent. They may talk too much and have difficulty falling asleep. Their concentration may be impaired and their memory poor. They may be essentially immobilized by their anxiety. Other symptoms include excessive perspiration, muscle-tension headaches, a quivering voice, sighing respirations, episodes of hyperventilation, abdominal pain, nausea, diarrhea, "butterflies" in the stomach, high blood pressure, rapid heartbeat, fainting episodes, frequent urination, impotence, or frigidity.

Anxiety has many causes. It can result from unconscious conflicts. It can be learned by example—by identifying with parents or others who are anxious. It can stem from childhood conflicts or from present-day situational problems. Some people get anxious about being anxious.

Spotlight 14.4. Christian Resources on Anxiety Disorders

Several resources on anxiety disorders are available. Collins' *Fractured Personalities* (1973), now out of print, offers a helpful Christian perspective on abnormality in general, although the classifications used are somewhat different than those in DSM III (he used DSM II). Although not as rigorous, one may also find help in Hyder (1971) and Narramore (1984). Kotesky (1983) and Backus (1985) include sections on anxiety disorders. Young's (1981) "Neurotic Christian" is helpful.

Anxiety can come from fears of inferiority, poverty, or poor health.

All children have experiences that create anxiety. Individuals who have had a particularly stressful childhood with many bad experiences generally suffer a great deal of anxiety. Much of that anxiety is not dealt with at the time it appears but is repressed. When individuals encounter situations and experiences that cause anxiety, the anxiety from their early childhood is also aroused. In most cases only the emotions from childhood are aroused; the specific event is not recalled. The repressed emotions seem to apply to the current situation, although they really do not—at least not in the proportion in which they are being experienced. This explains why we often overreact to certain situations. We are reacting not only to the current stresses but also to the repressed emotions of childhood. Anxiety from the current situation may also be partially repressed or it may be internalized, resulting in depression. Additional anxiety may be created as individuals become anxious over being anxious, or develop anxiety over a particular phobia or obsession they have, or feel anxious because they are depressed.

Conflicts may cause anxiety. Psychologists distinguish between approach-avoidance conflicts, approach-approach conflicts, and avoidance-avoidance conflicts. An approach-avoidance conflict exists when there is one goal with both desirable and undesirable qualities. An approach-approach conflict exists when there are two goals, both of which are desirable but which are mutually exclusive. An avoidance-avoidance conflict exists when there are two undesirable choices, and the individual cannot avoid dealing with one of them.

PHOBIAS

Phobic disorders are characterized by persistent avoidance behavior because of irrational fears of a specific situation, object, or activity. The individual recognizes that the fear is irrational. A diagnosis of phobic disorder is made only if the avoidance behavior is severe enough to interfere with social functioning. Agoraphobia is an irrational fear of leaving the familiar home setting. Individuals with agoraphobia may refuse to travel or walk alone, or even to be alone. They may develop much anxiety in closed or open spaces. The anxiety may become so intense that the individual feels a type of panic and will hyperventilate. Social phobia is fear of social situations in which individuals feel they might be humiliated or embarrassed. Social phobias involve anxiety about speaking or eating in public, writing in front of others, or using public restrooms. Simple phobia might more appropriately be called "specific"

Table 14.1

Phobias

Phobia	Morbid Fear of
acrophobia	high places
agoraphobia	leaving familiar places
algophobia	pain
anthophobia	flowers
astraphobia	thunder and lightning
belonophobia	pins and needles
claustrophobia	confined places
decidophobia	making decisions
entomophobia	insects
ergophobia	work
erthyrophobia	blushing in public
gephydrophobia	crossing bridges
hematophobia	sight of blood
heliophobia	sunlight
hydrophobia	water
iatrophobia	doctors
lalophobia	speaking
monophobia	being alone
mysophobia	dirt, contamination
necrophobia	dead bodies
nyctophobia	darkness
pathophobia	disease, suffering
ombrophobia	rain
phonophobia	speaking aloud
photophobia	strong light
taphophobia	buried alive
trichophobia	hair
toxophobia	being poisoned
xenophobia	strangers
zoophobia	animals
arachibutyrophobia	peanut butter sticking to the roof of the mouth

phobia. The irrational fear may have to do with animals, insects, water, closed spaces, or anything else. Animal phobia is especially common in childhood. Many adults have claustrophobia, becoming very anxious when confined to a small area.

OTHER ANXIETY DISORDERS

Panic disorder is actually an intense anxiety attack. The affected individual feels much apprehension, fearfulness, and impending doom. Associated symptoms include rapid heartbeat, shortness of breath, chest discomfort, a smothering sensation, dizziness, numbness, hot flashes, cold hands, sweating, faintness, and trembling. Feelings of unreality and fears of dying, of going crazy, or of doing something uncontrolled are common. Panic disorder often begins in late adolescence or early adult life, and occurs more commonly in women.

Obsessive-compulsive disorder is characterized by recurrent obsessions (irrational thoughts) or compulsions (irrational actions). The most common obsessions are thoughts of contamination, doubt, or violence. The most common compulsions include repetitive handwashing, checking, and touching.

Generalized anxiety disorder is characterized by chronic generalized and persistent anxiety. This diagnosis is not made if a definite stress precipitated the disorder (in which case it is called adjustment disorder). Symptoms of generalized anxiety include trembling, shaking, inability to relax, heart pounding, sweating, dizziness, upset stomach, apprehensive expectations (worries or ruminations), edginess, impatience, and irritability.

Mood Disorders

A second broad category of psychological problems encompasses the affective or mood disorders. These are characterized by either depression, elation, or some combination of these two extremes. Major mood disorders are subclassified as bipolar disorder, major depression, cyclothymia, and dysthymia (see tab. 14.2).

BIPOLAR DISORDER

The manic phase of the bipolar disorder is characterized by increases in mood, speech, and motor ability. The euphoric mood resembles the "high" of an amphetamine user. Manic individuals are habitually cheerful, demonstrating a contagious unrestrained good humor until frustrated. At that point their humor can instantly turn caustic as they become irritable and insensitive to others. In their euphoric mood they may show ambition, enthusiasm, optimism, effervescence, ecstasy, buoyancy, grandiosity, and inflated

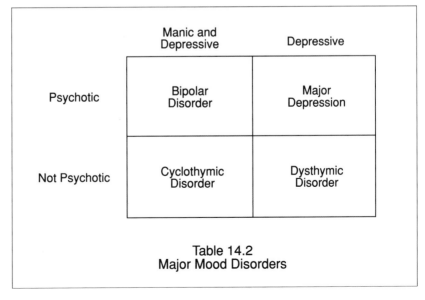

	Manic and Depressive	Depressive
Psychotic	Bipolar Disorder	Major Depression
Not Psychotic	Cyclothymic Disorder	Dysthymic Disorder

Table 14.2
Major Mood Disorders

self-esteem. In their uncritical self-confidence, their judgment may be so impaired that they make all sorts of extravagant business deals. Along with the euphoric mood comes extreme denial. The euphoric mood may in fact be a denial of an underlying depression.

Manic individuals characteristically talk rapidly and excessively. As their thoughts race their conversation frequently switches from one topic to another. Unable to sustain a continuous train of thought, they talk too loudly and often toss in jokes or hostile comments. Without evident talent they may start writing a novel or composing a song and may develop grandiose delusions. Their increased motor activity is evidenced in multiple activities, decreased sleep, and increased sociability (such as calling friends at all hours of the night). Manic individuals are intrusive, demanding, and domineering.

A depressive episode (whether caused by major depression or a depressed bipolar state) is characterized by a sad affect, painful thinking, physical symptoms, anxiety, and possibly delusional thinking. Affected individuals look sad. Women may stop putting on makeup. Men may stop shaving. Tearfulness may accompany a dejected or discouraged manner. Depressed individuals feel worthless, helpless, and hopeless. Guilt permeates their thinking. They are introspective in a derogatory sort of way. They lose their motivation and ability to enjoy pleasure. Withdrawing from people and feeling despondent and inadequate, they may eventually become suicidal.

Physical symptoms of depressed individuals include being restless or phlegmatic. They may think slowly and be unable to concentrate. Sleep disturbances are common. Appetite may be disturbed and weight may be gained or lost. Depressed individuals have very low energy levels and generally have a hard time getting started in the morning. They may become preoccupied with physical problems, such as headaches or constipation. Anxiety may be demonstrated by restlessness or increased irritability. Paranoid symptoms are especially common, including delusions of being persecuted because of some sin.

Depressive episodes may begin at any age, but manic episodes usually begin before age thirty. At least half of the individuals with an initial depressive episode have another depressive episode. The major complication of depression is suicide. Major complications of a manic episode are financial losses and other social consequences of impaired judgment.

Major depression

Psychiatrists treat more cases of depression than any other emotional disturbance. Eight to 10 percent of Americans suffer from a major depression at some time in their lives (Brown 1974). Many more persons have symptoms of depression but do not seek treatment.

Depression occurs more often in women and affects many people in the higher socioeconomic brackets. It occurs most often when individuals reach their forties or fifties but may occur during any period of life. When depression can be at least partially traced to difficult life events such as the death of a loved one, the externally triggered emotional response is said to be reactive and exogenous. Sometimes, however, feelings of depression have no apparent external causes. Such endogenous feelings can lead to chronic depression, sometimes lasting a lifetime.

Cyclothymia

Cyclothymia is characterized by at least a two-year history of both manic and depressive symptoms, not of sufficient sever-

La Migraine, a painting by Charles Aubry (1822) depicting a family coping with mother's headache.

ity to meet the criteria of a manic or depressive episode.

Cyclothymia is similar to manic-depressive psychosis but is much less severe. Throughout life such individuals are "high" and elated for a period of time, then thoroughly depressed for a period of time. Or they may remain mostly elated throughout life or mostly depressed throughout life. In other words, they can, throughout their lives, be high or low, or can alternate between the two extremes.

When cyclothymic individuals are elated, they are warm, ambitious, buoyant, optimistic, enthusiastic, outgoing, and likable. In severe cases, they may seem hypomanic or persistently euphoric. They may talk so much and so fast that they actually become hoarse, racing illogically from one topic to another as though unable to keep their minds on a single train of thought. Their speech is generally cheerful and effervescent, full of contagious humor until some frustration produces a flash of anger that turns the humor into hostile sarcasm. Wrapped up in their own achievements, they can be very insensitive to others, using religious jargon or making embarrassing comments. Since they have a tendency to blame others and possess little true self-awareness, their behavior can be exasperating to family and friends. Uninhibited by self-criticism, they may show poor judgment in their impulsiveness and self-confident drive. They may plunge into extravagant enterprises in an attempt to acquire needless possessions. Some act like exhibitionists, going nude or posturing seductively. Their tendency to maneuver or to exploit others without compassion can create havoc within a family.

When depressed, the same cyclothymic individuals are sad, hopeless, helpless, and despondent—performing at a low energy level. The recurring periods of high and low sometimes fluctuate rapidly, occasionally over weeks and months. The periods of depression are marked by reduced activity, pessimism, social withdrawal, guilt, depression, and anxiety. Hypochondriacal feelings may exist, such as diminished appetite, insomnia, or decreased sexual desire. Occasionally thoughts of suicide occur. Cyclothymic individuals continue to function during periods of depression, but only marginally.

The maniclike highs are commonly prized by cyclothymic individuals because they "feel so good," but are dreaded by family, friends, and associates. Conversely, low periods, disliked by cyclothymic individuals, provide welcome relief for family and acquaintances, since cyclothymic persons become less pushy and cease dominating conversations as they slow down to a state of mild to moderate depression. The elated periods are characterized by an enhanced sense of well-being. Optimistic and self-assured, cyclothymic individuals frequently make a number of commitments and may even fulfill them all. They may be viewed by others as capable and creative. With their increased motor activity, only a few hours of sleep seem to be adequate. During their high periods these individuals make expansive plans and can be financially and professionally successful. Problems arise when those plans are thwarted. Becoming irritable and suspicious, cyclothymic individuals may react in a socially inappropriate manner by being antisocial, impulsive, or explosive. Sexual or alcoholic excess may occur during that stage.

DYSTHYMIA

Dysthymia is essentially the depressive cycle of cyclothymia without the maniclike cycle. Dysthymia is an extended form of normal depression (see chap. 4).

WHY ARE CHRISTIANS DEPRESSED?

Depression is often the result of an adjustment reaction, the response of a basically healthy individual to a situational stress. Most people are able to deal with situational problems before their reaction develops into clinical depression. But, as already mentioned, too much in too short a time can overwhelm almost anyone.

A precipitating cause of depression in many Christians is a wrong perspective. In an affluent society with many temptations it is easy to develop the wrong focus. Psalm 73:1–3 records Asaph's depression stemming from his bad perspective: "Surely God is good to Israel, to those who are pure in heart. But as for me, my feet had almost slipped; I had nearly lost my foothold. For I envied the arrogant when I saw the prosperity of the wicked." When Asaph changed his perspective, his depression lifted: "When I tried to understand all this, it was oppressive to me till I entered the sanctuary of God; then I understood their final destiny" (vv. 16–17). In contrast, Moses was a man with a godly perspective. "By faith Moses, when he had grown up, refused to be known as the son of Pharaoh's daughter. He chose to be mistreated along with the people of God rather than to enjoy the pleasures of sin for a short time. He regarded disgrace for the sake of Christ as of greater value than the treasures of Egypt, because he was looking ahead to his reward" (Heb. 11:24–26). Moses recognized that the temporary pleasures of sin would not give lasting meaning to life. A healthy perspective leads us to invest in two things that have eternal significance: the Word of God and people.

Another precipitating factor in depression can be an attack by Satan, who seems to enjoy rendering Christians ineffective through depression. God wants us to confess our sins, deal with our problems, and not stay depressed. If the reason for discouragement and depression is vague, in all probability something is amiss. Those who feel helpless and hopeless often conclude that they are without Christ. With Christ, people sense their worth and know they can deal with their problems.

A major cause of discouragement among dedicated Christians is self-reliance. Clearly the Christian life can be lived joyfully only through the power of the Holy Spirit. Paul, who exuberantly exclaims, "I can do everything through him who gives me strength" (Phil. 4:13) and "for it is God who works in you to will and to act according to his good purpose" (Phil. 2:13) also records his discouragement from trying to live for God in his own energy (Rom. 7:14–24).

Psychotic Disorders

A third major division of abnormality is the psychotic disorders, in which the affected individual is in some way out of touch with reality. This category includes schizophrenia and the delusional disorder as well as several other disorders which will not be considered here.

SCHIZOPHRENIA

The best known of the psychotic disorders is schizophrenia, which has been studied and treated for many years. The classical symptoms are described by Bleuler (1950) as the "4 As": flat or inappropriate affect, loose associations, autism, and ambivalence.

Individuals with a schizophrenic disorder may ramble from one topic to another, making it impossible for others to follow their train of thought. The loose associations reflect an underlying thought disorder caused by a scrambling of neural transmissions. This is possibly precipitated by too much acute stress in an individual with a genetic weakness reared in a poor early environment. The underlying thought disorder is reflected in vague, overabstract, overconcrete, repetitive, stereotyped, or illogical communication. Facts may be obscured or distorted and conclusions reached based on inadequate or faulty evidence.

Individuals with a schizophrenic disorder generally have flat or inappropriate emotions. The schizophrenic may smile or laugh while relating a sad personal experience. Although certain antipsychotic drugs can produce some affective flattening, the blank, staring look is usually a symptom of the underlying schizophrenic disorder.

Autistic schizophrenics are caught up in their own world. Fantasies and daydreams increase as such individuals withdraw more and more from the external world. They may seem emotionally detached or preoccupied, becoming increasingly shy and socially regressed.

The ambivalence of schizophrenics may become so marked that they become immobilized when faced with choices. The ambivalence reflects an underlying disturbance of the will, often resulting in loss of motivation and goal-directed activity.

In addition to the four primary symptoms, secondary symptoms include delusions and hallucinations. A delusion is a belief held to be true in the face of solid evidence to the contrary. Common types of schizophrenic delusions include those of grandeur, persecution, or reference (thinking newspaper articles or television shows are making personal references to one). Some delusions are of thoughts being controlled, inserted, broadcasted, or withdrawn. Some delusions have jealous content.

A hallucination is hearing, seeing, or feeling things that are not actually present. Auditory hallucinations are by far the most common. Schizophrenic individuals may hear insulting statements, their name being called, or music no one else can hear.

Delusions and hallucinations are the result of the extreme defense mechanism known as distortion. Affected individuals reshape external reality to suit their own inner needs, frequently hearing voices from "God" or "demons." Other general symptoms of schizophrenia include peculiar behavior, poor personal hygiene, eccentric dress, impaired role functioning, and disturbances in motor behavior (mannerisms, grimacing, rigid posture, reduction of spontaneous movements).

Schizophrenia implies a lasting disorganization of a previous level of functioning.

By definition the symptoms must be present for six months before a diagnosis can be made. The degree to which the symptoms abate with treatment varies. Often an individual can return to near normal functioning in many respects although some symptoms remain. Individuals with any of the following are more likely to have a good prognosis: a clear precipitating event, an abrupt onset, an onset late in life, adequate functioning prior to the onset of the disorder.

Schizophrenia usually begins in adolescence or early adulthood. It occurs in 0.2 to one percent of the population, equally among males and females (DSM III-R 1987, 192). It is found more often among lower socioeconomic groups and biologically related family members, with a concordance rate significantly higher for identical twins than for nonidentical twins. The personality type most likely to develop schizophrenia is characterized by being suspicious,

---

Spotlight 14.5. Resources on Mood Disorders, Schizophrenia, and Substance Abuse

Three excellent books consider the mood disorders, a prominent problem among Christians. Minirth and Meier's *Happiness Is a Choice* (1978) and White's *Masks of the Melancholy* (1982) are excellent. Some will consider White a bit simplistic, but there is real practical wisdom in some of his comments. You may also want to consider Foster's *How to Deal with Depression* (1984).

Owens provides a vivid firsthand description of schizophrenia (*A Promise of Sanity* [1982]). The descriptions of her own schizophrenic thinking are perhaps unmatched in the literature, as well as the way she describes the effects of certain medications (although it should be noted that psychiatric medications affect individuals in different ways).

There is a wide variety of Christian resources available on substance abuse, most of them dealing with alcoholism and drugs on a popular level. Perhaps the best sources are Clinebell (1968), Lenters (1985), and VanVondervan (1985). Also see a series of articles entitled "Getting Free" (1988). On gaining a Christian perspective on drinking alcohol, consider Geisler (1982) and Stein (1975).

shy, introverted, withdrawn, or eccentric. Schizophrenics have a shorter life expectancy and an increased suicide rate.

Subtypes of schizophrenic disorders include the disorganized, catatonic, and paranoid varieties.

Disorganized schizophrenia is characterized by a silly affect. Other symptoms include grimaces, mannerisms, and extreme social withdrawal. This type of schizophrenia usually starts early in life and has the poorest prognosis.

Catatonic schizophrenia is characterized by psychomotor disturbances, excitement, stupor, and a rigid posturing known as waxy flexibility. Mutism is also common.

Paranoid schizophrenia is characterized by paranoid delusions of persecutory or grandiose content. Anger may be a prominent feature. This type of schizophrenia usually starts later and tends to remain stable over time.

THE DELUSIONAL DISORDER

A delusional disorder, like schizophrenia, is a psychotic disorder. They are both characterized by the person not being in touch with reality. The delusional disorder differs from schizophrenia in that, except for the paranoid delusion, thinking is clear and orderly. In other words, individuals with paranoia have only one aspect of their thinking out of touch with reality. They may feel spied on, conspired against, followed, drugged, or poisoned. They may have delusions of jealousy. The delusion tends to be chronic, in spite of facts to the contrary.

Stress and Adjustment Disorders

While most psychological disorders involve precipitating factors, stress and adjustment disorders are clearly related to the intense stress itself rather than some combination of stress and earlier factors.

The stress and adjustment disorders are characterized by a reaction to a life event without which the disorder would not have occurred. Post-traumatic stress disorder produces certain symptoms (anxiety, recurrent nightmares, sleep disturbances, trouble concentrating, guilt, depression) after occurrence of a traumatic event outside the range of usual experience (earthquake, flood, car accident, torture, airplane crash). Adjustment disorders occur when an individual's ability to function is significantly affected because of some identifiable stressor. Subtypes include adjustment disorder with depressive mood, adjustment disorder with anxious mood, adjustment disorder with physical symptoms, adjustment disorder with disturbance of conduct, and adjustment disorder with withdrawal.

Dissociative Disorders

Dissociative disorders are characterized by alterations in consciousness or identity producing such symptoms as amnesia, somnambulism (sleep walking), fugue (a type of amnesia), and multiple personality. The various forms of dissociation may begin and end gradually or abruptly. Dissociative disorders are related to a series of events beyond an individual's power of conscious recall.

In psychogenic amnesia there is a total loss of memory about events covering a period from a few hours (localized amnesia) to a whole lifetime of experience (general amnesia). Seemingly alert before and after the amnesia, affected individuals give no appearance of anything being wrong. Persons with continuous amnesia lose their memory for each event as it occurs; in systematized amnesia memory for specific, related past events is lost.

In psychogenic fugue individuals wander, sometimes for several days and often far from home, even totally establishing a new identity. During this time they forget their past but are unaware that they have forgotten anything. When they return to a normal state they do not recall the period of time covered by the fugue. They do not behave strangely or give evidence of acting out a memory of some traumatic past event.

Individuals with a multiple personality are dominated by a number of distinct personalities. The transition from one personality to another is sudden and often dramatic. Each personality is a complex set of associated memories with its own behavior patterns, personal relationships, and attitudes. Sometimes the individual in one personality state will have no recall of the other states. At other times a personality state is not bound by amnesia and that personality is aware of the existence and activities of the others. Often the primary personality is emotionally restricted, moralistic, and proper. The secondary personality, on the other hand, often exhibits diametrically opposite behavior and attitudes.

In depersonalization disorder a feeling of self-estrangement or unreality is present. Since such feelings are common, diagnosis is not made unless the feeling occurs at least six times during a six-week period, with each episode lasting thirty minutes or more.

The psychological conflicts that lead to dissociative symptoms are the result of earlier disturbances in growth and development. When faced with a situation that arouses excessive grief, despair, or anxiety, many people repress the memory of the disturbing events to get rid of the painful effect. Most people with amnesia develop symptoms in response to a difficult life situation. Individuals with multiple personalities or in a fugue state have repressed patterns of behavior that emerge into open expression in the dissociative state.

Somatoform Disorders

This group of disorders is characterized by physical symptoms for which there are no organic findings. The symptoms which arise from a displacement of psychological conflicts and anxieties are not under voluntary control. The subcategories of somatoform disorders are somatization disorder, conversion disorder, somatoform pain disorder, hypochondriasis, and body dysmorphic disorder.

Somatization disorder (Briquet's syndrome) is characterized by multiple physical complaints for which there is no physical explanation. The complaints are usually dramatic and vague, and refer to many organs. The symptoms usually begin during adolescence and may be first manifested as menstrual difficulties. Sexual problems (indifference, pain during intercourse) are often an associated finding. Perhaps one percent of American females have had this disorder.

In conversion disorder conflicts are represented as physical symptoms in portions of the body innervated by sensory or motor nerves. The symptoms usually symbolize a conflict or an unacceptable impulse. Symptoms include sensory complaints, paralysis, or loss of muscle control. Sensory symptoms include loss of feeling, blindness, and deafness. Disturbances of skin sensation may occur in any location, shape, or pattern, most commonly in the extremities. Partial or total deafness or loss of vision may be accompanied by sensory hallucinations. Hysterical pain in any part of the body may also occur, a common site being the abdomen, which has led to frequent misdiagnoses and unnecessary surgery. Paralysis may affect several parts of the body. For example, the vocal chords may be paralyzed; the individual is usually able to whisper but can make no vocalized sound. In chronic cases of paralysis, atrophy from disuse can

Spotlight 14.6. Resources on Stress, Dissociative, and Somatoform Disorders

The stress disorders have been considered by several Christian writers (Hart 1986; Walker 1984/85). Post-traumatic stress disorder is most likely after major catastrophes, and thus sources such as Bush (1979), Carlson (1955), and Price (1981) may be helpful. A number of psychologists have identified a subtype of post-traumatic stress disorder, called "postabortion syndrome." Many women have strong emotional aftereffects from abortion, which require solid Christian counseling. Perhaps the best overall source on this topic is Michels (1988).

Multiple personality has captured media attention, first by the release of the movie and book "The Three Faces of Eve" in the 1950s, then later with the movie and book "Sybil" in the 1970s. Christians have not given this disorder much attention, primarily because it has generally been considered a very rare disease. A vivid firsthand account by a Christian is *On Stage as One,* written anonymously with the help of Jan Meier. The forthcoming book was excerpted in *Christian Psychology* in 1985 and 1986.

As noted in chapter 13, multiple personality is sometimes confused with demon possession. A most interesting tape on determining whether a specific problem is possession or a multiple personality is available, taken from a session at the International Congress on Christian Counseling. It is entitled "Treatment for Multiple Personality Disorder: Integrating Alter Personalities and Casting out Spirits" (Friesen 1988).

One specific somatoform disorder, the conversion reaction, is graphically portrayed in Smith's *Winter Past* (1977). This popular book makes for most interesting reading, and she emphasizes how Christian counseling helped her overcome her struggles. Nolan's *Healing: A Doctor in Search of a Miracle* (1974) considers some faith healers to be dealing with psychological problems rather than actual physical problems. Also consider Myers (1978, 157–95) on the role of superstition in healing.

While mentioned only tangentially in this section, there are a number of books and articles on physical symptoms with psychological causes. One of the better ones is Guldseth (1969). Several sources also relate to the organic mental disorders, such as Brand and Yancey (1984), Jones (1981), and MacKay (1980). Also consider the *Theology Today* article "Senile Dementia and a Resurrection Theology" (1986). Chaney's (1981) book on mental health skills for clergy also contains a section on this topic.

occur in the affected muscles. Impairments of the power of voluntary motion include tics (muscular twitches), convulsions, and recurring peculiar movements or postures.

Individuals with a conversion disorder

show no major abnormalities in their mental status. The most characteristic behavioral feature is an indifferent attitude toward the conversion symptom and the disability produced by it. Sometimes the patient identifies with the symptoms of a person with whom the patient has had a close relationship. Such identification, commonly with a person who has recently died, may be accompanied by signs and symptoms of pathological grief. Hysterical symptoms tend to come and go in response to environmental stresses.

Somatoform pain disorder is characterized by pain in the absence of physical findings. The pain allows the individual to avoid some activity that is upsetting. It also allows the individual to gain support. Hypochondriasis is a preoccupation with bodily function or a fear of disease. The body dysmorphic disorder involves preoccupation with some imagined physical deformity.

The somatoform disorders may be confused with other kinds of abnormality. For example, what were once known as psychosomatic problems (now referred to as psychological factors affecting physical condition) involve actual medical problems that can be produced by stress. Examples include asthma, headaches, arthritis, ulcers, high blood pressure, and colitis. These are clearly organic in nature, while the somatoform disorders have little or no organic cause. We should also distinguish the somatoform disorders from organic mental disorders, which result from physical changes in the brain due to the use of drugs, head trauma, or other physical causes. The somatoform disorders must also be distinguished from fictitious disorders in which individuals consciously fake various symptoms.

Substance Abuse Disorders

Substance abuse disorders are maladaptive behavior patterns associated with the use of psychoactive drugs. The maladaptive behavior pattern is reflected in impaired social or occupational functioning, in failure to control or stop the use of the substance, and in withdrawal symptoms after cessation of use. Behavior may be impulsive or irresponsible, with failure to meet important obligations. Personality disorders, such as antisocial behavior, often occur in an individual who has a substance abuse disorder. A substance abuse disorder beginning early in life is often associated with failure to complete school and with low occupational achievement. Traffic accidents and physical injury and illness (such as malnutrition or hepatitis) are common complications.

The substance abuse disorders can be divided into substance abuse proper and substance dependency. Substance abuse implies a minimal duration of use for one month, social complications, and psychological dependency. Substance dependency, although similar to substance abuse, also involves tolerance (increasing amounts of the substance are required to achieve the desired effect) or withdrawal (adverse effects from cessation or reduction of the drug).

Alcohol dependency involves numerous physical complications. Cirrhosis, a fatal liver disease, is on the increase in the United States. Depressive symptoms common in alcohol dependency may partially account for the high rate of suicide among alcohol-dependent persons.

Amphetamine abuse involves psychological dependency or a pathological pattern of being intoxicated during the day. Social complications include fighting, loss of friends, a poor work record, and legal difficulties.

In cannabis (marijuana) dependency there may be a marked loss of interest in activities. Lack of motivation may become a significant problem along with other social complications.

Tobacco use disorder is an interesting new category of DSM III. Research (DSM III-R 1987, 182) has shown that chronic tobacco use predisposes an individual to a variety of physical diseases (bronchitis, emphysema, coronary artery disease, peripheral vascular disease). It has been estimated that 15 percent of deaths each year in the United States results from diseases either caused or aggravated by tobacco consumption. Tobacco use is considered a disorder if there is a repeated need to use the substance and distress is experienced with that need, or if there is evidence of a serious tobacco-related physical disorder in an individual who is psychologically dependent on tobacco.

DSM III-R specifies a separate category for the intoxicating effects of different drugs. Intoxication is maladaptive behavior, such as belligerence or impaired judgment, resulting from the ingestion or inhalation of a specific substance (alcohol, opioid, barbiturate, cocaine, amphetamine, marijuana, caffeine).

Alcohol intoxication may involve slurred speech, incoordination, unsteady gait, impairment in memory, mood lability, disinhibition of sexual or aggressive impulses, irritability, talkativeness, fighting, or interference with social and occupational functioning.

Alcoholics can often consume more alcohol than the average person before the symptoms of intoxication become evident. Medical complications (head trauma from falls, pneumonia or sunburn from exposure to elements, suppressed immune system) often result from alcohol intoxication. Prolonged periods of intoxication can lead to one of the other organic brain syndromes, such as Korsakoff's syndrome, in which the memory deficit is irreversible.

While most people are familiar with alcohol and drug intoxication, many do not realize that caffeine may also intoxicate. Caffeine intoxication may produce restlessness, nervousness, excitement, inability to sleep, flushing, gastrointestinal complaints, muscle twitching, or rambling conversation. Intoxication may occur from ingestion of as little as 250 milligrams of caffeine. A single cup of coffee contains 100 to 150 milligrams. Tea is about half as strong as coffee; cola is one-third as strong.

Withdrawal symptoms result from the cessation or reduction of a specific substance that was regularly used by an individual to the point of intoxication. The most common symptoms include restlessness, anxiety, irritability, insomnia, and impaired attention. The individual has a compelling desire to resume taking the substance.

Personality Disorders

Personality disorders are deeply ingrained patterns of maladaptive behavior, often present throughout life. Personality disorders are characterized by behavior patterns rather than by the symptoms (such as anxiety or depression) which typify the clinical syndromes. There is a spectrum of behavior involved, ranging from the full-blown personality disorder, which is fairly rare in the general population, to specific personality traits which are relatively common. Having one or two traits is normal but when there are enough traits to impair occupational or social functioning, a disorder is present. Most everyone has some trait of a disorder. In the following discussion, we will speak of both disorders and traits, but the distinction should be kept clear.

THE PASSIVE-AGGRESSIVE PERSONALITY

While it may sound like a contradiction in terms, some individuals are passively aggressive. The aggression is often unconscious, but surfaces in a passive manner. Passive-aggressive individuals feel resentful that they have not had their emotional needs met by others, and thus they passively manipulate.

Several behavior patterns are characteristic of passive-aggressive people. Obstructionism may occur. A wife might be angry over something that happened Saturday night and then make the family late to church the next morning when she cannot find her lipstick or shoes. This is especially likely if her husband is compulsive about being on time for church. Another way aggression might be expressed passively is by pouting. Instead of resolving a disagreement maturely, the passive-aggressive person will withdraw and sulk. Procrastination is another way of letting suppressed anger surface. A mother who asks her passive-aggressive son to mow the lawn may find him putting the task off. When he can no longer get away with that, the boy may resort to intentional inefficiency. He may mow the yard, but do a poor job. He is rewarded for his passive aggression if he is relieved of the task. Passive-aggressives tend to be chronic complainers who act slighted when someone disagrees with them or when they feel others are expecting too much of them. They often believe they are doing better work than what others think. They resent suggestions and criticize people in authority without reason.

THE OBSESSIVE-COMPULSIVE PERSONALITY

Obsessive-compulsive individuals are marked by inflexibility and perfectionism in a wide variety of situations. They have very strict standards that interfere with completing tasks. They tend to be preoccupied with order, scheduling, rules, and details to the point that they lose sight of the activity. They insist that others must do things their way. They are so devoted to work that they have little time for recreation and friendship. They tend to be indecisive, avoiding or postponing decisions as long as possible, and extremely scrupulous regarding their values (far beyond the demands of their faith or culture). They tend to be unaffectionate, unwilling to give of their time or money unless they can benefit in some way, and have problems throwing away worthless items.

While obsessive-compulsives are likely to become depressed, they are usually overly conscientious "workaholics." Doctors, lawyers, musicians, and computer programmers are particularly likely to have obsessive-compulsive traits. Men are more likely to have this disorder. Perhaps this personality disorder accounts for the high number of suicides among professionals. While they may appear to be dedicated servants of society, in actuality they have a subtle selfishness about them—they may be avoiding their family responsibilities so they can be approved by society or peers. They bury their emotions, trying to compensate for their own insecurity. Underlying all the hard work they usually feel inferior and are self-critical. They spend most of their lives working at a frantic pace to amass wealth, power, and prestige and thus convince themselves they are somebody.

THE HISTRIONIC PERSONALITY

Another extreme in personality is the histrionic, who is emotional, extroverted, dramatic, impulsive, naive, and frequently seductive. Such individuals tend to be attractive to the opposite sex and popular socially, possessing a great deal of charisma. While obsessive personality traits are more common in males, histrionic traits are more common in females. This is probably due in part to the stereotypical sex roles imposed upon males and females in our culture.

Spotlight 14.7. Christianity and Personality Disorders, 1

Many Christians manifest passive-aggressive or obsessive-compulsive traits. We need to guard against these tendencies because they can keep us from becoming the whole people that God intends.

The Christian with passive-aggressive traits is likely to be the half-hearted believer who irresponsibly "waits on the Lord" for everything while criticizing others as being "less spiritual." Such individuals may brag about being prayer warriors or even be attracted to full-time Christian employment in which they depend upon others for support, but do little to merit it.

Obsessive-compulsive Christians are quite different. In a study conducted by the authors over 75 percent of ministers leaned toward compulsive personality traits. Missionaries frequently fall into this category as well. Pastors and missionaries are particularly likely to give time to their work to the neglect of family and spouse. Of course many of them do spend time with their loved ones, but it is all too easy to disregard biblical priorities. Clearly the Bible says that taking care of one's family must be a top priority (1 Tim. 5:8). The Bible also says Christians should not be pastors unless their families are well governed and their children are well behaved. Those who cannot say no to parishioners' (or superior's) demands should not be pastors or missionaries. Those who neglect their families for the "Lord's work" are forgetting that the family *is* the Lord's work. Individuals who cannot accept this fact should stay single or at least not have children. Church leaders who spend all their time building bigger and better churches often do so out of selfish motives (although this may be unconscious). Missionaries may send their children to a distant boarding school so they can have more time for their work (although it may be quite appropriate to send teen-agers to boarding school if they so desire).

Some perfectionistic Christians may feel overwhelmed with anger toward God (for supposedly expecting so much of them), toward their children (for rebelling) and toward themselves (for not being perfect). They may become depressed and even attempt suicide. They may suffer immense pain and hopelessness because they forget that we are called to rest in Christ rather than be caught up in a never-ending round of activity.

Christians with obsessive-compulsive tendencies may become legalistic, absorbed in right and wrong because of their overly rigid nature, and unable to relax and have fun. Their conscience is stricter than God's guidelines in the Bible, as they fail to distinguish between true and false guilt (see chap. 13). They may carry a burden of false guilt about thoughts or actions that do not actually violate God's laws. Legalistic Christians need to be reminded of the grace and mercy of God, rather than be overwhelmed with the letter of the law (as the Pharisees were). Christians should relax and enjoy the abundant life God desires for them (John 10:10).

The histrionic is always seeking or demanding approval or praise from others. She is inappropriately seductive in her appearance or actions or is overly concerned with being attractive. She expresses exaggerated emotions, such as impulsively hugging those she knows only casually or sobbing uncontrollably over a minor incident. The histrionic may have temper tantrums, is uncomfortable when not the center of attention, or may express emotions in a shallow manner. Self-centeredness characterizes many histrionics, and they usually demand immediate gratification. Finally, the histrionic may be overly impressionistic in speech, giving little detail. Four of these traits are required for the disorder to be diagnosed.

Histrionics may act depressed, but they may do so because they recently read a book on depression ("theatrical depression"). They may act depressed to get attention or to punish a parent or spouse. They may also tell a counselor they wish to commit suicide. While this is usually a ploy to get attention, the counselor should take such comments seriously since a histrionic may accidentally succeed in a faked suicide attempt.

THE ANTISOCIAL PERSONALITY

Individuals with this disorder, sometimes referred to as sociopathic personalities, engage in repeated conflicts with other members of society. Basically they are unwilling to be loyal to individuals, groups, or social values. Selfish, callous, irresponsible, and impulsive, they are unwilling and relatively unable to feel guilt or to learn from experience, including punishment. Their failure to follow rules, however, is not a result of ignorance or lack of intelligence. They tend to blame others, rationalizing their antisocial behavior. They are unreliable, untruthful, unpredictable, and insincere. They have little or no plan for their lives, living only for pleasure and excitement.

By definition sociopaths have had conflicts with society early in life, engaging in a variety of socially unacceptable behavior prior to age fifteen, such as truancy, drug abuse, and burglary. It is a pattern of several different behaviors, not one criminal action, that marks the sociopath. This pattern continues into adulthood; thus this personality disorder cannot be diagnosed until age eighteen.

Perhaps the most prominent characteristic of the sociopath is the relative absence of anxiety and guilt feelings. The Bible speaks of people who harden their hearts until they no longer feel any guilt.

God attempts to convict people repeatedly of their need for salvation. Continual rejection, however, results in God's Holy Spirit no longer striving to convict people of their need. Some theologians have described this point of no return as the unforgivable sin. While the lack of conscience is a mark of the sociopath, some do come to know Christ as Savior and become progressively less sociopathic as they mature in Christ. Apart from salvation, few individuals with this disorder make any significant improvement, even with prolonged psychotherapy.

THE NARCISSISTIC PERSONALITY

This disorder combines several characteristics of other disorders. Narcissistic individuals are extremely self-centered, like histrionics. Like antisocial personalities, they lack empathy and often do not recognize when others are hurting.

Traits of the narcissistic personality include an overreaction to criticism in the form of humiliation, shame, or rage. Such individuals tend to exploit people for their own ends. They have an exaggerated sense of their own importance. They believe their difficulties are unique. They spend a great deal of time thinking about fantasies of power, success, brilliance, idealistic love, or beauty. They believe they deserve special favors, but show no inclination to return those favors. They want continual attention and praise, and may manipulate people to get positive comments. They do not recognize how others feel and are often envious.

The term "narcissistic" is taken from a Greek myth about young Narcissus, who sees his reflection in a pool of water and falls in love with it. Perhaps, as Lasch (1979) has stated, ours is a culture of narcissists. We may not all have the disorder, but many of us (including many Christians) have some of the traits.

Kilpatrick (1983, 57–60) sees the mod-

Spotlight 14.8. Christianity and Personality Disorders, 2

Within the Christian community, those with histrionic traits tend to emphasize emotional experiences rather than God's Word. They typically have many spiritual ups and downs, sometimes blaming the devil in order to exempt themselves from personal responsibility. Some become religiously grandiose and claim special powers and gifts. Even in church-related activities they unconsciously seek attention. They may become angry with God for not doing things their way, neglecting personal devotions whenever God does not do what they tell him to.

Pastors, pastoral counselors, and other church workers need to take special precautions when they see histrionics (Bustanoby 1988). A male church leader should insist that either women be counseled by other women, or leave the office door ajar with a secretary just outside. Histrionics may be seductive in order to prove that the counselor is just like every other male. A female histrionic who entices a man sexually may tell everyone that he seduced her and ruin his reputation. It is clear why the Book of Proverbs warns young men against the adulteress and her histrionic traits (Prov. 5:3–20).

Regrettably some pastors or evangelists use their positions of prestige and power to manipulate and control people. Many who use people "in the name of the Lord" to accomplish their selfish goals are self-righteous and have very little insight into their own disordered personalities. They have superficial relationships with their mates and children, not because they are absorbed with their work, but because they are serving their own interests.

Finally, a word on the narcissistic personality. Peck (1983) has proposed a variation of the narcissistic personality that he calls the evil personality. This disorder is marked by regular scapegoating and blaming others. Such individuals cannot tolerate criticism and are very concerned about their public image. They are extremely devious and occasionally have a mild disturbance in their thinking, somewhat like schizophrenia. Many are religious, yet they make devious behavior and scapegoating a way of life while attempting to give an outward appearance that nothing is wrong.

It is important to note that while Peck's proposed disorder is interesting, and it is good to find a psychiatrist who started from an essentially secular background affirm the reality of evil, he uses the term "evil" in an unusual manner. All of us can and do sin, not just those with severe disorders. Yet it may be true that some narcissistic individuals become "people of the lie" (to use Peck's phrase) who cover their sinful behavior with misleading and overtly untrue statements, projecting their own evil upon others.

Spotlight 14.9. Resources on Personality Disorders

One of the most complete Christian references on the personality disorders is Conver and Conver's *Self-Defeating Life-Styles* (1988), which surveys many of the personality disorders (though using popular descriptions rather than technical designations). Collins (1972, 139–47) also gives an overview of several personality disorders (using older DSM II terminology).

Seamands' *Healing Grace* (1988) deals with obsessive-compulsive traits. In his earlier books, Seamands addresses the performance-oriented, compulsive Christian briefly; here he gives book-length treatment to the problem.

Kotesky (1983, 228) describes the narcissistic personality in terms of the sin of pride. Shepperson (1984) portrays Jacob as going from narcissism to spiritual wholeness.

The obsessive-compulsive personality disorder is the subject of Beck (1981) and Gibson (1985), while the histrionic personality is analyzed in Armstrong (1983).

---

ern person as basically trying to be God (the original sin). A sense of responsibility to others is lost as the self becomes enthroned. Kilpatrick links this problem with the self-help movement and excessive emphasis upon self-esteem in modern psychology. While many psychologists have, indeed, encouraged people to look out for themselves and seek only personal gain, it is equally false to assert that all psychologists have done so. The Christian must resist the temptation to become narcissistic, even though everywhere our society seems to emphasize "looking out for number one."

The above discussion does not exhaust

Table 14.3

Major Personality Disorders

Disorder	Characteristics
Paranoid	Suspicion, mistrust of people, hypersensitivity
Schizoid	Withdrawn, reserved, seclusive
Schizotypal	Oddity of thinking and behavior (called simple schizophrenia in DSM II)
Histrionic	Overly emotional/expressive, egocentric, having poor sexual adjustment
Narcissistic	Grandiose sense of self-importance
Antisocial	Violation of the right of others
Borderline	Instability in a variety of areas
Avoidant	Hypersensitivity to rejection
Dependent	Failure to assume responsibility for one's own life
Obsessive-compulsive	Preoccupation with rules, order, and details
Passive-aggressive	Passive resistance to demands for adequate performance

Table 14.4

Major Sexual Disorders

Disorder	Definition
Trans-sexualism	Desire to be a member of the opposite sex
Fetishism	Abnormal sexual attraction to an object or nonerogenous body part
Transvestism	Practice of dressing like the opposite sex for sexual arousal
Pedophilia	Sexual preference for prepubescent children
Exhibitionism	Compulsive exposure of the genitals in public
Voyeurism	Observation of other people undressing or making love, especially from a secret vantage point
Masochism	Sexual arousal derived from having physical or emotional pain inflicted on one
Sadism	Sexual arousal derived from inflicting physical or emotional pain on others
Frotteurism	Fantasy of touching a nonconsenting partner
Frigidity	Inability to experience orgasm in sexual intercourse (used of women)
Impotence	Failure to maintain an erection during sexual intercourse (used of men)
Functional Dyspareunia	Pain experienced during sexual intercourse
Functional Vaginismus	Sudden and painful contraction of the muscles surrounding the vagina

the personality disorders, but provides a sampling of some of the personality problems people have. Table 14.3 briefly outlines major personality disorders, including several not considered in this book.

Spotlight 14.10. Resources on Other Disorders

The impulse control disorders have generally been neglected by Christian writers, but there are several good sources on gambling. As Christians observe the current trend toward legalizing state lotteries and other forms of gambling, they should consider the antigambling heritage Christians have held for centuries. McKenna (1977), a Christian leader who participated on a governor's committee which discussed this important topic, has written on the topic. Also see Alnor (1985). For a fascinating article on impulse control as it relates to evil in general, see McMinn (1988).

In recent years many resources on sexual problems, particularly homosexuality, have become available. Several sources on sexuality in general were considered in chapter 5. Wheat and Wheat (1981) is probably the best general book available (they also consider a number of sexual disorders). Three other key books that deal more specifically with sexual problems are Rekers (1982), Wilson (1984), and Mayo (1987).

Childhood and adolescent disorders have also been considered tangentially in a number of popular Christian books. One of the more extensive treatments of problems from a Christian perspective is Meier (1977). Eating disorders such as anorexia nervosa and bulimia, listed under childhood and adolescent disorders by DSM III-R are also popular topics that have received a great deal of attention. Two personal accounts by Christians are Christian and Johnson (1986) and O'Neill (1982). Other Christian sources on anorexia and bulimia include Vredevelt and Whitman (1985), Johnson (1984), Rowland (1985), Sabom (1985), and Thomas (1984).

Other Areas of Abnormality

This chapter has considered a mere fraction of possible disorders. DSM III-R contains many more that fall within several other general categories. Organic mental syndromes and disorders include many drug-related problems and brain disorders. The largest division of DSM III-R includes disorders usually first evident in infancy, childhood, and adolescence (several of these were considered in chap. 10). Disorders in the latter category are anorexia nervosa, bulimia (binge eating following by purging or self-induced vomiting), and pica (eating nonfoods, such as dirt or paint). The impulse disorders include pathological gambling, kleptomania (impulsive stealing), pyromania (setting fires impulsively), and the intermittent explosive disorder (uncontrolled assault or destruction of property out of proportion to the precipitating stressor). The sexual disorders are summarized in table 14.4. Clearly the many possible problems indicate how varied human behavior can be, for good or ill.

References

Adams, J. 1977. *Competent to counsel.* Grand Rapids: Baker.

Alnor, W. 1985. Atlantic City: The gamble that lost. *Eternity* (Apr.): 23–28.

Anonymous, A., and J. Meier. (In press.) *On stage as one.* (Excerpted in *Christian Psychology* 1985/86).

Armstrong, G. 1983. A psychological and theological understanding of the histrionic personality. *Pastoral Psychology* 31: 193–203.

Backus, W. 1985. *Telling the truth to troubled people.* Minneapolis: Bethany.

Beck, J. 1981. Treatment of spiritual doubt among obsessing evangelicals. *Journal of Psychology and Theology* 9: 224–31.

Bleuler, E. 1950. *Dementia praecox.* New York: International University Press.

Brand, P., and P. Yancey. 1984. *In his image.* Grand Rapids: Zondervan.

Brown, B. 1974. Depression roundup. *Behavior Today* 5: 117.

Bush, J. 1979. *Disaster response: A handbook for church action.* Scottdale, Pa.: Herald.

Bustanoby, A. 1988. Counseling the seductive female. *Leadership* 9: 48–54.

Carlson, A. 1955. *He is able: Faith overcomes fear in a foxhole.* Grand Rapids: Zondervan.

Chaney, D. 1981. *Mental health skills for clergy.* Valley Forge, Pa.: Judson.

Christian, S., and M. Johnson. 1986. *The very private matter of anorexia nervosa.* Grand Rapids: Zondervan.

Clinebell, H. 1968. *Understanding and counseling the alcoholic.* Nashville: Abingdon.

Collins, G. 1972. *Fractured personalities.* Carol Stream, Ill.: Creation.

Conver, C., and L. Conver. 1988. *Self-defeating life-styles.* Nashville: Broadman.

Cosgrove, M., and J. Mallory. 1977. *Mental health: A Christian approach.* Grand Rapids: Zondervan.

Darling, H. 1969. *Man in triumph.* Grand Rapids: Zondervan.

Dempsey, D., and P. Zimbardo. 1978. *Psychology and you.* Glenview, Ill.: Scott, Foresman.

Diagnostic and statistical manual of mental disorders. 3d rev. ed. 1987. Washington, D.C.: American Psychiatric Association.

Foster, T. 1984. *How to deal with depression.* Wheaton, Ill.: Victor.

Friesen, J. 1988. Treatment for multiple personality disorder. Session of International Conference on Christian Counseling, Nov. 12. Tape available from Fuller Theological Seminary, Pasadena, Calif.

Geisler, N. 1982. A Christian perspective on wine-drinking. *Bibliotheca Sacra* 139 (Jan.): 46–56.

Getting Free. 1988. *Christianity Today* 32 (Dec. 9): 29–44.

Gibson, D. 1985. Doubting Thomas, the obsessive. *Journal of Psychology and Christianity* 4: 34–36.

Guldseth, G. 1969. *God is for the emotionally ill.* Watchung, N.J.: Charisma.

Hart, A. 1986. *The hidden link between adrenalin and stress.* Waco: Word.

Hetherington, E., K. Camara, and D. Feathermore. 1983. Achievement and intellectual functioning of children in one-parent households. In *Achievement and achievement motives*, ed. J. Spence. San Francisco: Freeman.

Hyder, O. 1971. *The Christian's handbook of psychiatry*. Old Tappan, N.J.: Revell.

Jenkins, R. 1968. The varieties of children's behavioral problems and family dynamics. *American Journal of Psychiatry* 124: 134–39.

Johnson, R. 1984. Bulimia. *Cornerstone* 12: 29–30.

Jones, D. 1981. *Our fragile brains*. Downers Grove: Inter-Varsity.

Jones, S., and D. Workman. 1989. Homosexuality: The behavioral sciences and the church. *Journal of Psychology and Theology* 17: 213–25.

Kilpatrick, W. 1983. *Psychological seduction*. Nashville: Nelson.

Kolata, G. 1981. Clues to the causes of senile dementia. *Science* 211: 1032–33.

Kotesky, R. 1983. *General psychology for Christian counselors*. Nashville: Abingdon.

Lasch, C. 1979. *Culture of narcissism*. New York: Norton.

Lenters, W. 1985. *The freedom we crave*. Grand Rapids: Eerdmans.

MacKay, D. 1980. *Brains, machines and persons*. Grand Rapids: Eerdmans.

McKenna, D. 1977. *Awake my conscience*. Winona Lake, Ind.: Light and Life.

McMinn, M. 1988. The abiding Mr. Hyde. *Christianity Today* 32 (Nov. 18): 27–29.

Malony, H., ed. 1983. *Wholeness and holiness*. Grand Rapids: Baker.

Mayo, M. 1987. *A Christian guide to sexual counseling*. Grand Rapids: Zondervan.

Meier, P. 1977. *Christian child-rearing and personality development*. Grand Rapids: Baker.

Michels, N. 1988. *Helping women recover from abortion*. Minneapolis: Bethany.

Minirth, F. 1977. *Christian psychiatry*. Old Tappan, N.J.: Revell.

Minirth, F., and P. Meier. 1978. *Happiness is a choice*. Grand Rapids: Baker.

Myers, D. 1978. *The human puzzle*. San Francisco: Harper and Row.

Narramore, C. 1984. *The compact encyclopedia of psychological problems*. Grand Rapids: Zondervan.

National Institute of Mental Health (NIMH). 1985. *Mental health, United States, 1985*. Washington, D.C.: U.S. Government Printing Office.

———. 1988. Cited in the *Atlanta Journal* (Nov. 8): 1D.

Nolan, W. 1974. *Healing: A doctor in search of a miracle*. New York: Random.

O'Neill, C. 1982. *Starving for attention*. New York: Continuum.

Owens, C. 1982. *A promise of sanity*. Wheaton, Ill.: Tyndale.

Owens, T. 1984. Personality traits of female psychotherapy patients with a history of incest. *Journal of Personality Assessment* 48: 606–8.

Patterson, G. 1979. Treatment for children with conduct problems. In *Aggression and behavior change*, eds. S. Feshbach and A. Fraczek. New York: Praeger

Peck, M. 1983. *People of the lie*. New York: Simon and Schuster.

Pervin, L. 1978. *Current controversies and issues in personality*. New York: Wiley.

Poznanski, E. 1973. Children with excessive fears. *American Journal of Orthopsychiatry* 43: 428–38.

Price, M. 1981. Helping children cope with natural disasters. *Church training* (Sept.).

Provence, S., and R. Lipton. 1962. *Infants in institutions*. New York: International University Press.

Rekers, G. 1982. *Growing up straight*. Chicago: Moody.

Rowland, C. 1985. *The monster within: Overcoming bulimia*. Grand Rapids: Baker.

Sabom, W. 1985. The gnostic world of anorexia nervosa. *Journal of Psychology and Theology* 13: 243–54.

Seamonds, D. 1988. *Healing grace*. Wheaton, Ill.: Victor.

Sears, R. 1961. Relation of early socialization experiences to aggression. *Journal of Abnormal Social Psychology* 63: 466–92.

Sergovich, F., et al. 1969. Chromosomal aberrations in 2159 consecutive newborn babies. *New England Journal of Medicine* 280: 851–54.

Shepperson, V. 1984. Jacob's journey: From narcissism toward wholeness. *Journal of Psychology and Theology* 12: 178–87.

Smith, N. 1977. *Winter past*. Downers Grove: Inter-Varsity.

Spickard, A., and B. Thompson. 1985. *Dying for a drink*. Waco: Word.

Stein, R. 1975. Wine drinking in New Testament times. *Christianity Today* 19 (June 20): 9–11.

Stuart, R. 1970. *Trick or treatment.* Champaign, Ill.: Research.

Szasz, T. 1970. *The manufacture of madness.* New York: Harper and Row.

Thomas, D. 1984. Hope for binge eaters and other addicts. *Journal of Psychology and Theology* 12: 34–39.

Thomsen, M. 1984. Coping with depression. *Ministry* (Sept.): 4–6.

VanVondervan, J. 1985. *Good news for the chemically dependent.* Nashville: Nelson.

Vredevelt, P., and J. Whitman. 1985. *Walking a thin line.* Portland, Oreg.: Multnomah.

Walker, P. 1984/85. How you can overcome the power of stress. *Ministries* 3 (Winter): 34–37.

Wallerstein, J., and S. Blakeslee. 1989. *Second chances.* New York: Ticknor and Fields.

Weaver, G. 1986. Senile dementia and a resurrection theology. *Theology Today* 42 (Jan.): 444–56.

Wheat, E., and G. Wheat. 1981. *Intended for pleasure.* Rev. ed. Old Tappan, N.J.: Revell.

Wilson, E. 1984. *Sexual sanity: Breaking free from uncontrolled habits.* Downers Grove: Inter-Varsity.

White, J. 1982. *The masks of melancholy.* Downers Grove: Inter-Varsity.

Young, P. 1981. The neurotic Christian. *Journal of the American Scientific Affiliation* 33 (Dec.): 215–19.

15

Psychotherapy and Personal Counseling

M any people think that the discipline of psychology is synonymous with counseling and therapy. But psychology is much more than this. Psychology is the study of the psyche, the individual person, and encompasses all aspects of the person. Therapy and counseling can be seen as the art of helping people overcome their problems, and, more positively, helping them grow in mental, emotional, and spiritual health.

The term "psychotherapy" is often used to describe the process of helping people who have severe problems, such as those described in the previous chapter. Psychotic disorders and other major psychological problems require intensive treatment by professionals who have spent many years learning to deal specifically with those problems. Counseling, on the other hand, is a more general term referring to the process of helping people with more common problems such as marriage and family difficulties. Counselors may have as many years of training as therapists, but they are less likely to be oriented toward severe mental disorders. Therapy attempts to make relatively permanent changes, while counseling is oriented toward giving advice.

Yet the distinction is not that simple, as therapists and counselors both make use of conversational techniques; they both counsel and thus can each rightly be called counselors. In addition, counselors often use therapeutic techniques that were developed from working with the severely disturbed. Generally we can say that therapists are counselors but that not all counselors are therapists.

Therapists and Counselors

The term "psychologist" reflects a specific kind of training and should not be used too casually. Psychologists deal with all kinds of problems. Generally a clinical psychologist must have a doctorate in psychology, followed by an internship under a practicing psychologist. Psychologists must also be licensed by the state. Such a license

Spotlight 15.1. Training for Christian Counseling

Graduate programs in psychology have become increasingly diverse, so career objectives should be decided on before selecting a graduate training program. Christian students can get help in deciding on their career objectives from knowledgeable faculty members or career counselors at their college or university. A student's chances for admission to different kinds of programs can often be assessed on the basis of other students' experiences.

Currently there is much competition for acceptance into graduate training programs in psychology, with three to four applications per opening. Some programs average thirty to forty applicants per opening. American Psychological Association (APA) approval of a school for doctoral training in clinical or counseling psychology means that the school has voluntarily applied for examination and has met minimum standards of acceptability for specified training programs. It also means that the program has been in existence long enough to have granted some doctorates in that specialty. Some excellent departments of psychology may have applied for examination but have not yet been approved, or may not have had a doctoral program long enough to be eligible. Graduation from a program not having APA approval does not bar a person from a job or prevent licensing or certification. Most employers prefer to hire graduates from approved programs, however, and sometimes fellowships or internship opportunities are limited to APA-approved graduates.

In 1977 APA set up guidelines stating that only individuals who obtain a doctor of philosophy or doctor of psychology degree from a training program whose primary content is psychology should be designated "psychologists" by the agencies designated to license or certify psychologists. Study leading to the Ph.D. in psychology or the Psy.D. can be undertaken in at least four different kinds of settings: (1) state and private universities; (2) graduate-level training programs in a few Christian schools (such as the Rosemead Graduate School of Psychology in California); (3) schools of professional psychology, which have sprung up in various states such as California and Illinois and offer primarily a doctor of psychology degree oriented around the professional practice of psychology; or (4) doctoral programs in pastoral psychology at many seminaries and graduate schools of theology (for example, Western Conservative Baptist Seminary in Portland, Oregon, or Southwestern Seminary in Fort Worth, Texas). Many evangelical seminaries have begun Ph.D. programs in psychology.

Individuals designated "counselors" have usually completed a training program leading to a masters degree in psychology or a discipline such as social work, communications, or education. Programs with a specific Christian orientation include those at Wheaton College, Fuller Graduate School of Psychology, the Psychological Studies Institute, and Conservative Baptist Seminary.

often requires passing state examinations in psychological techniques and knowledge. Individuals with a masters degree in psychology may work under a licensed psychologist as "psychology assistants" or "psychology associates," but usually do so as part of their internship.

While psychologists have a doctoral degree in psychology, psychiatrists have a doctoral degree in medicine. Psychiatrists usually receive additional training in counseling and complete an internship, generally in a mental hospital, where they practice counseling techniques. Psychiatrists can prescribe drugs as part of therapy, but lack the broad background in psychological theory and research that psychologists have. They certainly can be as good at doing therapy as psychologists, but their training is different.

Marriage and family counselors deal with more common and less severe problems. Such counselors generally have at least a masters degree in counseling, though not always in psychology. (Some schools, for example, have separate departments in counseling; or other departments such as education offer these programs.) Many marriage and family counselors have doctoral degrees in counseling; this will eventually probably become a requirement. Most states also license marriage and family counselors. Counselors without a doctoral degree generally work under the supervision of someone who does.

School psychologists may have either a masters or doctoral degree in their area. Generally they work within school districts and deal with learning and behavioral problems of children in the school context. (Although parents may become involved in such counseling, the difficulty is usually identified in the school situation.) Most states require licensure of school psychologists.

Pastoral counselors comprise a fifth and very important category. In most states they must work under the auspices of a church organization (unless they are also qualified under another kind of counseling). The State of Georgia law related to the licensing of psychologists is fairly typical in this respect:

> Nothing in this Chapter shall be construed to limit the activities and services of a person in the employ of or serving for an established and recognized religious organization. . . . Provided that the

title "applied psychologist" is not used by a person not licensed and that the professional practice of psychology is not implied.

While they are not licensed and most states do not have specific educational requirements for this designation, they should have a seminary degree in pastoral counseling. They also need to have a good undergraduate preparation in Bible and theology as well as psychology and counseling. The best seminary programs in pastoral counseling also meet the requirements for marriage and family counseling licensure, as pastors often need skills in this area.

The above five categories do not exhaust the kinds of counselors; there are others beyond the scope of this discussion. These include psychiatric social workers, who usually have a masters degree in social work and have completed an internship in mental hospitals.

Psychiatric Hospitalization

Some Christians oppose psychiatric hospitalization under any circumstances. They say it is unspiritual to rely on psychiatrists since Christians should rely exclusively on the Lord.

Yet Christ said that those who are sick need a physician. Luke, who wrote a larger proportion of the New Testament (the books of Luke and Acts) than Paul, was a physician. God's use of miracles in the early church to prove that Christianity was true before the Scriptures were completed hardly justifies the insistence of some Christians that God heal them supernaturally. God heals most Christians through medical technology, expecting us to use the intelligence he has given us.

There are a number of advantages of hospitalization for treatment of severe anxiety or depression. Patients have a safe,

---

Spotlight 15.2.
Suggested Patterns of Referral*

1. Refer to *psychologists* those who are:

— suicidal or homicidal (a doctor or psychiatrist may prescribe medication as well)
— psychotic (usually a psychiatrist is also needed)
— phobic, particularly if problems are related to early childhood
— having sexual problems (again, a doctor or psychiatrist may be needed)
— experiencing other severe problems noted in chapter 14

2. Refer to *psychiatrists* those who are

— manic-depressive
— having physical problems related to psychological problems
— severely depressed
— hyperactive (a pediatrician may be helpful)
— having other severe problems noted in chapter 14

3. Refer to *school psychologists* those who are

— mentally retarded (or this is suspected)
— experiencing learning problems
— having behavior problems in school

4. Refer to *marriage and family counselors* those who are

— experiencing marital conflicts or are considering divorce
— having child-rearing problems
— suffering from other problems and the other professionals listed above are not available or appropriate

5. Refer to *pastoral counselors* those who are

— encountering problems that are both psychological and spiritual (may also need one of the other sources listed above)
— if qualified, they may also deal with the problems listed in category #4 above.

*Adapted from Dobson 1986 and the opinions of the authors of this text.

---

protected place to which they can retreat; intense therapy is possible; observation of daily routine is facilitated; and adjustments to medication can occur more often. The disadvantages of hospitalization are avoidance of responsibility, social stigma and rejection after dismissal, and cost.

Secular Counseling

Before describing the practice of Christian counseling we will take a brief look at several schools of thought in secular psychology and the therapeutic practices they posit. Such an overview of alternative therapies will help us appreciate both the uniqueness of the biblically based approach stressed in this book and the extent to which Christian counselors can make use of secular insights.

Psychoanalysis

The unconscious mind is the emphasis in psychodynamic therapy. As has been noted throughout this text, the unconscious mind is responsible for anxiety,

Sigmund Freud (1859–1939).

guilt, and the defense mechanisms. Here we will consider Freud's approach in depth, although it is not the only psychodynamic approach available (for another example, see Jung 1928).

The oldest recognized systematic approach to explaining and treating psychological problems is classical psychoanalysis. Modern psychoanalytic theory derives primarily from the work of Freud (1933). The theory places major emphasis on the role of the unconscious and of dynamic forces in mental functioning.

For Freud, the goal of treatment is to come to understand the role of the unconscious mind in current problems. By gaining insight into the unconscious, the individual becomes better able to face reality. Treatment using classical psychoanalysis usually requires a patient to lie on a couch facing away from the therapist while ther-

apist and patient, using several techniques, attempt to uncover subconscious conflicts. The patient is asked to talk about whatever he or she wishes, including memories and feelings. The therapist then asks the patient for thoughts, fantasies, and feelings associated with the material given (free association). Use is also made of the patient's unconscious disproportionate emotional response to the therapist (transference). For instance, the patient may unconsciously respond to the therapist as a father or mother figure. It is believed that such a response can be used to facilitate understanding of the patient's own unconscious feelings toward father, mother, or spouse.

The therapist observes and points out the patient's resistance to talk about or work through various areas of conflict. The therapist strongly emphasizes clarification of feelings. As awareness of feelings increases, the defense mechanisms that concealed them are also uncovered. Psychoanalytic theory states that as patients "experience" acceptance from the analyst, they accept and "love" themselves more and hence, with growing self-tolerance, their defenses against subconscious conflict diminish. The analyst and patient normally meet for one hour a day, five days a week. An average period of time for psychoanalytic therapy is three to five years, but some patients stay in analysis for much longer.

In the process of therapy catharsis may occur, in which the person being treated has a sudden rush of emotions accompanying a new insight. The new understanding of the unconscious mind then helps therapy to progress further and relief from problems becomes more likely.

Freud (1900) also made use of dream analysis in his attempts to deal with the unconsciousness. The dreams of clients

---

Spotlight 15.3.
A Christian View of Psychoanalysis

While Christian thought has been compared and contrasted with Freud's theories earlier in this book (see chaps. 1 and 13), here we wish to specifically consider the psychoanalytic concept of insight. Freud believed that insight into the conflicts of the unconscious mind was central to mental healing, but is this sufficient for the Christian?

While insight is a good first step in that we must recognize problems before we can solve them, it is a partial solution at best. Christianity provides the only adequate solution to anxiety and defense mechanisms. Christian theology gives a more satisfactory description of the self-deceit implicit in defense mechanisms and also gives us the answer to self-deception: forgiveness through Christ's death on the cross. Self-examination for hidden motives, confession of sin, and apology or restitution are all found in the Bible. These are also needed to bring emotional and spiritual healing and growth.

---

were analyzed for both manifest and latent content. The manifest content refers to the details that can be recalled from a dream. From the manifest content, the therapist tries to adduce meaning, including hidden and symbolically disguised messages. Freud tended to find a great deal of sexual symbolism in dreams. For example, any long round pointed object such as a rocket would be interpreted as a phallic symbol (representing the male sex organ). Interpreting dreams can obviously become very speculative, and few psychologists (other than those following Freud or Jung) make use of this method today.

Freud also made use of hypnosis in his early years of practice, but later dropped it in favor of free association. Classical hypnosis involves causing the patient to relax and enter an altered state of consciousness where the individual is more receptive and suggestible. Under the direction of the counselor the client then regresses to some point in childhood when a traumatic event occurred that is responsible for the present problem. By reliving that event, the individual may come to understand the causes of the current problem and be better able to resolve the conflict.

Some psychologists still use hypnosis, but usually in a different manner from the classical approach. In most cases, the person is placed in a relaxed state of consciousness and given suggestions that will help counteract current problems. For example, chain smokers might be given the suggestion that the taste of nicotine will make them violently sick. Such hypnotic suggestion can be effective, particularly if clients genuinely want to overcome their problem. This kind of hypnosis has more in common with the aversion techniques of behavioral psychology than psychoanalysis.

Christians are divided on the issue of hypnosis. Some believe the practice is dangerous because in such an open, altered state of consciousness there is the possibility of demonic influence. Others believe it is an acceptable practice if the counselor is a godly Christian and the hypnosis is prefaced by prayer. Still others, perhaps the majority, prefer other methods of counseling because hypnosis is not as effective as other approaches. There is some evidence that, in fact, genuine regression does not occur (Nash 1987).

It might also be noted that there is a distinctively Christian method of emotional healing called "memory healing" or "inner healing." Generally this approach shares with psychoanalysis an emphasis upon healing at the depths of one's being. Clients are encouraged to relax and are then asked to describe early problem experiences. As clients attempt to relive those experiences, the counselor encourages them to ask God to forgive those who wronged them (or to forgive themselves if they did the wrong). God is then asked to erase the pain of the memory; clients may imagine Christ helping them in the situation. The finest source on memory healing to date is Seamands (1985).

Transactional Analysis (TA)

There are several superficial similarities between transactional analysis and Freudian psychology. For example, the id, ego, and superego are similar to TA's child, adult, and parent ego states. Technically, however, it is not considered a form of psychodynamic counseling by most psychologists.

According to transactional analysis (Harris 1969), we have several basic needs. The first is stroke hunger, the need for another person's time, attention, and physical contact. A second is recognition hunger, which is satisfied when others recognize our existence. Structure hunger, or what to do with our time, is a third need. Another need is leadership hunger, especially the opportunity to help others structure their time. Our final need is excitement hunger, which is met by structuring time in ways that seem most exciting.

Transactional analysis uses a number of terms in a special way. For example, the script is a life plan, decided on at an early age, through which individuals meet their needs in the world as they see them from the vantage point of their "life position." A script is a life plan containing the significant things that will happen to a person. The four possible life positions are:

I am OK, you are OK.
I am OK, you are not OK.
I am not OK, you are OK.
I am not OK, you are not OK.

The importance of life position is that it helps determine the type of script a person will pursue throughout life. Games are a series of transactions occurring on two different levels of communication simultaneously, with an unexpected twist leading to a payoff—perhaps a particular feeling, such as guilt, depression, or anger. Three ego states form the basis for structural analysis. The first is "child," which encompasses the feelings, attitudes, and behavior patterns of a child under age six. The second ego state is "parent." That state reflects advice and values, the "shoulds" and "should-nots," and is programmed both socially and traditionally. The last state, "adult," is the aspect of ego that responds to reality. "Rackets" are the feelings individuals collect to justify the major actions in their life script.

Transactional analysis is contractual treatment in which patients specify what they expect to achieve in the therapeutic relationship; therapists accept or reject the contract, depending on whether they think they can help. Therapy begins with structural analysis—the identification and delineation of the three ego states in the individual and in others. Structural analysis is followed by transactional analysis, that is, analysis of the ego states from which transactions emanate and the ego states to which actions are directed (see fig. 15.1).

Although influenced by others, the ultimate choice of life script is that of the in-

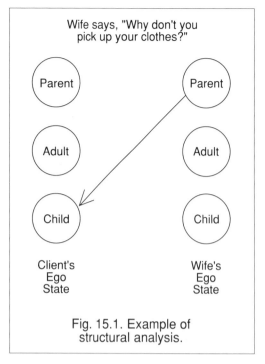

Wife says, "Why don't you pick up your clothes?"

Parent | Parent

Adult | Adult

Child | Child

Client's Ego State | Wife's Ego State

Fig. 15.1. Example of structural analysis.

dividual. Individuals choose the script best adapted to the life position already decided on, and the games and rackets that can readily be learned in accordance with family injunctions and their own wishes, needs, and desires. The alternative to game playing is an autonomous, self-chosen life pattern that can be changed to a more interesting and rewarding pattern at any time. From a Christian viewpoint, the problem with TA is that without Christ, change is difficult—and no one is really okay.

Behavior Modification

Behavior involves cognitive, motor, and emotional responses to both external and internal stimulation. Maladaptive behavior can be changed systematically by application of techniques derived from learning theory.

Behavior therapy emphasizes changes in overt behavior. Direct behavior modification leads to changes in feelings and attitudes. The therapist expects clients to set specific goals to aid in their own treatment. Behavior modification works particularly well with phobias and obsessive thinking.

Since behavioral theory was considered at length in chapter 6, we will only briefly review some of the methods and give an example of each. Basically all of the methods involve the idea of modifying a behavior by changing either the consequences of that behavior (what follows the action) or by changing the antecedents of that behavior (what occurs before the action). Rather than changing the unconscious mind, external behavior is to be modified.

One consequence that might be changed is reinforcement. For example, mentally retarded people can often develop new skills through the systematic reward of approximations of new behavior (shaping). Counselors may unknowingly use this technique by paying more attention to a client (a reinforcement) when important ideas are being discussed, and paying less attention with peripheral issues.

Extinction is the elimination of a reinforcement so that a given behavior will decrease. Those who have certain somatoform disorders may get reinforcement because of their imagined disability. The counselor may instruct the family and friends to ignore the client's comments about the problem and pay close attention when he or she speaks of improving.

Aversion therapy focuses on the use of punishment. Alcoholics have sometimes been treated with mild electrical shocks (not to be confused with shock treatment) when they taste alcohol. The idea is to develop a phobia to the smell and taste of the beverage. This can be effective if the individual genuinely wants to overcome the problem. Unfortunately the phobia can quickly extinguish if the client wants to subvert the treatment. Aversion therapy has been used with pedophiles (child mo-

Spotlight 15.4. Attention as Reinforcement in the Church

Pastors sometimes find themselves wondering how to react to testimonies or other comments in services that are not compatible with the theology of the church. For example, what should a pastor do when a visitor asserts publicly that a television program produced by a cult helped him a great deal?

The reaction of the pastor must be kind and yet clear. An "amen" not only affirms the speaker but may also be construed to affirm the cultic belief. Certainly it is important for the pastor to assess the situation accurately. A weak Christian who is sharing for the first time publicly might be told, "Thanks for your ideas. I'd like to talk with you further about that after the service ends." Sometimes silence (extinction) is appropriate. With more dogmatic assertions, confrontation may be needed, such as "I'm sorry, but those are not the beliefs of this church." Interrupting, a powerful punishment, may be called for in very difficult situations.

A chorus of "amens" following a testimony by a shy youngster may be reinforcing, while silence or murmuring can be effective extinction or punishment. This can be taken too far, of course, to the point where innovative ideas that are doctrinally sound will be dismissed simply because the congregation has not heard them before. The latter is probably more likely in rigid, legalistic churches.

---

lesters) and homosexuals with some success (Walen, Hauserman, and Lavin 1977).

Modeling involves observing and imitating desired behavior. This is used most in assertiveness training, where shy individuals learn to take the initiative and become more outgoing. The leader may display an assertive response in front of a group of clients (generally assertiveness training takes place in group therapy). Each client then takes a turn imitating the assertive behavior, and is encouraged and praised by the counselor and others in the group.

Desensitization is another method used by behavioral counselors for the treatment of phobias and is based upon classical conditioning theory.

Another method used by behavioral therapists is contracting, where the client and counselor agree on a specific plan and/or goal between counseling sessions.

For example, a person who is trying to stop smoking might agree to smoke five cigarettes less each day to obtain a certain reward. The written parent-teen-ager agreement mentioned in chapter 11 is also a contract.

There are Christian variations of behavioral therapy. Adams (1973), who is openly hostile to psychology, has developed nouthetic counseling in which desired behavior is rewarded while undesired behavior is punished. Adams insists that clients have "homework" that involves an agreement between the counselor and client. While Adams asserts that his is not a behavioral approach, these aspects are certainly behavioral! (To be fair, nouthetic counseling does involve more than behavioral methods, as will be noted later in this chapter.) Bufford (1981) has also outlined a Christian behavioral approach to counseling.

RATIONAL-EMOTIVE THERAPY (RET)

Rational-emotive therapy (or cognitive behavior therapy), pioneered by Albert Ellis (Ellis and Grieger 1977), is an extension of behaviorism that emphasizes the influence of beliefs upon behavior. A number of irrational beliefs have previously been noted (see chap. 7). These irrational beliefs must be located, confronted, and then replaced by more rational beliefs.

Rational-emotive therapy is active and directive. This school of thought operates on an A-B-C paradigm. "A" refers to events in a person's life; "B," to a person's thoughts about event "A"; "C," a person's emotions and behavior as a result of "B." When a highly charged emotional consequence (C) follows an activating event (A), "A" may appear to cause "C." Actually, however, emotional consequences are largely created by "B," the individual's belief system (see fig. 15.2).

The goal of therapy is to minimize a self-defeating outlook and help an individual acquire a more realistic, total philosophy of life. Pain may be alleviated in several ways, including diversion, satisfaction of demands, and convincing a person to give up demandingness. Counselees are taught basically how to think—to separate rational from irrational beliefs.

The rational-emotive therapist is infor-mal, active, energetic, and directive. Often a forceful approach is necessary to alter destructive patterns of behavior. Homework assignments and facing unpleasant events are part of the therapy. Individuals need to be shown that they are resistant to changing their outlook and behavior because change is difficult and because they prefer an instant solution rather than work to bring about change.

We can think of the irrational self-statements of RET as a sort of self-talk that is unproductive. What we tell ourselves about events often influences our reactions more than the events themselves. Backus and Chapian (1980) and Propst (1987) represent Christian variations of RET and the concept of self-talk.

Humanistic Counseling Approaches

The term "humanist" is used here in the psychological sense rather than the philosophical sense. A number of Christian writers have spoken out against secular humanism because of its ignoring or denial of God, which of course is incompatible with Christianity. Humanistic psychology, on the other hand, refers to the importance of the individual person and the positive value of human beings. It is therefore quite compatible with Christianity; in fact, we could even say that Christianity is humanistic because it underscores the importance and value of the person made in the image of God. On the

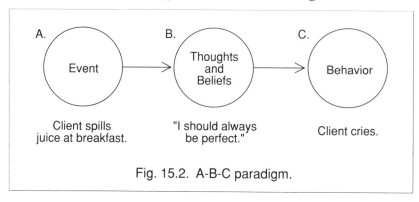

Fig. 15.2. A-B-C paradigm.

Spotlight 15.5. RET in the Church

A Sunday school teacher might make use of rational-emotive therapy by presenting some irrational self-statements (see chap. 7) to the class and then discussing them from a biblical perspective. Each of them might be evaluated using a Bible study. Sources that may help in this respect include Crabb (1977) and Backus and Chapian (1980).

Counseling pastors may also find themselves facing the irrational self-statements of clients. These are more likely to be implicit than overt. Such statements need to be analyzed and confronted. While pastors may help some in this area, extensive treatment of irrational beliefs and assumptions probably needs to be undertaken by professionally trained Christian counselors.

---

other hand, it must be admitted that many who hold to humanistic psychology are also secular humanists (as are many psychoanalysts, behaviorists, and others). The best-known humanistic counseling approach is client-centered therapy. We will also consider gestalt therapy in this section since it shares some of the ideals encouraged by humanistic psychologists.

CLIENT-CENTERED THERAPY

Rogers (1951) believes that all individuals possess a strong drive toward personal growth, health, and adjustment, which he calls self-actualization. Tension, anxiety, and defensiveness interfere with basic human drives. If these forces can be reduced or relieved, a person can experience personal growth. Neurotic individuals, according to Rogers, have lost sight of their own values and have taken on the values of others. The goal of client-centered therapy is to help people regain contact with their true feelings and values. Increased self-acceptance increases autonomy and reduces the destructive forces of anxiety; thus personal growth occurs.

In client-centered therapy the therapist needs to be honest, genuine, transparent, and totally accepting. According to Rogers, the growth potential of individuals is released in a relationship where a help-

ing person is experiencing and communicating realness, caring, and a deeply sensitive, nonjudgmental understanding. The client-centered approach is applicable to any relationship where persons want to understand and be understood and are willing to reveal themselves to some degree.

Client-centered therapists must have an unconditional positive regard for the other person. They must accept the client as a person regardless of how socially unacceptable that person's behavior and feelings may be. Therapists must possess empathy; they must try to understand as clearly as possible the feelings of the client. Finally, therapists must be genuine, able to be "themselves" in a session and express their thoughts and feelings without pretension. Client-centered therapy is especially effective for individuals with a poor self-image.

A major technique in client-centered therapy is reflection. This involves repeating what clients have said using different words and sometimes condensing and clarifying what they have stated. For example, a client might say, "I can't believe it! I got an A on my last psychology test!" to which the counselor would respond, "You feel elated." Feelings are important to

---

Spotlight 15.6.
Rogerian Techniques in the Church

Many churches make use of small groups, such as home Bible studies or Sunday school classes, in which interaction is highly desirable. Some of the methods mentioned in spotlight 16.3 might be used. On the other hand, specific ideas suggested by Rogers might be used to encourage interaction.

Unconditional positive regard is helpful. Reflection could also be used, which behaviorally would be understood as reinforcement, but in the Rogerian view would be a means of clarification, communicating that real understanding has taken place. A leader could reflect underlying feelings being expressed or even subtle theological implications in what is shared in a manner that would encourage others to speak up.

Reflection is a good technique for helping people really listen to one another, and could be used in testimony services, small groups, and personal evangelism. The pastor or member of a church board who uses reflection and clarification may be able to defuse a potentially explosive situation. The time taken to restate positions can give people an opportunity to think before reacting, as well as clear up possible misunderstandings or miscommunications.

---

client-centered therapists; thus they tend to use many "you-feel" statements.

Client-centered therapy has been accused of not doing enough; it basically assumes that clients can solve their own problems if accepted and affirmed. While some people can solve their own problems and there is value in just listening and accepting, most counselors feel this is insufficient. On the other hand, good listening skills and reflection can help establish rapport between any counselor and client. If nothing else, client-centered techniques can initiate the counseling process; once the relationship has been established other methods can be introduced.

McKenna (1977) has outlined a Christian approach to counseling called "The Jesus Model," that includes many components of client-centered therapy. For example, he explains Christ's encounter with the Samaritan woman (John 4:1–42) using many of the concepts of Rogers' approach,

although he notes other psychological and spiritual dynamics as well (McKenna 1977, 128–42). Rogerian counseling was central to the pastoral counseling movement in its formative period (see chap. 1).

GESTALT THERAPY

Gestalt therapy seeks to create experiences that increase self-awareness. Perls (1969) believes that people are kept from reaching their potential because they do not have the opportunity to discover fully who they are. Individuals are responsible for their own decisions and actions, and cannot blame society, parents, or past experiences for their problems. When individuals know and accept themselves to the fullest extent possible, they can overcome conflicts within their personalities so that psychological growth occurs.

According to gestalt therapy, people rarely tap the potential within themselves or between themselves and others. Our awareness is usually directed to a few areas that are consistent with our sense of identity, and then all experience is funneled through that self-concept. Limited self-concepts constrict awareness and inhibit experiences, so that awareness is not allowed freedom. Gestalt therapy attempts to counteract that limitation by broadening experiences.

Other Methods of Counseling and Therapy

REALITY THERAPY

The focus of reality therapy is responsible behavior (Glasser 1965). In pursuit of such behavior the "three Rs" must be observed: face reality; do right; and be responsible. According to reality therapy most psychiatric help is sought because of failure to meet two needs: love and self-worth. The focus should be on the present, not the past, and on behavior rather than on feelings.

Individuals must face reality and admit that the past cannot be rewritten. They must accept full responsibility for their present and future behavior. Unconscious motivations are no excuse for misbehavior. What is important are present attempts to succeed and intentions for the future. The therapist helps individuals devise specific plans for their behavior and make a commitment to follow through with those plans.

Human beings have a single most important social need—for identity. That intrinsic need is inherited and transmitted from generation to generation. The identity we develop comes from interaction with others as well as interaction with self. An identity change follows a change in behavior. To change what we are, we must change what we do and undertake new ways of behaving. Reality therapy focuses strongly on helping individuals understand and accept themselves as they are with their own limitations and abilities.

The therapist in reality therapy must be personal, encouraging the individual to make a value judgment and a plan to alter behavior. Making a commitment to a choice develops maturity; no excuses are accepted for not following through. Positive in approach, the therapist never focuses on punishment, attempting instead to lead clients out of a failure identity. In reality therapy, individuals are assisted in understanding, defining, and clarifying life goals (both immediate and long-term), in identifying the ways they hamper their own progress toward goals, and in comparing alternatives.

Of the various secular schools of thought, reality therapy seems to have had the greatest influence on Christian counseling. Its emphasis on responsibility and its attempts to distinguish between right and wrong are commendable; yet in reality therapy morality is relative because it is based on no absolute standard.

ADLERIAN PSYCHOTHERAPY

Adlerian or "individual" psychology was developed in 1911 by a contemporary of Freud. Alfred Adler (1927) agreed that human beings have inherent factors that affect their destiny but considered such factors social rather than biological. Rather than being mentally sick, individuals are merely discouraged because of their self-defeating inferiority feelings. Adler was a holist who thought a person could be understood only as an indivisible unity. He believed that all particular functions were subordinate functions of an individual's goals or style of life. Lifestyle was not synonymous with behavior; behavior can change throughout a person's life whereas lifestyle remains relatively constant.

To Adler, human beings are creative, self-determined decision makers who choose the goals they wish to pursue. The "dynamic striving" toward a self-selected goal gives an individual a place in the world. Life has no intrinsic meaning, according to Adler, but each person gives life meaning according to that person's own fashion. Because people grow up in a social environment, they search for significance by attempting to master their environment. If children perceive that they can achieve peace through useful endeavor they will pursue the "useful side of life." If they become discouraged, however, they will engage in disturbing behavior in an effort to find their place. Such children will usually use one of four approaches: attention getting, power seeking, revenge taking, or declaring defeat.

According to Adler, there are four levels of conviction in a lifestyle. The first is self-concept, the conviction people have about who they are. The second is self-ideal, the conviction of what they should be or are obligated to be to have a place. The third is a picture of the world, not a conviction of self but rather of what the world demands of a person. The last conviction is a personal code of ethics. Inferiority feelings develop when a discrepancy occurs between self- and ideal-self convictions.

Since psychological problems emanate from faulty perceptions, learnings, values, and goals, the goal of therapy is one of education or reeducation. People need to learn to have faith in themselves, to love, and to trust. Ideally, through psychotherapy their social interest is released so they can become fellow human beings who contribute to and feel a sense of belonging in their world.

Individuals utilize various problem-solving devices to protect their self-esteem, such as compensation, safeguards, excuses, projection, depreciation tendencies, and creating distance. To Adler the concept of the unconscious is not acceptable, so repression and sublimation are irrelevant. Being self-determined, human beings have no room for instincts, drives, libido, or other alleged unconscious motivation.

LOGOTHERAPY

Viktor Frankl has developed a form of psychotherapy that he terms "logotherapy." This approach emphasizes the importance of the meaning of life, as suggested by the title of his famous book *Man's Search for Meaning* (1959).

Frankl's ideas derive from his experience in German concentration camps during World War II. He noticed that some people admitted to the camps gave up and died soon after they arrived, while others survived incredible hardships. What was the difference between the two groups of people? Those who endured had something that provided ultimate meaning in life. There was something that provided transcendence, something beyond them that beckoned them onward. For Frankl, it was his psychological work; for others it was family; for still others it was religious faith.

Frankl believes that society is generally characterized by noögenic neurosis, or a search for meaning. In this quest for ultimacy, our spiritual nature is underscored; we are not just physical creatures. In therapy, the client is given the freedom to choose, but is then held responsible for the choices made. Frankl encourages the counselee to turn away from excessive emphasis upon self, sometimes fostered by other therapies as well as by the pervasive narcissism in our society, and instead to focus upon what is ultimate in life.

While Frankl is obviously not a Christian psychologist, his ideas are quite compatible with Christian thought. Many today search for meaning, meaning that only God can give. As Augustine states, there is a God-shaped vacuum that only God can fill. People continue to search until they find God or some substitute. Realizing the fact of that search and the need for an adequate answer for the meaning to life can be an important aspect of Christian counseling. Christ is the solution to man's search for meaning.

INTEGRITY THERAPY

O. Hobert Mowrer pioneered integrity therapy out of his personal experience. The relationship between his theory and Christian faith is perhaps best analyzed in his *Crisis in Psychiatry and Religion* (1961), while his personal experience leading to that theory is documented in *Abnormal Reactions or Actions?* (1966).

A successful behavioral therapist, Mowrer rose quickly among the ranks of counselors during the 1930s and 1940s. In 1953 he was elected president of the prestigious American Psychological Association. At that year's annual meeting of the association, he was to give two speeches and then be inducted into the presidency. The only problem was that he failed to show up because he was hospitalized for acute depression!

With time he improved and was able to address the 1954 APA convention. Over the next several years he came to have deeper insights into his recurring depressive episodes, realizing how important sin and forgiveness were. He proposed that feelings of guilt come from violations of the conscience while emotional problems are often due to sin. The solution for sin, and thus emotional problems, is for clients to recognize the presence of sin in their life, confess it, reject it, ask for forgiveness, and finally perform restitution or make penance.

While much of Mowrer's integrity therapy is compatible with the heart of the Christian message, he categorically rejects Calvinist theology as too deterministic. He believes it advocates cheap grace and leads to excuses instead of the confession and forsaking of sin.

While Mowrer holds to a number of principles that are found in Christian theology, his ideas are not without their limits. Most Protestants would agree with the idea of restitution but not the idea of penance (we cannot justify ourselves—only Christ can). We must also question the assumption that all mental illness is due to sin; there can be powerful influences from early childhood as well as organic causes (see chap. 14). Sin can cause psychopathology, but there can be other causes as well. A specifically Christian version of integrity therapy is Adams' nouthetic counseling, which combines elements of behaviorism and integrity therapy within a Christian framework.

Physical Interventions

In addition to verbal counseling, psychiatrists also make use of certain physical treatments of disorders, particularly for depression. These include medications, shock therapy, and psychosurgery.

PSYCHOACTIVE DRUGS

One of the most significant discoveries of the mid-twentieth century has been the psychoactive drugs. A number of medications, such as Elavil, Trofanil, Norpramine, and others, are used to treat severe depression. Lithium salt has been very effective in helping manic-depressives control their extreme mood swings. The major tranquilizers are often used to help people suffering from severe anxiety, while megavitamins and hormones may help depression and other mental disorders. Thorazine, Haldol, and other medications may help schizophrenics.

Medication alone is usually insufficient; counseling is also needed to supplement medical therapy. But the advent of psychoactive medications has resulted in a dramatic reduction in long-term in-patient treatment. Many who had no hope before can now respond to counseling once extreme symptoms are under medical con-

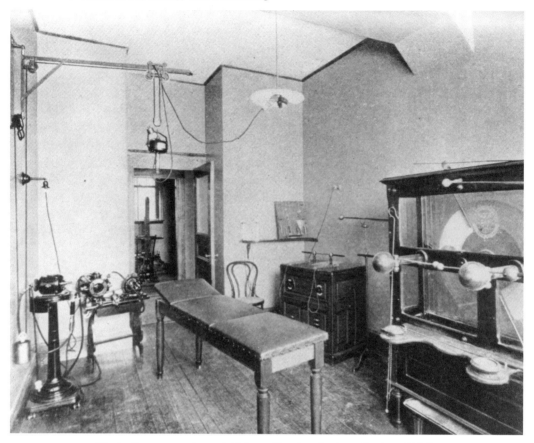

Electrotherapy equipment (Adams Nervine Asylum, Boston, 1904).

trol. Schizophrenics who are completely out of touch can hardly respond to counseling, but with help from medication they are sometimes able to begin listening, learning, and changing.[1]

SHOCK TREATMENT

Electroconvulsive therapy (ECT, or "shock treatment"), introduced in 1938, was once used extensively to treat emotional disorders, especially psychotic disorders. After the phenothiazines and antidepressant drugs were introduced in the early 1950s, the use of ECT began to decline. In certain cases it has dramatic results, but the nature of the treatment and reports of alleged memory impairment associated with it have turned many against it.

1. For a detailed description of psychoactive drugs, see Minirth and Meier 1978, 213–24.

Today shock therapy is rarely the first line of treatment chosen for depression. It is sometimes given to patients who are resistant to or have had adverse reactions to antidepressants. ECT is sometimes used for suicidal crises because antidepressants do not take effect for a period of two to three weeks. Usually five to eight treatments are given for depressive disorders. Following a course of ECT, 30 to 40 percent of the patients will relapse within a year because the root psychological and spiritual causes of the depression were not uncovered and resolved.

ECT has proven to be relatively safe over the years, with a declining death rate of one in ten thousand in earlier years to one in forty thousand treatments. Transient memory loss definitely occurs with the use of ECT, increasing in severity with the number of treatments given. Since depression alone also causes impairment in memory, all such memory loss may not be due to ECT. Actually, some patients have improved memory after ECT because the depression lifts. Generally, ECT is not used unless a severely depressed person is resistant to all other forms of therapy and is determined to commit suicide.

PSYCHOSURGERY

Attempts to influence the mind through surgery have met with much resistance in the Christian community, and rightly so. Prefrontal lobotomy (cutting the frontal lobe of the brain to make people more compliant and relieve their emotional pain) was introduced by a Portuguese neurologist, Egas Moniz, in 1935. Today it is less popular because of the advent of psychoactive or psychotropic medication. If psychosurgery is used, it most commonly involves destruction of very minute areas of the brain to accomplish very specific effects. It is also used to treat lesions in the temporal lobe of the brain which may cause marked changes in behavior. In contrast to their normal behavior, such patients may become irritable and aggressive. The surgical treatment of a specific temporal lobe lesion is vastly different from the prefrontal lobotomies done in the 1930s and 1940s. It is also important to distinguish between psychosurgery and brain surgery. Psychosurgery involves destruction of brain tissue to ameliorate some psychological problem, while brain surgery generally involves removal of foreign matter such as a tumor.

Christian Counseling

Christian counseling utilizes a variety of therapeutic approaches, as is true of secular psychology and psychiatry. In spite of a basic unity derived from their oneness in Christ and their acceptance of the Bible as an absolute standard, Christian counselors differ in personality, the training they have received, their experience, the setting in which they practice, and the kinds of counselees who come to them for help. However, a few basic characteristics distinguish true Christian counseling. In essence, the counseling process can be understood as a three-part ministry. Basically, a counselor performs the following functions:

> Listens to the counselee.
> Helps the counselee gain insight.
> Helps the counselee formulate a specific plan of action.

Listening

Simply talking to another person often relieves problems. True friendship is built when one person listens to another and shows genuine concern.

Caring, although intangible, is readily sensed by people, particularly those with problems. People tend to gravitate toward those individuals who are warm, understanding, accepting, and personal—and who will listen to them. Unless counselees develop a caring relationship with a counselor, they are seldom motivated to change. Listening is one of the best ways to express concern or caring.

Good listening techniques must be learned. For example, when working with two people at once, try to talk to only one person at a time and not engage in two conversations. It is important to avoid interrupting a person who is speaking. A good listener does not tune in to only part of the conversation, argue mentally while the other person is talking, and jump to conclusions before that person finishes. Care should be taken not to appear restless or to convey disinterest through facial expressions. A warm smile, eye contact, and interest shown by every movement are marks of a caring listener. Counselors must not let their own biases affect therapy. Counselees can usually tell if they are being "pigeonholed" mentally or labeled by a counselor as they speak, especially if the counselor uses emotionally charged words in response. Also, it is wise for the counselor to avoid making notes.

Spotlight 15.7. The Uniqueness of Christian Counseling

Whether the counselor is a minister, psychologist, psychiatrist, or social worker, certain principles make Christian counseling unique.

First, Christian counseling accepts the Bible as the final standard of authority. Christians are not left to be "tossed back and forth" but can look to a final authority. Relying on the Holy Spirit to guide them through the Bible, Christians are not dependent on their own consciences to direct their behavior. If conscience agrees with the Word of God, it is valid; if not, conscience is invalid. The Bible not only gives insights into human behavior but also puts everything into proper perspective. It tells who we are, where we came from, and our nature and purpose.

Second, Christian counseling is unique because it depends not only on the human will to be responsible, but also on the enabling, indwelling power of the Holy Spirit to conquer human problems. Although all of us are responsible for our actions, even Christians can choose to act irresponsibly. Through God's power, however, we no longer need to be slaves to a weak will, our past environment, or social situations. Although problems do not disappear when we accept Christ, we gain new power to deal with them.

Third, Christian counseling is unique because although by nature human beings are selfish and tend to ignore or hate God (Rom. 1:28–32), Christians through faith receive the Spirit who gives them victory in overpowering their sin nature.

Fourth, Christian counseling is unique because it effectively deals with the counselee's past. Many traditional personality theories (particularly psychoanalytic theories) deal exclusively with the past. Because Christians find themselves forgiven for past life events, they can be guilt-free (1 John 1:9) and look forward to the future (Phil. 3:13–14). Even if some past events require insight and specific prayer to remove resentment and bitterness, believers have a secure position in Christ.

Fifth, Christian counseling is unique because it is based on God's love. God loves us (1 John 4:10) and as his love flows through us we love others and care for them (Rom. 12:9–21). A Christian counselor feels a spiritual relationship to other Christians and helps them to grow in Christ as they solve their problems.

Sixth, Christian counseling is unique because it deals with the whole person. The Christian counselor is aware that the physical, psychological, and spiritual aspects of human beings are intricately related.

Helping People Gain Insight

The key to counseling is to help a counselee gain insight. Once people gain insight into the true nature of their problem, much of the problem may be resolved. A counselor can often help by maintaining a balance between focus on the past and attention to the present by clarifying the difference between feelings and behavior, and by using appropriate directive and nondirective techniques.

PAST VERSUS PRESENT

In counseling today the pendulum seems to be swinging from focusing on the past to focusing on the present. One extreme position has always blamed the past for present problems; the other has avoided the past and focused almost entirely on the present. For example, reality therapy emphasizes that the past is past and can never be changed. In general, past experiences should not be used as excuses to avoid present responsibility. Christian counseling endeavors to deal with present behavior, but sometimes it is appropriate to do something about unresolved issues from the past. Overall, taking a balanced view tends to work best.

For a Christian, of course, the past is forgiven. "If we confess our sins, he is faithful and just and will forgive us our sins and purify us from all unrighteousness" (1 John 1:9). "But one thing I do: Forgetting what is behind and straining toward what is ahead, I press on toward the goal to win the prize for which God has called me heavenward in Christ Jesus" (Phil. 3:13–14). Although the past is forgiven by God, guilt may still haunt an individual consciously or subconsciously, and hence must be dealt with in counseling.

FEELINGS VERSUS BEHAVIOR

Although one extreme in counseling focuses entirely on feelings and another entirely on behavior, Christian counseling must treat both. It is important to let counselees ventilate their feelings. This helps them cope with the internalized anger that causes depression and helps to bring anxiety from the subconscious to the conscious, where it can be dealt with appropriately. It also helps counselees feel that the counselor cares for them and understands them. The Christian counselor must move beyond attention to feelings, however, to deal with behavior. After all, people have little direct control over their feelings but maximum control over their behavior. Troubled individuals generally benefit from developing new interests and activities.

It is often possible to change feelings by changing behavior. Memories and feelings from the past recorded in the brain (in the subconscious) can be replayed later. One way to change feelings is to reprogram the mind by studying the Scriptures: "Do not conform any longer to the pattern of this world, but be transformed by the renewing of your mind. Then you will be able to test and approve what God's will is—his good, pleasing and perfect will" (Rom. 12:2).

DIRECTIVE VERSUS NONDIRECTIVE TECHNIQUES

Conventional psychiatry is essentially nondirective. The therapist does not attempt to tell patients what they should do, but rather operates on the principle that once patients understand why things have gone wrong, they will change; insight supposedly leads to changed behavior. Directive counseling, on the other hand, attempts to teach patients better ways to meet their needs. If counselors are too directive they defeat their own purpose, though, because only personal decisions will last. But counseling that is not sufficiently directive confuses counselees, since they are left with too few guidelines to follow.

Spotlight 15.8.
Christian Counseling by Radio

In the 1960s, long before non-Christians considered the use of radio counseling, Clyde Narramore had a nationwide radio program entitled "Psychology for Living," in which he answered letters from people with personal problems.

In the 1970s Dobson's "Focus on the Family" was born. Though some of the earlier programs included a live call-in format, the use of recording tapes made this impossible later. Dobson continues to invite psychologists and counselors as guests on his program from time to time, and his own psychological background comes through regularly. The counseling of listeners through correspondence is another very beneficial aspect of his radio ministry.

With the 1980s came a third radio ministry, this one a daily call-in program live by satellite. The "Meier–Minirth Clinic" offers psychological and spiritual advice and counsel.

Radio counseling is, of course, no substitute for personal counseling and other kinds of therapy, but many call who would not come for counseling, and thousands more listen to the helpful advice. In addition, many come to consider counseling as a legitimate alternative as a result of listening.

Christian counseling generally uses an "indirect-directive" approach. The Christian counselor should be able to recognize clients' problems and then guide them in solving those problems. Because the Bible serves as the standard of authority, Christian counseling is directive. Its goals are to help counselees solve their problems in accordance with the will of God and to help them grow spiritually. Yet the preferred approach is indirect because the counselor generally uses indirect techniques (questions, suggestions, listening) to help the counselee reach appropriate decisions. The Christian counselor thus uses indirect techniques for a directed end.

Jesus Christ was directive at times and nondirective at other times. He helped others obtain valuable insights through both statements and questions. His statements were stern and rebuking at times but kind and gentle at other times. The Gospel of Mark records approximately twenty questions asked by Christ. Some of those questions were matter-of-fact, intending to teach others or help them gain insight, but at least five of them were rebuking in nature (three directed at the Pharisees and two at the disciples). Questions often force people to reach their own conclusions; they are valuable tools when used by an experienced counselor.

BALANCE

Balance, the key to spiritual and emotional maturity, is also the key to successful Christian counseling. Jesus Christ demonstrated how to be both direct and indirect in helping people gain insight (see John 3), how to focus on the present without excluding the past (see John 4), and how to emphasize spiritual aspects without neglecting physical and psychological aspects (see John 5).

Formulating a Plan of Action

After serving as a good listener and guiding individuals in discerning the nature of their problems, a counselor should assist clients in formulating a specific plan to deal with those problems. Troubled individuals seldom realize that they may have subconsciously planned out in great detail a course of action destined to destroy them.

In formulating a new plan, counselees should make a list of alternatives for dealing with their problem and for being mentally healthy. To foster creativity, evaluation should be done only after the list is completed. After considering perhaps several dozen alternatives (likely ones, seemingly impossible ones, even totally illogical ones), a specific plan of action should be drawn up consisting of five to ten of the best alternatives. As the reality therapists insist, the plan needs to be specific, including, for example, a detailed exercise program or a set number of social contacts for the week. It may include some direct courses of action to deal with a particular problem, such as confronting in an assertive manner a friend with whom the counselee is angry.

It is important that the counselee make a commitment to the specific plan and adhere to it for a set period of time. As goals are met and problems are solved, feelings will change.

Christian counselors should suggest that time be spent each day reading the Word of God. Memories and feelings stored in the brain may constitute a faulty belief system from the past on which counselees are still acting. As individuals meditate on the Word and apply it to their lives, their belief systems and feelings will change. For example, a grown man may have doubts about his salvation because his father did not accept him as a child. As he spends time in God's Word, he will real-ize how much God loves and accepts him, and his faulty belief system will change. A husband's faulty belief system may cause him to be unloving toward his wife. As he grows in God's Word and realizes how God wants him to love his wife, his marriage will improve as his faulty belief system changes.

In helping a counselee formulate a plan, the decision-making process must be given some thought. The three criteria for making a right decision are feelings, logic, and God's Word. Many faulty decisions are made because feelings are considered first, logic second, and God's Word last. Although feelings are the most unstable, unreliable, and changeable standards, many individuals base their entire lives on them. Logic, far more stable than feelings, should be relied on by Christians for the many decisions not spoken of specifically in the Bible. God gave us logic and wants us to use it. The danger with logic is that people are basically selfish, so that without the guidance of the Holy Spirit, people tend to choose a selfish course. The best criteria for making decisions are God's Word (used in conjunction with prayer), the conviction of the Holy Spirit, and advice from other Christians.

Do Counseling and Therapy Work?

Surprisingly this question was not seriously addressed until the early 1950s when Eysenck (1952) suggested a negative answer. He stated that those who received no therapy recovered more quickly than those who did. However, there were serious flaws in Eysenck's research. His data were taken not from random samples of carefully controlled participants, but rather from insurance company records from 1946. His measure of success was how quickly people went back to work, while the definition of "doing nothing" was getting medical treatment from doctors. A valid conclusion from his study might be that people in the 1940s went back to work sooner if they went to a medical doctor than if they received counseling—a hardly surprising conclusion, but one that is far removed from his original assertion!

While the original studies were flawed, the question of whether counseling works is an important one. Some, such as Mischel (1968, 103–48), have emphasized the limitations of at least certain kinds of counseling, most have continued to affirm the value of counseling. Perhaps the best conclusion is that many methods of counseling can be effective, but a particular approach is better for certain kinds of problems than others, for certain kinds of counselors than others, and for certain kinds of clients than others.

Seamands (1988) points out the fact that if we believed all the Christian counseling books, we would conclude that every Christian approach works in virtually all situations. But the pervasive effects of the sin nature and traumatic childhood experiences are not erased simply because the counselor is a Christian. Worthington's (1986) research reveals that most Christian counseling is done by clergy and they are not doing as well as many other counselors.

However, this is not grounds for giving up on Christian counseling. We may legitimately ask if these clergy are as well trained in counseling as secular counselors. We may also ask how well they have integrated their faith into their counseling. Perhaps many are imitating the secular professionals yet lack the training. The research usually has relied upon surveys, not actual counseling experiences. Perhaps it would be more fair to compare the counseling of graduates of Christian APA-accredited schools, such as Fuller and Rosemead, with graduates of secular APA-accredited schools, making sure that the

graduates of the former do indeed include distinctively Christian ideas in their counseling.

In the meantime, it is helpful to offer several guidelines for obtaining good Christian counseling (Campolo 1988, 213–14). First, decide what kind of help is most appropriate. Second, if repressed memories are part of the problem, be sure the counselor refers to God's forgiveness. Third, get counseling from someone who is not antagonistic to Christianity. Fourth, a marriage counselor must prize marriage to the same degree the Bible does. Fifth, be sure the counselor's philosophy of life and spirituality are compatible with yours. Finally, trust your instincts—the Holy Spirit may be warning you to avoid a particular counselor, even if that individual is a Christian.

Eclectic Counseling

Most psychologists, including Christian counselors, do not rely upon a single theory or approach to counseling. The predominant approach to counseling and therapy is *eclectic*, involving a combination of theories, methods, and viewpoints. Among those theories, methods, and viewpoints must be those found in the Bible.

Four kinds of eclecticism can be noted. First, there is research-based eclecticism, where certain methods are identified as most effective for certain problems on the basis of systematic research. For example, phobias have generally been best treated by behavior therapy, specifically desensitization.

A second level of eclecticism is experiential/pragmatic. By experimenting in one's own counseling or by talking to other counselors, approaches that are more likely to succeed for certain problems can be ascertained.

Third, there is rational eclecticism, where counselors study different methods and by thinking them through conclude

---

Spotlight 15.9.
Professional Associations

Before Christian professionals begin a private psychological practice they should establish a reputation. First, they should affiliate with a local church. Second, they should associate with a local professional group. A group of psychologists or psychiatrists, or perhaps a Christian counseling organization, can provide a network of interaction while serving as a basis of support and professional responsibility. Third, Christians should join the appropriate national organization of their profession, such as the American Psychological Association or the Christian Association for Psychological Study. Counselors need to be aware of what others in the community are doing and build solid relationships with other professionals. Opportunities to share needs, obtain supervision, and learn of referral availabilities come through professional associations. Christian counselors often have significant opportunities to witness within these professional groups while developing their own approach to counseling. Finally, Christian counselors should meet whatever local, state, or national guidelines apply to their practice.

---

that certain approaches fit their particular philosophy better than others or make more sense for certain problems than others. For example, the Christian counselor usually emphasizes the importance of distinguishing whether a given problem is primarily spiritual, mental, or physical before determining treatment.

Fourth, there is mystical eclecticism. Most often associated with memory healing (Seamands 1985; McDonald 1981), this approach notes that God can and (if allowed) will intervene directly in the counselor's thinking (as well as the counselee's) during the process of counseling to show what approach is needed. God sometimes mystically puts it all together, revealing the problem and/or solution quite apart from rationality, research, or prior experience. Certainly, this should not be the predominant form of counseling, but it should be allowed to function as God directs.

It might also be noted that almost everyone who follows the eclectic approach also tends to have one or more "fall-back"

theories. In a specific situation with a client, the counselor will tend to search through the theoretical options. Often one approach definitely fits the problem and counseling can proceed. But when a client's problem does not fit one of the options comfortably, there is the tendency to force the new situation into an existing theoretical mold. If the fall-back theory is behaviorism, the counselor will seek out the specific behaviors involved, as well as the contingencies producing that behavior. If the fall-back theory is psychoanalysis, the counselor relies upon defense mechanisms or Freudian stages to interpret the problem. Those with a Rogerian fall-back theory will tend to do less interpreting and more reflecting until the problem is clarified. Christians sometimes use the doctrine of sin as their fall-back theory, concluding that some specific sin must be rooted out that will explain the problem. In any fall-back situation, there is a real danger of distorting the problem and thus the possibility of helping the client is less likely. While fall-back theories are probably necessary, the good counselor will keep current by reading recent textbooks and journal articles, consulting with colleagues, joining professional associations, and perhaps attending conferences so that the number of fall-back situations will be minimized.

There is certainly a great need for Christian counseling in churches, in Christian mental health centers, in Christian colleges, on mission fields, in every context. The Christian counselor must combine faith with counseling techniques in the most effective manner.

References

Adams, J. 1973. *Christian counselor's manual.* Grand Rapids: Baker.

Adler, A. 1927. *The practice and theory of individual psychology.* New York: Harcourt, Brace, and World.

Backus, W., and M. Chapian. 1980. *Telling yourself the truth.* Minneapolis: Bethany.

———. 1987. *Christian counseling and psychotherapy.* Grand Rapids: Baker.

Bufford, R. 1981. *The human reflex.* San Francisco: Harper and Row.

Campolo, T. 1988. *Twenty hot potatoes.* Dallas: Word.

Collins, G. 1975. Pulpit and the couch. *Christianity Today* 19: 5–9.

———. 1980. *Helping people grow.* Ventura, Calif.: Vision.

Crabb, L. 1977. *Effective biblical counseling.* Grand Rapids: Zondervan.

Dobson, J. 1986. Keys to a family-friendly church. *Leadership* 7: 12–21.

Ellis, A., and R. Grieger. 1977. *RET.* New York: Springer.

Eysenck, H. 1952. The effects of psychotherapy: An evaluation. *Journal of Consulting Psychology* 16: 319–24.

Frankl, V. 1959. *Man's search for meaning.* New York: Pocket.

Freud, S. 1900. *The interpretation of dreams.* London: Hogarth.

———. 1933. *New introductory lectures on psychoanalysis.* New York: Norton.

Gibson, D. 1985. Adlerian psychotherapy. In *Baker encyclopedia of psychology,* ed. D. Benner. Grand Rapids: Baker.

Glasser, W. 1965. *Reality therapy.* New York: Harper and Row.

Harris, T. 1969. *I'm ok, you're ok.* New York: Harper and Row.

James, M. 1973. *Born to love.* Reading, Mass.: Addison-Wesley.

Jung, C. 1928. *Contributions to analytical psychology.* New York: Harcourt Brace.

McDonald, R. 1981. *Memory healing.* Atlanta, Ga.: RLM Ministries.

McKenna, D. 1977. *The Jesus model.* Waco: Word.

Minirth, F. 1977. *Christian psychiatry.* Old Tappan, N.J.: Revell.

Minirth, F., and P. Meier. 1978. *Happiness is a choice.* Grand Rapids: Baker.

Mischel, W. 1968. *Personality and assessment.* New York: Wiley.

Mowrer, O. 1961. *The crisis in psychiatry and religion.* Princeton, N.J.: Van Nostrand.

———. 1966. *Abnormal reactions or actions?* Dubuque, Iowa: Brown.

Murphree, J. 1975. *When God says you're ok.* Downers Grove: Inter-Varsity.

Nash, M. 1987. What, if anything, is regressed about hypnotic age regression? *Psychological Bulletin* 102: 42–52.

Perls, F. 1969. *Ego, hunger, and aggression: The beginning of gestalt therapy.* New York: Random.

Propst, R. 1987. *Psychotherapy in a religious framework.* New York: Human Sciences.

Rogers, C. 1951. *Client-centered therapy.* Boston: Houghton-Mifflin.

Seamands, D. 1985. *Healing of memories.* Wheaton, Ill.: Victor.

———. 1988. Saturday plenary session. International Congress on Christian Counseling, Atlanta, Ga., Nov. 12.

Walen, S., N. Hauserman, and P. Lavin. 1977. *Clinical guide to behavior therapy.* Baltimore: Williams and Wilkins.

Worthington, E. 1986. Religious counseling. *Journal of Counseling and Development* 64: 421–31.

16

Group and Family Counseling

Group Counseling

Maintaining small face-to-face groups can facilitate the growth and development of many organizations, including the church. One important reason small groups are needed is that many communication problems exist (Balswick and Balswick 1989). Poor communication interferes with good relationships in general; this is why communication often becomes an important emphasis in group counseling.

Why Communication Is Difficult

Communication on intimate levels is difficult to attain in a modern industrial society where productivity is overemphasized and human activity is measured in quantitative terms. For example, workaholics, who must labor compulsively to feel good about themselves, are models of success in much of our culture. This product/ task orientation is a primary factor undermining close relationships.

This product/task orientation also stresses cognitive forms of communication in spite of research indicating that people rarely attend to verbal or cognitive communication alone. As Ralph Waldo Emerson said, "When the eyes say one thing and the tongue another, a practiced man relies on the language of the first." Hence, with a culture largely encouraging a reading of the verbal component of communication but with most individuals reading the nonverbal or body language component, a dichotomy is produced that actually discourages intimacy and open communication. In addition, the rapid expansion of knowledge hinders genuine one-on-one or small-group communication.

How Small Groups Function

Small groups can, by facilitating genuine communication, counter the tendency in our society toward depersonalization. Essentially, small groups provide an environment in which people can practice communicating accurately with each other.

The New Testament reveals the importance of small-group interaction. Christ chose twelve disciples with whom he maintained a close relationship. Later, the first churches met in houses (Snyder 1975, 69), relying on small-group dynamics for encouragement and growth. A recurring concept in the New Testament letters to the earliest churches is that of the church as the body of Christ, growing up with all parts in close communication and dependence on each other. For example, Ephesians 4:15–16 pictures each part of the body preparing for its own unique work of service while contributing to the growth of the whole.

Another important concept is that of the priesthood of all believers. Priests are individuals appointed to represent God's people in matters related to God (Heb. 5:1). Christians are referred to in the New Testament as "a chosen people, a royal priesthood, a holy nation, a people belonging to God" (1 Pet. 2:9). Each believer can minister to another in the relational context of love and unity. Growth occurs when Christians speak the truth in love and build each other up with humility, gentleness, and patience. A properly functioning "growth group" in a church is not simply a Bible study with a discussion tacked on. It is intended to help participants learn, live, and resolve their problems.

A healthy small group can accomplish other goals, of course, including evangelism. Jesus' first concern for his small group of disciples, as shown in John 13:34–35, and 17:22–23, was that unity be expressed in their love and commitment to one another. He knew that such unity would attract people to the gospel message. The twelve disciples passed that pattern on to the first-century church (Acts 4:32–33).

Spotlight 16.1.
Small Groups in the Church

In recent years many churches have begun to use the small-group approach for Bible study, discipleship, changing habits, and developing relationships. Actually small groups have long been with the church in the form of board meetings and Sunday schools. Earlier antecedents include the class meetings of Wesley's time (Snyder 1980; Davies 1984). The early church met in homes, not church buildings. Small groups can be a key to revitalization of the local church.

Perhaps the finest source on small groups in the church is *Getting Together* (1982) by Griffin. He divides such groups into three categories: the task group, the relationship group, and the influence group. A church committee is likely to be a task group, while a group to help church members stop smoking would be an influence group. The relationship group emphasizes the building of Christian community in a small-group setting.

Dozens of books on the topic of small groups in the church exist. Other good resources include *Growth Groups* by Dibbert and Wichern (1985) and *Five Audiences* by Hartman (1987).

Participation in a small group can give an opportunity for self-understanding which may be of more value than the feedback the secular world provides. The warning in Romans 12:3 not to think of ourselves more highly than we ought, but rather to think of ourselves "with sober judgment," is given in a context of the body of Christ and of gifts given to members. To maintain a healthy, accurate self-perspective, we need feedback from an intimate group. Galatians 6:3, which reminds us that it is easy for Christians to deceive themselves, is also set in the context of a group experience. An accurate self-identity is directly related to effective interpersonal communication.

Christians are instructed in such passages as Philippians 2:4–8 and Galatians 6:2 to serve by bearing each other's burdens. We can assume the burdens of another only with an accurate understanding of the personality and needs of that person. The small-group relationship affords opportunities to discover and minister to the needs of others. By contrast, too many churches follow the practice of listing congregational needs on a Wednesday night prayer list or in a bulletin circulated to the whole congregation, with the hope that someone will be motivated enough to pray or take action. Burdened individuals seldom feel touched through a broadcast type of ministry. Small groups can provide a means for local churches to minister to their own people.

Advantages of Group Treatment

Small-group counseling is effective in dealing with psychological problems as well as interpersonal problems. Interpersonal problems have been the major focus of group therapy in the past. For example, individuals with poor social skills have often been helped through group sessions to develop healthier patterns of interaction, to be more vulnerable, and to discuss problems along with giving others encouragement. For such interpersonal development, a small group serves as a laboratory or a workshop of social skills effectiveness.

Psychological problems can be dealt with at the same time as interpersonal problems. Harry Stack Sullivan and other interpersonal theorists indicate that individuals as they manifest themselves in social relationships also reflect the underlying dynamics of their internal function. Hence individuals are apt to display in small-group situations the very problems that occur within themselves. As they continue to deal with those problems within an accepting, supportive, and interpersonal situation, these individuals progress toward becoming whole persons while they are developing healthy interpersonal dynamics.

An important reason for considering a group counseling approach is efficiency. With traditional counseling, one individual to one counselor, twenty persons needing contact would require twenty contacts. Perhaps half of the population in the twenty-to-thirty-year age bracket is undergoing a significant psychological distress. With so much demand for professional counseling, the one-to-one option is simply not realistic for every contact. A group counseling format with one leader or facilitator to six to eight participants provides considerable flexibility and allows more people access to counseling.

In a group situation, individuals are confronted with many novel stimulations or options for their behavior. If that response is acted out in the group, it may be reinforced so that the individual has a greater probability of achieving new behavior. The six or eight models of behavior offered by members of the group make it more likely that new behavior will actually be incorporated into an individual's

---

Spotlight 16.2. Encounter Groups

In the late 1960s and 1970s there was a strong movement toward encounter groups, small groups that sometimes took on therapeutic emphases. Generally such groups, which still exist on some campuses, emphasized utter honesty and intimate relationships with other group members. Similar groups can be found in many metropolitan areas today.

Are such groups beneficial? They may help people share more, but they can also be dangerous. Some may not be able to cope with the utter honesty required. Sometimes participants verbally attack one another or apply artificial labels to other group members. Any positive consequences from such groups may be short-lived.

One of the authors of this text participated in an encounter group during his college years. The participants were all Christians and nearly all were psychology or sociology majors. We met once a week in a professor's apartment and looked forward to those times when we could be totally open with one another. There were times when someone would have a new insight accompanied by crying and warm expressions of affection. The Bible was central to the discussions, and a strong bond of Christian love permeated the group.

One member of the group also participated in a secular encounter group at a nearby university. She reported that there was extreme verbal abuse in her group, including insults and obscenities. From her account, the purpose of the group appeared to be tearing down one another which would supposedly be followed by the development of a more realistic self.

Encounter groups and their contemporary equivalents may be positive or negative. If you decide to participate in such a group, be sure to follow the guidelines noted in spotlight 16.3.

---

lifestyle. Thus, although a one-on-one situation is more confidential, a group situation is better able to provide novel behavior for individuals to draw on for their own lives.

A small group also offers the advantage of catharsis of emotions. In Western culture the importance of discharge of affect or feeling has been deemphasized. Males in our culture are encouraged to deny feelings and to rechannel them into "productive outlets." Females are discouraged from being honest or genuine in their emotions, which often leads to hysterical or otherwise inappropriate releases for emotions. Inexperience with appropriate expressions of feelings produces a lack of intimacy between persons, including spouses. A group counseling format can reduce the fear of expressing feelings and offer retraining in appropriate emotional expression.

Effective Group Leadership

The leader in a group counseling situation should demonstrate certain characteristics, foremost among them being mental healthiness. Preferably, leaders themselves should have experienced group therapy and be trained in leadership of small groups.

Leaders should take the role of facilitators, moving the group from a traditionally structured learning orientation toward a process-learning orientation (see tab. 16.1).

In traditional learning, roles are precisely defined: leaders are the teachers or sources of information while listeners are the students. Leaders are seen as authorities who must have respect and cannot be anything but experts. The learning in such situations is usually based on respect for the authority of the leaders, that is, on how well they demonstrate their knowledge of the material and on their ability to provide answers. Often the leaders respond on the basis of abstract information not gained within the context of the group.

In contrast, facilitators should be process-oriented leaders whose role is to facilitate the networks of relationships developed as a result of the interaction of the participants. A leader can be a learner and the learners can be leaders. The leader's primary function is to provide a continual focus on the problems at hand rather than becoming abstract. The leader should formulate problems and facilitate problem formulation but does not have to be an expert. The leader does not have to provide the answers. Commitment to the group is taken as commitment to the learning process. Participants develop problem-solving skills and standards for their own solutions.

In a process-learning group participants should generally be oriented around a desire to explore and develop their own problem-solving mechanisms. In traditional learning, where members work with what is external and abstract, they try to

---

Table 16.1
Traditional versus Process Learning

Traditional Learning	Process Learning
Roles are precisely defined. Leaders teach; members listen and learn.	Roles are determined by involvement and interaction. Leaders can be learners; members can be teachers.
The leader is "the authority." He must be an "expert" and command the respect of members. He provides all of the "answers." Learning is based on his authority, knowledge, and command of content (information).	The leader helps to formulate problems and assists in the development of problem-solving skills. He helps others "learn how to learn." Learning is based on each member's commitment/involvement in the learning process. Each member develops personal problem-solving skills.
Members work with external and abstract data (content) provided by the leader. The leader defines what needs to be learned.	Members work with external and internal data. Members determine what they need to learn. Members consult the leader for assistance.
Members seek to know themselves by measuring themselves against an ideal type. They are externally oriented to performing for the expectations of others.	Members seek to know themselves by the choices they make, the relationships they enter, and the knowledge they seek. They are internally oriented and establish their own performance standards.
Major learning problems involve the accumulation and storage of external information, and the acquisition of "right answers." Motivation is difficult, and memory difficulties destroy effectiveness.	Major learning problems involve communication (increasing understanding), involvement (participation), and transparency (vulnerability). The emphasis on developing problem-solving skills maintains motivation to learn and acquire relevant knowledge.

gain as much as possible from the leader, who defines what should be learned. Rather than finding themselves through the time spent in the group, participants measure themselves against the leader as an ideal type, and are oriented toward performing to meet the leader's expectations. In traditional learning formats, students face the problem of how to store and utilize information provided by an expert. Often they feel a need to be perfect and fulfill the expert's expectations. Motivation becomes a problem and a student may forget much of the material learned during traditional sessions.

Most of the material conveyed in a classroom, if not rehearsed, is lost within one or two days. In a traditional learning situation, therefore, it is important continually to go over what has been provided by the expert. "Experts" seldom take the memory-decay factor into consideration and tend to provide more abstract material than people are capable of accumulating or storing.

In a process-group context, participants work with both what is external and what is internal. That is, they define their own educational needs and develop their own learning methods. The group leader, as a facilitator, helps to focus the members' definitions of their own goals. Some people who come for counseling are fearful and may seek a strong, traditional leader. Assessing potential group members may require an evaluation of their motivation to work on their problems. The more motivated they are to solve their own problems, the more likely they are to make behavioral changes. Good prospects for a group are those who seek to know themselves through the choices they make, the relationships they enter into, and the knowledge they seek.

Each individual's responsibility for personal choices is emphasized throughout the Bible. A small group functions as a realm in which individual members can become more responsible for their choices and understand more fully why they make certain choices. Participants should be encouraged to set their own performance standards. The more individuals grow in areas of vulnerability, communication, and participation, the more they develop problem-solving abilities applicable outside the group.

Stages of Group Function

Group processes generally go through four stages.[1] The first stage is one of negotiation of goals and values within the group. In one to four sessions the participants usually can evaluate the level of participation, the style of communication, and the degree of vulnerability they want. During those first sessions, the group leader must develop an atmosphere of openness, genuine communication, and warmth. The group leader may choose to begin the first session with a brief personal history, oriented primarily around "here-and-now" facts. Abstract facts are less appropriate than issues with which the leader is dealing at the current time. Then each group member should be asked to discuss personal history during the next one or two sessions. The second and third sessions usually include some discussion about goals that the group might set. The facilitator should not serve as the expert in setting goals even if the group wants expert input. Rather, members of the group should discuss and select the goals.

During the first stage a junior leader may emerge. The signal of a change to the second stage of group function is usually characterized by sharper discussion among group members as to who will be the junior leader. This stage is often

---

1. See Griffin 1982; Dibbert and Wichern 1985 for slightly different analyses of the process.

termed the conflict stage, during which some anger toward the leader surfaces as the group begins to confront the issue of how vulnerable to each other they will be. One hears a number of questions at this stage: "What will I really get out of this group?" "How well can I get to know you in ten weeks?" "How well can I get to know you since we will be students here for only four years?" Such questions indicate that the goals have been negotiated, but now the individual members must take responsibility for how much they will invest and how vulnerable they will be.

In the conflict stage the message should be communicated that the group leader is there to help each person work through problems and solve them more effectively. If the group leader can communicate that message, the group will progress to the third stage. If not, the group will remain in the conflict stage and seldom make progress beyond a trading of expert, abstract knowledge.

The third stage of group function is the resolution or growth stage. By this time the group facilitator can often take a back seat to the group. The leader's primary role continues to be helping individual members analyze their own communication styles. A wise leader will not be overly active, but rather will allow group members to develop skills of encouraging each other and being genuine in relationships. Since groups often suggest that they should have a party, the stage of resolution has sometimes been called the "party" stage. But having a party or extragroup activities can adversely affect group function.

The group resolution phase generally leads to an anticipation of the group's ending, which initiates the termination phase. During this final phase, group members must deal with separation and the anxieties separation may involve. Will they continue as a group? Will they meet again? How will they continue to know each other? How will they deal with loss of the valuable relationships gained during the group meetings? In this stage the leader should not provide assurances or false promises. There should be a meaningful balance of dealing with the anxiety plus recalling the warmth that each group member has felt during the period. But there should be no false hope that the group or individual relationships will somehow continue in the leader's absence.

Dynamics of Change in Groups

For most groups of eight to ten people the best setting is a small room no larger than fourteen by fourteen feet. For a beginning group leader, a smaller group of perhaps only six might be better. The setting should be informal, with people sitting on the floor or in comfortable chairs. The room should not be open to passersby or other disruptive influences; individuals in the group must be able to communicate freely in an atmosphere of confidentiality.

Generally group sessions should last no longer than ninety minutes and no less than sixty minutes. Sometimes it is difficult to get group members to move into appropriate group function. A ninety-minute period seems to offer the greatest flexibility.

Two important rules govern the group process. The first rule, having to do with confidentiality, should always be discussed during the first session. The group leader should lay down the rule that all material presented in the group must stay in the group. Group members may practice skills learned within the group but they are not to discuss or talk about group members outside of the group. Further, group members should not discuss group matters outside of the group.

The second rule concerns regularity of attendance. If group members are to bene-

> ## Spotlight 16.3.
> ## Small Group Guidelines
>
> The perspective of this chapter is quite consistent with Rogers' (1970) use of small groups for therapeutic purposes. However, there are some dangers in small groups that should be recognized (Back 1972). These dangers can be minimized when certain guidelines are followed:
>
> 1. Avoid labeling behavior and people. Labeling changes people's perceptions of others and themselves and may actually make genuine self-expression less likely.
> 2. Make verbal participation voluntary for group members. Never coerce others into talking about a topic.
> 3. Make sure the group has a good leader who is able to take charge if things get out of control.
> 4. Maintain confidentiality. Free expression should be encouraged in the group, but what is discussed should not go outside the group. This requires mature members.
> 5. Avoid embarrassment and putting people on the spot. Be kind in your honesty.
> 6. Only include people who are emotionally balanced. Those who have severe emotional problems require professional counseling and perhaps group counseling with other emotionally disturbed people.
> 7. Keep the group spiritually based. Make regular use of Bible study and prayer.

fit, each individual member must make a commitment to be at the meetings consistently. Probably no more than two absences should be allowed for every ten sessions. Regularity depends on commitment. The issue of commitment is usually dealt with during negotiation of rules.

It is usually suggested that when members must miss a meeting, they contact another group member or the leader at least twenty-four hours in advance to explain why they cannot attend. In a group that lasts as long as ten or more meetings, any individuals who must drop out should give notice at least two sessions before leaving the group. Advance notice allows the whole group to deal with any anger or conflict. Frequently individuals come into conflict with one another but should not leave a group session with the conflict unresolved. If individuals are allowed to drop out of the group without returning to deal with the conflict, all the members suffer.

Conflict often arises when individuals are resistant to insight about communication or participation. Another source of conflict is a defensive relationship, in which the beliefs, attitudes, or values of one individual are projected onto another. Such conflicts lead to confrontations. It is important that the confrontations occur, because they facilitate growth and development. Hence the group leader should be capable of modeling an appropriate style of confrontation within a caring context. Anger, especially uncontrolled, explosive anger, has no place in a group session. In so-called encounter groups, many individuals have been hurt by the unwise expression of anger. An important task of the group leader is to monitor and manage anger within the group.

During the first three sessions it is important for the leader to model skills of listening, empathy, and encouragement while working on the development of these skills within the group members. One way to do that is to ask the group members to evaluate their own style of communicating, noting such points as body language, tone of voice, modulation and rapidity of speech, and eye contact with other group members.

The leader might also call attention to whether certain individuals dominate the discussion group or sit passively and quietly. Commenting about individual styles within the group may provide certain signals important in facilitating group function. Such communication, evaluation, and participation during the first sessions allow individual members to formulate their own goals. Members may not be aware of their tendency to take responsibility for other group members, particularly to defend another group member when they themselves are identifying with the reason that individual has been confronted.

Generally, when good listening skills, empathy, and encouragement are present, a group will be in a "here-and-now" mode. The individual members tend to relate their own experience to what is happening at that particular moment in the group. Often such a response is indicated by an "I-feel" statement. The individual is talking about the problem that the group is currently working on. "There-and-then" statements are apt to be abstractions and represent defensiveness, which prevent a group from working. When individuals are quoting material from authorities, they seldom relate it to the work that the group is currently doing. If during the early sessions the leader fails to provide "here-and-now" modeling, but rather continues to quote experts and provide "there-and-then" information, the group may never emerge from the conflict stage. Participation in such a group may be a very frustrating experience for the members.

Within any group, some individuals will have an external orientation; that is, they believe that trustworthy knowledge is external to themselves and must be objective. Such individuals frequently like to quote the experts and usually want an expert to lead their group. They are attracted to name personalities and are apt to pay little attention to their own feelings or to the feelings of those around them. They are often excellent candidates for learning interpersonal skills through group counseling. They are very difficult to work with, however, because of their extreme demand for external information and "there-and-then" function. In contrast, internal-oriented individuals tend to believe that knowledge is gained by balanced evaluation of objective facts and internal experience. Hence they are apt to be aware of some of their own feelings and attitudes and feel good about using them as sources for action and judgment. They have a healthy self-concept or self-esteem, but may have particular areas they would like to work on.

For healthy group function, groups should be balanced between those individuals with an external orientation and those with an internal orientation. A leader can always check the "here-and-now" functioning by asking the group, "What are we doing now?"

Premarital Counseling

Whom Should a Christian Marry?

Christians should consider several principles in deciding whom to marry.

Spotlight 16.4.
A Premarital Counseling Inventory

The Scripture may be used profitably in every form of counseling, including preparation for marriage. Because the Word of God has been a source of understanding, behavior change, and decision making for centuries, its importance in premarital counseling is not to be underestimated.

In my marriage counseling I have found the suggested inventory helpful in isolating a number of key factors which allow couples to gain insight into the realistic demands of marriage as well as to estimate the maturity of prospective mates. Too often couples enter into marriage without objective assessment of each other since the roles of the relationship before marriage are so different from those required afterward. Using the Bible as the basis for such an assessment helps to assure one that his insight is reality-based rather than the kind of superficial "starry eyed" understanding with which too many individuals, even Christians, begin marriage.

This inventory is taken from Proverbs, a book rich in wisdom and insight into many kinds of human problems. Proverbs contains statements on a wide variety of human relationships, and many such inventories could be developed on a number of topics. Since an important goal of prenuptial counseling is objectifying the demands of marriage, this kind of inventory is particularly valuable.

Proverbs 31:10–31 should be read and discussed verse by verse by the counselor and counselees as they take the inventory. Preferably a recent translation should be used. A separate inventory should be completed by each counselee, evaluating both the prospective mate and self in these marriage-related activities. This should occur with discussion limited first to the meaning of the question and then to the actual responses when the inventory is completed by both.

After the prospective husband and wife have finished, the results may be compared and discussed. Since the text speaks of the wife's role, the wife's self-evaluation and the husband's evaluation of his wife-to-be might be compared first. Afterward, the two evaluations of the husband-to-be can be compared and discussed. The counselor especially will want to determine the *basis* for the decision on each characteristic; that is, both may feel one has a noble character, but what specific evidence caused each to assume that such noble character exists? If a lack is indicated in a characteristic, the counselor could discuss how that lack would surface within the marriage relationship.

Differences between evaluations should be noted, particularly for consistently low self-evaluations and consistently high evaluations of the future spouse. The complementary effects of a lack in one spouse and presence in the other also might be considered, although differences might suggest areas of future conflict. These should be discussed, with emphasis upon long-range relationships and how these differences in evaluations could affect the marriage over the years.

This particular form is not, of course, exhaustive of biblical content regarding marriage but can be a good beginning for further biblical analysis of the marital partners. Additional items from other passages might be added, although these might be considered more informally after the initial assessment. Some verses on subjects such as divorce and remarriage should be phrased according to the counselor's biblical understanding of these issues. After considering the verses in Proverbs, the couple generally will understand the approach and continue the assessment with other verses without need of formal test items.

The Desirable Husband or Wife		Does Future Mate Have This Quality?			Do I Have This Quality?		
verse	quality	usually	some-times	rarely	usually	some-times	rarely
10	noble character	☐	☐	☐	☐	☐	☐
10	seen as worth a great deal by spouse	☐	☐	☐	☐	☐	☐
11	fully trustworthy	☐	☐	☐	☐	☐	☐
12	brings best out of spouse	☐	☐	☐	☐	☐	☐
12	willing to help spouse for the rest of life	☐	☐	☐	☐	☐	☐
13	works with hands around house	☐	☐	☐	☐	☐	☐
14	willing to sacrifice for family	☐	☐	☐	☐	☐	☐
15	willing to rise early (for example, to feed baby)	☐	☐	☐	☐	☐	☐
16	spends money wisely	☐	☐	☐	☐	☐	☐
17	a hard worker	☐	☐	☐	☐	☐	☐
17	does his/her best	☐	☐	☐	☐	☐	☐
18	plans ahead for possible problems	☐	☐	☐	☐	☐	☐
19	happy with being own sex	☐	☐	☐	☐	☐	☐
20	generous to needy, not self-centered	☐	☐	☐	☐	☐	☐
21	able to provide comfort for family	☐	☐	☐	☐	☐	☐
23	builds up spouse, not tearing down the other	☐	☐	☐	☐	☐	☐
24	able to support family in case of death of spouse	☐	☐	☐	☐	☐	☐
25	has dignity	☐	☐	☐	☐	☐	☐
25	basically happy	☐	☐	☐	☐	☐	☐
28	praises accomplishments of spouse	☐	☐	☐	☐	☐	☐
30	fully devoted to God	☐	☐	☐	☐	☐	☐
31	receives praise from family and others	☐	☐	☐	☐	☐	☐

Marry a growing Christian. The New Testament warns against being "yoked together" with unbelievers (2 Cor. 6:14). Less marital conflicts can be expected in a marriage where the husband and wife are mature believers.

Marry someone who treats others with respect. Observing how a person treats the parent of the opposite sex, for example, gives clues of future behavior as a mate.

Marry someone who is not overly critical. "Why do you look at the speck of sawdust in your brother's eye and pay no attention to the plank in your own eye? How can you say to your brother, 'Let me take the speck out of your eye,' when all the time there is a plank in your own eye? You hypocrite, first take the plank out of your own eye, and then you will see clearly to remove the speck from your brother's eye" (Matt. 7:3–5).

Marry someone who has conquered sensual and materialistic drives. "Dear friends, I urge you, as aliens and strangers in the world, to abstain from sinful desires, which war against your soul" (1 Pet. 2:11). Lust wars against the mind, emotions, and will, making us weak and unstable. Another drive that needs to be conquered is a focus on material things. "No one can serve two masters. Either he will hate the one and love the other, or he will be devoted to the one and despise the other. You cannot serve both God and Money" (Matt. 6:24). A Christian should marry someone who no longer has sensual or material objectives as a central focus, but rather a focus on Christ.

Marry someone who agrees with you on biblical husband/wife roles within the marriage.

Suggestions for Counselors

Examine the couple's degree of commitment to God and to each other. Decisions need to be made on the basis of commitment, not emotions. Commitment means being willing to accept each other, recognizing that no one is perfect. Such commitment is not based on physical attraction or even tender affection (Gk. *phileō*), but on love which comes from God himself (Gk. *agapē*). Such love seeks the welfare of others, works no ill, and seeks opportunities to do good.

Help couples contemplating marriage to learn good techniques for communication. To listen during conflicts, to acknowledge a degree of truth in complaints, and to state one's own case in an adult, tactful manner should be learned before marriage.

Encourage couples to build a strong foundation on the Bible. Spiritual maturity produces stable marriages and the Bible gives a couple a common basis for decision making. It can serve as a "higher court" when disagreements do arise. Good materials are available for Bible studies on marriage-related topics.

Provide information on sexual matters. Many couples need to learn sexual anatomy and physiology, birth control methods, and good love-making techniques in marriage. Few realize that satisfying sexual contact starts hours before intercourse itself with a good attitude. Men may need to be reminded of the importance of such simple things as being clean and clean-shaven, while women may need

---

Spotlight 16.5.
Communication in Marriage

Couples may be married for years but have never learned to communicate their feelings. Sometimes they can communicate how they feel about their mate to a third party, such as a friend, pastor, or psychiatrist, but they have tremendous difficulty communicating their feelings to each other face to face.

When a husband and wife come to my office for conjoint therapy, they consistently tell me (rather than their mate) how they feel about each other. At this point I ask the communicating mate to turn to the other person and express the feeling directly.

Many of the couples I have counseled have told me that the forty-five minutes in my office is the only forty-five minutes during the week that they are able to communicate honestly with each other. But the longer they are in therapy, the more they learn to communicate intimately and honestly at home.

In the first few sessions of marriage counseling I usually confront and direct them, but the longer a couple is in therapy, the more I can just sit back and observe them doing therapy on each other. I only need to add occasional interjections to bring something to their awareness that they have missed.

Some couples who have been sexually impotent for months regain their sexual function after six months or so of communication therapy—even if the subject of sex seldom comes up. Sexual function is a symptom of a couple's verbal communication ability, emotional intimacy, and spiritual closeness. Many times an improved spiritual relationship with God also seems to improve a couple's sexual intimacy.

to know about artificial lubricants. It may be helpful to warn a couple of some of the common sexual problems in marriage, such as premature ejaculation, impotence, or orgiastic dysfunction.

Marriage and Family Counseling

In 1860, only one in every thousand marriages ended in divorce each year. Today, approximately one in fifty end in divorce (Rascheke 1987; Cherlin 1989). Overall about one-third of marriages end in divorce (Balswick and Balswick 1989, 261). At a typical counseling center, half of those coming for counseling come primarily because of marital conflicts and another one-quarter come because of marital-related conflicts. It is estimated that over 20 million couples in the United States are unhappy and unfulfilled.

The Bible presents a strong case for sexual fidelity in marriage. Many Christians regard such passages as Ephesians 5:23–24 as a biblical basis for maintaining clearly defined sex roles in marriage. The Bible definitely regards the family as a divine institution. Like the church, which will prevail because God ordained that it should do so, the family is likely to endure in spite of many pressures.

The existence of such pressures has produced a serious need for marriage and family counseling. The American Association of Marriage and Family Counseling has greatly increased in membership in recent years, and more psychiatrists and psychologists have been entering the field. Many medical schools in the United States offer courses in family and marital counseling. Within the major secular approaches to psychology, such as transactional analysis, reality therapy, behavior modification, gestalt therapy, and even psychoanalysis, psychiatrists have become more interested in family counseling. Journals focusing attention on this area

include the *Journal of Marriage and the Family,* the *Family Coordinator, Family Process,* and the *Journal of Marriage and Family Counseling.*

Christian counselors have always tried to help individuals apply biblical principles to their lives so that they can experience improved marital and family relationships. Evangelical pastoral counselors do most of the premarital counseling in America today and in addition often help couples through what they say from the pulpit. Christian professionals (psychiatrists, psychologists, and counselors) are increasingly called on by Christians experiencing marital difficulties. Bill Gothard and the Christian Family Life seminars have also helped many individuals who are experiencing marital difficulties.

The Functions of a Healthy Family

Families fulfill a number of important functions. First of all, within a family needs for affection are met. For husbands and wives the family also provides an appropriate means of satisfying sexual needs. Another function obviously is child bearing and rearing. A family also serves as an efficient economic unit. Finally, the family is a smaller arena where religious, philosophical, and social ideas and practices are taught and tested. In a well-adjusted family, the adults are reasonably healthy mentally and able to agree or disagree constructively. Discipline is appropriate and avoids extremes. Material needs are met. Communication is open and the roles of individuals are well defined.

Most healthy marriages function effectively in three critical dimensions. Power is the first area to be clarified: who is in charge and how that person functions are issues important to family health. Intimacy is another area that needs definition. Changes in emotional and geographic distance are significant as family members

---

Spotlight 16.6. Norman Wright on Marriage Counseling

H. Norman Wright, a teacher at Biola College and Talbot Seminary, has authored scores of books on marriage and family relationships and offered workshops nationwide. In one of his books (1979, 14–19) he considers the five levels of intimacy described below, in greater detail.

Two key books provide an overview of Wright's approach and should be on every Christian counselor's bookshelf. In *Marital Counseling* (1981), he outlines a detailed summary of his basic counseling strategy, which combines behavioral and cognitive techniques with a biblical perspective. *Premarital Counseling* (1981) gives a comprehensive overview of how Wright does this kind of counseling in his church. His approach incorporates group counseling, large amounts of reading, and personal counseling.

---

struggle with their need for and fear of closeness. A third area to consider could be termed inclusion-exclusion, having to do with relationships with in-laws, friends, and coworkers. In healthy relationships the solutions are not static but constantly changing to meet the needs of the family at different stages.

Five characteristics are consistently found in mentally healthy families. Children in homes where the following qualities exist generally develop into happy, mature, emotionally and spiritually whole adults.[2]

1. *Love.* Parents express genuine love and affection for each other and their children.
2. *Discipline.* Discipline is considered essential; it is fair, quick, and to the point.
3. *Consistency.* Parents consistently enforce rules.
4. *Example.* Parents live up to the standards that they expect their children to observe.
5. *Authority.* Parental authority is es-

2. These characteristics are elaborated in Meier 1977, 81–90.

tablished and respected and the husband has the final authority in the home.

Marital Classification

Marriages may be compared on the basis of several criteria. Marriages classified by the level of intimacy include the conflict-habituated marriage, the devitalized marriage, the passive-congenial marriage, the vital relationship, and the total marriage (Cuber and Haroff 1963). A conflict-habituated marriage is held together largely by fear of loneliness, but may also be held together by conflict. A devitalized marriage is often held together by the children; although free of a lot of overt conflict, it is devoid of zest. A passive-congenial marriage is a "pleasant marriage" with some sharing of interests but without much intimacy; most of the interests of each individual center outside of the marriage. In the vital type of relationship at least one major area is of common interest or at least one major goal is pursued in common. Finally, in a total marriage, most of the interests, activities, and goals are pursued in common.

Another way to classify marriage is by

personality style. Individuals usually marry someone who meets not only certain conscious requirements but certain subconscious requirements as well. For example, a man with a lot of obsessive-compulsive traits may marry a woman with hysterical traits because she helps him to enjoy life. He may not be aware of that motivation, but just knows that he likes her. Or a depressive with masochistic traits may be drawn to a paranoid with sadistic traits, though unaware of a subconscious need to be hurt.

Goals and Roles

In individual marital counseling only one member of a couple comes in for counseling, hoping to find healthier ways to cope. In collaborative marital counseling the husband and wife see different counselors. The counselors may get together at times to discuss the case. In concurrent marital counseling one counselor sees both husband and wife but at separate times. In conjoint and combined marital counseling both partners are separately seen at times by one counselor, but they are also seen together.

GOALS OF MARRIAGE COUNSELING

The goals of family counseling are as follows:

1. To resolve interpersonal conflicts and to help a couple agree or disagree constructively. To improve communication.
2. To encourage each individual to meet the emotional needs of the mate.
3. To clarify role relations.
4. To build Christian values in the family.
5. To strengthen the ability of each member to cope in a healthy manner with stresses (from within or without).

ROLES OF MARRIAGE COUNSELORS

The roles of marriage counselors could be listed as follows:

1. They stimulate healthy interactions.
2. They serve as observers.
3. They participate in the family interactions.
4. They help to temper the destructive features of conflicts. They encourage sympathy. They help couples realize that they are on the same team, so to speak.
5. They help couples see the real conflicts. They challenge denials and rationalizations. They point out games that have become destructive such as See What You Made Me Do, If It Weren't for You, Look How Hard I've Tried, Ain't It Awful, I'm Only Trying To Help You, Poor Me, and Kick Me. Counselors need to be careful lest couples involve them in such games as Courtroom, as each one tries to win the counselor to their side.
6. They are educators at times.
7. They should be examples of mental health.

Special Problems in Marriage Counseling

Common problems for which couples come for counsel include role conflicts, financial problems, sexual problems, in-law conflicts, and child-rearing problems. A Christian marriage counselor may need to help a couple better understand scriptural role differences between husband and wife. A healthy marriage is one in which there are clear role definitions but also much flexibility. Marriage counselors often need to educate couples to help them deal with a sexual conflict. They may need to help a newlywed couple realize that good love making is a slowly learned process.

Spotlight 16.7. Qualities Essential in a Christian Counselor

An accepting attitude. For persons seeking advice, an attitude of unconditional acceptance on the part of the counselor is essential. An effective counselor understands that problems are normal, and are among the means God uses to conform us to his image. People grow when they are accepted unconditionally.

Good listening skills. Effective counselors listen with interest, showing warmth in their expression and manner. Without interrupting they allow their counselees to finish sharing what they perceive their problems to be before helping them to gain insight.

Knowledge of proper technique. Effective counselors know the proper approach and the appropriate time to use it. At times a probing question will be received when a direct statement would be rejected. At other times it is important to be direct and confrontational.

Appropriate use of Scripture and prayer. A godly counselor knows the proper time and technique for using Scripture. After rapport is established, it can be extremely beneficial to point to Scripture appropriate to a particular problem. Counselees often benefit from meditation on the Word and from prayer at an appropriate time.

Personal approach. According to Glasser (1965) most people who need psychological help have been unable to fulfill two basic needs in life: love and self-worth. A warm, personal, caring counselor can help supply these needs. Individuals who sense that a counselor is personally interested in them and their problems are able to be more open and honest.

Unshockable response. Effective counselors are not shocked by anything people tell them. Counselees must feel free to share their problems and guilt. If a counselor were shocked by such confessions, people would be afraid to share intimately and thus be prevented from dealing with their problems. Christ was not shocked by what people said because "he knew what was in a man" (John 2:25). When responding to the Samaritan woman at the well, for example, he was not shocked about her past but dealt with her in a straightforward and effective manner (John 4).

Confidence. Effective Christian counselors have confidence in Christ, in their ability through Christ, and in what Christ can accomplish in someone else. Counselors should offer people realistic hope that they can be helped. "So do not throw away your confidence; it will be richly rewarded. You need to persevere so that when you have done the will of God, you will receive what he has promised" (Heb. 10:35–36).

Sense of humor. Because counselors deal with many serious problems on a daily basis, a sense of humor is necessary for their personal release. An effective counselor often encourages a sense of humor in others. Obsessive-compulsive individuals, for example, can be helped by learning to laugh at their perfectionistic attempts.

They may need to help couples work through financial problems due to poor planning and budgeting, or child-rearing problems due to differences in parenting in the homes in which husband and wife were reared.

Special problems may be encountered. A marriage counselor may eventually realize that a sadomasochistic couple is actually happy being unhappy and probably will not change. In what might be called the "alcoholic wife syndrome," a woman

Spotlight 16.8. Case Study: When Love Is Gone

A twenty-nine-year-old woman, whom I will call June, came to see me at my office and spent our first forty-five-minute session talking about her husband. He had been reared by a domineering, overprotective mother and a weak, passive father (which is the case in many mental illnesses). His mother had spoiled him all his life, giving him everything he wanted. She had also done most of his thinking for him, so that he had developed a very passive and dependent personality. He had been married previously and this was his second marriage. He was drinking quite a bit, smoking pot with great regularity, and skipping work (calling in "sick") at least one day a week. He was spending nearly all of his free time "with the boys," almost totally ignoring his wife.

His wife sat in my office, telling me that unless I could dramatically change him within the next few weeks she was going to divorce him. I was supposed to accomplish this in spite of the fact that he had refused to come in with her for sessions.

In reality, there are only three choices for any person involved in an unhappy marriage: (1) get a divorce—by far the most immature choice; (2) tough out the marriage without working to improve it—another immature decision but not quite as irresponsible as divorce; and (3) maturely face up to personal hangups and choose to build an intimate marriage out of the existing one—the only really mature choice to make.

June was fairly certain that she should divorce her husband because she did not love him any more. I asked her if she would be willing to act like she loved him for a couple of weeks to see if the feeling would follow. She agreed to try it. She even came up with some good ideas about how she would go about it.

In individual sessions we dealt with some of her own problems. I was not surprised to find out that she was very similar in personality to her husband's domineering mother. She personally thought of ways to turn the leadership in the home back over to her husband. She acted as though she trusted him to handle the finances (even though she really did not).

To her amazement, within a week she started to regain her love for her husband. He responded to her changed attitude toward him by actually becoming more responsible. He even requested to come with her to her therapy sessions.

I saw them together (which is the only good way to do marriage counseling) once a week from then on for a period of several months. After several sessions of open, three-way discussion, June's husband became bitterly aware of the fact that he was an overgrown, spoiled child who was married to a substitute mother—and he wept. But from that awareness came genuine growth, as he assumed adult responsibilities for the first time and as June relinquished her mothering instincts toward him.

Both of them learned to get in touch with angry feelings and to talk them out with each other rather than to allow their anger to accumulate inside until they acted it out immaturely. I taught them the principle found in Ephesians 4:26: "'In your anger do not sin': Do not let the sun go down while you are still angry." Married couples should never go to bed at night with angry feelings still pent up inside. They need to sit down and talk things out calmly and openly. It promotes real trust and unity.

I cannot take the credit for inventing the technique of restoring love by acting as if you love someone. It is a technique that God himself uses in Revelation 2:4–5. In this passage of Scripture, Christ compliments the local church at Ephesus for several things, but then tells them that he holds something against them: they have forsaken their first love.

Christ then shares with them three steps that will enable them to rediscover the original love for him that they lost: (1) *"Remember* the height from which you have fallen." Christ wants them to remember what it was like when they were intimately in love with him. (2) *"Repent."* Christ asks them to *choose* to love him intimately again. (3) *"Do the things you did at first."* Christ suggests they do the things they had done when they were intimately in love with him. He knows that the feeling of love will follow if they only act as they did when they loved him earlier.

June seemed to be headed for divorce when I saw her for the first time in my office. Six months after termination of therapy, I received a letter from the couple thanking me for helping them build an intimate marriage out of apparent disaster.

may have a history of having been married to several alcoholics. If her mate stops drinking she may even divorce him and then marry another alcoholic. Consciously she may repeatedly criticize her husband while subconsciously wanting to be married to an alcoholic who mistreats her.

A problem often seen is a lack of balance between dependence and independence. Another special problem centers around confession. How much should a couple tell each other about past sins? No answer to that question is automatically right or wrong, but a counselor can help explore possible subconscious motives (such as a need to hurt the mate) behind the desire to confess.

Suggestions for Marriage Counselors

When a couple comes in for marriage counseling, establish what their objectives are in the first session. Counselors must be realistic in the objectives they try to help a couple reach.

Make it clear that each spouse must assume responsibility for changing self, not for trying to change the other person.

Help couples to communicate better. Couples should be taught first of all to listen to each other, then to recognize elements of truth in what the other person says. An accusation may not be totally true but will usually contain a degree of truth. After listening and recognizing a degree of truth in an accusing statement, the individual should be encouraged to state how he or she sees the situation.

Help couples to grow in Christ and in his love. Without Christ a couple even through counseling may be gaining more "weapons" with which to argue. Growing in Christ can make individuals less selfish and thus resolve many marriage problems automatically. What is it like to live with a person whose personality is characterized by love, joy, peace, patience, kindness, goodness, faithfulness, gentleness, and self-control? The fruit of the Spirit are character traits that result from knowing Christ and growing in him.

Finally, experiment with various techniques. For example, it may be helpful to have both individuals write down what they like and dislike about their mate and then share their lists. Or it may be helpful to have both individuals make a list of their mate's needs and how they can help meet those needs, or to make a list of their own needs and how those needs can be met. Or have a couple share with each other why they feel the other is their perfect completion, or what is their biggest concern or worry in life. It is often helpful to teach couples to use "I" statements rather than "you" (accusing) statements, to use statements that reflect feelings (as "I felt hurt when . . ."), to stick to the present, to attack behavior rather than character, to discuss only one issue at a time, to deal with conflicts promptly, or to speak in an adult manner (controlling aggressive emotions and behavior).

Ethics in Counseling and Therapy

There has been an increased concern in recent years with the issue of ethics in the practice of counseling and therapy. Some popular movies portray male psychologists who are sexually involved with their female clients. Although this is certainly an ethical issue, such incidents are probably rare. There are other ethical concerns that are more likely to affect the Christian counselor. For example, details of a particular counseling situation should remain confidential.

McLemore (1985, 720–22) notes that ethics is an area of philosophy, and thus psychotherapy is at least as much encouraging a client to adopt certain philosophical assumptions as it is using a scientific process. By its very nature, this philoso-

Spotlight 16.9. Some Biblical Examples of Good Counseling

One way to learn to be a good counselor is to study examples found in Scripture. Solomon comes to mind immediately. The Book of Proverbs, with which Solomon is intimately associated, contains many of God's thoughts on counseling. Its wealth of wisdom for Christian counselors covers topics such as the cultivation of wisdom and rules for child development and mental health. Solomon's therapeutic approach was directive because his counsel agreed with the counsel of God.

In the New Testament, Paul is an example of a wise counselor. One can see in his writings to early Christians some of the ideas later developed by Freud. Freud's id roughly corresponds to what Christians call the "old nature." Freud's superego corresponds roughly to the conscience. The ego corresponds to the will. In one passage Paul writes: "May your whole spirit, soul and body be kept blameless" (1 Thess. 5:23). He refers to the body, soul (mind, emotions, and will), spirit, flesh, a good but weak law of the mind, an evil law of the members, a supreme law of the Spirit, an eternal deadening law, and how all those factors interrelate.

Jesus Christ, of course, was the Counselor of counselors. We can all learn from him, because he had perfect insight into human problems and was able to share that insight with others. He was an expert at asking questions, using them to teach, to rebuke irresponsible behavior, and to help others gain insight. He genuinely cared for others, giving them a feeling of self-worth. Because of his warm and personal concern for them, people were able to deal with their problems and not feel threatened. He could be matter-of-fact, rebuking, or friendly, as appropriate.

Jesus Christ could counsel others because of his close relationship with God the Father and because he understood human problems. He not only knew what people needed to do to deal with their problems, but also knew how to motivate people to change. Often he would lay down guidelines or formulate a plan to help individuals deal with their problems.

Christ was a master counselor with perfect balance. He knew when to be directive and when to be suggestive. He knew when to deal with the past and when to deal with the present. He knew the importance of feelings, but he also knew how to effect behavioral changes.

phizing is subjective and beyond scientific validation. For the Christian, biblical and theological concerns influence the philosophy imposed upon the client.

One ethical concern underscored by McLemore is the subtle coercion that takes place within the counseling context. To what extent is the consent a client gives for being influenced an informed consent? Does the client have any idea how likely the advice given will actually work? Does the client know the alternatives and the disadvantages as well as the advantages of following the advice given?

Christian counselors should also be concerned about the issue of malpractice. Popular author and pastor John MacArthur, pastor of Grace Community Church in California, was charged with contributing to the suicide of a young man in 1979. While MacArthur was eventually acquitted, the case does raise the important issue of how accountable pastors and Christian counselors are for the results of their counsel. Most malpractice suits are filed not for deliberately injuring the client, but for failing to do enough (negligence) (McLemore 1985, 722). This is one reason why good counseling training is increasingly important. Of course, a good educational background is important for a better reason than just avoiding a lawsuit; adequate preparation is also more likely to make a counselor more effective in general.

References

Back, K. 1982. *Beyond words.* New York: Sage.

Balswick, J., and J. Balswick. 1989. *The Family.* Grand Rapids: Baker.

Barna Research. 1987. *Combined data analysis of teen sexuality in the evangelical church.* Glendale, Calif.: Barna Research Group.

Cherlin, A. 1989. *Marriage, divorce, remarriage.* Cambridge, Mass.: Harvard University Press.

Cuber, J., and P. Haroff. 1963. The more total view. *Marriage and Family Living* 25: 140–45.

Davies, J. 1984. Small groups: Are they so new? *Christian Education Journal* 5: 43–52.

Dibbert, M., and F. Wichern. 1985. *Growth groups.* Grand Rapids: Zondervan.

Glasser, W. 1965. *Reality therapy.* New York: Harper and Row.

Griffin, E. 1982. *Getting together.* Downers Grove: Inter-Varsity.

Hartman, W. 1987. *Five audiences.* Nashville: Abingdon.

Kephart, W. 1981. *The family, society, and the individual.* 5th ed. Boston: Houghton Mifflin.

Kinsey, A., et al. 1953. *Sexual behavior in the human female.* Philadelphia: Saunders.

McLemore, C. 1985. Moral and ethical issues in treatment. In *Baker encyclopedia of psychology,* ed. D. Benner. Grand Rapids: Baker.

Meier, P. 1977. *Christian child-rearing and personality development.* Grand Rapids: Baker.

Raschke, H. 1987. Divorce. In *Handbook of marriage and family,* eds. M. Sussman and S. Steinmetz. New York: Plenum.

Ratcliff, D. 1984. A premarital counseling inventory based upon Proverbs 31. *Journal of Pastoral Practice* 7: 46–49.

Rogers, C. 1970. *Carl Rogers on encounter groups.* New York: Harper and Row.

Snyder, H. 1975. *The problem with wineskins.* Downers Grove: Inter-Varsity.

———. 1980. *The radical Wesley.* Downers Grove: Inter-Varsity.

Wright, H. 1979. *The pillars of marriage.* Glendale, Calif.: Regal.

———. 1981a. *Marital counseling.* Denver, Colo.: Christian Marriage Enrichment.

———. 1981b. *Premarital counseling.* Rev. ed. Chicago: Moody.

Afterword

We hope that, by reading this book, you have begun to see how the study of psychology can be helpful in your personal Christian walk as well as in church life. Psychology is helpful in spotting problem areas and in providing constructive alternatives.

This may be a good time for a caution: psychology should never be the heart of any Christian's life or work. The only adequate foundation is Jesus Christ. Only through prayer, Bible study, and a daily walk with the Lord can the church and the individual Christian mature. However, psychology can be a tool to help us in this process. Only through the work of the Holy Spirit can we help build the kingdom of God, but God can use what psychologists have discovered to aid in this process.

Many of the ideas found in this book are not in their final form. Many are more suggestive than definitive. You may need to experiment a bit and refine applications so that they fit your situation. The theories upon which they are based are not fixed laws but guiding principles that are

generally based upon the best research conducted to date. However, there will always be more research and additional refinement to psychological theory. As a result, this book is incomplete. Any book on psychology is incomplete because we will never, in this life, know everything that God has revealed. But perhaps what this book contains will help you be more effective in your Christian life and work. That is the prayer of the authors.

Finally, we must again underscore the centrality of the Bible in using and understanding psychology. Perhaps a book review, written by one of the text's authors, best emphasizes this important aspect.

The Bible is an enigma of sorts, lacking the identification of an editor or author. Indeed even the title is obscure, as it means "sacred book." Here we find a combination of history, poetry, and letters that is unmatched both in its literary value and psychological insight. While essentially religious in outlook, it goes much further in its implications to incorporate every area of life, including psychology.

The Bible is actually a compilation of many smaller booklets. Some include the name of an author almost parenthetically, while others give no author at all. The lack of stated authors and editor almost makes it appear that the writers may not have wanted to take full credit for their work; perhaps this implies that it may not have been completely their own work. The consistent message throughout the work implies the possibility of a single individual behind all of the writings.

The Bible begins with a provocative account of early history, including a most interesting but brief account of the earth's origins. Soon after the first section, which is called "Genesis," the book bogs down a bit into the details of early Jewish customs and laws. While this section is a bit difficult, with study a number of psychological and moral insights can be found.

Following the law section, the book again continues the historical overview of the Israelite nation. The personality profiles are lifelike and heavily laden with insight into human nature and personality.

About halfway through this compilation are several booklets of poetry, one a missive about suffering, another a lengthy series of songs. The songs are followed by a very insightful series of proverbs, primarily short tidbits of wisdom. Again,

here is some great psychology, foreshadowing the findings of much modern research. Another book of poetry is called "Ecclesiastes"—a somewhat melancholy philosophy, as is another later book titled "Lamentations." The first major section of the Bible concludes with a number of "prophets."

A second section, shorter than the first, is designated the New Testament in contrast with the first section called the Old Testament. This is a rather confusing comparison, since the "new" section is nearly two thousand years old. Either the "new" is relative to the more ancient writing of the "old," or it may refer to a new way of living which is emphasized throughout the second section.

The New Testament begins with several books on the life of a man named Jesus. He was indeed a remarkable man, being able to perform miracles and reportedly possessing both a divine and human nature. Here the editor could have done more work by combining the four accounts of his life. Yet, one gets the impression that something might have been lost in such editing—each account is separately authored and reveals distinctive perspectives about Jesus and his life. The multiple accounts approach was also taken in the Old Testament, where Chronicles constantly overlaps with several previous books.

The remainder of the New Testament is composed of letters that describe the events of the early group of followers of Jesus after he died. The followers stated, and provided much evidence for Jesus coming back to life after his death. While an incredible conclusion, this reviewer finds the claim quite believable. Both the accounts of Jesus' life and later letters are loaded with psychological and religious insight, and well worth the reading.

Such a fine book is not above criticism, however. Those who do not believe in God would probably find this book intrusive with its basically theistic approach to life. One also wonders why an index is lacking. The reviewer also found himself troubled at points by the implied need to change in his personal life as the result of reading certain sections. The need to change is a dominant theme of the book.

This is definitely the finest work the reviewer has ever read, psychological or otherwise. The Bible is loaded with psychological insight; this book is where psychology and Christianity integration should begin. It is indeed inspired writing and highly recommended.

Appendix: *Self-Change Projects*

Most people would like to change something about themselves. This self-help project uses behavior modification (see chaps. 6 and 15) to promote self-change. The first section will help you to either increase something you desire to do more often or decrease something you would like to do less often. The second part should be used if you have a problem common among college and seminary students: test anxiety. It can be used to overcome other kinds of common fears as well.

These procedures have been used to change many kinds of behavior. For example, it has helped students stop nail biting, reduce weight, stop smoking, and decrease their arguing with family members. It has also helped people increase the time spent reading the Bible and studying for class. Of course the person must *want* to change before the procedure can work.

The methods described have been tested over a number of years by scores of students in classroom and counseling situations. They are almost always successful. When people report that they have not worked, it is usually because the instructions were not followed completely. You may need to refer back to previous chapters to better understand the concepts involved. Therefore, if you are careful, success is virtually assured. This project is designed for typical people with typical problems. People with more severe difficulties should be referred to a professional counselor.

Many have found that this project works better when done with the help of others. A close friend or spouse can provide support that will make the project more likely to succeed. Groups of people with the same problem can provide an atmosphere of expectancy as well as give additional attention and praise for desired changes (see chap. 16).

Increasing or Decreasing Behavior

Step 1: What Is Happening Now?

1. Specifically describe the present behavior. Try to describe it in such a way that it can be observed and counted.

2. Describe the contingencies surrounding the present behavior. For example, under what circumstances does it occur: only at certain times or places? If you want to decrease behavior, what rewards are operative at the present time? If you want to increase behavior, what might be preventing the behavior at present?

3. Gather data on the number of times the behavior occurs at the present time. It may be happening more or less than what you think it does, so take a few days to actually quantify it. DO NOT GUESS. You may find that a pocket counter will help. This is an important step because you cannot tell if the project works unless you have this information. State how many times the behavior occurred each day for the period of one week.

Step 2: What Are My Plans?

1. Specifically state your goal(s) for the project. The goals should be stated as observable and countable behavior. Each goal should be small enough to be practical. If you decide to take smaller steps toward an ultimate goal, list each step. Specify exactly what you want. If there are things that hinder the accomplishment of the goal (such as current punishments), state how you plan to change these.

2. List at least three positive reinforcers which you can use to help motivate you. Reinforcers are things that you desire a great deal, yet you can do without if need be. Reinforcers are tangible privileges or objects. Students commonly use favorite foods, talking with a friend, playing a game, listening to records or television, new clothes, being alone, and so on. Do

not hesitate to use all three reinforcers if you need to.

3. You may find it helpful to use "tokens" (substitutes for actual reinforcers). Many people give themselves tokens when the desired behavior occurs, and then at the end of the day give themselves the actual reinforcer in exchange for the tokens. You may find it helpful to have another person give you tokens and reinforcers.

4. Write a contract, stating your goal(s), reinforcers, and tokens (if any). The contract should specifically state what is to be accomplished at each step of the project for you to be able to receive the reinforcement. Sign and date the contract.

Step 3: How Am I Doing?

1. Begin doing what you agreed to do in the contract. Keep a careful daily record of your progress. Just being able to see the results on paper can itself be reinforcing.

2. How are things going? Does the contract need to be revised? If there are several steps in your program, you should now go on to the second step—*if* you have been successful so far. If you are not successful at this point, you need to consider breaking down the desired goal into smaller steps. You may also want to consider using another reinforcer.

3. Continue to keep track of the results each day. As you are able to meet a goal consistently for at least a couple of days, move on to the next step.

Step 4: How Do I Stop the Project?

1. After you have reached your final goal for several days consistently, you need to begin to terminate the intervention. This is where many people run into difficulty because the temptation is to terminate too quickly. Plan on several days during which you will gradually do away with the intervention.

Perhaps the best way to terminate is to

"thin" your reinforcement. This refers to giving yourself reinforcement only occasionally for the desired behavior. For example, you might cut out three slips of paper and mark an *X* on one of them. Then put them in something so you cannot see them and draw one out each time you normally would receive a reinforcer. If you get the one with the *X* on it, you get the reinforcer; otherwise you get none. After doing this a few days, you might add a couple more pieces of paper without *X*s on them. Eventually you can give yourself the reinforcer just once in a while and forget the slips of paper. This procedure is sometimes called "intermittent reinforcement." Describe how you plan to thin out your reinforcement.

2. After your reinforcement was eliminated, did things go back to the way they were before? If they did, you may need to start the program again, or at least one of the last stages with drawing slips of paper. For a few problems you may have to have some reinforcement indefinitely. If so, try to substitute a more natural reinforcer if you can.

Continue to keep track of your behavior for at least a week or two after you remove the reinforcement. Note any changes or restarts of the program.

Overcoming Test Anxiety

Many college students report a great deal of anxiety about tests. If anxiety precludes doing a good job on the test, it may need to be reduced. Sometimes anxiety can be so overwhelming that the person forgets everything that was studied.

Behavioral psychology suggests that relaxation exercises combined with the specific situation creating the anxiety can help reduce anxiety. Some psychologists prefer that the person imagine the situation, then combine relaxation with the situation imagined, while other psychologists believe the person should be in the actual situation while doing the relaxation activities.

Learning How to Relax

Many people do not know how to relax. One of the most successful methods used by psychologists is tensing and releasing different muscle groups in the body. After systematically going through each muscle group, tensing and releasing each one, the entire body feels much more relaxed. If you practice this process at least once a day, eventually you will be able to relax all the muscles at once by just beginning the process.

At least once a day (more often if you can), try doing the following exercises:

1. Tense your forehead as tightly as you can for several seconds. Then gradually release the muscles. Keep releasing more and more.

2. Tense your jaw as much as possible. Then gradually relax the muscles, more and more until your jaw begins to sag.

3. Tense your hands and arms for several seconds. Then release the muscles gradually. Keep releasing until they are limp.

4. Tense your neck and shoulder muscles. Then let the muscles go, more and more. You can feel them relax as you let go.

5. Tense your stomach muscles very tightly. Then let go. Continue to relax them.

6. Straighten out your legs and point your toes as far as you can. Hold them for several seconds, then relax the muscles more and more.

7. Now try doing all of the above at once, tensing each muscle as much as possible. After a few seconds, let go. Continue to let go more and more, feeling greater and greater relaxation in each muscle.

Identifying Feared Situations

Most students report that the situations that create test anxiety can be listed in the following order, from the most feared to least feared situations:

A. actually taking a test
B. having the test handed out
C. sitting down to take the test
D. entering the room to take the test
E. walking down the hall toward the class to take the test
F. thinking about taking the test a few hours before
G. studying for the test

Imagining and Relaxing

Now try imagining level G in the previous section. Try to picture it as clearly as possible. If you begin to feel anxious, use relaxation procedures.

After you can imagine level G without feeling anxious, go to level F. Again try to picture that situation as intensely as possible. If you start to feel anxiety, go through the relaxation exercises again. Eventually you will be able to imagine level F without anxiety.

Now go to level E, imagining it as clearly as possible. Again, if you start to feel anxiety, use the relaxation procedures. Continue with this procedure, working your way up the ladder until you come to level A. When you can imagine level A without anxiety, you have finished this step.

Relaxing in the Actual Situation

Sometimes the imagining and relaxing does not completely get rid of the anxiety in the real situation of taking the test. In this case, you should try relaxing in the actual situation.

1. Role play the different levels with another person, again imagining you are in the real situation. At each step, if you feel anxiety, perform the relaxation procedures.

2. Begin at level E and actually walk down the hallway as you would if you were going to take the test. Pretend you will be taking the test in a moment as you walk. Stop and do the relaxation exercises if you feel anxiety. Then move on to level D, entering the actual classroom you will be taking the test in. Continue to imagine it is an actual test day. If you feel anxiety, stop and do your relaxation exercises. Continue on in this manner until you are actually sitting in your seat in the classroom, imagining the test is before you.

3. If you still feel anxiety while taking the test, you should try doing the relaxation exercises *during* the test if possible. If you are not pushed for time, you may be able to close your eyes and do several of the relaxation exercises when you feel extreme anxiety. Even if the test is timed, it may be better to take a minute or two relaxing and get several questions correct, than to not relax and miss everything!

4. A few people have such extreme fear and anxiety about tests that even these procedures are not sufficient. In such cases, it is best to see a qualified counselor about the problem.

Other Applications

The principles of imagining and relaxing (or experiencing and relaxing) can be applied in other situations. Many students have fears that keep them from being their best.

To apply these ideas to other situations, use the following steps:

1. Make a list of different situations, listing them in order from most feared to least feared (as we did with test anxiety).

2. Practice the relaxation exercises until you either know them by heart or can

relax instantly without having to go through them.

3. Imagine the least feared situation. If you begin to feel anxiety, do the relaxation exercises. After you can imagine that situation without anxiety, move up to the next most feared situation and imagine it. Con-tinue this process until you can imagine the most feared situation without anxiety.

4. If you still feel fear in the actual situation, you can combine the relaxation procedures with role playing or the actual situation as mentioned in the test anxiety example.

Glossary

absolute threshold—the magnitude of a stimulus strength when a stimulus is strong enough to be detected 50 percent of the time.

accommodation—the process of modifying previously developed cognitive structures on the basis of new experiences.

acting out—performance of maladaptive behaviors in order to relieve the tension of unacceptable urges.

adaptation—reduction in the firing rate of receptor cells in response to a constant stimulus.

affect—a feeling or emotion.

afferent fibers—sensory nerves that conduct impulses from the body to the central nervous system.

algorithm—set of procedures that guarantee the solving of a problem.

altruism—concern for the well-being of others.

amnesia—loss of memory sometimes including that of personal identity.

anorexia—prolonged loss of appetite.

anorexia nervosa—pathological fear of weight gain leading to excessive dieting, profound weight loss, and malnutrition.

approach-approach conflict—conflict which exists when there are two desirable but mutually exclusive goals.

approach-avoidance conflict—conflict which exists when there is a single goal with both desirable and undesirable qualities.

avoidance-avoidance conflict—conflict which exists when there are two undesirable choices.

archetype—hidden symbol in the individual unconsciousness which derives from the collective unconsciousness.

assimilation—the process of altering new perceptual cognitive elements to make them more similar to already familiar elements.

autonomic nervous system—that portion of the nervous system that regulates involuntary action.

aversive conditioning—counterconditioning which associates an undesirable state with an unwanted behavior.

axon—long unbranched fiber extending from the cell body of the neuron which conducts impulses away from the nerve cell.

baseline—in operant conditioning, the rate of responding or how many times a response occurs over a given unit of time.

blocking—sudden cessation of the flow of thought or speech.

bulimia—binge eating followed by purging or self-induced vomiting.

case study—an in-depth account of a given individual.

castration anxiety—a preschool boy's realization that he is a competitor with his father for the mother's attention.

catatonia—schizophrenic condition marked by muscular rigidity, lack of awareness, and lack of response.

catharsis—in psychoanalysis, the patient's sudden rush of emotions accompanying a new insight.

central nervous system—the brain and spinal cord.

cerebellum—portion of the brain responsible for the regulation and coordination of voluntary movement.

chaining—in operant conditioning, the acquisition of a series of behaviors one step at a time.

clairvoyance—supposed ability to see or know things out of the range of normal perception.

classical conditioning—conditioning in which the experimenter produces a subject's response whenever desired by presenting an unconditional stimulus to form a new association between the conditioned stimulus and the conditioned response.

cognition—both the process of knowing and the product of the act of knowing.

cognitive dissonance—inner tension resulting from the attempt to hold two contrasting thoughts at the same time.

collective unconsciousness—Jung's concept of an endowment each individual receives from experiences which other individuals have had throughout human history.

communication—the process by which individuals give and receive cognitive and other information.

compartmentalization—the unconscious experiencing of attitudes as though they are unconnected and unrelated.

compensation—an unconscious striving to make up for inferiority feelings.

compulsion—an irrational action.

condensation—the reaction to a single word, phrase, or idea with all the emotions unconsciously associated with a complex group of ideas.

confabulation—replacement of fact with fantasy in the memory.

consciousness—the variation of the psychological and physiologic dynamics of the brain.

conservation—the principle which states that the amount of a substance is unchanged even though its appearance may be changed.

contracting—agreement between client and counselor on a specific plan and/or goal between counseling sessions.

control group—the norm or standard against which observations of the experimental group are compared.

correlation—a statistical index which measures the relationship of two factors.

critical features—the most obvious features of an object, action, or idea.

deductive reasoning—process in which data are combined and conclusions are drawn from those facts.

defense mechanism—unconscious pattern by which the psyche defends itself from conflict and anxiety.

defensive devaluation—continual criticism of others in order to cover up unconscious inferiority feelings.

delusion—a belief held to be true in the face of solid evidence to the contrary.

dendrite—short branching fiber projecting from the cell body of the neuron which conducts impulses to the nerve cell.

denial—the disavowal of something disturbing.

dependent variable—variable that is expected to change as a result of variations in the independent variable.

depth perception—the perception of spatial relationships in three dimensions.

diathesis—the predisposition or vulnerability an individual may have for a particular disorder.

discriminating stimulus—stimulus which sets the stage or provides the occasion for an organism to emit a voluntary operant response.

displacement—the transference of an emotion from its original object to a more acceptable substitute.

dissociation—the separation of psychological activities from the rest of the personality so that they function independently.

distortion—a gross reshaping of external reality to suit one's own inner needs.

eclectic—selecting the best of various forms of therapy.

ectomorph—individual with a fragile, thin body who is inhibited and scholarly.

efferent fibers—motor nerves that conduct impulses away from the central nervous system to an effector.

ego—the negotiator between the id and the superego.

electra complex—romantic and sexual feelings in a girl for her father, first evident between the ages of three and six.

endomorph—individual with a soft, round body who is sociable and affectionate.

epistemology—the philosophical study of the origin and nature of knowledge.

evaluative reasoning—process of judging the appropriateness of a new idea or concept.

evoked companion—the sense of self being with others which exists even when the infant is alone.

experimental group—the group directly tested by the experimenter.

externalization—the experiencing of inner thought processes and feelings as though they are occurring outside the self.

extinction—the elimination of a reinforcement so that a given behavior will decrease.

fixation—powerful attachment to a person, thing, or behavior.

free association—in psychoanalysis, the patient's expression of thoughts, fantasies, and feelings.

Freudian slip—a slip of the tongue that reveals unconscious thoughts.

fugue—disturbance of consciousness in which individuals perform acts of which they seem to be aware but of which they later have no recall.

games—a series of transactions occurring on two different levels of communication simultaneously.

ganglion—aggregate of nerve cell bodies outside the brain and spinal cord.

generalization—process in which behavior in response to a given stimulus can be prompted by a similar stimulus.

gestalt rules—rules that are used by individuals as they organize their perceptions.

grand mal—form of epilepsy characterized by severe seizures and loss of consciousness.

gray matter—gray nerve tissue of the central nervous system, composed of nerve cells and fibers and supportive tissue.

groupthink—extreme concern within a group that everyone reach full agreement.

habituation—the process by which the nervous system ignores sensory input.

hallucination—false perception of something not actually present.

heuristic—rule of thumb that generally leads to the best answer.

higher-order conditioning—process by which a series of conditioned stimuli serves as a substitute for other originally conditioned stimuli.

histrionic—overly emotional.

homeostasis—state of physiological equilibrium.

hypnosis—an altered state of consciousness in which an individual is receptive and suggestible.

hypochondriasis—preoccupation with bodily function or a fear of disease.

hypothalamus—part of the brain regulating body temperature, hunger, thirst, and other autonomic activities.

hypothesis—tentative idea which is tested for its agreement with known facts.

iatrogenic—used of imagined ailments induced in an individual by autosuggestion.

id—innate basic drives.

idealization—the overestimation of the admired attributes of another person.

image—the mental picture of an actual sensory experience.

independent variable—variable which an experimenter changes in the experimental group.

inductive reasoning—process in which inferences about the unknown are formulated on the basis of what is already known.

inoculation—process in which an individual is presented with a weakened form of an idea and is then asked to give a strong refutation of it.

insomnia—the inability to sleep.

intoxication—maladaptive behavior resulting from the ingestion or inhalation of a specific substance.

introjection—the redirection toward self of the feelings one has toward another person.

introspection—the process of self-observation in which the individual experiences an event and then attempts to describe it.

intelligence quotient (IQ)—measure of intellect derived from scores on an intelligence test.

isolation—the splitting off of an unacceptable emotion from conscious thought.

lability—tendency to discharge emotions or feelings.

law of effect—law which states that the stimulus-response bond, or learning, is strengthened by reward or satisfaction.

learned helplessness—passive resignation which is learned when an individual is forced to endure repeated aversive events.

learning—a relatively permanent change in behavior as a result of experience.

learning curve—graph demonstrating progress in learning, showing steady increase at the beginning and a leveling off at the end.

limbic system—portion of the brain governing basic activities such as self-preservation, reproduction, and the expression of fear and rage.

mania—hyperactive, excessively excited state.

marasmus—condition in which an infant refuses to eat and becomes increasingly emaciated.

medical model—model of personality which states that outward behavioral difficulties are merely symptoms of a deeper underlying cause.

medulla oblongata—portion of the brain stem that controls respiration and circulation and contains reflex centers.

mental retardation—below-normal general intellectual functioning beginning before age eighteen which is associated with impairment in adaptive behavior.

mesomorph—individual with a strong, muscular body who is courageous, aggressive, and active.

modeling—the observation and imitation of desired behavior.

mutism—condition of being unable to speak.

negative reinforcement—the removal of an unpleasant or aversive situation as the result of a given behavior.

neuron—nerve cell.

nonverbal communication—any expression that does not rely on words or word symbols.

noogenic neurosis—society's search for meaning.

normal neurosis—psychological problem that is socially acceptable.

objectivity—the degree to which different individuals scoring a test obtain the same results using the same scoring methods.

obsession—an irrational thought.

Oedipus complex—romantic and sexual feelings in a boy for his mother, first evident between the ages of three and six.

operant conditioning—conditioning in which the experimenter takes a response that the subject already has and strengthens it by reinforcing it every time it occurs.

operant level—the rate at which a freely available response occurs when its consequences are neither positive nor negative.

overcompensation—the attempt to make up for deficiencies in socially unacceptable ways.

overlearning—process in which information to be learned is rehearsed to the extent that it can be recalled and then is rehearsed several more times.

paradigm—the overall assumptions and general approach that psychologists share.

paralanguage—those aspects of communication that are vocal but nonverbal.

parapsychology—the study of phenomena that cannot be explained by natural laws.

penis envy—a preschool girl's feeling of deprivation which is eventually resolved by identification with the mother.

perception—the interpretation and organization of neural impulses into an internal representation of reality.

peripheral nervous system—that part of the nervous system comprising the cranial nerves, the spinal nerves, and the autonomic nervous system.

perseveration—uncontrollable repetition of words or gestures.

personality—the ingrained pattern of behavior, thought, and feelings consistent across situations and time.

petit mal—mild form of epilepsy characterized by occasional spasms and lapses of consciousness.

phallus—technical term for the male sex organ.

phobia—irrational fear of a specific situation, object, or activity.

phoneme—basic sound unit of a language.

pica—the eating of unnatural nonfood items.

placebo—a neutral substance that may induce change because of an individual's confidence in it.

precognition—knowledge of something prior to its occurrence.

primary cause—a specific condition that must always be present for a disorder to occur.

proactive inhibition—process in which material already in the memory interferes with new material learned.

projection—the unconscious attribution of one's own impulses or wishes to someone else.

psychoanalysis—method of psychotherapy designed to bring unconscious material into consciousness.

psycholinguistics—the psychological study of language and speech.

psychology—the scientific study of the behavior and thinking of organisms.

psychosomatic reaction—a physical malady related to prolonged stress associated with other negative emotions.

punishment—the presentation of an aversive stimulus that decreases the probability of a response.

rackets—the feelings an individual collects in order to justify major actions in a life script.

rationalization—the articulation of self-justifying explanations instead of the real reasons for one's actions.

reaction formation—process in which attitudes and behavior contrary to an individual's true feelings or unconscious impulses are adopted.

reflection—psychotherapeutic technique in which the therapist repeats what the client has said using different words and clarifying what has been stated.

reflexivity—the tendency of participants in experiments to think about the experiment and thus change their behavior from what it would be otherwise.

regression—reversion to a less mature pattern of behavior.

rehearsal—the repetition of information in short-term memory which aids the transfer of information to long-term memory.

reinforcer—any stimulus that follows a response and increases the probability of its occurrence.

reliability—the degree to which individuals obtain the same relative scores each time they are measured.

repression—the unconscious exclusion of painful thoughts from the consciousness.

reticular activating system—specialized system running throughout the entire brain stem which monitors incoming information and relays important stimuli to higher centers.

retroactive inhibition—process in which new material learned interferes with retrieval of indexed material in the memory.

reward—any positive consequence of a behavior.

RIGS—representations of interactions that are generalized, or models the child develops in the course of interactions with others.

ritual—a compulsive behavior performed to temporarily ease intense guilt feelings.

satiation—condition in which a previously desired object is no longer desired because so much has already been acquired.

scalloping—the dramatic increase of a reinforced behavior shortly before a fixed interval is completed.

script—a life plan determined at an early age through which an individual meets needs.

secondary reinforcer—anything consistently associated with a reinforcer which in time itself becomes reinforcing.

self-actualization—a strong drive toward personal growth, health, and adjustment.

self-talk—cognitive activity in which individuals give themselves certain messages.

sexualization—an individual's focus upon personal sexual prowess in order to alleviate inferiority feelings or hostility toward the opposite sex.

shaping—in operant conditioning, the process in which approximations of a desired target behavior are reinforced until that behavior is learned.

social loafing—phenomenon in which people tend to exert less effort when working with others in contrast to more effort when working alone.

sociopath—individual (usually a male) who exhibits a lack of conscience for wrongdoing.

somnambulism—sleep walking.

standardization—the administration of the same test under the same conditions to a large representative group.

sublimation—transformation of a consciously unacceptable drive into a socially acceptable form of behavior.

superego—the socially acquired conscience.

superstitious behavior—behavior that is accidentally reinforced and as a result later reoccurs.

synapse—the space between the dendrites of one neuron and the axon of another neuron.

telepathy—the transference of thoughts between people by inexplicable means.

template—a complete mental pattern for a given object or idea.

thalamus—portion of the lower brain that relays sensory stimuli to the cerebral cortex.

theory—a prevailing concept that guides research.

transference—in psychoanalysis, the patient's unconscious disproportionate emotional response to the therapist.

transitional object—any object that aids a child in being separate from the parent by symbolizing the care and security provided by the parent.

UBO—ultimate background object, or a primitive experience of God during infancy.

undoing—the carrying out of unconscious acts or verbal communications in order to negate a previous mistake.

validity—the extent to which an instrument actually measures what it is intended to measure.

white matter—white nerve tissue of the central nervous system composed largely of myelinated nerve fibers.

Index of Names

Index of Subjects